GRAND STAND

C

ENTRANCE

33

41

Indianapolis Motor Speedway

INDY SPLIT

THE BIG MONEY BATTLE THAT NEARLY DESTROYED INDY RACING

JOHN OREOVICZ

octanepress.com

Octane Press is based in Austin, Texas

Printed in Canada

CONTENTS

ACKNOWLEDGMENTS

This book would not be possible without the friendship and support of Bruce R. McCaw.

I also want to thank Robin Miller, Nigel Roebuck, Gordon Kirby, Alan Henry, Maurice Hamilton, David Tremayne, and David Phillips —journalists who inspired me to want to follow in their footsteps, documenting the history of auto racing. The best editors also deserve mention, and mine included K. Lee Davis, John Zimmermann, and Mike Kerchner.

Finally, a round of applause for the team at Octane Press.

FOREWORD

FIGHTING FOR RELEVANCY

By all rights and considering the longevity, history, dramatics, and sheer speed, open-wheel racing should be so far ahead of NASCAR that it would take the world's finest telescope for the stock car set to even see the back of the IndyCar field.

But because open-wheel racing has, for the most part, been run by the wrong people for most of the past century, IndyCar lags behind NASCAR in American awareness, sponsorships, television ratings, and attendance.

A litany of poor choices at the top helped derail the United States Auto Club (USAC); then Championship Auto Racing Teams (CART) got greedy after successfully taking over, only to see Tony George's Indy Racing League (IRL) do a poor imitation of its predecessor. Today, we've got the NTT IndyCar Series, and while it's got great racing and stout fields, it's become a tiny niche sport in the USA.

John Oreovicz was too young to grasp the politics of the USAC-CART split, but he was right on top of the CART-IRL war that ravaged open-wheel racing. In this book, he's documented all the stupid decisions, infighting, jealousy, incompetence, and arrogance of both civil wars. His own experiences as a writer covering CART and IRL, plus talking to the people in the trenches and looking back at their words in the newspapers of the day, have provided an in-depth look at what went wrong.

It's a little disconcerting to read if you're an IndyCar fan, because you might have forgotten all the idiocy, but it's the unabridged truth about what was once the pinnacle of motorsports and is now fighting for relevancy.

Robin Miller
March 2021

INTRODUCTION

AUTHOR'S PERSPECTIVE

It's fair to say that over almost half a century, I developed a love-hate relationship with the Indianapolis Motor Speedway (IMS).

I was a ten-year-old VW Beetle enthusiast when my family moved from Pennsylvania to West Lafayette, Indiana, in 1974. Within a year, my fifth-grade class (like every fifth-grade class in the state) took a field trip to the Speedway and the IMS Museum. The race cars in the museum were cool, though I can't remember any of them specifically. What really caught my attention was the Buick Century pace car. Actor James Garner was the driver in '75, and his brand-new series *The Rockford Files* happened to be my favorite television show.

My parents were English/Communications professors at Purdue University, and they had gotten me a subscription to *Road & Track* to encourage me to read. As luck would have it, there was extensive coverage of the Indianapolis 500 in the September 1975 issue. That same issue included a two-page color photograph of Niki Lauda winning the Monaco Grand Prix in the Ferrari 312T, sparking my interest in Formula 1 and in racing journalism. I still have my original copy of the magazine.

Mom and Dad drove Volvo station wagons and Toyota Camrys; they had no interest in racing or cars. But they encouraged me to pursue my passion. If they knew friends were going to the Speedway, they asked if I could be included. My first day at IMS with cars on the track was Bump Day 1977, the day Janet Guthrie became the first female qualifier in the history of the Indianapolis 500. As a young Formula 1 fan, the only two names I really recognized were Mario Andretti and Clay Regazzoni.

I discovered I could ride my bike across the Wabash River to City News in downtown Lafayette, and I began to monitor the USAC championship through Indianapolis newspapers. My growing interest in Indy car racing in the late 1970s coincided with the original USAC vs. CART split. Even though I was just a high school kid, I studied the roots of the conflict, and I was as fascinated by the politics, the personalities, and the posturing as I was by the cars and the competition.

I attended the 500 for the first time in 1978, and I've been back for most of them ever since. As a fan throughout the '80s, it was a rite of passage to occasionally skip school or work and head to the track to watch practice on a sunny day. Pole Day was also fun, especially those years when you'd get to hear Tom Carnegie's unmistakable voice belt out "It's a new track record!"

We never bought race tickets in advance, so we'd find some from a scalper, then cruise 16th Street or Georgetown Road until they stopped traffic in the middle of the night. We'd get a bucket of chicken from the KFC at 16th and Warman, and make sure our coolers were stocked for the long day ahead. Sometimes we'd even grab a couple hours of sleep before they detonated the early morning bomb and started letting cars into the infield.

I was usually the most sober member of our group, but I still managed to forget where we parked in 1988, making for a long hike around the exterior of the track on a very hot day. The heat took its toll on my friend Dave Everhart's '62 Ford Thunderbird, which burst a coolant hose while we were creeping along in traffic on Georgetown Road. We got the car onto the sidewalk and out of the way, and luckily enough, the man who owned the house we stopped in front of worked at a nearby auto parts store. He was kind enough to pick up a replacement hose after hours, and we were soon on our way. Hoosier hospitality!

Those are the kinds of memories that made me fall in love with the Indianapolis 500, the Speedway, and Indy car racing as a whole. I started traveling to races outside of Indianapolis in the mid-eighties, starting with Milwaukee and Road America, Cleveland and Mid-Ohio. Then I got more ambitious. Nazareth and even Toronto were drivable from Indy in a day. The auto parts company I worked for had a store in Signal Hill, California, so I flew out and attended the Long Beach

Grand Prix. I loved the way modern Indy car racing had evolved into a blend of road-racing circuits and ovals, with increasingly high-tech cars and a spectrum of interesting drivers from around the world mixing it up with the established American stars.

As I followed the sport through the 1980s, it was clear the CART-USAC conflict was not totally resolved. The Indy 500 was sustained by CART's growth, yet a crucial part of CART's success was the inclusion of the Indy 500 in its championship. There was an uneasy coexistence, but still a lot of hard feelings on the USAC side that occasionally flared up during the month of May at IMS.

In the early 1990s, I decided to pursue a journalism degree to try to make a living writing about Indy car racing. It looked like my timing was good; in 1993, Nigel Mansell competed in the CART series, which of course included the Indianapolis 500. He was the reigning F1 World Champion, and he brought Indy car racing unprecedented worldwide interest. The Speedway doubled the size of its pressroom, and it also hired me as an extra Media Center intern for the month of May for $1,200. With encouragement from beat writers Gordon Kirby, Robin Miller, and David Phillips (and an indirect assist from Mansell), my career as an Indy car journalist was underway.

This, unfortunately, is where the story takes a turn. Despite the success of the CART-sanctioned series, newly appointed IMS President Tony George didn't like what he saw. George's vision of Indy car racing featured a much greater emphasis on oval tracks and American drivers. He wanted simpler, less expensive racing cars, and he wanted to overhaul the way engines were sold and serviced. To those who enjoyed Indy car racing's evolution and growth in the 1980s and into the '90s, it looked like George wanted to take the sport back to the '50s.

George's ascension to a position of IMS leadership and his subsequent formation of the Indy Racing League as a new series around the Indianapolis 500 brought decades of simmering tension to a boil. It was the nuclear blast that rocked the sport of Indy car racing to its foundation. Many of George's goals were worthy or admirable, but the path he chose to pursue them was incredibly destructive and the timing could not have been worse. The CART-IRL split of 1996 halted Indy car racing's upward trajectory by creating unrest among the competitors and a range of emotions from confusion to hostility from fans. The '96 split was a civil war and an ugly divorce, all wrapped into one.

I witnessed Indy car racing's growth when I was a fan; as a journalist, it was my job to document and analyze its decline. Covering the CART side for *National Speed Sport News*, it wasn't that noticeable through the end of the 1990s. The series still had full fields of pedigreed drivers with name-brand sponsors and strong manufacturer support, playing to packed grandstands around the world.

In retrospect, Greg Moore's death in the final race of the 1999 season represented more than the loss of the sport's brightest young star. It was truly the end of an era, and CART arguably never really recovered. Chip Ganassi took his team back to the Indianapolis 500 in 2000 and won. Roger Penske went back in '01 and won. A trickle of CART teams switching loyalty to the IRL became a flood, and by January 2004, CART was toast. Sitting in a federal courthouse, covering a hearing to auction bankruptcy assets was certainly something I hadn't envisioned all those years ago when I dreamed of writing about Indy car racing.

It took another four years of IRL vs. Champ Car before the sport finally came together under one umbrella, a period I spent with a foot in both camps writing for ESPN. Those were strange times; a lot of trash talk emanated from each side, with seemingly little to brag about from a pair of dueling eighteen-car series. The split took a toll on anyone who cared about Indy car racing. Friendships were strained. Historic venues and events were lost, key sponsors and manufacturers departed. The Speedway eventually won the war, but at what cost? NASCAR was the only real winner in the Indy car split.

I started writing this book in 2017, but in reality, I've been working on it since 1978. I've dedicated much of my life to Indy car racing, both as a fan and as a member of the media covering the sport. This is not my life story, but it is effectively a journal of how I spent my life.

Robin Miller's Foreword expresses the agony that longtime Indy car fans suffered for so many years. But Roger Penske gave this often-frustrating narrative an upbeat ending when he acquired the Indianapolis Motor Speedway, the IndyCar Series, and Hulman & Co. in 2020. The Hulman-George family could not have found a more suitable buyer in Penske—a man with a deeply personal interest in preserving the Speedway, the Indy 500, and the sport of Indy car racing.

Penske played many roles in his fifty-year history as a competitor in the Indianapolis 500, and he was often portrayed as a villain. But he ultimately emerged as a hero, and Indy car fans around the world can be thankful for that.

John Oreovicz
February 2021

CHAPTER 1

POSTWAR ROOTS

The Indy car "split" didn't start in the 1990s, when Indianapolis Motor Speedway President Tony George formed the Indy Racing League (IRL).

Nor did it begin in the 1970s, when a group of racing team owners joined forces under the Championship Auto Racing Teams (CART) banner and gradually began to take over governance of the sport.

To understand the fundamental conflict that kept Indy car racing's collective engine misfiring for so many years, you have to go all the way back to November 14, 1945. On that day, a businessman from Terre Haute, Indiana, named Tony Hulman purchased the Speedway from World War I hero Eddie Rickenbacker, sparking what turned into a seventy-five-year stewardship of the Indianapolis Motor Speedway (IMS) by Hulman and his descendants.

Through three generations, the Hulman-George family became an entrenched force in American automobile racing, using the power and stature of the Speedway to seize control of the open-wheel segment. That position of power also often put the Hulmans, as de facto managers of the sport, into conflict with the participants—a struggle that was not truly resolved until 2008.

While the Indianapolis 500 maintained its status as the world's largest single-day sporting event, Indy car racing as a whole—as a unified national series of races that crowns an annual champion—often appeared to be stuck in neutral. In the 1990s, Hulman's grandson Tony George formed the Indy Racing League around the Indianapolis 500 and went

1

into direct competition with the seemingly successful PPG/CART IndyCar World Series. In what commonly became known as "the split," Indy car racing was seriously damaged, allowing NASCAR-sanctioned stock car racing to emerge as America's favorite motorsport.

Even though the CART-IRL split finally ended in 2008, prevailing economic conditions and lingering tension within the Hulman-George family continued to prevent the unified IndyCar Series from achieving its potential. When legendary Indianapolis 500 competitor Roger Penske purchased the Speedway and the INDYCAR organization from Hulman & Co. in 2019, it finally gave the Indy car community genuine closure from the split and confidence that the sport would have strong leadership and financial support long into the future.

This is how it all happened.

———

Measuring 2.5 miles in length with a rectangular shape and four lightly banked ninety-degree turns, the Indianapolis Motor Speedway was constructed on a tract of farmland five miles west of downtown Indianapolis in 1909. By the time the first "International 500-Mile Sweepstakes" was staged on Memorial Day 1911 with a record prize of $25,000 on offer, the track had been resurfaced with 3.2 million paving bricks, and was given the obvious nickname "The Brickyard."

Although the Indianapolis 500 was not staged in 1917 and '18 due to World War I, the Speedway was a successful business entity through the mid-twenties despite the fact that the facility was utilized only one month out of the year. In 1927, however, the last of the four original track founders were ready to divest, and they sold the track to Rickenbacker, who raced four times in the Indianapolis 500 with a best result of tenth place in '14 before gaining fame through his conquests as a fighter pilot in World War I. When the international conflict ended, he entered the auto industry as a builder of luxury cars; a Rickenbacker sedan, with "Captain" Eddie at the wheel, served as the pace car for the 1925 Indianapolis 500.

Many of the great Indianapolis traditions we now take for granted were established during Rickenbacker's ownership in the 1930s, including the presentation of milk and the Borg-Warner Trophy to the winner in Victory Lane. But the Indy 500's upward trajectory was interrupted by World War II; the annual race was canceled from

1942-45, prompting Rickenbacker to explore the potential sale and redevelopment of the IMS property. The track lay dormant for several years until three-time Indianapolis 500 winner Wilbur Shaw revived interest when he made a promotional film for the Firestone Tire and Rubber Company at IMS in November 1944.

After Shaw ran a second tire test for Firestone in early 1945, he immediately arranged a meeting with Rickenbacker, who at that point was heavily involved in developing Eastern Airlines and appeared ready to sell the Speedway. Several proposals were already being floated for redevelopment of the land, but Shaw wanted to see IMS survive as a racetrack. He was discouraged to see the beloved facility in a state of disrepair, and he began thinking about how to save the track and the "month of May."

"There were big crevices in the track surface on the turns, which had to be patched before we could start the test, and grass was growing between the bricks on the main straightaway," Shaw wrote in his 1955 memoir *Gentlemen, Start Your Engines*. "The old wooden grandstands looked as if they were about to fall apart. Apparently, no maintenance work of any kind had been done for almost four years. It reminded me of a dilapidated back house on an abandoned farm. The depressing scene actually haunted me in my dreams for several nights.

"To me, the track was the world's last great speed shrine," he added. "I felt that all I was, or ever hoped to be, I owed to the Indianapolis 500-mile race. I accepted the situation as a personal challenge and started a one-man crusade to get the job done."

Shaw first attempted to put together a consortium of buyers, but his primary goal for the Speedway was to save and grow the Indianapolis 500 rather than allowing it to be used as a test facility or for promotional purposes. He eventually identified Hulman as a prospect who met his objectives of "having no business interests connected to the auto industry, who would be free to do whatever was necessary for the good of the Speedway and racing in general."

Anton "Tony" Hulman Jr. was born into one of Terre Haute, Indiana's most prominent families in February 1901. German immigrants, the Hulmans settled in Terre Haute in 1850, and by the turn of the century, Tony's grandfather Herman Hulman had built Hulman & Co. into a major wholesale dry goods grocer. Tony graduated from Yale and married an even wealthier heiress from Evansville, Indiana, named Mary Fendrich. A proud Hoosier, Hulman first attended the Indianapolis 500 in 1914.

In the 1920s and '30s, Tony was the driving force behind the impressive national success of Hulman & Co.'s Clabber Girl brand of baking products, and he was well prepared to take over the multimillion dollar family business when his father died in 1942. When the opportunity to acquire IMS arose, Hulman believed that applying the same kind of energy and marketing acumen that worked so well for Clabber Girl to the 500-mile race would maintain the event as an Indiana institution. With a small group of associates, including his longtime financial man Joe Cloutier, Hulman met with Shaw at the Hulman & Co. office in Terre Haute in September 1945.

Shaw had audited IMS records dating back to 1928 and was convinced that the right buyer could sustain the Speedway as a viable business. "With proper management, I don't see how you can fail to make money on your investment," he told Hulman at the end of the two-hour meeting.

Terms were agreed, and the contract transferring ownership was signed in a boardroom at the Indianapolis Athletic Club on November 14, 1945. Tony Hulman acquired the Indianapolis Motor Speedway for approximately $750,000, and as chairman of the board, he immediately named Wilbur Shaw as president and general manager.

"I don't care whether or not I make any money out of it," Hulman stated to the press. "The Speedway has always been a part of Indiana, as the Derby is part of Kentucky. The 500-mile race should be continued. But I don't want to get into something which will require additional capital each year to keep it going. I'd like to make sufficient income so we can make a few improvements each year and build the Speedway into something everyone can really be proud of."

While Hulman became famous as the man who saved the Speedway, Shaw's role in ensuring the future of the Indianapolis 500 cannot be understated. Shaw was Hulman's point man on the grounds, and he and the IMS crew had a mammoth job on their hands getting the facility ready for participants and spectators for May 1946. Two grandstands needed to be replaced, and the Pagoda scoring tower and seven other wooden grandstands required substantial repairs. A postwar steel shortage caused delays that put the rebuilding project on an even tighter time frame.

The success of the 1946 race was crucial to the future stability of the track, and all the way up to race day, Hulman still harbored doubts whether the tradition of the Indianapolis 500 could be revived. But Shaw's unwavering confidence was justified, because local media estimated attendance at 165,000, the largest crowd in the history of the Indianapolis Motor Speedway.

True to his word, Hulman reinvested in the track after that profitable 1946 race. His regime also promoted the Speedway and the Indy 500 like never before through a partnership with the IMS Radio Network, which was formed in 1952 and eventually grew to include more than 1,200 affiliate stations. Alice Greene, a copywriter at Indianapolis radio powerhouse WIBC coined the phrase "The Greatest Spectacle in Racing," which was quickly made famous by Sid Collins, the "Voice of the 500." Spectators at the track were kept up to date over the public address system by the booming call of local television sportscaster Tom Carnegie.

The most visible sign of change at IMS was the construction of a new Master Control Tower, built from 1956-57 to replace the old Japanese-style Pagoda that had housed race officials since 1926. Additional grandstands were erected and others upgraded, and all of the track, except for the main straight, was repaved with asphalt prior to the '56 race. Full paving was completed in 1961, with the exception of a three-foot section of bricks denoting the start/finish line. In addition, a dedicated pit lane was constructed, separated from the track by a grass verge and a low concrete wall.

"I don't believe there has been a year gone by that we haven't spent a considerable amount of money trying to improve facilities around the track, and also, in a slight way, try to increase the seating capacity," Hulman said in a 1970 interview. "I believe since we've been here, there's been a natural growth to the 500-mile race. The number of race fans must be increasing over the country, and we would like to accommodate as many as we can here. It's always been our desire and interest to make the 500-mile race the largest race of its kind in the world. If we can hold that, certainly we're making every effort in that direction."

Hulman was content to generally remain in the background, but he was forced into a more public role when Shaw was killed in a plane crash in northern Indiana on October 30, 1954. That included Hulman taking over as the man in charge of giving the traditional command of "Gentlemen, start your engines!" at the start of the Indianapolis 500.

The reluctant IMS front man soon took on important additional responsibilities after 1955 unfolded into the deadliest year in the history of auto racing. In the space of sixteen days, two-time world champion Alberto Ascari died in an accident at Monza, Italy; Bill Vukovich, winner of the Indianapolis 500 in 1953 and '54, was killed in a crash while leading the '55 race; and an unspeakable tragedy shook the 24 Hours of Le Mans when Pierre Levegh's Mercedes-Benz was launched into a spectator area, killing Levegh and more than eighty spectators.

These incidents prompted Switzerland to ban most forms of motor racing, and within two months, the American Automobile Association— which in 1909 had formed a contest board to sanction the Indianapolis 500 and other key American races—announced its withdrawal from all racing activities.

Hulman acted quickly. He put up $5,000 in seed money and recruited the necessary staff to create a new sanctioning organization known as the United States Auto Club. Initially run out of the IMS office at 444 N. Capitol Avenue in downtown Indianapolis, USAC eventually moved to the Town of Speedway near IMS and would serve as the sanctioning body of the Indianapolis 500 into the 1990s.

USAC also took over sanction of midget and sprint car racing, the traditional path to Indianapolis. But the "Championship Trail," comprised of the Indy 500 and a handful of other races staged on oval tracks one mile or longer, was the group's bread and butter. The Milwaukee Mile was paved in 1954, and it was joined in the rotation in '57 by a paved mile in Trenton, New Jersey. Still, dirt ovals, including State Fairground tracks in Indiana, Illinois, and California that formed the backbone of the schedule since the late '40s, made up the majority of the USAC slate until well into the '60s.

Despite the death of Vukovich, auto racing grew in popularity as the 1960s dawned, with the Indianapolis 500 leading the charge. The event had truly developed into "The Greatest Spectacle in Racing" as the rough-and-tumble drivers and evocative cars of the era known as "Roadsters" quickly developed a loyal following. Vukovich, considered the greatest American driver of his time, is credited for coining the term "Roadster"; it denoted a front-engine car with a tubular space frame chassis and solid axles front and rear, with a massive seventy-gallon fuel tank hung off the back. A four-cylinder Offenhauser engine was mounted to the left of the chassis centerline, while the driver was seated to the right, helping to balance weight distribution. The steering mechanism, transmission, and torque tube driveline produced by Halibrand were pretty much standardized.

The Roadster era, generally defined as 1952-66, was in many ways a high-water mark for the U.S. racing car trade. Until the '50s dawned, the cars that competed at Indianapolis often dated to the late '30s. But led by men like Frank Kurtis, Eddie Kuzma, and A.J. Watson, a cottage racing car industry in California burgeoned in the '50s, which was made possible by the affordability and reliability of the ubiquitous Offenhauser engine. By 1953, the "Offy" powered the full field at Indianapolis and would continue to dominate the race through the mid-sixties.

Frank Kurtis founded Kurtis-Kraft in the late '30s and was soon the leading supplier of Offenhauser-powered midget racers. He began constructing "big" cars for Indianapolis competition in 1952, and Vukovich was dominant in Kurtis roadsters from 1952-55, winning the "500" in commanding fashion in '53 and '54. "Vuky" appeared destined to be the first driver to win Indy three straight years, but instead his life ended when he was swept into another driver's accident while he was leading the fifty-seventh lap of the 1955 race.

Led by Vukovich, the drivers of the 1950s were perhaps even more captivating than the cars. Vukovich was peerless at Indy in the first half of the decade, leading an amazing 485 of the 647 laps (75 percent) he completed from 1952-55. He remains the only driver to lead the most laps in three consecutive years (1952-54), and he won the '53 and '54 races by a combined total of nearly five minutes. He also set one- and four-lap qualifying records in 1952 and '55 and started from pole position in '53.

The death of the two-time defending Indy 500 champion, caused when a pair of relatively inexperienced drivers overreacted to Rodger

Ward's crash in Turn Two during the 1955 race, remains one of the darkest moments in IMS history. But Vukovich wasn't the only driver killed in action at Indianapolis in the '50s; five others perished in practice, including Jerry Unser, the brother of future Indy champions Bobby and Al Unser. Pat O'Connor died during the '58 race.

Other legends endured. Troy Ruttman was barely twenty-two years old when he won the 1952 race; nearly seventy years later, he remains the youngest winner of the 500. Jim Rathmann notched three second-place finishes at Indy ('52, '57, and '59) as a precursor to his win in 1960. Pat Flaherty was a part-time racer who was tending bar at his Chicago tavern when he overheard patrons discussing the fact that team owner John Zink did not have a driver for the 1956 race. Flaherty and Zink inked a one-race deal, and Pat led 127 of the 200 laps on the way to victory.

Famous as one of Indy's toughest characters, cigar-chomping Jimmy Bryan was the winner of the 1958 race, leading 139 laps. Bryan finished in the top six at Indianapolis in four of his nine 500 appearances, scored twenty-three race wins in seventy-two Indy car starts, and was a three-time national champion, but he was killed in action at Langhorne Speedway in 1960. Another popular driver who failed to survive the era was Melvin "Tony" Bettenhausen, who made fourteen starts at Indianapolis from 1946-60 with a trio of top-four finishes before being killed at the Speedway in '61.

Victory in the tragic 1955 race went to Bob Sweikert in a Kurtis, but Watson, his chief mechanic, thought he could improve on the Kurtis product. The resultant Watson roadster had a lighter frame and a lower center of gravity, and it became the dominant chassis at the Speedway through the mid-sixties. The exception came in '57 and '58, when George Salih and Quinn Epperly designed and built what became known as a "laydown" roadster due to its seventy-two-degree canted engine that gave a lower frontal area. Veteran Sam Hanks won the 500 in '57 and famously announced his retirement from driving in Victory Lane. Hanks remained closely involved with Indianapolis and USAC, driving the pace car from 1958-63 and serving as the IMS director of competition through '79.

Driven by Jimmy Bryan, the Salih car won Indy again in 1958, but Watson-produced roadsters—or copies—took over through '64. Watson built a total of twenty-three chassis, and his cars served as the inspiration for a handful of "clones," including the Trevis that A.J. Foyt drove to the first of his four Indy wins in 1961.

One car from the 1950s proved to be well ahead of its time. Fred Agabashian made eleven Indianapolis 500 starts from '47 to '57 and was known as one of the era's best qualifiers, but his most famous achievement was qualifying a Cummins diesel-powered Kurtis on pole for the '52 race. The Cummins engine was also notable for featuring the first use of a turbocharger at Indianapolis, a power-boosting device that would not return to IMS for another fourteen years. From the inception of the race in 1911 up to the '70s, the Indy 500 was frequently a catalyst for racing car innovations that often trickled down to production automobiles.

With new talent, including A.J. Foyt, Jim Hurtubise, Eddie Sachs, and Parnelli Jones poised to emerge as stars, the Indianapolis 500 and the USAC Championship Trail were riding a wave of success as the 1960s dawned. The sport would continue to prosper throughout the next decade, but substantial changes were coming to the cars that competed at Indy, and USAC struggled to keep pace.

CHAPTER 2

THE FIRST FOREIGN INVASION

B y the early 1960s, "rear-engine" racing cars (with the engine behind the driver but ahead of the rear axle line in a midship position) were nothing new. Dr. Ferdinand Porsche's spectacular Auto Union Grand Prix cars of the '30s utilized a true rear-engine concept, and a rear-engined car designed by Harry Miller—the dominant American racing car designer/ engineer of the '20s and '30s—qualified for the Indianapolis 500 for the first time in 1939. Miller's influence on Indy car racing would carry through the '70s in the form of the Offenhauser engine, which started life as a Miller-designed four-cylinder power unit for marine use.

Despite the success of the Auto Unions, front-engine cars ruled Formula 1 in the post–World War II period, until the U.K.-based Cooper Car Company produced a competitive rear-engine car in 1957. Stirling Moss scored the first modern-era F1 win for a rear-engine car in a Cooper entered by Rob Walker at the '58 Argentine Grand Prix, and works Cooper driver Jack Brabham swept to the F1 World Championship in '59 and '60. Ferrari was the last front-engine holdout, but when F1 introduced a new 1.5-liter engine formula in 1961, the Scuderia created an effective rear-engined chassis, featuring a distinctive shark nose that powered American Phil Hill to the championship crown.

In October 1960, the Cooper team took advantage of a two-month gap in the Formula 1 schedule between the Italian and United States Grands Prix to schedule a private test at the Indianapolis Motor Speedway. Brabham had never seen the track before, but he reached 144.8 miles per hour during the two-day session at IMS while running his unmodified F1 Cooper on pump gasoline. Brabham's speed wasn't too far off the official track record of 149.601 mph set by rookie Jim Hurtubise earlier that year.

Armed with that knowledge, Brabham (who would clinch his second straight F1 World Championship with a fourth-place finish a few weeks later in the 1960 USGP at Riverside Raceway) and team principal John Cooper figured the tiny, rear-engine Cooper could be competitive at Indy with a few tweaks and a bit more horsepower. The rear-engine revolution that had shot through F1 since the late '50s, resulting in Cooper's two straight championships, had not yet reached USAC Championship racing. But that was about to change.

For May of 1961, the Cooper F1 car was fitted with offset suspension components to optimize the handling for an oval track, along with a Climax four-cylinder engine bored out from 2.5 to 2.7 liters. It produced 252 horsepower on the dyno, compared to around 410 for the best Offenhausers. Of course, the traditional front-engine roadsters that the Offys powered weighed quite a bit more—1,500 to 1,600 pounds. The Cooper had just 1,000 pounds spread over its 93.5-inch wheelbase. But the Offy was unbeaten at the Speedway since 1946, when George Robson won the Tony Hulman–led postwar resurrection of the Indianapolis 500 in a car powered by a six-cylinder Sparks engine.

Brabham was treated with respect by the close-knit USAC community. They viewed his tiny, green-and-white Cooper as a novelty until "Black Jack" qualified it thirteenth fastest with a four-lap average of 145.144 mph. People started doing the math. They saw the Cooper was much easier on tires than the roadsters, and realized Brabham might have to make one fewer stop for fuel than his rivals.

"World's Road Racing Champion Jack Brabham and his rear-engine Cooper-Climax have the American racing fraternity plenty 'shook up,'" wrote *Indianapolis Star* Sports Editor Jep Cadou in mid-May. "For the first time in at least fifteen years, a foreign entry is given an excellent chance of winning the 500-Mile Race by top American drivers and mechanics. This represents a sharp change in thinking among the racing fraternity in the last two weeks."

"Sure, he's got a damned good chance," defending Indianapolis champion Jim Rathmann told reporters. "If he can get by with one less stop than the rest of us, then we'll really have to hustle when we're on the track to make up for the difference."

"I think Brabham has a real good chance to beat us," added fellow veteran Don Branson, who qualified on the middle of the front row. "It's just like the old story of the tortoise and the hare."

Excessive tire wear forced Brabham to make more pit stops than expected, but he still brought the underpowered Cooper home in ninth place, completing the five hundred miles about eight minutes behind winner A.J. Foyt. He won $7,250. "All we need is more power and we can win with this car," said Brabham. "I honestly believe a three-liter, rear-engine motor car is capable of lapping here at 150 miles per hour. I'm certainly not sorry we came here, and I never drove against better chaps."

"Jack Brabham is a real professional," noted Foyt at the Victory Banquet. "I really admire you guys. You did a great job coming over here like this. We were really worried about you, I'll tell you."

Chris Economaki's race report in *National Speed Sport News* made the same observation. "The speed of the ultra-light Cooper, and its handling qualities with the rear-mounted engine and independent suspension, has led most of the experts to predict that there would be more such foreign entries next year, and certainly some experimenting with rear engines by American builders of these machines."

Other notables saw the writing on the wall. "I'm glad it's here," A.J. Watson told *Sports Illustrated*. "For years we've been scared to try anything new. Now we are simply going to have to," said the most successful car builder of the roadster era.

But surprisingly, that didn't happen immediately. The only men smart enough to pick up on the trend were Mickey Thompson and Dan Gurney. Like Hill, Gurney was one of a handful of Americans who were respected competitors in European road racing; he graduated to F1 in 1959, so he had firsthand knowledge of how rapidly rear-engine designs were showing their superiority. The versatile Californian made his first Indianapolis start in '62, driving a rear-engine car constructed by hot rod and land speed record legend Thompson and powered by a Buick V8 engine. While the Thompson effort was not as competitive as Brabham and Cooper had run a year earlier, the experience drew Gurney to conclude that the right engine and chassis would make a rear-engined car highly competitive at Indianapolis and other USAC tracks.

He invited Colin Chapman, founder of road and racing car manufacturer Lotus Cars, to attend the 1962 Indianapolis 500. Gurney paid Chapman's expenses, with the ultimate goal of using his contacts at the Ford Motor Company to source an engine for a Lotus-built chassis designed for Indy. Soon after Gurney scored the first of his four career F1 victories (and the only win for Porsche) in the French Grand Prix at Rouen in July 1962, he and Chapman flew to Detroit for a meeting with Ford executives.

"We had both lived through the rear-engined revolution when it came to F1, and it was clear to me that someone was going to do the same at Indianapolis," Gurney said. "That challenge really appealed to Colin, and I thought it would also appeal to Ford."

As luck would have it, Ford was entering the most prolific period of motorsports involvement in the company's history. Rebuffed by Enzo Ferrari in his attempt to acquire the famous Italian sports car marque, Henry Ford II took Ford into competition with Ferrari on the track. He commissioned an assault on the 24 Hours of Le Mans that ultimately resulted in four consecutive overall wins between 1966 and '69; Ford also provided the £100,000 seed money that created the Cosworth DFV, the most successful F1 engine of all time with 155 Grand Prix wins from 1967-83.

The basic terms for a Lotus-Ford Indianapolis program were agreed upon by September 1962. Following the United States GP at Watkins Glen in October, the Lotus F1 team traveled to Indianapolis, where Jim Clark lapped the Speedway at around 143 mph, just three mph slower than the slowest speeds in the Indy 500 field. This was significant because Clark's car was fitted with a standard F1-spec 1.5-liter Coventry Climax V8 that produced just 175 horsepower, less than half the output of the dominant Offys. The test convinced Lotus and Ford more than ever that they could be highly competitive at Indianapolis when on similar or equal horsepower terms.

And so it proved. Using a slightly downsized and race-modified version of Ford's 260-cubic-inch production V8, Clark qualified fifth and finished second on his Indianapolis debut in the 1963 Indy 500, his Lotus beaten only by emerging star Parnelli Jones and his Watson roadster. Jones's car appeared to be leaking oil late in the contest, but he was never black-flagged, leading some to conclude that USAC officials unfairly favored the American driver and car. Rival driver Eddie Sachs complained to that effect, claiming he crashed on Jones's oil, and Jones responded by slugging Sachs in the jaw!

As newcomers, Chapman and Lotus chose not to force the issue, but there is no question that some ill will toward the rear-engine "funny cars" was apparent; something as simple as the British Racing Green color of the Lotus entries was considered unlucky by veteran drivers like Foyt and many other IMS old-timers. But Clark used the perceived snub as motivation. In August 1963, the Scotsman drove his Lotus to an unchallenged victory at the Milwaukee Mile, earning the first Indy car win for a rear-engine car.

Clark qualified his Lotus on pole position for the 1964 Indianapolis 500 but retired early when his car suffered a Dunlop tire failure. Two of the twelve rear-engine cars in the race were involved in a multicar pileup on the first lap that killed rookie driver Dave MacDonald and popular veteran Sachs; that fiery inferno prompted the switch from gasoline to methanol fuel prior to the '65 season.

In 1965, Clark was quietly motivated when Foyt remarked, "I'm just glad to bring the track record back to the United States" over the IMS public address system after the Texan edged him for pole position. The comment only intensified the Scotsman's desire to beat the locals at their own game. On Firestone tires and running a new Lotus chassis with an uprated Ford engine, Clark dominated the 500, leading 190 of 200 laps on the way to an easy win. Twenty-seven of the thirty-three cars in the '65 field featured rear-mounted engines, and the days of the roadster were clearly numbered.

Gurney recalled the reaction to Indy car racing's rear-engine revolution in Andrew Ferguson's book *Team Lotus: The Indianapolis Years*. "The Indy establishment was very insulated from the real world outside," Gurney said. "The first time we drove up to the Speedway, we arrived at the entrance at the corner of 16th Street and Georgetown Road and there was a sign reading: 'Indianapolis Motor Speedway—Racing Capital of the World.' Colin instantly took exception and began grumbling.

"Going into Indy racing with something so entirely new was one hell of a challenge," Gurney added. "Above all, it was fun tweaking the establishment's tail. Obviously, we came in for some comments from the traditionalists about how favored we were, being allowed to run those kiddie cars in amongst the big roadsters. But the interesting feature there was that when more established U.S. drivers began to run the rear-engined cars, they quickly discovered that these things were not viceless either—they really were not on the sweet spot all the time. When they appreciated that we had to work at it too, we were regarded with perhaps a little more respect."

Those foreign funny cars were accompanied by a wave of international F1 drivers in the mid-sixties. Clark was the most notable; he concentrated on Formula 1, where he was a two-time world champion, but he also made five Indianapolis 500 starts from 1963 to '67, leading four of those races and adding second-place finishes in '63 and '66 to his '65 victory. Due to a scoring controversy, to this day, some still believe Clark is the rightful winner of the 1966 race. Other F1 world champions who moonlighted at Indianapolis included Brabham, Jackie Stewart, Graham Hill (who won the '66 race after Stewart dropped out of the lead late in the contest), Denis Hulme, and Jochen Rindt.

Spurred on by the wholesale switch to rear-engine cars, designers explored even more radical solutions. In 1966, Albert Stein produced a twin-engine car that featured air-cooled Porsche 911 flat-sixes mounted both fore and aft of the driver. A year later, STP boss Andy Granatelli commissioned a Paxton chassis powered by a Pratt & Whitney turbine engine normally used in helicopters, with the driver seated alongside the engine. The strangely quiet machine was dubbed the "Whooshmobile," and after allegedly sandbagging in practice and qualifying, '63 Indy winner Jones sped from sixth to first on the opening lap. Flabbergasted pole winner Mario Andretti flipped the turbine driver a one-finger salute while he was being passed exiting Turn Two. "Very rarely have I ever thought a race was in the bag until I saw the checkered flag waving," said Jones, who led 171 laps. "Only I never got there." The turbine car ground to a halt with just three laps remaining when a six-dollar bearing failed, leaving Foyt, at the height of his career, in position to inherit his third Indianapolis win in seven years.

USAC imposed restrictions to cut the power of the turbines, but for 1968, Lotus produced a wedge-shaped chassis to house a rear-mounted turbine engine. Clark tested the car at Indianapolis, but was killed a few days later when his Lotus Formula 2 car crashed in a race at Hockenheim, Germany, on April 7. Joe Leonard qualified a Lotus turbine on the Indy pole, but once again, defeat was snatched from the jaws of victory when Leonard's leading car broke on a Lap 191 restart. Although the turbines didn't dominate like Jones had done in '67, USAC restricted the power-plant even more and the radical technology disappeared for good after a brief two-year appearance, which included the tragic death of Lotus driver Mike Spence in May 1968. It was the first fatality at IMS since 1966, when Chuck Rodee died in a crash during qualifications.

Meanwhile, the ancient Offenhauser that dated to the '30s got a new lease on life to compete with the Fords when turbocharged versions of the venerable four-banger appeared at Indianapolis in 1966. Bobby Unser won the '68 race in an Eagle chassis built by Dan Gurney's All American Racers (AAR) that utilized a turbo Offy, and by the end of the decade, the Ford V8 was also being turbocharged. A.J. Foyt's '69 pole speed topped 170 mph, an increase of more than twenty mph from a decade earlier when Jim Hurtubise topped the 150-mph barrier for the first time.

Aside from engine development, a tire war between Firestone and Goodyear also contributed to the escalating speeds. Goodyear entered USAC Championship racing in 1964, and for the next ten years, Good-year and Firestone were unofficially the biggest-spending sponsors in the sport, contracting the top drivers of the era for huge amounts of money. Foyt was the first to switch to Goodyear; Andretti remains synonymous with Firestone to this day. Bobby and Al Unser's mother, Mary, famously created a pair of half-Goodyear, half-Firestone jackets so she and her husband could equally support both of their sons, who were on opposite sides of the tire war.

Foyt was without a doubt the driver of the decade, scoring three of his four Indy 500 wins (1961, '64, and '67) as well as five of his seven USAC national championships. To this day, Foyt remains the driver most closely associated with the Indianapolis 500. He made a record thirty-five starts at the Speedway between 1958 and 1992, and he later became the race's first four-time winner with his victory in '77. Foyt, known as "Super Tex," also earned four Indy poles between '65 and '75, led a record thirteen races for a total of 555 laps, and set career marks for laps completed and races led. He is the only driver who won the 500 in front- and rear-engine cars.

Foyt developed a close friendship with Tony Hulman and the Hulman-George family, and he has been the Speedway's biggest cheerleader for decades. "I won a lot of races, but the world knows me because I won Indianapolis," he often says. "The world doesn't know me because I won at Daytona or Le Mans or Pocono. Indianapolis made A.J. Foyt what he is today."

Jones was revered as one of the top drivers of the era and was in position to become Foyt's chief rival, but he never ran a full season of USAC competition and stopped racing open-wheel cars altogether after his 1967 Indianapolis heartbreak. Parnelli never started lower than fifth at Indy, and he was the first driver to achieve the 150-mph milestone in qualifying. He led five of his seven Indianapolis starts, utterly dominating the '63 and '67 contests. He also shared '61 Rookie of the Year laurels with Bobby Marshman—another budding star of the '60s who was killed in an Indy car accident at Phoenix International Raceway in 1964.

Jones turned down the opportunity to race alongside Clark for Lotus in Formula 1, and ultimately, Jones switched his focus to Trans-Am road racing and SCORE off-road competition. Parnelli retired from driving in 1970, and like Gurney, also left his mark on the sport as a constructor. The Vel's Parnelli Jones (VPJ) team crafted a series of race-winning Indy cars in the '70s and even took on the challenge of Formula 1. That short-lived venture sparked the initial development of a turbocharged version of the Ford-Cosworth DFV engine that transformed Indy car racing.

In Parnelli's wake came a new generation of driving talent that formed the foundation of the USAC series for decades, led by Andretti. Mario was an Italian immigrant who rose quickly through the East Coast midget and sprint car ranks to reach championship cars by the age of twenty-four. After finishing third at Indianapolis in his first start in 1965, he went on to win the USAC national championship as a rookie, and his career skyrocketed. He claimed pole at Indianapolis in '66 and added a second

USAC crown, followed by another Indy pole in '67. Andretti finally won the 500 in 1969 in his fifth start, along with his third USAC title. An intense and sometimes bitter rivalry with Foyt was kindled in this period.

Amazingly, Mario would never claim victory at IMS again, and his legendary bad luck at Indianapolis (the so-called "Andretti Curse") is an ingrained part of Speedway lore. Mario focused on Formula 1 in the 1970s, and in '78—driving for Lotus—he became just the second American driver to claim the world championship. Remarkably, Andretti's victory in the '78 Dutch Grand Prix at Zandvoort remains the last F1 win for the USA.

Bobby and Al Unser were the second generation of racers from an Albuquerque, New Mexico, family that dominated the action at the Pikes Peak International Hill Climb for decades. Brash older brother Bobby arrived first, followed a few years later by the much more taciturn Al. The Unser brothers had different styles on the track as well, Al's somewhat conservative approach a marked contrast to Bobby's hard charging.

Gordon Johncock, Johnny Rutherford, and Lloyd Ruby were other top drivers who made their Indy car debut in the 1960s. Meanwhile, Gurney never won the Indianapolis 500 as a driver, but he finished second in '68 and '69 and third in 1970, the year he retired from the cockpit. Gurney left a lasting impression on the sport with a legacy of technical innovation and leadership; Eagle cars designed and built by his California-based All American Racers team won the race in '68 and '75 with Bobby Unser behind the wheel; an Eagle fielded by Patrick Racing claimed the tragic '73 race, driven by Johncock.

Aside from this crop of appealing new stars, rapidly rising speeds and the constant element of danger were undoubtedly factors in the growth of the Indianapolis 500 in the 1960s. Because tickets for the race itself consistently sold out a year in advance, the four qualification days attracted huge crowds, with Pole Day attendance estimated at up to two hundred thousand. Twenty-five years into the Tony Hulman era, the Indianapolis Motor Speedway was still growing in popularity and could justifiably back up one of its many trademarked claims as "The Greatest Race Course in the World."

But the USAC Championship Trail, in need of consolidation and refinement, was searching for an overall identity. In 1968, for example, the USAC schedule included twelve races on paved ovals, eleven on road courses (including doubleheaders at Indianapolis Raceway Park [IRP] and Canadian venues Mosport and St. Jovite), four on dirt ovals, and the Pikes Peak Hill Climb.

USAC's flirtation with road racing may have been influenced by the rear-engine revolution. IRP joined the schedule in 1965, and between then and the end of the decade, the series experimented with road races at ten different venues. But the number of road races dwindled to two in 1970. Then in '71, road races were dropped altogether, and the dirt races (still featuring front-engine cars) were broken off into a separate USAC-sanctioned category outside the Indy car championship.

Taking the dirt tracks out of USAC's top championship is a decision that rankles some to this day. But at the time, auto racing was being billed as "The Sport of the '70s," and the marketers believed that dirt tracks and front-engine cars with technology that had barely evolved since the '40s were old-fashioned or anachronistic. At the same time, NASCAR was also in the process of streamlining its schedule and phasing out dirt tracks from the top-level Grand National series, so USAC's action was not untimely nor unexpected.

While rear-engine cars took over from front-engine cars at the championship level within a five-year period, no such rear-engine revolution took place in the sprint car and midget categories, which may be a bigger factor in the evolution of American motorsports than anyone could have understood at the time.

A full ten years passed since Clark, Gurney, and Lotus-Ford came to and nearly conquered the Indianapolis 500 and USAC championship racing before a rear-engined sprint car finally began to make an impact. Tom Sneva, a high school math teacher and coach from Spokane, Washington, who moved to Indianapolis to make a full-time career out of racing, gained attention by winning a series of USAC sprint car races in 1973 on paved ovals with a rear-engine '66 Huffaker Indy car chassis that Carl Gelhausen converted for sprint car use. Perhaps wishing to prevent another design revolution, USAC promptly banned rear-engine sprint and midget cars in '74.

Whether it was a coincidence or not, beginning in the 1970s, USAC sprint and midget racing failed to produce future Indy car stars at the rate it managed up through the '60s. We can speculate, but will never know if USAC's failure to bring its grassroots series philosophically and technically in line with its top-level Indy cars was part of what ultimately caused a mass migration of USAC stars to NASCAR in the '80s and '90s. But it was a decision that USAC felt it needed to make at the time.

"Today, some point to this ruling as the blow that ended the flow of USAC sprint car drivers into championship racing, a tradition that dated back to the beginning of the sport," observed longtime racing journalist Chris Economaki in his autobiography titled *Let 'Em All Go!*. "From that standpoint, yes, it was probably a factor. However, from the standpoint of the survival and well-being of sprint car racing, it was the proper move . . . besides, great racers figure out how to win. The severing of the connection of short track racing and Indy car racing wasn't simply a matter of front-engine or rear-engine experience; it's vastly more complex than that."

Still, many believe it was an important factor, including Mario Andretti—a winner in everything from midgets to Formula 1 and regarded as perhaps the most versatile racing driver the world has seen. "The path to Indy car changed with technological advances," Andretti said. "When I started, racing sprint cars was the easiest way to get involved in racing the Indianapolis 500, and it's not anymore. There's no question about it, when rear-engine cars came into the circuit, it changed the picture dramatically because it was a huge change. It's a totally different skill.

"The way you drive a rear-engine car as opposed to a sprint car is different," Mario added. "Lloyd Ruby tried to run a rear-engine car in some of the dirt races and some rear-engine sprint cars were built, but somehow it doesn't work. We could see the disparity between the two and it changed the picture."

Jim McGee was Andretti's crew chief during the racer's breakthrough years on Clint Brawner's Dean Van Lines team in the mid-1960s. This launched a career that saw McGee emerge as Indy car racing's most successful mechanic/team manager with ninety race wins and four championships. McGee believes the advent of the rear-engine revolution was a crucial factor in Mario's rapid success at the championship level.

"The timing was good for him," McGee said. "In the years preceding the rear-engine cars, it was tough and you needed big, strong burly guys who could manhandle those cars. There was no power steering, and the racetracks they ran were full of chuckholes. It was a muscle sport, and when the rear-engine cars came along they made it more of a finesse sport. Mario was kind of on equal footing because all the veterans were on a learning curve too, but he had the advantage of probably having a better car than a lot of those guys. He figured out how to make it work. Mario was really into the chassis and what it took to make it go fast—springs, roll bars, and that kind of stuff. He kept his own setup records, and I think he was one of the first drivers that tried to understand what was going on with the car. The others tended to just jump in the car and drive the hell out of it. If you could survive, you won, and if you didn't, you went home."

The world was rapidly changing as the 1970s loomed, and USAC—governing a sport that relied on technology like no other—was beginning to lag.

CHAPTER 3

DECLINE IN THE 1970s

The Public Health Cigarette Smoking Act passed by Congress in 1970 stipulated that tobacco companies could no longer advertise on American radio and television as of January 2, 1971. But there was nothing stopping them from utilizing sports marketing to promote their products, and outside of Virginia Slims's sponsorship of women's tennis, motorsports sponsorships soon became the preferred vehicle of choice.

Brought together by legendary driver and team owner Junior Johnson, NASCAR entered into what would prove to be a highly lucrative relationship with the R.J. Reynolds (RJR) Tobacco Company that spanned more than three decades. From 1971 to 2004, NASCAR leased RJR the naming rights of its top-level Grand National Series, which became known as the Winston Cup Series. At the same time, NASCAR eliminated races of less than 250 miles and those run on dirt tracks from the Cup schedule. This heralded the start of NASCAR's modern era.

Over the next three decades, RJR increased its annual contribution to the Winston Cup Series points fund from $100,000 to $17.5 million. RJR also backed initiatives including the Winston Million (a prize of $1 million to any driver who won three of four designated races, a feat accomplished by Bill Elliott in 1987 and Jeff Gordon a decade later) and the event that continues today as the NASCAR All-Star Race. RJR sponsored Winston Cup Series races at Talladega Superspeedway and Riverside Raceway, while dozens of short tracks around the country received a fresh coat of red and white paint as RJR successfully extended its support of the sport to the grassroots level.

Winston wasn't the only tobacco company that pushed into American motorsports in 1971. Liggett & Meyers Inc. entered the SCCA Can-Am Challenge, using its L&M brand to sponsor Jackie Stewart in a Lola entered by Carl Haas in one of his earliest team ownership ventures. More significantly, Philip Morris USA inked a deal with USAC to become title sponsor of the Marlboro Championship Trail, putting $100,000 toward the prize fund of a twelve-race championship, with all events on paved ovals.

Marlboro was set to increase its stake to $150,000 in 1972 until Brown & Williamson Corp. announced "total commitment, and a long-term one at that" to enter Indy car racing using its Viceroy brand to sponsor what was called the Vel's Parnelli Jones Superteam. The Viceroy program included an extensive print advertising campaign based on the theme of auto racing and drivers. Jones, the former Indianapolis 500 winner turned team owner, lured Mario Andretti away from Andy Granatelli's STP team to join forces with Al Unser (winner of the '70 and '71 Indianapolis 500s as well as the '70 USAC title) and defending USAC national champion Joe Leonard to create the sport's first three-car team. Successful crew chief George Bignotti led the effort, using radical new cars designed by Maurice Phillipe, the man behind the wedge-shaped Lotus 72 chassis that won Formula 1 championships in the hands of Jochen Rindt and Emerson Fittipaldi.

Marlboro believed its contract with USAC prevented the involvement of any competing tobacco companies, but USAC refused to block Viceroy's entry. Terms had already been agreed upon for 1972 and contracts prepared, but Philip Morris representatives never signed them and the sponsorship was terminated.

"The writing was on the wall for Marlboro," observed *Motor Sport* magazine. "They did not need very much imagination to see that a good proportion of the races they were sponsoring are likely to be won by cars backed by a rival and the idea did not appeal. Marlboro have thus withdrawn their sponsorship from USAC, who presumably will now have to look for a backer in a different field." USAC would not land another title sponsor until 1978, when the national championship was renamed the Citicorp Cup for a single season.

In actuality, the VPJ "Superteam"—with Viceroy sponsoring Andretti and Unser and serving as an associate on Joe Leonard's Samsonite Special—failed to live up to the hype, though Leonard won three of ten races to claim his second consecutive USAC championship in 1972. The complex Parnelli chassis soon discarded the unusual dihedral wings, torsion bar suspension, and camber compensators, but it never achieved the record-setting speeds being run by the latest McLaren and Eagle Indy cars. Despite the star power of Unser and Andretti, Viceroy-sponsored cars won just three USAC races between '72 and '75.

The Eagle and the McLaren chassis were contemporary wedge-shaped designs with the radiators moved from the nose of the car to the sides. Jim Hall had developed the first wings on his Chaparral sports cars in the mid-sixties, and by 1970, rudimentary wings were commonplace at Indianapolis. McLaren gained an advantage in '71 by utilizing a clever way of pushing its rear wing farther back by integrating it with the engine cover and bodywork.

Dan Gurney's All American Racers, makers of the Eagle, found an even more effective trick. Frustrated by a lack of speed while testing its 1971 car at Phoenix, Gurney had his crew fabricate a piece of scrap aluminum into a long L-shaped strip that was pop-riveted to the trailing edge of the rear wing. Bobby Unser ran a few test laps and immediately knew he had something special on his hands.

"He said that the rear of the car stuck so tight that he had a big push and that he didn't want to go as fast as he could have for fear of showing his cards," recalled Gurney in a 2000 interview. "Right away, we realized that we had discovered something really powerful."

The small aerodynamic appendage became known as the Gurney Flap, though it is sometimes still referred to as a "wickerbill" because that's the code name AAR used to back up their explaination that the aluminum strip was installed to reinforce the thin, trailing edge of the wing. "We used it to great advantage for a whole season before our competition caught on," Gurney said.

Meanwhile, turbocharging the four-cylinder Offenhauser and four-cam Ford V8 brought massive horsepower gains. Engine builders pushed the limits with huge amounts of turbo "boost," creating in excess of 1,000 horsepower and producing record speeds. But these overstressed powerplants blew up with comical regularity, detracting from the quality of racing in the early 1970s.

The final piece of the speed puzzle was the tire war waging between Goodyear and Firestone that ultimately produced treadless "slick" racing tires. Put together, the combined effect of horsepower, tire grip, and aerodynamic downforce was staggering. Bobby Unser's 1972 Indianapolis pole speed was 195.940 miles per hour, an amazing seventeen mph faster than the year before and twenty-five mph faster than 1970!

Aside from Unser's unbelievable pole speed, the 1972 Indianapolis 500 is also notable for being Roger Penske's first victory in the race he holds most dear. Born to a wealthy Cleveland area family, Penske was a successful driver in his own right before he retired in '65 at the age of twenty-eight to focus on his business interests. He started out with a Philadelphia Chevrolet dealership, and in '66, he formed Penske Racing. The team was small but efficient, with a tight bond between Penske, chief mechanic Karl Kainhofer, and driver Mark Donohue, a Brown graduate who brought an analytical, engineering-driven approach to the team. Donohue and Penske competed in the SCCA Can-Am and Trans-Am series as well as in the USRRC Road-Racing Championship before entering an Eagle with a Chevrolet stock-block engine in three USAC road course races in '68. The following year, Team Penske made its Indianapolis debut, with Donohue claiming Rookie of the Year honors. Donohue scored Penske's first Indy car win in the inaugural Schaefer 500 at Pocono Raceway in '71, but it was the '72 Indianapolis win that really put Penske Racing on the map. Donohue's 162.962-mph average remained the race record for nearly twenty years.

"We had committed to our sponsor (Sun Oil/Sunoco) that we would try to win it in three years," Penske related. "We did that, and that was the kickoff. I think at that point we started to bring the sport to a higher level. We brought some technology; we started to look at data. Mark was an engineer from Brown, and certainly that was part of it. He obviously brought an air of professionalism. I think the people at Indy thought we were the college guys with the crew haircuts and the polished wheels. We used to clean our garage out every night, and that was something people didn't understand. But we were committed. We weren't out there to have fun—we were there to go racing."

Jerry Grant broke the magic 200-mph barrier in the fall of 1972 at Ontario Motor Speedway, and it seemed inevitable that the mark would soon fall at Indianapolis, especially when Gordon Johncock was timed at 199.4 mph in a Goodyear tire test at IMS in March 1973. But the month of May 1973 would instead be remembered as one of the grimmest in Indianapolis Motor Speedway history.

For starters, it rained, and it rained a lot. The lack of practice time meant that no 200-mph laps were attained, though Johnny Rutherford set one- and four-lap track records of 199.071 and 198.413 mph respectively en route to pole position. The first qualifying day was marred by the death of popular veteran driver Art Pollard in a violent Turn One accident; it was the second fatality at Indianapolis in just over a year, following on the heels of a practice accident that killed Jim Malloy in 1972.

Scheduled for Monday, May 28 (the observed Memorial Day holiday), the fifty-seventh Indianapolis 500 would require three days to complete amid more rain and misfortune. A damp track pushed back the start by nearly four hours and the sky was still heavily overcast when the field finally rolled out for the traditional parade and pace laps and settled into formation to approach the green flag.

Since 1934, Indianapolis tradition dictated that the lineup be comprised of eleven rows of three cars. At fifty feet in width, the Speedway was considered a narrow track, and by the '70s, modern race cars were nearly twice as wide as those that raced forty years earlier. They were also much more difficult to control under acceleration, with highly boosted engines that released an onslaught of horsepower like a light switch when the turbocharger spooled up. On top of that, the Indy 500 is also notable for attracting inexperienced or part-time competitors, some of whom race only once or twice a year.

In 1973, the field approached the rolling start too slowly, and a multi-car accident unfolded. A McLaren driven by Salt Walther was launched into the catchfence on the outside of the front straight, showering grandstand occupants with burning methanol fuel and debris. Twelve spectators were injured, three severely. Walther, meanwhile, was lucky to escape serious injury, suffering major burns but no broken bones.

The race was red-flagged to clean up the track, but another round of rain arrived, ending hopes of restarting the race. Tuesday's 9:00 a.m. start was delayed to 10:15, and then it started raining again as the cars were running the pace lap. Finally, on Wednesday, the green flag flew at 2:10 p.m. However, due to the many unpredictable delays, local media weren't promptly informed of the start time, and many fans were still streaming into IMS.

On the fifty-eighth lap, Swede Savage appeared to get loose in Turn Four, and his car shot to the inside of the track where it made head-on contact with a concrete wall at an impact speed of close to 200 mph. The car exploded into flames and flooded the track with debris, causing an immediate red flag.

At the time, Dr. Stephen Olvey worked under Dr. Thomas Hanna for the IMS Medical Staff. "It resembled a plane crash more than it did a car wreck," wrote Olvey in his book *Rapid Response*. "When the smoke settled, only his seat, still burning with him in it, remained on the race track. The rest of the car was completely torn apart and scattered throughout the exit of Turn Four. Remarkably, he was still conscious when rescuers arrived."

Aside from suffering terrible burns, Savage sustained severely broken legs, a broken arm, bruised lungs, and other internal injuries. But Olvey, who was Savage's resident physician in the Intensive Care Unit at Indianapolis Methodist Hospital, revealed that his July 2 death was the result of hepatitis-contaminated plasma, not his grievous injuries.

Savage's accident itself wasn't the last awful moment from the month of May 1973. When the race was red-flagged, Armando Teran, a crewman for Savage at Patrick Racing, began running north up the pit lane toward Turn Four to try to aid his driver. Teran was struck from behind by an IMS Safety vehicle responding to the accident, killing him instantly.

After yet another lengthy delay, the race resumed. Al Unser led until his Offenhauser engine failed, putting Johncock in front until the next round of rain rolled in and Pat Vidan waved the red and checkered flags at the end of the 133rd lap. At 332.5 miles, it was the shortest 500 in history to that point.

The Indianapolis Motor Speedway and USAC came under serious fire in the aftermath of May 1973, with Indy car racing as a whole arguably at its lowest point since the tragedy-ridden '55 season. "Now, following a 57th '500' blighted by death and severe injuries, scorched by flame and postponed and shortened by rain, the track and the race are being fashioned by some as anachronisms overdue for extinction," ran the start of a fourteen-part series in the *Indianapolis Star* written by Dave Overpeck and titled "The Troubled 500."

"The Tony Hulman regime is under attack as never before in its 28-year stewardship," Overpeck continued. "It is accused of ignoring safety considerations, being impervious to the legitimate concerns and well-being of its patrons, imperious in its dealings with outsiders and concerned only with attracting bigger crowds and accumulating more money. . . .

"In fact, it is time to question if the Hulman regime, made up of people who have been involved in raising the Speedway and the 500-Mile Race to their undreamed-of heights, has not become so inbred and insulated to outside influences after 28 years that it has come to view itself as omnicient and has become incapable of making needed changes."

There was plenty of blame to throw around in the summer of 1973. The drivers were quick to defend the winged 200-mph cars, and pinned the cause of the twelve-car start line crash on the slow approach to the green flag.

"I talked with several drivers after the race and they were all doing different things at the start—changing gears, trying to get the boost in—that all ought to be done before they get the green flag," said USAC chief steward Dick King. "Everybody should be in fourth gear and should have the turbocharger boost in. They have to be going fast enough that they've done that."

King, despite his role as USAC chief steward, did not have any significant influence at the Indianapolis 500. Rather than relying on the USAC crew used at every other venue on the championship trail, IMS maintained its own crew of stewards and observers for the month of May. The IMS chief steward since 1958 was a man named Harlan Fengler, who gained a disporoprtionate amount of power and was generally viewed with disdain by the modern-day Indy car competitors.

Fengler, who competed twice at Indianapolis in the 1920s (once as a driver and once as a rider), wound up being the fall guy who took the rap for the events of May 1973. Two months prior to the '74 race, he was replaced by former USAC President Tom Binford, who would hold the role of Indianapolis 500 chief steward through '95—when his own tenure would also end in controversy, though thankfully, not in tragedy.

Binford's first task was to restore a state of calm to the Speedway in the wake of the previous year's trauma. "The Speedway management felt a change was needed," Binford wrote in his autobiography. "The racing fraternity felt that the media's massive reaction to the 1973 race wasn't good for the sport, and I tried to convey to the drivers that we all have some responsibility to provide a 'good show' for the fans and for each other. I think the heat on the event from 1973, plus an approach of reaching out to the racers, went a long way toward improving the race in 1974."

USAC mandated immediate changes to the cars, reducing the width of the rear wing by nine inches, cutting fuel capacity from seventy-five to forty gallons, and shifting the fuel tanks away from the right side of cars. There were also changes at IMS prior to the 1974 race. The concrete retaining wall around the outside of the track was raised, and the wall inside of Turn Four was reprofiled to prevent a repeat of Savage's vicious accident. That also created a wider pit entry that extended to the exit of the fourth turn. In addition, the Speedway for the first time utilized a starter stand, with flag man Vidan perched fifteen feet above the track and Binford another seven feet above him. The traditional eleven rows of three remained, but the rows were spaced one hundred feet apart instead of the previous fifty. The final change had little to do with safety: the 500 would henceforth be scheduled on the last Sunday in May instead of May 30.

Speeds at Indianapolis dropped by about ten mph in 1974, and in general, Indy car racing's safety record improved dramatically for the remainder of the decade. The 500 continued to be plagued by rain, shortened to 435 miles in '75 (the images of winner Bobby Unser splashing his Eagle through the deluge show how quickly the storm moved in) and an all-time low of 255 miles in '76, when Johnny Rutherford's McLaren was out front when the race was declared official.

By 1977, drivers were knocking on the door of 200 mph at Indianapolis once again. The honor finally fell to Tom Sneva, who ran a pair of 200-mph qualifying laps in his Penske Racing McLaren. Driving a Penske chassis a year later, Sneva posted the first full 200-mph qualification run, averaging 202.156 mph. The former schoolteacher won consecutive USAC championships for Penske in '77 and '78 but was released by the team at the end of his second title campaign, his fate sealed by Penske's recruitment of promising newcomer Rick Mears.

The 1977 Indianapolis 500 was significant for a couple of other reasons, most notably that A.J. Foyt became the first four-time winner of the famous race. In addition, the field featured its first female qualifier: thirty-nine-year-old Janet Guthrie. An aeronautical engineer turned sports car racer, Guthrie's spot in the '77 Indy 500 set a precedent that today still makes the race unique as one of the few sporting endeavors where men and women compete on equal terms. A year later, Guthrie finished ninth at Indy, a record that stood until eclipsed nearly thirty years later by Danica Patrick—who cites Guthrie as a key influence in her decision to become a race car driver.

Given Guthrie's presence, Tony Hulman had to make a change to his well-rehearsed pre-race command. "In company with the first woman ever to qualify at Indianapolis," he said, "Gentlemen, start your engines!" But the female racer's arrival wasn't welcomed by all.

"They told me women can't do it, women don't have the strength, women don't have the endurance or the emotional stability and we're going to endanger our lives," Guthrie recalled. "Most of the oval track drivers had never had the experience of running with a woman driver, and they were sure they weren't going to like it. But that got calmed down within the course of the races that I ran. The 'first woman' thing was more of a responsibility.

"The public, I think, needed to be convinced," Guthrie continued. "Of course the late 1960s and '70s were the glory days of the Indianapolis 500, when ninety cars were entered, when just qualifying fast enough to put a car in the field was a major accomplishment for any driver. Those were the days of Johnny Rutherford, Mario Andretti, and A.J. Foyt. So qualifying for the first time was really a major moment of my life."

Al Unser claimed his third Indy 500 triumph in 1978, and he went on to become the only man to sweep USAC's Triple Crown in the same year with additional victories in the Pocono 500 and the California 500 at IMS clone Ontario Motor Speedway. The other important aspect of Unser's '78 Indianapolis win is that it was the first for the Ford-Cosworth DFX engine. A few years earlier, Vel's Parnelli Jones Racing built a Cosworth-powered Formula 1 car in California and fielded it with Andretti driving from late '74 to early '76, when costs drove the team out of F1.

However, VPJ came up with the idea of modifying the 3.0-liter Ford-Cosworth DFV Formula 1 engine for Indy car racing. They cut the capacity to 2.65 liters, added a turbocharger, and installed it in a modified Parnelli F1 car. Al Unser won three races in 1976 in the Parnelli VPJ6B-Cosworth, prompting Cosworth to poach Parnelli's key engine men and develop its own Indy car engine that became known as the DFX.

McLaren modified an M23 F1 chassis for a Cosworth DFX installation and was very successful with its M24 in USAC competition. A year later, Penske Racing turned its DFV-powered F1 contender into the PC6-Cosworth Indy car, winning many races in 1978 and '79. By '81, Cosworth powered thirty of thirty-three cars in the Indianapolis 500 field, and the Offenhauser four-cylinder was finally obsolete, after a remarkable fifty-year run.

Dormant in the first half of the 1970s, the battle over engine regulations really ramped up after the Cosworth came on the scene as USAC tried without success to keep the ancient Offy and aged Foyt/Ford V8s competitive with a modern product. The struggle to create an equivalency formula between engines was a major point of contention over a number of years in the late '70s, and in '78, the Offenhauser faithful actually staged a strike. By then, all participants lost confidence in USAC and its ability to provide a level playing field. Even before the advent of the Cosworth, many competitors were upset by USAC's constant adjustments to boost levels and the implementation of pop-off valves to regulate boost. The addition of fuel mileage regulations confused matters even more.

Competitors generally weren't happy with the way the USAC series was performing commercially, either. Few races outside the Indianapolis 500 were televised, and the 500 was still broadcast via tape delay through 1985. Purses were small, and the championship featured just thirteen to fourteen oval races throughout the mid-seventies until a '78 expansion brought road racing—including a pair of late-season races at Silverstone and Brands Hatch in England—back into the equation.

USAC started exploring a greater presence for road racing in 1974, but instead of integrating it into the Indy car Championship Trail, it entered into a partnership with the Sports Car Club of America to co-promote and sanction the North American Formula 5000 Championship, which featured single-seat, open-wheel cars powered by five-liter V8 engines. F5000 had what *Road & Track* called "excitement, competition and color, [but] it didn't have the names that draw the fans." *R&T* went on to say "a merger looked like good business for both sides."

So the SCCA turned over key sanctioning duties to USAC and, in return, opened the rule book to allow turbocharged Champ Cars to compete in F5000 races. USAC loosened the reins on its drivers and allowed them to participate in more events, and the two sanctioning bodies commenced work on a common car that would likely have utilized something similar to the five-liter stock-block engines used in F5000.

"A common formula was, and is, a must," commented USAC executive director Dick King in mid-1975. "Road racing is a viable part of the sport and our drivers wanted to try it. And we had to do something to bring the cost of the sport down. A common formula should be the answer."

"We want to get to that North American Championship," added Cameron Argetsinger, chief of the SCCA. "I'd like to see a common formula by 1977, but 1978 is probably more realistic. Whenever it happens, it will be the biggest thing in the history of racing in this country."

The mooted consolidation of Formula 5000 and USAC Champ Cars had the potential to create a golden era for American open-wheel racing. USAC boasted names like Andretti and Foyt, as well as the Unser brothers, Rutherford, Johncock, and Sneva. Meanwhile, Brian Redman was dominating F5000, winning three straight championships between 1974 and '76 over strong fields that included stars like Jody Scheckter, David Hobbs, Sam Posey, Jackie Oliver, and Vern Schuppan. Andretti and Al Unser were both F5000 race winners in Viceroy-sponsored cars entered by the Vel's Parnelli Jones team.

Yet somehow, by the end of 1976, USAC and the SCCA were again bitter enemies and Formula 5000 was dead. "Under the unsure, part-time guidance of the SCCA, Formula 5000 slipped into the same kind of disrepute that killed the Can-Am two years before," wrote Gordon Kirby in the *Autocourse 1976-77* annual. "Despite the establishment of an entrant's organization known as the North American Grand Prix Association (NAGPA), which addressed the issues of promotion, sponsorship, and prize money, Formula 5000 died because circuit owners said it was not promotable." By the end of '76, the SCCA had announced plans for a "new" Can-Am, featuring rebodied F5000 cars. In retrospect, it is tempting to wonder what would have happened if those exploratory efforts more than forty years ago would have resulted in the SCCA and USAC successfully creating a unified open-wheel racing series that included road, street, and oval circuits.

All in all, the late 1970s were a volatile and difficult time for Indy car racing in almost every respect. And then Tony Hulman died.

CHAPTER 4

THE BIRTH OF CART

After A.J. Foyt became the first four-time Indianapolis 500 winner in May 1977, Tony Hulman did something unusual: he rode around the Indianapolis Motor Speedway perched on the open roof of the Oldsmobile pace car with his good friend, sharing in Foyt's record-setting triumph. A slow victory lap for the winner was a long-established Indy tradition, but caught up in the excitement of Foyt's historic win (and still clutching a cigarette), this was the first time that the Indianapolis Motor Speedway chairman included himself in the celebration.

"I will never forget that day in 1977 for as long as I live," said Ralph Hansen, who was Hulman's personal assistant from 1970-77. "Tony was overjoyed by A.J.'s win. None of us knew that this would be Mr. Hulman's last Indy 500, but I can testify that he was truly thrilled that Foyt won, and in my ten years of being his friend, I don't know if I ever saw him more excited and happy than when A.J. got the checkered flags and drank the milk."

Hulman was seventy-six years old and in apparent good health, so his death on October 27, 1977, during planned heart surgery at St. Vincent Hospital in Indianapolis came as a shock to his family, the Speedway, and the racing world as a whole. He was the man who was credited with almost single-handedly saving the Indianapolis Motor Speedway and building the Indianapolis 500 into the world's largest single-day sporting event.

Those who knew Hulman remember him as a shy man who was uncomfortable in the spotlight, especially when it came to public speaking.

But he was also a man of extraordinary charisma who had a unique ability to put anybody in his presence at ease.

Hansen became acquainted with Tony and Mary Hulman when he attended Indiana State University in Terre Haute, where he was the president of the Delta Pi chapter of the Theta Chi fraternity. The Hulmans lived just two doors down from the Theta Chi house on Sixth Street, and in October 1969, Hansen invited them to join him and his fraternity brothers at the house for dinner. Mr. Hulman was happy to accept.

About two months later, on January 7, 1970, the Theta Chi house burned to the ground. Hulman quickly offered to help. He arranged accommodations for the displaced members at a nearby hotel he owned, the Terre Haute House, and made certain that dinner was prepared for the brothers each night. He also assisted in obtaining the bank loan the fraternity needed to rebuild, and furnished the new house with items including desks and beds.

Upon graduating from ISU in 1970, Hansen became Mr. Hulman's assistant until his death. Hansen spent hours traveling with Hulman, often in Hulman's immaculately polished Beechcraft D18S aircraft (tail number N500). He has many fond recollections of the impact the Indianapolis Motor Speedway owner had on people.

On one occasion in 1977, Hulman's commitments nearly kept him from celebrating one of the most significant milestones in IMS history—the first two-hundred-mile-per-hour qualifying lap. "Tony had an event to attend in Greencastle, where DePauw University was dedicating the fine arts building and art collection donated by Mr. and Mrs. Hulman," Hansen said. "Mr. Hulman was not very eager to go because it was the morning of Indy 500 qualifications. He asked me to drive him to the event and we took his personal car, a dark blue Cadillac Seville, instead of his Oldsmobile pace car.

"We were listening to qualifying on WIBC while we were on the interstate on the way home," he continued. "Tom Sneva was qualifying and was the first driver ever to break the two hundred barrier. Mr. Hulman was upset he was not there and kept telling me to drive faster. I admit I was pretty darn nervous driving a hundred miles an hour with Tony Hulman as my passenger. Sure enough, just after I said to

Mr. Hulman that I was probably going to get a ticket, here comes an Indiana State Police car off an entrance ramp.

"He pulled up behind us, but Mr. Hulman told me to stay put. Tony got out of the car, which is frowned on these days by police, and spoke to the officer for about thirty seconds. The State Trooper pulled in front of us with lights flashing and siren blaring and Tony said to me, 'Follow him!' I was as nervous as hell driving that fast with such a famous passenger, and as we passed the next entrance on the interstate, here comes another Indiana state police car. He pulled in right behind us and both State Troopers took us right into the Speedway main tunnel. I had white knuckles from gripping the steering wheel so tight, but Mr. Hulman got to congratulate Tom Sneva when we arrived. Tony Hulman was absolutely *the* most powerful man in Indiana, and the State Police rightfully treated him as such!"

Although Hulman's passing was sudden and unexpected, business went on as usual at IMS. Mary Fendrich Hulman, Tony's widow, took over as chairman of the board of Hulman & Co., and Hulman's longtime right-hand man Joe Cloutier assumed presidency of the track. But a long-term succession plan within the Hulman family was in question, in part due to events that occurred early on May 31, 1976.

In 1957, Tony and Mary's daughter Mari married Elmer George, a sprint car driver of the era who made three Indianapolis 500 starts between '57 and '63. After retiring from driving, Elmer worked at a variety of jobs for IMS, and by the mid-seventies he was a vice president of the IMS Radio Network. Between '57 and '62, Elmer and Mari had four children—daughters Nancy, Kathi, and Josie, and on December 30, 1959, a son christened Anton Hulman George.

Mari George filed for divorce from Elmer on May 3, 1976, and a few weeks later, the contentious split turned deadly. According to police records, after an argument broke out in a Turn Two suite at IMS following the rain-shortened '76 Indy 500, an angry Elmer George traveled to Terre Haute to confront Mari's alleged boyfriend, a horse trainer named Guy Trollinger who worked for the Hulmans and lived at the family farm.

Sometime around 1:00 a.m., George attempted to break into the house, and gunfire between the two men broke out with as many as seventeen shots fired. George, forty-seven, died from multiple gunshot wounds. Trollinger was initially charged with assault and battery with intent to kill, but a hastily convened Vigo County Grand Jury dropped the charges, essentially concluding that Trollinger killed George in self-defense.

We can only speculate whether Elmer George would have made an impact on the future of the Indianapolis Motor Speedway or USAC; details of the relationship between Tony Hulman and his son-in-law are not well-known. Though they never married, Trollinger would remain Mari Hulman George's partner until the day she died in 2018. In any case, uncertainty over the long-term management of the sport increased on April 23, 1978, when eight USAC officials died when their private plane crashed in rural Indiana when they were returning from a race in Trenton, New Jersey. The group that perished included USAC Technical Director Frankie Delroy, starter/flag man Shim Malone, and Vice President of Public Affairs Ray Marquette.

With all the drama that was happening off the track, the last thing USAC and IMS needed was dissention among the competitors. But that is exactly what was brewing by the late 1970s. Team owners began to express their dissatisfaction that so much emphasis was placed on the Indianapolis 500 at the expense of a full series of strong Indy car championship races. They thought USAC needed an expanded, diversified series of races with much stronger commercial backing and media coverage, which the team owners believed was necessary for their survival as business entities.

As Formula 1 technology continued to creep into Indy car racing, the cars were becoming more expensive to develop and build, and purses were not keeping pace with the increased costs for the competitors. The participating teams also believed that engine rules needed to be brought in line with the times. Turbocharger boost regulators, known as pop-off valves, were introduced in 1976, and boost limits were frequently raised and lowered over the next few years. Sometimes pop-off valves were required in races, then only in qualifying as fuel mileage limits were used to control boost in the races. At the peak of the crisis, USAC's vacillation got to the point where boost and fuel mileage regulations often differed on a day-to-day basis. Insiders recognized that it was a thinly disguised ploy to keep the old-timers with their Offenhauser engines happy and competitive.

"The economics were impossible," recalled Parnelli Jones, who transitioned from driving into team ownership in the 1970s. "If we had $500,000 in sponsorship, we were spending $1 million, and if we had $1 million in sponsorship, we were spending $2 million. We could never get ahead. Every year was costing us more money."

This constant and unpredictable change not only created higher costs for the owners, it hurt the quality of competition. USAC's 500-mile races often featured only five or six finishers, most of them many laps behind the winner. The mileage restrictions resulted in several races from 1976-78 being determined by attrition and competitors running out of fuel in the closing laps.

For example, thirty cars started the 1978 California 500 at Ontario Motor Speedway—"the first time in 30 years that a USAC 500-miler has been without a full complement of 33 starters," according to the report in *Autosport* magazine—but only five were running at the finish, with second-place finisher Gordon Johncock no less than five laps behind winner Al Unser at the checkered flag. The last of the five running cars was forty-two laps down, yet credited with sixth place, and there were an amazing thirteen engine or engine-related failures. The severe attrition and small number of finishers detracted from Unser's achievement of becoming the first (and still only) driver to sweep a Triple Crown of 500-mile races in the same season.

"The lack of cars can probably be attributed to the four-cylinder revolt since quite a few of the regulars passed up the Cal 500 because they didn't want to tow 2,000 miles to run for twelfth place," wrote Robin Miller in the *Indianapolis Star*. "But as it turned out, all you needed was two working cylinders and you could have finished no worse than seventh.

"The USAC Board of Directors holds the future of championship racing in its shaky hands. It's got a big meeting scheduled here this weekend when it will decide whether or not the four-cylinder engines will continue to compete or become large boat anchors. And if it doesn't make the right decision, the whole ship may sink."

Earlier in 1978, Dan Gurney, the driver turned car builder/team owner, wrote a seven-page letter to his fellow team owners known as the "White Paper" that compared USAC racing to Formula 1. He noted that F1 experienced considerable growth and gained stability after the team owners, led by Brabham owner Bernie Ecclestone, banded together to form the Formula One Constructors' Association (FOCA) to take over greater control of the commercial side of the sport. Gurney proposed that the Indy car team owners form a FOCA-like alliance to take over promotion of the sport, while leaving technical sanctioning of the races to USAC. "Let's call it CART, or Championship Auto Racing Teams," he suggested.

Gurney explained his rationale in an interview with journalist/ historian Gordon Kirby: "Indy was the hub around which the USAC championship revolved. The tradition at Indy was to have one race a year, and it was a big one that paid a great purse and had tremendous history. It was just a great event. At the time it was far and away the biggest in the world of racing. Maybe Le Mans came close, but Indy was the big one.

"USAC was a child of the Speedway," he continued. "USAC was there to run the month of May, and it also was allowed to have its own additional other races that made up the national championship series. That was fine, not a problem, but the rest of the championship series was bogged down. It didn't have any leadership and was more or less derelict. There was not much linkage between all the other races and the Indy 500. The rest of the races were sort of orphans that nobody paid attention to. Nor had anybody heard the word 'marketing.' The waters were stagnant.

"You can't run the business of a racing team with just one big race a year and the rest of them are a bunch of losers, unless you're doing it as a hobby and not as a real business," he concluded.

DAN GURNEY'S "WHITE PAPER"

Gentlemen:

Over the past 3 or 4 years I've had conversations with almost all of the car owners and team directors. I've had talks with drivers, with sanctioning body directors, with track owners and promoters and big sponsors and fans and other interested parties. Generally there is agreement that something is wrong with our sport—it is not reaching its full potential by any means, and there is great need for a change!

Early in my discussions I realized that we are so intent upon racing each other that we do not stop to look and analyze our situation. In frustration I decided that things must get worse before we will all wake up. Our sport has the potential to be financially rewarding and healthy from a business standpoint for all participants. Many of the car owners and team directors are excellent and very successful businessman in their own lives outside of racing. We as businessmen should be ashamed of ourselves for being involved in a prestigious sport such as Championship racing with all its potential while it is as weak and disorganized (sick) as it presently is. It is truly strange that with all these "heavyweights" involved, we still do not have our act together. ("Divide and conquer" still seems to be working doesn't it?)

O.K.! What shall we do about it? First let us digress for a moment. Let's study some history. Back in the early '70s, the status of Formula 1 Grand Prix racing was similar to our own USAC Championship racing right now. The crowds were quite small, sponsors were hard to find, the news media was not overly interested, expenses were high and going higher and the entire scene was one of disorganization.

It was at this moment in time that the desperateness of the situation made them unite and form an organization called the Formula 1 Constructors' Association (F1CA or FOCA). They appointed a man named Bernie Ecclestone as the chief of operations officer and negotiator and they made a solemn pledge to abide by his decisions 100%. They rolled up their sleeves and proceeded to up-grade the entire sport to the point where the paying spectator crowds are much, much larger, sponsors are numerous and happy to be involved, the media is vigorous in covering all the events on TV and so are weekly magazines and daily newspapers on a world wide basis, and money is coming back to the constructors and track owners in the form of larger ticket sales, more sponsorship, more prize money and expense money and the spectator is getting a much bigger, better spectacle for his ticket money.

The obvious fact is that the FOCA has transformed the Formula 1 Grand Prix racing scene from what was a weak and scattered group of teams without any bargaining or negotiating strength into a bona fide business. They did it by uniting and making that "no turning back" commitment. They speak with one voice (that of the Chief negotiator) and that voice has gained authority by leaps and bounds.

Now, it is true that the Championship racing scene is somewhat different from Grand Prix racing and therefore it will require a slightly different organization to bring about an improvement. I only mention the FOCA organization as an example of something that has succeeded, on no uncertain terms. I think everyone agrees that the cost of Championship racing has escalated to the point where it is virtually ridiculous, and at the same time, many of the rewards have not increased at all, but have actually declined when you consider the effects of the general inflation in the U.S. economy.

At the moment we the car owners are the ones who have put forth by far the most effort, by far the most financial stake with little or no chance for return and yet, because we have been so busy fighting with each other, we have let the track owners or promoters and the sanctioning body lead us around by the nose while they reap the benefits. USAC for instance negotiates with TV as though it had the TV rights, which in fact, if it came to a showdown, would turn out to be ours. (The car owners and teams.)

It is obvious that if Long Beach (Formula 1's United States Grand Prix West) can afford to pay approximately $1,000,000 per race after only 5 years of existence (established 1974) and maximum paid attendance of 70,000 so far, that Indy with its 600,000 plus audience (200 1st weekend qualifying, 100 2nd weekend qualifying, 300 Race Day for 600,000 paid attendance) and its 60-year tradition and international TV coverage, could afford to spend over $2 million on the purse, if it were to be fair. As Mr. Lindsey Hopkins said, "We are the ones who did more to build the stands at Indianapolis than anyone else. IMS should thank us each year, in addition to our thanking them."

In all of our discussions, as car owners and team leaders, we have agreed that it is essential that we continue to support USAC as the sanctioning body for Championship racing. The only improvement will be that USAC will work for us and support our cause and our policies as well. It should be clearly understood that the purpose of this organization is to make racing better in an overall way. Not just for the car owners and drivers, but also for the track owners and promoters and the sanctioning body and the sponsors and supporters and last but certainly not least, the racing fans and paying spectators.

In the final analysis of course, large crowds of paying spectators are the keys to success for all. Track owners and a sanctioning body who aggressively promote these big events—which by contract will feature the teams and driving stars, will get the crowds . . .which in turn excites the sponsors and TV networks and the crowd, etc., thereby upgrading the entire sport business. It is my firm belief that rather than cutting the cost of racing, which in itself is nearly impossible, it is far more important to make money more readily available by increasing the popularity and prestige of the sport with the general public.

Tracks that refuse to put forth the necessary enterprise and promotion in order to meet the minimum purses should not be allowed to hold races. Another alternative is to allow our organization (this idea borrowed from the FOCA) to take over the track on a reasonable lease arrangement and we can do the promotion and the running of the race where we feel it can be successful. Still USAC sanctioned, of course. For instance, the German GP at Hockenheim will be promoted by the FOCA this year, 1978.

Now, how do we get there from here? As I see it, the first step is to analyze the situation, get together and form the organization. (Let's call it C.A.R.T., or Championship Auto Racing Teams.) Once we agree to the fact that CART is needed then we must outline what we want to do and how we should accomplish it. I believe that the organization can be operated by a staff of three people. One director/negotiator, one secretary and a staff accountant and gopher if needed. He will need an air travel card, a telephone credit card and an expense account. It is rumored that Bernie takes none of this, he only works on a 2% commission of everything that is done through the FOCA.

It appears that a "show down" with the Indianapolis Motor Speedway is or should be the first target. They are the ones who can afford it. We should re-negotiate the TV contract (our rights—not theirs) and we should double the purse. Other tracks should be negotiated with on the basis of what is a reasonable amount of revenue to come from all sources such as TV, gate receipts, advertising sponsors, etc. The entire picture should be shared from the standpoint of cooperation rather than killing each other.

We must work together to learn how to upgrade the overall marketing— advertising. If CART can send in drivers and media material beforehand to the newspapers, the TV stations, the Chamber of Commerce as well as various civic organizations and schools, etc. then we should do so. It is vital that we solve the riddle of getting more money coming in from spectator and sponsor advertisers, and TV networks so that there is a bigger pie to carve up . . . the only way our demands for more money in the form of a prize fund can have any validity is if the money is there in the first place. Unless we reach the point where we can see the books of these various tracks, we will be negotiating from a position of ignorance. It seems to me that we could all be further ahead if we worked together rather than be divided. We must see the tax returns and books.

With the correct program of exposure, a fuel company can still get the right sort of benefits from being the exclusive Championship series sponsor. Cigarettes, Whiskey, Banking, Unions . . . we need a very aggressive sales promotion team with super people heading it. How do we finance this CART operation? Entry fees? Percentage of the purse? Etc. I'm open for suggestions. Someone (our man from CART) must be part of all Dick King's negotiations with track promoters and television people and series sponsors etc.

Gurney's "White Paper" rambled and lost focus at times, but the key points were clear for all to see. As the 1978 season rolled on, the idea of an owners' group gained momentum. A series of meetings throughout the summer and autumn of '78, generally in hotel lobbies and conference rooms, resulted in the formation of Championship Auto Racing Teams, or CART. Twenty-one entrants, including Penske Racing, Patrick Racing, Team McLaren, Chaparral Racing, All American Racers, Foyt-Gilmore Racing, and Fletcher Racing as the principal members, paid a $7,500 fee to join the group.

With Roger Penske and fellow team owner U.E. "Pat" Patrick as point men, CART proposed a revised structure to govern the sport. CART's concerns centered around marketing, including television, but the new group made clear it wanted USAC to retain control of actually running the races. "CART is in no way making any demands on USAC," said Penske. "All of us have too much at stake to do anything to harm racing."

At this point, Foyt was hopeful that CART could bring some much-needed structure and stability to the rules, particularly in terms of the engine and fuel regulations. Foyt was incensed by USAC's recently announced 1979 rule package, which mandated an even narrower rear wing and altered boost levels, allowing additional boost and extra fuel for the four-cylinder Offenhauser cars. During the September 1978 Gould Grand Prix race weekend at Michigan International Speedway (a 75-lap-150-mile oval race won by Foyt), A.J. blasted the USAC board as "idiotic."

"There have to be some changes made," Foyt said. "Apart from three or four of them, USAC's board of directors don't know anything about racing. It's no good having guys from the midget and sprint divisions telling us how to run championship racing. They don't have any idea what our problems are. We are the guys with millions of dollars invested, and we should be making our own rules.

"So a lot of us owners have gotten together, and we'll probably have our own group make the championship rules," he added. "Now I don't mean we're gonna get rid of USAC or anything like that. We need them as a governing body because there are an awful lot of things they do real well. But that don't include making the rules."

CART continued to maintain that its members were simply seeking additional representation within the framework of USAC. Patrick presented CART's six-point plan to overhaul the USAC Championship Trail to the twenty-one-man USAC board at an emergency meeting on November 18, 1978, proposing the following:

1. An eleven-man board to be formed with six CART members and five from the USAC ranks with this board to be totally independent from the USAC board.
2. All races to be USAC sanctioned.
3. The eleven-man board would be responsible for the following areas:
   a. Rule changes with these 1979 proposals: seventy inches of boost for eight-cylinder engines, seventy-four inches of boost for four-cylinder engines, 1.8 miles per gallon fuel allotment, and the rear wing to remain at the 1978 width of forty-three inches.
   b. A maximum of fourteen races per season, with a minimum thirteen days between races.
   c. The following purse guidelines: 150-mile races are guaranteed $75,000 plus television and accessories, 200-mile races are guaranteed $100,000 plus television and accessories, 500-mile races are guaranteed a 20-percent increase over 1978, and all road races will be sanctioned for a minimum of $125,000.
   d. The board shall negotiate television and series sponsorship.

USAC quickly rejected the CART plan, so CART responded with a counter. "We offered to comprise the board of six CART and six USAC members with [USAC President] Dick King sitting in as a non-voting chairman," Patrick said. "I got another phone call from Reynold [Mac-Donald, USAC board chairman] and was told that compromise had been vetoed unanimously."

In fact, USAC accepted CART's proposal for technical changes, and said it would modify the 1979 rules it announced in September (eighty inches of boost for all competitors, 1.5 miles per gallon fuel economy requirement and thirty-six-inch wide rear wing) to match CART's proposal. But it stood firm on relinquishing any additional control.

"We are in accord with some of their objectives and in fact we took some steps at our September meeting to relate to some of those objectives," MacDonald said. "We feel we must continue to function in the best interests of all our members. These include not only car owners, but also drivers, mechanics, race organizers, manufacturers, and sponsors."

Motivated by USAC's firm resistance, CART acted quickly. CART President Patrick announced that his group would break away from USAC and stage its own series of Indy car races in 1979. "There's no longer a USAC Championship division as far as we're concerned," Patrick told the *Star*. "We've been fair and we've tried to act like gentlemen. But the people spending the money (the team owners) have no vote in the rules. We have no input into what USAC says or does. And effective today, we are going to control our destiny.

"We've already got two dates at Phoenix and Michigan, and we've talked to the promoters at Atlanta and Ontario," he added. "We're prepared to lease tracks and do whatever we have to do to get good races."

Penske later explained his reasoning for the split. "Indy car racing, as I saw it, was on a decline under the United States Auto Club," he told *Indy Car Racing* magazine in 1983. "Not because there weren't dedicated, good people, but because they were planted in sprint cars, stock cars, and everything else. They had a charter and covered all types of racing, and it was obvious the attention and the ability to go out and put the thing together just wasn't there. The fields were short. That's how we were going along—two races at Trenton, a race at Texas, and no crowds. Pat and I decided one night in New York that we had to do something about it. What we have to do is make it a viable sport which can generate tremendous fan interest."

With the benefit of hindsight, Gurney believes the initial USAC-CART split could have been averted if USAC and the Indianapolis Motor Speedway had been a bit more flexible and open-minded about the changes CART hoped to implement. Instead of looking at the big picture, he suggests that IMS looked inward to protect its own power base.

"If the Speedway wouldn't take hold and provide real leadership to the rest of the circuit, just to survive, somebody else was going to have to do it," Gurney said. "We asked the Speedway to understand the predicament that we were in. We talked to them and they essentially were happy with the status quo. As far as they were concerned they were okay, and yet they would not relinquish the control that USAC had over the rest of the races.

"We said, 'Look at what has happened to these other sports and entertainment businesses,'" Gurney continued. "Golf was in the age of Arnold Palmer and Jack Nicklaus, and Mark McCormack and his management group (IMG) were showing golf and tennis and other sports that things were booming because there was leadership. We could see that, and we said to the Speedway, 'Let's have a heart and discuss this thing.'

"We were trying to be genuine, professional teams and were watching other sports blossom and get big recognition on television and everywhere else. We asked, 'Where were we headed?' And they told us they had no plans. We had never targeted the Speedway for attack; we only asked them to provide the leadership. There was never any discussion about doing something that would harm the Speedway. I never heard one tiny hint that that was the case.

"I thought the potential was so much bigger than what had been achieved and that it would be good for everybody," he concluded. "It would raise all boats and it would be terrific, and I still believe that. Had the Speedway just taken a moment to look into their crystal ball at the future, things might have been different and we could have all worked together."

An underlying reason for the tension between the car owners and the governing body was a changing of the guard in the owners themselves. When USAC took over control of the sport in the 1950s, car owners, including J.C. Agajanian, John Zink, and Al Dean, were often wealthy sportsmen who financed race teams out of their own pockets, more or less as a hobby. For the new breed of owners, racing was a business every much as it was a sport, and as such, they needed their on-track exploits to at least be self-sustaining, if not profitable.

Men like Gurney, Colin Chapman, Jim Hall, and Bruce McLaren revolutionized the sport not only with the technologically advanced racing cars they produced, but with the business-first mindset they possessed. At the same time, Penske was among those who were instrumental in establishing the advent of corporate sponsorships to support the increasing costs. Penske sold his first sponsorship to DuPont Corp. in the early 1960s and his Formula 1-based Cooper sports car was rechristened the Zerex Special. When Penske won a series of high-profile races in the controversial car, Dupont gained far more publicity out of the sponsorship than the $5,000 it invested.

The flashpoint that ignited the conflict in philosophies was the rear-engine revolution of the 1960s, but the animosity among the old guard was still bubbling away in the late '70s, as noted by historian Forrest Bond. "USAC saw the new cars and the new owners as violators of sacred tradition, and ultimately as revolutionaries," Bond wrote. "Conversely, the new owners saw USAC as out of touch with reality, resisting change at Indy simply because it was change, and obstinately converting midgets and sprints into vintage racing."

Robin Miller highlighted the owners' unhappiness with the financial structure of the sport in a December 3, 1978, column in the *Indianapolis Star* titled "Speedway Purse: $1 Million Crumbs." Miller noted that the Indianapolis 500 purse had not significantly increased in ten years, and purses for the other races on the USAC Championship Trail had also failed to keep pace with the cost of competing.

"Amid the civil war between USAC and CART, one should consider this possibility," Miller led. "What would happen if the Indianapolis Motor Speedway began paying its participants justly?

"That's right, what if the sixty-third Indianapolis 500 upped its purse to $4 million instead of $1.1 million? Would the car owners that have broken away from USAC to form their own organization be satisfied enough to get back together and go racing?"

Miller estimated that IMS brought in more than $10 million in ticket sales alone for the month of May, yet after the ABC television payout, the Speedway's actual contribution to the $1.1 million purse was something like $300,000. He pointed out that for the other two 500-mile races on the USAC schedule (Ontario and Pocono), the participants ran for a guaranteed purse of 40 percent of the gate, which by his estimation worked out to about $4 million at Indy. He noted that while the Indianapolis 500 purse had risen by 1.4 percent since 1974, NASCAR's Daytona 500 purse soared by some 300 percent in that same period.

"So maybe if you gave the owners a chance to make a little money—or just break even—it would encourage new faces, or at least keep the old ones smiling," he concluded. "It's billed as the greatest, and it's way past time the wages met the effort. It's about time for Indy to catch up with reality."

Instead, it was business as usual at 16th and Georgetown. Meanwhile, Patrick and his cohorts were busy working on creating their own series of Indy car races. By mid-December, they inked a deal for the Sports Car Club of America (SCCA) to sanction CART's still-unsettled slate of events. Among the signatures on the SCCA contract was that of Foyt, still the sport's most recognizable star.

Less than two months later, and not for the first time, Foyt changed his mind. He defiantly quit CART and returned to the USAC fold on January 31, 1979. "I left because the original goals of CART have changed, and I don't like some of the politics that have been played," Foyt fumed. "They used me to get CART formed and now there are only one or two guys doing all the talking. They're on an ego trip to conquer the racing world, but I have no desire to do that."

Speaking to Dick Mittman of the *Indianapolis News*, Foyt added, "I just feel I've been with USAC for many years and I wasn't going to throw it down the drain. There were too many quick decisions . . . right now, looking at CART, I would say USAC is in better shape. Stop and count and CART will have a hard time getting twelve to fifteen cars for a race. I know a couple teams who'll pull out.

"CART is not strong enough to do anything about Indianapolis," he continued. "Indianapolis is the greatest race in the world. It always has been its own organization, and I can't see any reason for it to change. They are going to have a full field."

CART ultimately produced a ten-race schedule for 1979 that opened at Phoenix International Raceway (PIR). The slate also included stops at Atlanta International Raceway, Trenton International Speedway, Michigan International Speedway, Watkins Glen, and Ontario Motor Speedway.

CART's teams and drivers also expected to compete in the Indianapolis 500, part of a seven-race 1979 USAC National Championship that opened at Ontario on March 25 and also included events at Texas World Speedway, the Milwaukee Mile, and Pocono Raceway. "We'll abide by the Speedway's regulations," said Patrick.

CART was first out of the gates in 1979 with the Jimmy Bryan 150 at Phoenix on March 11. Roger Penske entered a pair of brand new Penske PC7-Cosworths for veteran Bobby Unser and rising star Rick Mears. Patrick Racing fielded Cosworth-powered Penske PC6s for Gordon Johncock and Wally Dallenbach, the McLaren factory team entered an M24-Cosworth for Johnny Rutherford, and two-time defending USAC champion Tom Sneva wheeled a highly modified McLaren M24 for Jerry O'Connell's Sugaripe Prune team. Other top contenders included Danny Ongais in Ted Field's Parnelli-Cosworth and Al Unser, driving a Lola-Cosworth for sports car legend Jim Hall. Seven Offenhauser-powered cars were entered.

It was almost miraculous that the CART contingent was even able to get to PIR at all after (believe it or not) a second consecutive winter of intense flooding. Development of the Avondale/Goodyear area was a distant dream at that point, and overflow from a nearby reservoir created three one-hundred-yard wide streams blocking the entrance to the track that left the CART event in doubt less than a week prior to the race. The main road from Interstate 10 to PIR had been washed away in early 1978, and floods also destroyed the replacement four-lane dirt road in February '79, causing the cancellation of the annual Copper World Classic. When several CART teams showed up early to test on the Tuesday of race week, they had to park their haulers several miles away and tow the cars into the track behind pickup trucks and station wagons.

PIR owner (and CART member) Bob Fletcher pulled out all the stops, and with plenty of assistance from Maricopa County, a new three-lane temporary road was constructed by Friday morning. "It's incredible, I'll admit," PIR General Manager Dennis Woods marveled. "Those guys really busted their tails. The fact that people told us there was no way makes it even better."

After a five-month buildup and war of words in the press, the race itself was almost anticlimactic. The most notable aspect was that 114 days into its existence operating a racing series, CART's first-ever event went off without controversy or dispute—for the most part.

Johncock took advantage of a pace car miscue to leapfrog ahead of Rutherford and Mears for the final fifteen-lap sprint to the finish. Mears snuck past Rutherford for second with just three laps remaining, and he crossed the line about six car lengths behind Johncock. Al Unser was fourth, and Bobby Unser was a lap down in fifth.

Johncock won $18,670 for barely an hour of work, which was witnessed by a reported eighteen thousand spectators (a good crowd for PIR in those days) and a nationwide NBC television audience. But the real winner of the day was CART, which proved that even in its infancy, it could put on a show comparable to the standard established by USAC since it took over sanction of the sport in 1956.

Two weeks later at Ontario Motor Speedway (OMS) against a comparatively lackluster field, Foyt unsurprisingly dominated the Indy car portion of USAC's Datsun Twin 200s. Twenty-two cars took the start, but sixteen of them were older Offenhauser-powered models; Foyt's Parnelli was the only current chassis among the four Cosworth-powered entries. Foyt collected $17,760 after besting Johnny Parsons, Bill Vukovich Jr., and Sheldon Kinser. The crowd was announced as twenty thousand, which was claimed as the largest ever for the March race at OMS.

Victory Lane at Ontario therefore had a familiar look, but already there were clear signs that USAC's days of sanctioning top-level racing were numbered.

CHAPTER 5

THE FIRST SPLIT:
CART VS. USAC

March 25, 1979 should have been an enjoyable day for A.J. Foyt since it was one of the most successful and record-breaking days of his long career. Yet he was mad as hell.

After claiming victory in a 200-mile USAC Indy car race in his Parnelli-Cosworth at Ontario Motor Speedway, Foyt triumphed in the second half of the doubleheader—a USAC-sanctioned 200-mile stock car race—making him the first such double winner in club history. It was the legendary Texan's record-extending 62nd win at the championship level and 151st overall in USAC competition.

Having switched sides back to USAC after initially breaking away as part of the upstart CART organization, Foyt angrily believed that CART's drivers and teams had boycotted the Ontario weekend.

"To me, what they did was detrimental to racing," Foyt declared, failing to mention that he and his fellow USAC competitors did not take part in CART's inaugural event two weeks earlier at Phoenix. "This was an FIA [sanctioned] race, so they could have driven here under their own licenses. I felt they all should have been here.

"As far as I'm concerned, I'd like to see Indy turn down their entries," he fumed. "How do you think their sponsors would like that?"

One man who recognized the potential adverse effects of the intensifying USAC-CART conflict was Indianapolis Motor Speedway President Joe Cloutier, who told the *Indianapolis News* the split was "not good the way it is."

Indianapolis Motor Speedway

57

"It definitely has drawn attention that isn't good," Cloutier told reporter Dick Mittman. "It's probably made it a little more difficult to get cooperative effort from the outside. Many car sponsors have backed off until this is settled. Maybe it would be better for racing to do more of its own financing . . . we all must recognize that this is a sport and not a business venture. No one can go into it and make money."

The CART teams again stayed away from USAC's next event, the Coors 200 at Texas World Speedway on April 8, 1979. Temporarily parking the Parnelli, Foyt ran his faithful Coyote chassis and Foyt/Ford V8 for the last time, leading eighty-three of one hundred laps to take the laurels over Gary Bettenhausen.

Even though they had submitted entries to the Indianapolis 500, with the month of May looming and all the rhetoric in the air, there was still uncertainty over whether the CART teams would actually participate. As usual, turbocharger boost rules were a sticking point; USAC had cut boost for V8 racing engines to fifty inches in an effort to create parity with the less expensive stock-block engines it favored. CART had continued with the 1978 boost level of seventy inches, producing as much as two hundred horsepower more than running USAC specifications.

CART strove to eliminate the perception that it would boycott the biggest event in championship racing. Speaking to reporters in New York on April 18, Pat Patrick said, "We've submitted forty-four entries to meet the tech requirements at Indy, and we are going through with our plans to race there. I'll admit to being approached by a television network and another track to hold our own Memorial weekend race, and they are viable proposals, but we never indicated we'd pull out of Indianapolis."

When Patrick and five fellow team owners arrived at Atlanta Motor Speedway for CART's Gould Dixie Twin 125s two days later, they received telegrams from USAC and IMS informing them their Indianapolis entries had been rejected because they "were not in good standing with USAC." The entries from Penske Racing, McLaren Racing, Hall Racing, Patrick Racing, Fletcher Racing, and All American Racers represented eight drivers and a total of nineteen cars.

Dan Gurney spoke for the rejected owners. "USAC appears to be using the Indianapolis 500 as a pawn in its efforts to destroy CART as a viable racing organization," he said. "We will not let this happen. They have attempted to eliminate six of the top racing teams in the world. What do they mean 'not in good standing'? We're not even members.

"We submitted forty-four entries for the Indianapolis 500, and that's the race we plan to run," Gurney continued. "They accepted our entries, and we've dedicated every effort to run there. We're trying to upgrade motor racing, and we have, in our opinion, the best cars and drivers in the world. And we will continue to direct our efforts to making the sport of Indy car racing better for everyone. We trust the fans will recognize that as well."

USAC President Dick King remained optimistic when he talked to the media. "This doesn't mean the situation is not reversible if some type of conciliatory agreement is reached," he said. "We have tried since last winter, when negotiations fell apart, to reach an agreement with all parties." King added that USAC is the sole authority to reject entries for the Indianapolis 500—"not the Speedway."

"The USAC board feels they [CART] have taken actions and publicly stated things that are detrimental to USAC," King noted. "We have acted in a manner we think is in the best interests of the race and everyone involved."

Patrick said he and Penske had met with King and Indianapolis 500 Chief Steward Tom Binford for five hours in Detroit on April 17. Patrick believed CART and USAC had forged a deal to work together moving forward, only for King to inform him during an April 20 telephone conversation that the USAC board had rejected not only the proposal, but the six key CART team entries as well.

"I don't want to go into details, but we talked about schedules and rules," Patrick told Robin Miller. "It was an equitable deal for both sides, and that's why we were so shocked about what happened.

"I look at this as a last-ditch effort by USAC to break us up," Patrick added. "But it's just like when A.J. Foyt jumped ship and went back to USAC. It's making us stronger."

Binford confirmed that in a subsequent interview with the *Star*'s George Moore. "I think the compromise we discussed would have met the needs of both organizations," he said. "It wouldn't have solved the problems, but it would have been the basis for further negotiation."

Patrick and the CART group disputed King's notion that USAC was the ultimate arbiter of entries for the Indianapolis 500 and fired off a telegram to IMS President Cloutier and Hulman & Co. board chairman Mary Hulman.

"First, we must know whether USAC is acting in behalf of the Indianapolis Motor Speedway with regard to the above referenced entries for the 500-Mile International Sweepstakes," read the missive. "If USAC is acting in your behalf with regard to those entries, we must assume until notified otherwise that the entry blanks as submitted are still pending with the Speedway, since it is our understanding that the right to refuse any entry is reserved to the Speedway.

"If USAC is speaking in your behalf with regard to these entries, we must request immediate clarification of the grounds of the rejection for the entries. Since some twenty-five CART entries have been accepted and a select few refused, none of which are USAC members, we must immediately know the basis of this distinction. Failing a satisfactory response to these inquiries, we will be compelled to resort to our available remedies."

Cloutier's April 24 response also came in the form of a telegram, in which he restated a passage from the Indianapolis 500 entry blank giving USAC sole authority to approve all entries.

"I have stated throughout that all sanctions lie with the United States Auto Club," he added. "I prefer an amiable settlement between the United States Auto Club and CART."

On that very same day, 500 Chief Steward and USAC board member Binford resigned as president of ACCUS (Automobile Competitor Commission for the United States, an umbrella company of sanctioning bodies that is also the official U.S. liaison to world motorsport), handing that role to NASCAR founder William "Big Bill" France. USAC Chairman of the Board Reynold MacDonald also submitted his resignation, citing a conflict of interest and adding: "The present split between USAC and CART has created a personal problem."

CART's response to the rejection of its entries was to file suits against USAC and IMS in United States District Court, seeking a preliminary injunction from Judge James F. Noland that would set aside the rejection of the six CART teams and associated drivers from the Indianapolis 500.

Driver Johnny Rutherford also filed individual suits. CART's attorneys contended that the exclusions constituted illegal restraint of trade under the Sherman Antitrust Act, and the plaintiffs (specifically the drivers) would suffer irreparable harm to their careers if they were not permitted to participate.

"We are not seeking to stop the Indianapolis 500, but to prohibit the Indianapolis Motor Speedway and the United States Auto Club from excluding our members from participating in it," commented CART attorney John W. Frasco.

CART attorneys filed a motion to compel when Cloutier refused to answer nine questions posed during a deposition about IMS's revenues and gate receipts and the sponsorship value of competing in the Indianapolis 500. Still, talks between Binford, King, and Patrick, along with their respective counsel, extended well into the night of May 2, the eve of the scheduled hearing in Judge Noland's court.

In a packed courtroom, IMS attorney Harry Ice demonstrated the rancor bubbling underneath the surface in his opening remarks. "This handful of race car owners do not come into this court with clean hands," he said. "They have boycotted both USAC races this year and threatened to boycott the Indianapolis 500. Even when they turned their entries in, Mr. Patrick presented a veiled threat when he said they turned in their entries only to avoid disqualification. The actions of the plaintiffs in this case are detrimental to the integrity of the operation of the Indianapolis 500."

The hearing dragged on through a second nine-hour day of testimony from Gurney and King when Judge Noland, who was scheduled to appear at a judiciary conference in Chicago the following week, took the unusual step of continuing the proceedings into Saturday morning. Six additional witnesses testified (Binford; Patrick; drivers Rutherford, Wally Dallenbach, and Al Unser; and radio broadcaster Doug Rea), and after just forty-two minutes of deliberation, Noland delivered a verdict on May 5 that cleared the way for the rejected six teams to move their cars and equipment into their garages at the Speedway to begin practice.

"If only CART entrants were excluded, the court might let monetary damage decide this matter," Noland wrote in his judgment, citing the appellate court case of *Fox-Valley Harvestone v. A.P. Smith Harvestone Products*. "But because of the irreparable harm that could be suffered by these drivers—the keystones of these teams—there is no way the driver plaintiffs can sit out the Indianapolis 500. The defendants' action was too severe, and I therefore order that the six teams be reinstated and treated like any other entrant.

"The plaintiffs have no accurate remedy by law and the threatened injury to the plaintiffs outweighs the threatened damage of the defendants," he added. "Therefore, a preliminary injunction was granted in the best public interest."

However, CART didn't win all points of its complaint. "The plaintiffs have not provided sufficient proof that there was a *per se* violation of the Sherman Antitrust Act," observed Judge Noland. "There is considerable evidence that the owners tried to coerce the IMS management into rule changes, and the court will keep this under advisement."

The decision was perceived as a major victory for CART, but as USAC President King was quick to point out, the fundamental conflict between the two groups had not been resolved. "We must make it clear that the differences between USAC and CART have not been settled," he stated. "We made every effort before the matter ever went to court to resolve those differences, but we were unsuccessful.

"As we understand it, the decision pertains only to the Indianapolis 500 for 1979," King's statement added. "And while the teams will be able to compete, the court did not exonerate the six car owners, which was the group against which the USAC board's original action had been taken. At no time did the USAC board take any action against these drivers. USAC does not harbor any resentment or bitterness, and we plan to conduct this event in the same manner as we would any other race on our schedule."

Behind the scenes, a CART insider dredged up an old story about King serving nine months in a New York state penitentiary after being convicted for larceny in 1957 and attempted to plant it in the media. King immediately offered his resignation when news outlets picked up the story, but it was unanimously rejected by the twenty-one-man USAC board on May 11. In fact, King's nomination to replace MacDonald as chairman of the USAC board was confirmed at this meeting.

Once track activity was under way, the lower boost levels dropped speeds by about ten miles per hour, with Mears taking pole position for

Penske at 193.736 mph before a first day qualifying crowd estimated at 125,000. With substantially less boost than one year earlier, the speeds were actually higher than expected and afterward, Mears made a point of saying that he had been running legal boost levels all week.

The meaning of his remarks became clear by the second weekend of qualifying as illegal manipulation of the USAC-issued turbo boost pop-off valve became rampant. Late on the third day of qualifying, USAC announced it had disallowed the qualifying time posted by driver Dick Ferguson because the car owned by Wayne Woodward featured "a deliberate attempt to override the pop-off valve." Ironically, the Woodward/Ferguson entry had been loyal to USAC for the first two races of the 1979 season.

Ferguson's team wasn't the only team that was "cheating" the valve by welding a bolt or washer into the wastegate pipe to artificially build pressure in the exhaust system. But they were the only ones singled out. "We should have caught it in the qualifying line, but that's why we have a backup check," said Binford.

Woodward and Ferguson threatened legal action but first took their case to the media. "There's no rule that says anything about restricting or plugging that pipe," pleaded Woodward. "A.J. Watson showed me how to do it, and it's a fact that half the guys have been doing it all month. There's no rule regarding what size hole you've got to have. Some guys have washers with little pinhole openings. Others have half-inch holes and some guys just plugged up the pipe like we did."

"Some guys gained as much as eight miles per hour today doing the very same thing we did, and all we picked up was two miles per hour," added Ferguson. "And you're telling me I was the only one that cheated? We did it out in the open because we didn't feel we were doing anything wrong. But I'm a nobody, and I guess they figured they'd just set the rules by me."

By the time the track opened for the final qualification day, two more cars were disqualified for pop-off valve violations, and what should have been a thrilling Bump Day was marred by conflict and distrust between the competitors and USAC. Particularly aggrieved were a group of bumped drivers who claimed that their boost levels had not been illegally altered. Bumped driver John Martin circulated a petition requesting that the Indy 500 field be increased to thirty-nine cars.

"We got rooked," Martin said. "We've just plain been eliminated due to the incompetence of the USAC technical staff. They were told before the first weekend of qualifications how the boost was being overridden and they didn't do anything about it."

On the Monday of race week, USAC rejected seven official protests filed by bumped teams or drivers. Then on Tuesday night, USAC President King announced a proposal to add a special extra qualifying session on Carb Day (Thursday) for eleven entries that were bumped from the field on the final weekend. Any of the cars that could equal or better the slowest qualified speed (Roger McCluskey at 183.908 mph) would be added to the field. But there was one proviso: All thirty-three qualified entries had to approve, and owner Doug Biederstedt and owner/driver Jim McElreath refused to sign.

The protests went to USAC's court of appeals, where a three-man committee ruled that the Speedway should invoke its special entry blank powers to grant the eleven affected entries the extra qualifying session. On Saturday morning—the day before the race—eight drivers made attempts. Two (Bill Vukovich Jr. and George Snider) met the minimum speed standard, while Bill Alsup crashed heavily. Meanwhile, attempts by Woodward and Ferguson to be reinstated to the field were finally denied at the eleventh hour by Marion County Circuit Court Judge Michael T. Dugan. The 1979 Indianapolis 500 would feature thirty-five starters, the first time the field included more than the traditional thirty-three cars since 1934.

After the month-long Indy 500 build-up—not to mention the six months of tension and legal battles that preceded it—the race itself was somewhat anticlimactic. Al Unser dominated the first half in the new John Barnard–designed Chaparral 2K out of the Jim Hall stable until a transmission seal failed. Brother Bobby Unser took over at the front, but he also encountered gearbox problems, losing top gear with about twenty laps remaining.

That opened the door to victory for Mears, Unser's Penske Racing teammate. Just twenty-seven years old when he won at Indianapolis for the first time, Mears came from Bakersfield, California, and made his name racing dune buggies in the desert before impressing in Super Vee and Formula 5000 cars. He was discovered by motorsports helmet and safety equipment manufacturer Bill Simpson, and throughout 1976 and '77, he coaxed some notable performances out of a series of well-used McLarens and Eagles. That caught the eye of Penske, who was looking for a part-time driver to share a car with Mario Andretti in '78, when Andretti concentrated on Formula 1 and won the world championship.

"It was a part-time deal, but I knew a part-time ride with Penske would be better than a full-time ride with most anybody else, especially at that stage of my career," Mears recalled. "Evidently he was talking to some other guys, but they didn't want a part-time ride. Are you kidding? Part-time was fine with me."

Mears made the most of the opportunity. He qualified on the front row at Indianapolis in 1978, and won his first Indy car race at Milwaukee not too long after. Mears won two additional races in '78, then three more, including Indianapolis on the way to the '79 CART championship. Mears, known as "Rocket Rick," was soon established as the Penske team leader, and by the time of his surprise retirement in '92 after a comparatively short career, he won three CART-sanctioned championships and twenty-nine Indy car races.

Amazingly, Mears and Tom Sneva (whose career accomplishments include claiming the 1977 and '78 USAC championships, the '83 Indianapolis 500, and three Indy poles) were honestly the only drivers who rose to star prominence in the 1970s to challenge the established nucleus of Foyt, Andretti, Johncock, Rutherford, and the Unser brothers. Pancho Carter came closest; the second generation driver won the '72 USAC midget and '74 and '76 sprint car titles, but he managed only one race win at the Indy car level.

Sneva, as mentioned earlier, came to prominence in a rear-engine sprint car that was quickly outlawed by USAC. Mears came from a totally different background; his desert racing background effectively taught him the dynamics of a rear-engine car with wings. Once he made the transition to circuit racing, he graduated to Indy cars within the space of about eighteen months.

No matter what path he took to Indy cars, Mears was the bright new star that the sport needed. But his long-term participation in either series was called into doubt during the winter of 1979-80, in part due to the simmering American open-wheel war.

"When CART and USAC had their feud, you didn't know which one was going to go, and I wanted to get a foot in the door somewhere," Mears related. "Then I received a call from Bernie Ecclestone about running Formula 1, and I started looking in that direction."

Aside from forming and leading the increasingly powerful Formula One Constructors' Association, Ecclestone owned the Brabham F1 team. Brabham won a handful of races in the 1970s with drivers Carlos Reutemann and Niki Lauda, who helped groom young Brazilian prospect Nelson Piquet into a winner. Piquet put together a breakout season in '80, taking his first Grand Prix win and challenging eventual champion Alan Jones down to the wire. Piquet went on to earn twenty-three race wins and three F1 championships, in 1981, '83, and '87.

In early 1980, Mears ran a pair of tests for Brabham in preparation for an entry in the U.S. Grand Prix West at Long Beach in a third Brabham. Mears was competitive with Piquet when the pair tested at the Paul Ricard circuit in France, and a couple months later, he outran Piquet in a subsequent test at Riverside Raceway just prior to the Long Beach race. But Mears decided to stay with Penske in CART and his potential F1 career never materialized.

"For some reason, a lot of people hold F1 in higher esteem than other things," Mears noted. "The first thing I found out when I got into Indy cars is that a race car is a race car and a driver is a driver. There are no supermen in this world. There's still a mystique and curiosity about F1, however, so doing the tests satisfied my ego. I knew I could be competitive if I wanted to do it. But I wasn't crazy about some of the attitudes in that series. I enjoyed being able to run ovals and road courses, and frankly, I liked knowing there was a 7-Eleven on every corner.

"The money in F1 was a little better, but by the time we did the test at Riverside, CART was taking off and I felt like you had to be a more well-rounded driver to win the CART championship," he added. "To me, CART was more competitive and more challenging, so I made a decision not to do Formula 1. I made the right call for me and I don't regret it one bit."

Despite Mears's vote of confidence, Indy car racing was still in a very shaky state heading into 1980. With the young Penske driver as champion, CART had successfully staged its inaugural championship and revealed that it signed PPG Industries as the series sponsor for $250,000. On the USAC side, Foyt cruised to victory in five of the seven races over limited opposition to claim the '79 USAC championship as his seventh and final overall title. Both series announced plans for competing 1980 championships, with the assumption that the CART teams and drivers would again compete at Indianapolis.

Meanwhile, the Indianapolis Motor Speedway had a new man in charge. During the same week that CART announced its PPG title sponsorship, John Cooper was named IMS president. Cooper was part of the formation of USAC in 1956, and he went on to forge a close friendship and long association with NASCAR founder Bill France. That connection sparked hopes of an Indy car merger or reconciliation.

"This USAC-CART dispute has been going on one year now, and it's not going to go away," Cooper said. "I don't think a Henry Kissinger type is going to come down out of the clouds and solve this thing. I'm not that guy, but I'll do my share.

"I've been around to several races this year, and other than the Indianapolis 500, they weren't good races, by and large," he added. "It doesn't seem championship racing can have two circuits."

True to his word, Cooper immediately went to work behind the scenes, and by Christmas of 1979, representatives from CART and USAC were again meeting face-to-face. Could the new IMS president succeed where his predecessors had failed by bringing Indy car racing back together as one unified organization?

CHAPTER 6

THE BRIEF CRL TRUCE

With John Cooper newly installed as Indianapolis Motor Speedway president, there were clear signs in early 1980 that relations were thawing between USAC and CART. Throughout December 1979 and into January, factions from both parties had four face-to-face meetings and on January 24, Cooper announced that the invitation criteria for the sixty-fourth running of the Indianapolis 500 would be changed, ostensibly to accomodate the CART teams. Under the '79 rules, only teams that competed in all three USAC Triple Crown races (500-milers at Indianapolis, Pocono, and Ontario) would be extended automatic invitations to Indianapolis in 1980, but Interscope Racing and driver Danny Ongais were the only CART regulars that fulfilled that requirement.

"There was a possibility [the CART entrants] wouldn't be invited, but I've been doing a lot of soul-searching lately," Cooper said. "This is a major sports entertainment, and the paying customers want to see the entertainers. In this case, it's the drivers and they didn't bring this feud about, so why should they be penalized along with the fans? It's really the only fair thing to do given the current Indy car scene and the fact no ground rules were established at this time last year."

The Goodyear Tire and Rubber Company also attempted to end the rift. As the only tire supplier to the sport since Firestone's withdrawal in 1974, Goodyear was in a powerful position. When the peace talks were dragging in January 1980, Goodyear announced that it would no longer provide free tires to all competitors. "Basically, we never got involved before because we'd hoped a settlement would have been reached by now," said Goodyear racing director Leo Mehl. "If they would get back together, Goodyear would probably take a different stance in regards to selling tires."

Mehl was a driving force in getting the warring factions together, but just when it appeared peace was at hand, USAC once again withdrew from the conversations. The chief stumbling block was the make-up of the so-called Championship Car Council, a board of six made up of three team owners from USAC and three from CART. "We don't see any way that would work because you've got to have more representation than just owners," commented USAC President Dick King.

The impasse prompted Foyt to temporarily resign from USAC. He believed that a meeting between himself and CART's Pat Patrick in Houston in December 1979 created the impetus for the latest round of unification talks, and he was upset that he was left out of the subsequent discussions.

"It bothers me I was never considered in the decision," Foyt said. "I felt Patrick and myself could have made a workable deal, but nobody bothered to ask my opinion. There has to be a reason I was ignored, and it makes me wonder if maybe USAC didn't want to get back together.

"USAC made a lot of bad decisions last year and I kept my mouth shut, but maybe it's time for the old wives' tale about the new broom that sweeps clean. Maybe it's time they took a broom and swept out the USAC office."

Cooper then tried a different tact. Instead of reaching out to Penske or Patrick or USAC executives, he created a detailed, eleven-page unification plan that he presented to the respective competition directors of CART and USAC—Wally Dallenbach and Roger McCluskey. Cooper's proposal highlighted three key areas:

- Formation of a twelve- to fourteen-race series to be known as the Championship Racing League (CRL), sanctioned by USAC
- A seven-member board of governors that would be the sole body within USAC to set policies for Indy car racing. The board would initially be composed of three representatives

from CART and three from USAC, with the seventh the unanimous choice of the other six. In the future, the board would include three elected car owners, one elected driver, one elected track operator/promoter, and the USAC president, with the seventh member once again agreed upon unnimously by the other six

- Establishment of a $1 million point fund, projected to grow to $2 million within three years

"If it doesn't sell, we should at least find out who it is that doesn't want to get Indy car racing back together," Cooper remarked.

McCluskey and Dallenbach initially consulted each other and recommended the expansion of the board to ten members, composed of five car owners, a driver, a mechanic, an Indianapolis Motor Speedway representative, a promoter of a non-500-mile race, and USAC President King. USAC gave the tentative okay to this modified plan on Cooper's established deadline of February 20.

CART wanted additional clarification about the autonomy of the board of governors, but Patrick told the *Indianapolis Star* that CART was also in favor of moving forward as the CRL. "That's all we've ever wanted, to be autonomous in setting policy," Patrick said. "If we are interpreting Mr. Cooper's proposal right and this is true, we say, 'Let's go racing, together, now.'"

In early March, Cooper confirmed that Indianapolis 500 tickets were selling at a pace faster than a year earlier. But he continued to express concern about the split, telling *Indianapolis News* reporter Dick Mittman he was "disappointed" that the Indy car peace talks had stalled once again. This time, USAC resisted, citing differences in the two groups' philosophy about turbocharger boost, though CART made clear it would acquiesce to running USAC's preferred forty-eight inches of boost for V8 engines at Indianapolis. CART still allowed V8 engines (including the Cosworth) sixty inches of boost.

"What should be going on in my view is that CART and USAC should be hammering things out," Cooper said. "It seems they are just stalking each other. An encouraging thing is that the attorneys are in discussion, but endless talking is not good.

"Damn, we've got to get something going!" he added. "Everyone is sick of it. If they open the season with separate series, I'm afraid we'll go through another season without getting back together."

The boost issue was complicated by Porsche's widely publicized plan to enter Indy car racing. The German manufacturer had developed a 2.65-liter version of the turbocharged flat-six engine used in the 911-based 935 sports car in endurance racing and expected to be permitted fifty-four inches of boost. Interscope Racing, a team formed by entertainment industry magnate Ted Field, was contracted to run the Porsche engine with Ongais as the driver, initially using the team's proven Parnelli chassis prior to the completion of a radical new car that came to be known as the "Batmobile."

Ongais was an interesting character, to say the least. He was a motorcycle racing champion in his home state of Hawaii in the early 1960s before transitioning into drag racing, where "The Flyin' Hawaiian" compiled an enviable record in cars with the National Hot Rod Association (NHRA) into the '70s. Ongais then turned to circuit racing after hooking up with Field in '75; he burst into prominence by winning his first USAC-sanctioned Indy car race at Mosport Park in '77 before breaking through for five wins in '78.

By then he was already thirty-six years old, so Ongais was therefore not particularly young, nor did he possess a dynamic personality; he was an introvert who tended to be constantly at odds with the media covering the USAC series. But no driver of the era exemplified "checkers or wreckers" as much as Ongais did during his brief time at the forefront of Indy car racing, and he was a fan favorite for that "win or bust" style.

He reportedly eclipsed the track record when Porsche tested its engine in the Parnelli at Ontario Motor Speedway in early 1980, drawing attention and concern from Foyt. After USAC technical chief Jack Beckley and Foyt's engine expert Howard Gilbert visited Porsche's headquarters in Stuttgart, Germany, USAC announced in mid-March that it would restrict the production-based Porsche engine to forty-eight inches of boost. "The engine is a 161-cubic-inch, double-overhead cam just like the Cosworth," Beckley said. "I know they're not very happy. They were told there was no guarantee, but fifty-four inches was a figure we'd start with."

Porsche was furious, claiming that the fundamental design of its flat-six engine could not be modified to accomodate the lower boost level. "Forty-eight inches is just not possible for us," stated Jo Hoppen, manager of special vehicles for Porsche-Audi USA. "It's a disaster for us. We took USAC engine people to Europe; we asked them to come over. We were open enough so they could see anything they wanted to see. This is highly unusual, but we did it. Then for them to cut us back to forty-eight inches before we get on track is highly unfair. Under the circumstances, we can't go on."

USAC President King publicly professed his desire for Porsche to reconsider. "I hope they are still coming," he said. "We want them, and if they don't come this year, I hope they come in '81. We're hopeful they are going to continue with their program—it could be a darn tough engine."

Interscope reportedly tested the Parnelli-Porsche with forty-eight inches of boost at Ontario, leading Field to believe that the car could still be competitive, but Porsche ended the program. Top driver Johnny Rutherford declared that USAC's decision on Porsche was "the dumbest damn thing I've ever seen in my life."

As April approached, the impasse between the two groups continued. At Indianapolis, where he was testing the Hall Racing Chaparral, Rutherford unloaded on USAC. "It's a bit bewildering to understand why USAC would suddenly decide to stick in an extra stipulation to the get-together which in effect puts us right back where we were," Rutherford told reporter Dick Mittman. "Somebody's hiding something over there, I reckon. We don't know what it is, but it sure is funny that they would go right down to the wire with us and suddenly change their minds or kind of wrangle it around where it comes out the same way as it was before. That's the reason CART came into existence anyway."

Finally, on April 2, a marathon meeting in Hot Springs, Arkansas, resulted in a truce, and the official announcement of the Championship Racing League. The race schedule was not finalized as series leaders scrambled to assemble a slate of around fifteen races from the twenty-seven combined events that CART and USAC were planning. But competitors from both sides revealed their intention to participate in the April 13 CRL opener, adhering to CART boost rules, at Ontario Motor Speedway. As part of the compromise, CART rules would be utilized at some circuits, while USAC rules (restricting V8 engines to forty-eight inches of boost) would be in effect at Indianapolis, Pocono, and selected other races.

"Both CART and USAC are to be highly commended for putting aside their differences and forging an agreement," stated Goodyear's Mehl.

The CRL would be administered and sanctioned by USAC, with team owners Penske and Patrick added to the USAC Board of Governors. A separate six-man board of governors for the CRL was comprised of King, Penske, Patrick, and Foyt, plus additional car owners Rolla Vollstedt and Jim Hall. Strangely, given USAC's concern about giving too much power to the competing teams, both of the group's board nominees (Foyt and Vollstedt) were car owners.

"USAC did what we asked for seventeen months ago, and that was to give us a voice in what's going on," Patrick remarked. "I'm glad it's over with, and I think it's good for the sport. Now I just want to get the details worked out and go racing."

Ultimately, it was USAC that finally bent, by changing the group's by-laws to allow the creation of the separate board of governors to administrate Indy car racing. "It's like a strike, and I don't think anybody benefits from a strike," King observed. "I don't think you'll ever win in a situation like this. It hurts the business."

Regarding running the 1980 season to two sets of rules, King added, "It's a way to get together. It will create some difficulties, but we can do it. If it brings peace in the family, it's the thing to do. I'd like to put the last seventeen months in the past and go forward with the program."

With the focus back on the track, Rutherford set the tone for the 1980 season by dominating the Ontario opener. Driving the Chaparral 2K developed throughout '79 by Al Unser, Rutherford enjoyed a three-mph advantage over the field in qualifying and won the 200-mile race by more than a lap over Tom Sneva.

The Chaparral arguably represented Indy car racing's last "eureka" moment in terms of advanced technology. Inspired by the Lotus 79 Formula 1 car that Mario Andretti drove to the 1978 world championship, the 2K brought the "ground-effect" concept of using the entire underside of the car as an aerodynamic surface to Indy car racing. Unser often showed plenty of speed but suffered bad luck throughout '79 before winning the final race of the season at Phoenix. Surprisngly, he split with Hall, believing that the car's primary designer John Barnard was not receiving the credit he deserved. With the bugs worked out, the 2K dominated in Rutherford's hands.

At Indianapolis, there was little of the controversy or rancor that permeated Gasoline Alley a year earlier. Rutherford and the Chaparral were invincible all month, the Texan claiming pole position before leading 118 of the 200 laps to take his third Indianapolis win at a canter. Tom Sneva mesmerized the crowd by driving from thirty-third and last on the grid to finish second. A confident twenty-five-year-old named Tim Richmond finished ninth to garner Rookie of the Year honors. After running out of fuel on the last lap and stopping on course, Richmond memorably hitched a ride back to the pits on the sidepod of Rutherford's winning car. Richmond ran fewer than ten career Indy car races in 1979 and '80 before focusing his attention on stock cars. He earned his first NASCAR Cup Series victory in '83, and he looked set for superstardom when he won seven races for the emerging Hendrick Motorsports team in '86. Richmond missed the first third of the '87 season due to undisclosed health problems; he was later diagnosed with AIDS. Despite what at the time must have been mysterious circumstances, Richmond won the first two of his eight Cup Series starts in '87. He died in August 1989.

Bobby Unser scored victories for Penske Racing at Milwaukee on June 6 and June 22, 1980, in the Pocono 500. At the start of the Pocono weekend, the CRL board agreed to adopt USAC's lower boost specifications for the next three years. But just one day later, the CRL was suddenly looking very fragile.

Cooper, citing dissatisfaction with the make-up of the six-man CRL Board of Governors, announced that the Indianapolis Motor Speedway was shopping the sanction of the Indianapolis 500, and that IMS had already approached all of the other American members of ACCUS involved in race sanctioning (NASCAR, SCCA, NHRA, and IMSA) with an invitation to bid for the contract.

"As we plan for 1981 we want to be sure that we explore all of the options available to us to assure fans, participants, and sponsors that the 500 will continue to be run in a fair and ethical manner," Cooper stated. "There is growing evidence to the effect that USAC has become an organization governed by selected car owners. That, of course, would not meet our criteria of having an independent authority sanction the 500. If USAC can dispel that notion, we will certainly consider continuing our twenty-five-year association with them."

It was little more than a thinly veiled threat to USAC: Remove power from the team owners, or lose control of the Indy 500. At the time, many believe Cooper's actions were motivated by his close relationship with NASCAR founder Bill France Sr., whose family had maintained complete control over the administration of NASCAR since its formation in the late 1940s. France expanded his power base by building Daytona International Speedway in '59 and Talladega Superspeedway a decade later, eventually developing a portfolio of tracks under the International Speedway Corporation banner. France also had experience dealing with competitor unrest; when tire problems prompted thirty-seven drivers to withdraw from the inaugural event at Talladega in '69, he ordered the race to be run anyway and substantially weakened the drivers' union.

Cooper believed that the Hulmans had the potential to follow the France family model, with the same level of broad, reaching power over all nonparticipatory aspects of the sport.

Indianapolis newsman Robin Miller reached out to France when Cooper and IMS made their announcement. "When NASCAR was formed [in 1947], the car owners all sat down in a room to make the rules," France told him. "After several hours, they came out with no agreement, and I learned right then that it was gonna have to be one man who told the people what the rules were gonna be. And if they didn't like it, they could go home. I think John is smart by doing this before it gets carried away, and I'm behind him 100 percent."

Miller also sought out Cooper's rationale for launching what he called "a left hook from the heavyweights out on 16th Street."

"The participants deserve an independent authority, and I guarantee you we'll have it," Cooper declared. "You just can't have car owners writing the specifications and hiring the officials for all the participants. I listened to competitors complain all week at Pocono about a certain team getting away with breaking the rules. Well, I don't know whether the rules were being broken or not, but I do know that it's impossible to have officials who are working for the participants. It's like having Roger Staubach [longtime Dallas Cowboys quarterback] hire the referees."

Penske put the blame on USAC, pointing out that USAC could have nominated figures other than team owners as representatives for their two seats on the board of governors. He was also upset because Cooper had essentially authored the CRL plan yet turned down an opportunity to sit on the CRL board.

Indianapolis 500 Chief Steward Tom Binford also weighed in. "I would hope that this would be the impetus for USAC to make reforms which would make it acceptable and to broaden its board to include representation from other areas," he told the *Indianapolis News*. "USAC wasn't formed to be beholden to any particular faction of racing, including promoters. Tony Hulman did make formation of USAC possible, but he had only one vote on the board, and the Speedway control of the organization was very subtle indeed. He did not wield a heavy hand. Many times I urged Tony to take a stronger position than he did on some things. On the other hand, I don't think any one promoter should dominate the sanctioning body."

Robin Miller was pointed in his description of what happened at an emergency meeting of the USAC board on June 30, 1980. "With the Indianapolis Motor Speedway holding a gun at its head, the United States Auto Club's Board of Directors voted to sever its ties with the CRL and restructure its policy-making to a twelve-man Competition Commission in hopes of pleasing IMS President John Cooper and thereby retaining the Indianapolis 500 as its chief client," he wrote.

"This action, in addition to abolishing the CRL, cancelled the fruits of an agreement reached after seventeen months of strife. And in the process, the scars of the USAC-CART war were once again ripped open."

Penske confirmed that he and the other CART team owners would fulfill their commitment to the promoter of a July 13 CRL race at Mid-Ohio Sports Car Course to be run under USAC sanction. But he declared that CART never went away and vowed to resuscitate the organization to take whatever steps were necessary to restart its own championship series. CART soon announced it would stage seven additional races in 1980, beginning with a 200-miler at Michigan International Speedway on July 20.

"Maybe I won't get invited back to Indianapolis, but I'll be a bigger man than they are for it," Penske said. "Right now I'm just at the end of my rope." He later added, "For a while there, when we had the CRL, we were going to a divorce counselor. But all of a sudden, we found out it didn't work, and we had to move on our own way."

Cooper called the CRL board "just five car owners willy-nilly and Dick King" but claimed he had no interest in becoming a France-like czar over the sport. "I don't have control, and I don't want control," he said. "But I do want someone to grab hold and put it together. Nobody was exerting leadership in Champ Car racing in the '70s as compared with NASCAR's Bill France or IMSA's John Bishop."

While CART acted quickly and decisively to reinstate its championship, USAC failed to organize any other Indy car races in 1980. Rutherford took a total of five race wins and earned the CART-sanctioned championship over Bobby Unser.

The events of June and July 1980 had successfully kept USAC in sanctioning control of the Indianapolis 500. USAC made some radical changes for '81. Dirt racing hadn't been a part of USAC's top level since '71, but the newly created USAC Gold Crown Series featured three events on dirt miles. The first Gold Crown slate started with the '81 Indianapolis 500, staged another 500-miler for Indy cars at Pocono four weeks later, then made stops at Springfield, Du Quoin, and the Indiana State Fairgrounds. The championship would then wrap up with the '82 Indianapolis 500.

USAC also announced in January 1981 that only "production-type" engines would be allowed for the Indianapolis 500 starting in '82, making the dominant Cosworth powerplant ineligible.

"The production-based engine formula for 1982 could produce one of the most exciting eras yet in championship racing," Cooper said in early '81. "And we anticipate many entries built to those specifications for our 1981 500, which will be run under the same basic specifications as last year. The announcement by USAC seems to be the kind of bold move that most participants and fans have been asking for."

But after watching a few tailenders struggle to make a stock-block engine finish a race—or simply reach a competitive speed—USAC quietly reversed course and reinstated the Cosworth in August 1981. "I'm thrilled, and not just for my team but for everybody in our situation," said Roger Penske. "I think it's obvious our rules the past two years have made for some great racing, and I'm happy we'll be keeping them in 1982."

A floundering USAC was forced to fill out the field for the 1981 Pocono 500 with nine front-engine dirt cars. Perhaps fittingly, the race was shortened by rain; Foyt was the victor in what was the last of his sixty-seven Indy car race wins, a record that still stands. Foyt's victory was also notable as the first for March, the English chassis constructor that would soon dominate the sport.

The 1981 Pocono 500 was the last Indy car race besides the Indianapolis 500 that was run under USAC sanction for nearly fifteen years. George Snider was declared the 1981-82 USAC Gold Series champion following the initial thirteen-month season, and dirt racing was quietly dropped from the slate. The Indianapolis 500 was the only race in the Gold Crown series from 1983-95. CART was firmly in charge of the sole remaining season-long Indy car championship. From that point forward, CART's teams and drivers would continue to participate in the Indianapolis 500, which became a points-paying round in the PPG Indy Car World Series. For 1981, PPG upped its contribution to the season-end points fund to $1 million.

After nearly two years of conflict, USAC and CART had reached an uneasy truce that would last more than a decade. In short, the Indianapolis 500 needed the name-brand value of the drivers and teams in the CART series to remain relevant, and CART needed the Indianapolis 500 for legitimacy.

The overt fighting may have ceased, but the bad feelings persisted. John Cooper left his executive role at IMS in 1982, moving on to hold a variety of roles for International Speedway Corp., including serving as president of Daytona International Speedway from 1987-90. Soon enough, a new generation of Hulman-George family leadership would be added to the mix.

CHAPTER 7

THE SECOND
FOREIGN INVASION

If the rear-engine revolution of the 1960s marked the first time Formula 1 technology made a major impact on American open-wheel racing, a second British invasion that started in the late '70s and carried through CART's transformation of the sport over the next decade went a long way toward defining Indy car racing as we know it today.

The first element was the advent of the F1-derived Cosworth DFX engine in the late '70s, as described in chapter 3. While that was happening in America, Colin Chapman and Team Lotus were using the trusty Ford-Cosworth DFV engine to lead another chassis design revolution in F1 with the Lotus Type 78 and 79 models that originated what became known as "ground-effect" aerodynamics. Front and rear wings had been used to create downforce in racing cars since the midsixties, but Chapman's concept shaped the entire bottom surface of the car into an airfoil. Lotus then discovered that the downforce produced by the floor increased dramatically when they sealed off the outer edges of the car with "skirts," sliding vertical panels that prevented air escaping to the side.

Even when the competition tried to copy the basic ground-effect concept, the compact size of the Cosworth V8 gave the Lotus cars an advantage over those from Ferrari, Alfa-Romeo, and Matra that utilized flat-twelve or V12 power. Until 1.5-liter turbocharged engines were developed into reliable form, the winning combination in F1 was a Lotus 79–inspired ground-effect chassis paired with a Cosworth DFV; Lotus dominated the Formula 1 field in 1977 and '78, with Mario Andretti (who focused on F1 from 1975-81, cutting back to part tme in Indy cars) claiming the '78 F1 World Championship. Aside from being the only American world champion besides '61 titlist Phil Hill, Andretti's victory more than forty years ago in the '78 Dutch Grand Prix remains the last F1 race win for an American driver.

The Lotus 79 created the basic blueprint for almost every Formula 1 and Indy car design since then: a very slim central tub, with all the fuel in a single tank immediately behind the driver; water and oil radiators mounted in aerodynamically sculpted sidepods, with a carefully contoured floor shaped for downforce; and front and rear wings to balance or trim the car aerodynamically. The 79 soon spawned a series of copycats and imitators, both in F1 and Indy car racing, starting with the Chaparral 2K designed by John Barnard that won the 1980 Indianapolis 500 and CART championship with driver Johnny Rutherford. Aside from safety developments, the 2K is arguably the last example of significant advancement in the basic concept and layout of an Indy car chassis.

Barnard went on to pioneer carbon fiber chassis construction in 1981 in his work with the McLaren F1 team (a major safety advance that took a decade to gain acceptance by CART), and while working for Ferrari in the late '80s, he was instrumental in the creation of the sequential shift gearbox with steering wheel paddle activation—another innovation that quickly gained widespread use in many forms of racing but was not legalized in Indy car racing until 2007. But before all that happened, Barnard also played a small role in the rapid rise of an English constructor that would soon dominate the Indy car chassis market.

U.K.-based March Engineering was formed in 1970 by a group that included future FIA President Max Mosley and designer Robin Herd. March set out to provide a customer car alternative to prospective F1 team owners who did not have the required budget to construct their own chassis. March also built cars for a variety of other series, including Formula 2, Formula 3, and the SCCA Can-Am championship.

March never achieved notable success in F1 (the marque scored two race wins, most notably the 1976 Italian Grand Prix, where Ronnie Peterson triumphed in Niki Lauda's comeback from his fiery accident six weeks earlier), but the company was approached by Indy car team owner Sherman Armstrong in September 1979 about creating a chassis for CART series competition. Armstrong stipulated that Barnard must be part of the design team.

However, Barnard soon joined the McLaren International F1 team, where he created the revolutionary carbon fiber MP4/1 chassis that debuted in 1981. Before his departure, he was able to provide March with some basic input that resulted in the one-off Orbitor chassis, based on March's 792 F2 car tub, that failed to qualify for the '80 Indianapolis 500 in the hands of Howdy Holmes. Later that year, veteran mechanic George Bignotti was called in to help make the car more competitive, and Gary Bettenhausen finished third in the '80 CART season finale at Phoenix in the Orbitor.

Bignotti began working on Indy cars in the mid-fifties and gained fame as A.J. Foyt's chief mechanic during Foyt's impressive run at the top of the sport in the early 1960s. They teamed to win thirty-two races, including the '61 and '64 Indianapolis 500, as well as four USAC national championships between '60 and '64. But the partnership between two strong personalities dissolved midway through the '65 season, and Bignotti won the '66 Indianapolis 500 with Graham Hill when Bignotti moved on to wrench cars for New Orleans oil magnate John Mecom. Near the end of the decade, Bignotti teamed up with Al Unser, and a joint move to Vel's Parnelli Jones Racing netted them back-to-back Indy wins in 1970 and '71. Bignotti then built Patrick Racing into a powerhouse later in the '70s.

Though still very much hands-on in terms of working on the cars, Bignotti was about to embark into team ownership with Dan Cotter. After working with the Orbiter, Bignotti envisaged subcontracting March to build his own chassis, but March instead convinced him that it should take over the entire project. The March 81C Indy car was a strengthened version of the company's 811 F1 car.

The legendary mechanic has a humorous recollection of his early dealings with the Brits. "Sherman Armstrong flew me over to England on the Concorde, and I stayed four days working in the shop," Bignotti recalled. "I gave them a $30,000 deposit for three cars, but a month later, I got a telegram from them saying that due to financial problems, they were going to give the first car to the Whittington brothers (a trio who allegedly funded their racing careers by dealing vast quantities of marijuana). They had gone over there with a briefcase of funny money and dumped $100,000 on the table, so they got the first two cars and I got the third one."

Bignotti's car was late to arrive, so his driver Tom Sneva missed the first few days of practice for the 1981 Indianapolis 500. But the two-time Indy pole winner quickly got up to speed and was the fastest second day qualifier. From the twentieth starting position, Sneva whipped quickly through the field in the race in his 81C and led twenty-five laps before being sidelined by a failed clutch just short of half distance. The speed of the March was obvious, and orders poured in quickly. March had three cars in the '81 Indianapolis 500 field; that number grew to seventeen the following year. By '84, March supplied thirty of the thirty-three cars on the Indianapolis grid, even including the cars fielded by Team Penske, which briefly ceased production of its own Indy car chassis at its facility in Poole, England.

Rival English car builder Lola returned to Indy car racing in 1983, providing a Cosworth-powered chassis for the new Newman/Haas Racing team. Through the end of the '80s, March and Lola retained almost exclusive control over the Indy car chassis market. Remarkably, Gordon Johncock's victory in the '82 Indianapolis 500 in Patrick Racing's Indianapolis-built Wildcat chassis was the last for a made-in-America entry in the great race until 2003, when a G Force chassis designed in England but manufactured in Braselton, Georgia, triumphed.

"From the Duesenberg brothers and Harry Miller through Fred Offenhauser and the likes of Frank Kurtis, A.J. Watson, Ted Halibrand, George Bignotti, All American Racers, Vel's Parnelli Jones, and many other engine, chassis, and component builders, Indy car racing enjoyed a thriving cottage industry of homegrown talent," observed writer/ historian Gordon Kirby. "Over many decades, the industry infused Indy car racing with pride and helped provide a fan base among the employees, family, and friends of these car and engine builders. It also helped generate plenty of commercial interest from the American automobile industry.

"But over the last thirty years, all that has been lost to overseas car and engine builders and engineers. It's hard to say whether or not it was an inevitable evolution or something that a more savvy leadership might have been able to manage more effectively, but it's certainly true that the focus of today's American racing industry has migrated to North Carolina and NASCAR."

The fundamental changes to the sport in the 1980s encompassed more than cars. Fueled by the demise of the SCCA's "new" Can-Am championship, a wave of new teams from a road-racing background entered the PPG IndyCar World Series in the first half of the decade.

Carl Haas began selling gearbox parts out of his parents' Chicago basement in 1952 to support his sports car racing hobby. He eventually became the U.S. distributor for Hewland gearboxes, as well as racing car constructors, including Elva and, most famously, Lola. The Lola marque actually won its Indianapolis 500 debut in '66 and continued to have a presence in Indy car racing for several years; Penske Racing's first Indianapolis 500 entries in '69 and '70 utilized Lola chassis, and Al Unser won the Triple Crown of 500-milers in '78 in a Lola.

Haas and Lola would be intrinsically linked for more than forty years, and for much of that period, he operated what was effectively Lola's American factory racing team, fielding cars in the SCCA Can-Am and Formula 5000 series. In partnership with Chaparral founder Jim Hall, Haas/Hall Racing dominated F5000 in the mid-seventies, winning three consecutive championships with driver Brian Redman. That success continued in the "new" Can-Am that replaced F5000 in 1977, where Patrick Tambay, Alan Jones, and Jacky Ickx all claimed series titles for Haas.

One of Haas's rival team owners in the second iteration of the Can-Am was Paul Newman, the Academy Award–winning actor. Newman began racing cars in 1972, three years after completing the movie *Winning*, in which he starred as Frank Capua, a struggling racing driver who turned his career around by winning the Indianapolis 500. The movie's subplot involved a three-way love triangle between Capua, his wife Elora (played by Newman's real-life spouse Joanne Woodward, whom he married in '58), and rival Luther Erding, portrayed by Robert Wagner.

Newman and Wagner attended the Bob Bondurant racing school to prepare for the movie, and while Wagner deferred to a stunt driver, Newman chose to perform many of the high-speed racing scenes himself. IMS President Tony Hulman and several contemporary Indy car personalities made cameo appearances in *Winning*, including Dan Gurney and Bobby Unser; Capua's Indianapolis winning "Crawford Special" was modeled after the Rislone Eagle that Unser drove to victory in the actual 1968 race.

Filming *Winning* was an experience that resonated with Newman for the rest of his life, to the point where he embarked on a successful second career as a racing driver. Newman piloted a Lotus Elan to victory in his first-ever Sports Car Club of America race in 1972 before graduating to a series of ever-more powerful Datsun sedans and sports cars while winning four SCCA National Championships between '79 and '86. After turning professional, he starred in the SCCA Trans-Am Championship, with two race wins and half a dozen podium finishes. Newman's greatest accomplishment as a driver was a second-place finish in the '79 24 Hours of Le Mans in a Porsche 935. He remained active in endurance racing well into his later years, making his last professional start at the Rolex 24 at Daytona in 2006 at the age of eighty-one.

When he was racing, Newman kept a low profile at the track and maintained an intense focus on the task at hand. He competed under the name P.L. Newman to avoid drawing attention to his status as a Hollywood icon. "I had a great deal of fun filming *Winning*, but I never really had a chance to stretch my legs out and find out what I could do in a car," Newman said. "It actually took me three years of rearranging my schedule before I could find time to get my license and everything. After that, I never did a film between April and September or October. Racing was all I did."

In 1977, Newman cofounded Newman-Freeman Racing, which fielded Lola Can-Am cars driven by Elliott Forbes-Robinson, future Indy car driver Danny Sullivan, and future F1 World Champion Keke Rosberg. Newman was among many competitors who griped about how Carl Haas Automotive withheld the latest and greatest parts from Lola customers, so he was surprised to receive an offer from his cigar-chomping rival in late '82.

"Carl and I didn't have what I would call a dynamite relationship, and when I left the Can-Am, I really was going to get out of racing," Newman told Gordon Kirby. "Then Carl called and said, 'How would you like to go Indy car racing?' And smoke started coming out of my ears. I said, 'Are you nuts? I shouldn't even be listening to this invitation.' Then he said, 'What if I could get Mario Andretti to drive?' And I said, 'Where would you like to meet?'"

It took Lola almost a year to get to grips with modern ground-effect Indy car technology, but Andretti still won a pair of races in 1983 before grabbing six wins and the CART series championship for Newman/Haas in Lola's new T800 in '84. By the end of the decade, Lola had supplanted March as the dominant Indy car chassis manufacturer, supplying twenty-four of the thirty-three Indianapolis starters in '89.

Newman/Haas was not the only team that looked to Indy cars as the new Can-Am faded sharply in the early 1980s. Gerald Forsythe sponsored rookie driver Scott Brayton in the '81 Indianapolis 500, and in conjunction with his brother John, he stepped into CART team ownership in '82, taking a lucky first win at Road America with Mexican ex-F1 driver Hector Rebaque. Forsythe's team made a bigger impact in '83, when Italian rookie Teo Fabi earned pole position at Indianapolis, won four races, and finished second to Al Unser in the CART championship. Forsythe withdrew from racing at the end of '85, but would return in a much more serious manner after nearly a decade away.

Rick Galles was an Albuquerque auto dealer who backed the career of local star Al Unser Jr., propelling the next-generation star through Super Vee and Can-Am into Indy cars by the age of twenty-one. And Red Roof Inn hotel magnate Jim Trueman formed Truesports Racing to field Indy cars for Bobby Rahal, a Chicago native who successfully raced his way through the European formula car ladder in the late 1970s before returning home to star in the Can-Am series.

When the Can-Am faded and eventually folded, it also left a number of road-racing venues in search of replacement events. Several of them soon landed with the growing CART organization. Road America joined the PPG IndyCar World Series schedule in 1982, along with a unique event staged on the runways of Burke Lakefront Airport in Cleveland, followed by Mid-Ohio Sports Car Course and Laguna Seca Raceway a year later. The '83 season concluded with a race on a temporary circuit in the parking lot of Caesar's Palace in Las Vegas. The Portland road course and street races at the Meadowlands complex near New York City and through Tamiami Park in Miami were added by the end of '85. But the most important addition to the PPG IndyCar World Series schedule during this fertile growth period for CART was the Long Beach Grand Prix (LBGP).

The inaugural LBGP was run September 28, 1975, as an SCCA Formula 5000 race to test the circuit and event infrastructure prior to a full-fledged Formula 1 Grand Prix planned for the Spring of '76. That first F5000 race was staged as the SCCA and USAC were completing their second year of co-sanctioning the U.S. Formula 5000 Championship, with the eventual goal of creating a common formula that would feature oval and road-racing catagories within an overall North American Championship (as discussed in chapter 3).

Of course those efforts failed. But somehow, this dysfunctional period produced the first Long Beach Grand Prix. Christopher Pook, an Englishman who operated a travel agency in Long Beach, believed a big-time car race—specifically, a Formula 1 World Championship Grand Prix—would attract attention to the downtrodden port city and pave the way toward redevelopment of the city center. He got key support from famous California racers Dan Gurney and Phil Hill, and armed with a number of ingenious ideas that would redefine the notion of a street race, set to work. Most notably, Dr. Peter Talbot created a design for precast concrete blocks that would deflect errant cars without introducing the hazards of steel Armco barriers. Around two thousand of these twelve-foot long, thirty-four-inch high blocks weighing eight thousand pounds each were craned into position lining the two-mile circuit, with key impact areas protected by around twenty-five thousand banded tires.

There were other areas in which Pook blazed new ground. He attracted the support of Toyota for that first F5000 race and staged a celebrity race using equally matched Toyota Celicas; the participants included Phil Hill, Dan Gurney, and Bob Bondurant. From small seedlings, Toyota grew to be the title sponsor of the Long Beach Grand Prix and rapidly expanded its involvement in American motorsports over the next forty years.

The F5000 race was successful enough to gain Formula 1's approval, and the inaugural United States Grand Prix West was contested on March 28, 1976, and won by Clay Regazzoni. Pook struggled initially to keep the event financially afloat, but he got a stroke of luck when Andretti won the '77 F1 race after a tense battle with Jody Scheckter and Niki Lauda. Andretti was at the height of his F1 career and that victory—still the only Formula 1 win on U.S. soil for an American driver—gave the LBGP the publicity boost it needed to survive, and indeed thrive, into the '80s. But Pook eventually decided the price Formula 1 was asking had gotten too high, and it was the exact set of circumstances necessary to give the event a makeover into the Toyota Grand Prix of Long Beach.

"The costs of the purse and of the transportation of cars, equipment, and officials is what broke our back," Pook told *Indy Car Racing* magazine. "The price had crept over the $2 million mark, and with an Indy car race, we'll be able to reduce the cost of our tickets, attract a larger crowd, and still be able to pump half a million dollars into promotion."

CART's debut at Long Beach came on April 1, 1984, when, perhaps appropriately, Mario Andretti drove a Newman/Haas Racing Lola to victory before fifty-six thousand fans. Recast as an Indy car race with the likes of Andretti, Mears, Rutherford, Sneva, and the Unsers—drivers more familiar to American fans—the Long Beach GP grew to be the most important road race in the CART series, demonstrating the potential for street racing in urban areas. Fueled by Southern California's love for cars and car culture, Long Beach developed into a popular festival where the racing often came second to the people-watching and the party. That concept, when properly executed in the right markets, would prove to be a vital element in the event development side of Indy car racing as we know it today.

The composition of the Indy car championship changed significantly in the 1980s. As late as '76, every round of the USAC Championship Trail was staged on an oval track, and even in '80, the year that included the briefly unified Championship Racing League, nine of the twelve Indy car races run were staged on ovals. Up to '89, three 500-mile oval races, including Indianapolis, still formed the core of the CART schedule, but nine of the fifteen events were run on road or street courses, along with only six ovals, a trend that was not lost on Indianapolis Motor Speedway management.

With that gradual shift to road racing came a wave of international drivers, led by Fabi and Australian Geoff Brabham, the eldest son of Indy car rear-engine trailblazer Jack Brabham. The most notable import was Brazilian Emerson Fittipaldi; the 1972 and '74 Formula 1 world champion embarked on a second career in America in the mid-eighties that was capped by a pair of victories in the Indianapolis 500 and the '89 CART championship. Fittipaldi had actually tested an Indy car at the peak of his F1 career while he was driving for McLaren, which then also still fielded entries in the USAC Indy Car Series.

"In September 1974, I drove Johnny Rutherford's Indy 500 winner at Indianapolis," Fittipaldi recalled. "I liked the car very much, but because the car was very fragile, I decided not to race it. I drove two days and went quite fast. My style of driving allowed me to adapt very quickly to high-speed corners. Johnny was very good to me, and A.J. Foyt was there as well. They took me around and showed me the track. The car had big wings, lots of downforce, and a lot of power—about 1,000 horsepower!"

After a brief retirement, Fittipaldi embarked on the second stage of his driving career a decade later in CART. The former F1 champion showed enough promise and commitment in his first few Indy car starts for small teams that he was hired by Pat Patrick in late 1984 to replace injured driver Chip Ganassi. That was the start of a very successful five-year partnership between Patrick and Fittipaldi, who scored his first CART-sanctioned race win at Michigan Speedway in '85.

Fittipaldi was not the first foreign driver to pursue a career in America racing Indy cars. But as a two-time F1 champion, he was the most notable since Jack Brabham, Jim Clark, Graham Hill, and Jackie Stewart were regular participants in the Indy 500 in the 1960s. Unlike those other champions, Fittipaldi raced Indy cars full time, and his success in CART in the late '80s and early '90s blazed a trail for a wave of international talent, including fellow Brazilians Roberto Moreno, Raul Boesel, Mauricio Gugelmin, Gil de Ferran, Hélio Castroneves, and Tony Kanaan.

Fittipaldi was also instrumental in bringing Philip Morris and its Marlboro brand back into Indy car racing. Marlboro was first associated with Fittipaldi with the McLaren F1 team in 1974 and '75; a new tie-up with Philip Morris USA supported Fittipaldi at Patrick from 1985-89 and the sponsorship followed the driver when he moved to Penske Racing in 1990. The Marlboro Team Penske association lasted through 2009 when tobacco sponsorships of teams or sporting activities were outlawed in America. Given R.J. Reynolds's long and successful role in helping build NASCAR from 1971 into the twenty-first century with its Winston brand, one can only wonder what kind of potential Indy car racing could have achieved had Marlboro maintained a steady participation, rather than stepping away for more than a decade as the result of USAC's handling of Viceroy's entry into the sport back in '72.

The Cosworth DFX was finally vanquished as well. Mario Illien and Paul Morgan, a pair of former Cosworth engineers, teamed up in 1984 to form U.K.-based Ilmor Engineering. They forged a partnership with Roger Penske, who attracted financial support from General Motors, resulting in a Chevrolet-badged Ilmor engine built to 2.65-liter turbocharged specifications for Indy car competition that debuted in '86. Penske Racing did the development work on the new engine, but it was made available to other competitors in '87. The Ilmor engine soon overtook the by-then long-in-the-tooth Cosworth as the most effective powerplant in the CART series.

Ilmor's desire to keep a tight grip on its intellectual property was intensified by an incident in 1989, when Patrick Racing provided Alfa Romeo with several Chevrolet engines to "reverse-engineer" in an effort to make Alfa's underpowered engine more competitive. For quality control, Ilmor already strictly limited the number of engines it supplied, but motivated by the contractual breach by Patrick, the company created a great deal of controversy and ill will among the old guard by instituting a system of engine leases in '90. Instead of selling parts to outside engine builders, Ilmor leased turn-key engine packages to a limited number of customers and provided a dedicated engineer to every team using its engine. The initial fee for a lease package was $120,000 per engine plus rebuilding costs. Al Unser became the focal point of the Ilmor lease controversy when he was unable to acquire a Chevrolet engine for the 1991 Indianapolis 500.

Under CART's leadership, Indy car racing grew quickly in the 1980s. PPG's championship points fund increased to $2 million over the course of the decade. According to Goodyear's annual report on auto racing attendance, CART nearly tripled its spectator count, from 788,000 in '80 to 2.28 million in '89. Per event attendance jumped from an average of 66,000 in '80 to more than 152,000 by the end of the decade.

While remaining under USAC sanction, the Indianapolis 500 also enjoyed a robust decade, with many races from the 1980s fondly recalled as classics. In his third decade of competition at the Speedway and back in Indy cars full time, Mario Andretti was still often the man to beat at Indy. He also continued to suffer his legendary IMS bad luck. He was at the center of the disputed '81 race; in fact, after finishing second to Bobby Unser, he was declared the victor when the official results were posted the next morning because Unser was judged guilty of passing a line of cars under caution. But 138 days later, on October 9, the decision was reversed in Unser's favor by a three-man USAC appeal board, and the driver was fined $40,000. Andretti still wears the '81 Indy 500 winner's ring he was awarded.

That wasn't Mario's only Indy disappointment in the 1980s. He was holding off Danny Sullivan at the 120-lap mark of the '85 race when Sullivan spun while trying to pass in Turn One. Sullivan kept his car off the wall, pitted for tires during the yellow flag he caused, then executed a clean pass on Andretti twenty laps later and drove away to win for Team Penske. Sullivan's famous "Spin and Win" marked the last time that an Indy car appeared on the cover of *Sports Illustrated* magazine, and the handsome driver quickly developed into a mainstream star, even making a guest appearance on the television crime drama *Miami Vice*.

Andretti then dominated the 1987 race, leading 170 of the first 177 laps. But when he eased his pace in the closing laps to conserve his car, it created a harmonic imbalance that caused his Ilmor/Chevrolet engine to drop a valve. Al Unser started that May on the sidelines, but he ended the month as the second four-time Indianapolis winner, driving to victory in a backup Team Penske entry that had been serving as a show car in a Pennsylvania hotel lobby.

Rick Mears and Gordon Johncock waged what was then the closest finish in the history of the Indianapolis 500 in 1982, with Johncock prevailing over Mears's obviously faster car by 0.16 second. Mears earned his second and third Indy wins in '84 and '88 and came close to notching another in '86. He also started from the pole in '82, '86, '88, and '89, and won the CART championship in '81 and '82. He no doubt would have accomplished even more had he not missed nearly two full years after smashing his feet in an '84 accident at Sanair Speedway in Quebec.

Drivers were pushed increasingly forward in the cars in the early years of the ground-effect era, resulting in several drivers—including Mears, Danny Ongais, and Derek Daly—suffering severe injuries to their feet and ankles in the early '80s.

A poignant moment came at the end of the rain-delayed 1986 race; after prevailing in a late race duel over Mears and Kevin Cogan, Bobby Rahal took a victory lap of the Speedway with frail team owner Jim Trueman, who died of cancer ten days later. Rahal was a consistent performer throughout the '80s, winning the CART series championship in '86 and '87. Remarkably, the '86 race marked the first time that the Indianapolis 500 was broadcast live. Since '65, the race had been run on a same-day tape-delay basis during prime time on the ABC network.

By then, two eagerly awaited newcomers were already established in Indy cars: Michael Andretti and Al Unser Jr arrived in 1983, and they quickly became star performers in their own right. Although USAC had not produced many true stars in the '70s, the sheer number of drivers who began to make their mark in the CART series in the '80s—all of whom came from road-racing backgrounds, whether they were American or foreign—was impressive. And thanks to a collective effort between CART and USAC led by Doctors Terry Trammell and Steve Olvey to improve the safety of the cars, longtime icons like A.J. Foyt, Johnny Rutherford, Al Unser, and Mario Andretti were able to extend their driving careers into their fifties.

CART also attracted a prominent new manufacturer. Almost a decade removed from its last flirtation with Indy car racing, Porsche made a full-fledged entry into CART series in late 1987, building its own chassis and engine. The bulky Porsche chassis was soon discarded in favor of a March, and Teo Fabi scored the first and only win for the March/Porsche at Mid-Ohio in '89. But the Porsche program was shut down after an uncompetitive '90 campaign.

At roughly the same time, Ferrari explored the possibility of going Indy car racing. In a feud with Formula 1 management in the mid-eighties, Enzo Ferrari commissioned a Ferrari V8 engine and chassis for the CART series, to be fielded by Bobby Rahal and the Truesports team. The Ferrari Indy car was tested at the Fiorano circuit by Michele Alboreto, but never entered in a race. The engine ultimately served as the basis for Alfa Romeo's generally unsuccessful Indy car program that ran from 1989-91.

By the end of the 1980s, Indy car racing under CART's stewardship appeared to be in better shape than at any time in the history of the American open-wheel competition, dating to the turn of the twentieth century. But the litany of changes in that decade that swept through a long-established form of racing—to the cars, to the engines, to the venues, to the make-up of the driver line-up—didn't always resonate well with the old guard at USAC and the Indianapolis Motor Speedway. And as the '90s loomed, a new generation of Hulman family leadership was deemed ready to assume control at IMS.

CHAPTER 8

ON A WORLD STAGE

I ndy car racing's first foray outside the United States during the Hulman-George era came in 1957 and '58 when an event billed as the "Race of Two Worlds" was held at the Monza circuit in Italy. In addition to the familiar road course used for the Formula 1 Italian Grand Prix, Monza also featured a 2.64-mile banked oval, and it was on that track that the Automobile Club d'Italia hoped to stage a competition between the top cars and drivers of the day from F1 and the USAC Championship Trail.

From 1950 to 1960, the Indianapolis 500 was actually counted as a points-paying round of the F1 World Championship. Alberto Ascari was the only F1 regular to actually compete at Indianapolis in that time, finishing thirty-first in a Ferrari in '52 during the year he claimed the first of his two consecutive F1 titles. Oval racing was still viewed as an American curiosity that had not caught on around the world.

Monza, with considerably steeper banking and constant radius 180-degree turns, was a much faster oval than the Indianapolis Motor Speedway. Pat O'Connor topped 170 miles per hour at Monza in a test a few weeks before he set pole position at Indy in May 1957 with a four-lap average speed of 143.94 mph. Those uncharted speeds, along with the rough condition of the Monza banking, were likely factors in why only ten American entries materialized for the June 23 race. F1 had even slimmer representation; the Grand Prix contingent was convinced that their smaller, less powerful cars would have no chance against the brutish American roadsters on the high-speed oval.

Associated Press

With heavy attrition predicted, the five hundred miles were split into three heats. Tony Bettenhausen took pole position at 177.046 mph (a speed not achieved at Indianapolis until 1971!) before Jimmy Bryan claimed the first two heats. A cautious second place behind Troy Ruttman in the third heat was enough for the three-time USAC National Champion to clinch the overall victory. Clint Brawner, chief mechanic for Bryan's Dean Van Lines Special, later called it the most meaningful victory of his career, even greater than his triumph in the '69 Indianapolis 500 with Mario Andretti.

Hoping to attract a bigger crowd, the Italian organizers convinced Ferrari and Maserati to enter cars in the 1958 race, with the Maserati to be shared by Stirling Moss and Phil Hill. Five-time F1 champion Juan-Manuel Fangio was lined up to drive Brawner's Dean Van Lines car, but the entry was an early DNF (Did Not Finish) after qualifying third. Jim Rathmann won all three heats, averaging 166.721 mph over the five hundred miles, but despite the speed and spectacle, "The Race of Two Worlds" was never run again. In fact, Indy cars would not race again on the European continent until 2001.

There were other sporadic trips outside the USA, starting with a nonchampionship event won by Jackie Stewart on the Fuji, Japan, road course in 1966. USAC also made a one-off trip to race on an oval in Rafaela, Argentina, to open the '71 season, with Al Unser claiming both 150-mile heats. A championship round was added at Canada's Mosport Park in '67 and '68 as part of USAC's limited embracement of road racing in the second half of the '60s, but Mosport disappeared from the Championship Trail until returning in '77 and '78. The '78 season also featured an international foray to England, where A.J. Foyt and Rick Mears won races at Silverstone and Brands Hatch, respectively.

CART's initial venture outside the United States took the PPG Series to Mexico City for races in 1980 and '81 at the Autodromo Hermanos Rodriguez road course. Both were won by Mears and Team Penske; Roger Penske reportedly led a wild celebration after one of the victories that included a borrowed bus and copious quantities of tequila. The Mexican event failed to gain traction despite the emergence of local star Josele Garza, who managed to slip past USAC's minimum age requirement to claim Rookie of the Year honors in the '81 Indianapolis 500 as a nineteen-year-old. Twenty years would pass before CART would revisit Mexico.

Canada returned to the schedule in 1984 with a trip to Sanair Speedway, a tiny tri-oval in the Quebec province. Although CART ran three races at Sanair, the track is most notorious for a crash that nearly ended Mears's career. Practicing for the '84 race, Mears made a rare error in judgment passing a slower car, and his Penske March was pitched into a guardrail lining the inside of the track. All twenty-seven bones in Rick's right foot were broken, his left foot was similarly smashed, and both of his Achilles tendons were detached. When Mears finally reached a hospital in Montreal after a tragicomic trip that involved multiple ambulances and a forestry helicopter, doctors wanted to amputate his feet. But after the driver's condition stabilized under the care of CART medical director Dr. Stephen Olvey, Mears was flown on Penske's jet to Indianapolis where orthopedic surgeon Dr. Terry Trammell performed a series of procedures that rebuilt his feet and salvaged his career.

For the last of Sanair's three-year run, CART added a second event in Canada. Plans for an Indy car race in downtown Toronto through the grounds of the Canadian National Exhibition (CNE) were discussed as early as 1967; a decade later, an effort by the Labatt Brewing Company to move the Canadian Grand Prix F1 race that it sponsored to the CNE was rejected by the Toronto City Council. In '86, Labatt's major rival Molson Brewery finally succeeded in bringing a race to Exhibition Place with an event that was officially called the Molson Indy Toronto.

Quickly dubbed "the Indy" by locals, the Toronto race was an immediate success. Road racing long enjoyed strong fan support in Canada, and by the mid-eighties, the F1 Canadian GP (staged in Montreal since 1978 after being spurned by Toronto) had already developed into what the *Montreal Gazette* called "Canada's most important tourist event in terms of economic impact and international media coverage." By then the PPG CART IndyCar World Series also featured a very compelling product for road-racing fans, with increasingly high-tech cars and engines and a mix of well-known star drivers from North America and abroad.

Helping matters even more, the inaugural Toronto Indy was memorable, with Bobby Rahal overcoming a stop-and-hold penalty for passing the pace car to triumph over Danny Sullivan and Mario Andretti.

Molson was an incredibly effective sponsor, creating its own television production company called Molstar Sports and Entertainment, and a second Molson-sponsored Canadian Indy car race was added in 1989. The Molson Indy Vancouver enjoyed a fifteen-year run before redevelopment of the city for the 2010 Winter Olympic Games forced its cancellation.

CART's first truly international venture would not come for another two years when the series traveled to Australia to open the 1991 season on a street course in the Gold Coast resort area. For CART, this was a coup, as the Australian organizers, with considerable (and controversial) government assistance, paid a healthy sanction fee and assumed all transportation costs for the competitors. However, the Surfers Paradise race cost Queensland taxpayers an average of A$20 million per year through '97 until International Management Group took over promotion of the event and it finally became profitable, in part due to the inclusion of the popular Australian V8 Supercar Series as a supporting act.

Through the first half of the 1990s, the three street races in Australia and Canada made up the international aspect of the sixteen-race CART schedule. The schedule itself stabilized considerably in this period, with the same sixteen venues (including six ovals, a consistent number since the mid-eighties when second races at Phoenix and Michigan were dropped to accommodate other events) featured from 1992-94. A successful street race in downtown Miami was added in '95 before the event moved to the newly built Homestead-Miami Speedway a year later.

As the CART schedule developed and stabilized through the 1980s, the Indianapolis Motor Speedway went through a change of leadership. With her health failing, Tony Hulman's widow Mary Fendrich Hulman stepped down as chairman of IMS and Hulman & Company in May 1988, passing the responsibilities to her daughter, Mari Hulman George. Then, on December 11, 1989, just weeks prior to his thirtieth birthday, Mari's son Anton "Tony" Hulman George ascended to the role of IMS president following the death of eighty-one-year-old Joe Cloutier. Mary Fendrich Hulman died in '98.

In the Hulman tradition, George stayed close to home when he was growing up, attending Indiana State University in Terre Haute prior to taking on a series of roles in the family businesses intended to groom him for leadership. George also raced on the side, competing sporadically in the Firestone Firehawk Sports Car Series and the CART-sanctioned American Racing Series (later renamed Indy Lights), a feeder formula created by Pat Patrick in 1986 that used a spec March chassis with Buick V6 power to prepare drivers for Indy cars.

At the time of his ascension to the IMS presidency, George was eight months removed from a contentious divorce, following a stormy six-year marriage to his first wife, Lisa Clark. Sordid details of George's first marriage emerged during the trial, including the couple's use of marijuana and cocaine and George's efforts to have his wife institutionalized. Just six weeks after his divorce from Clark was finalized, George married Laura Livvix and he eventually adopted her eight-year-old son Everette "Ed" Carpenter.

The Livvix family hailed from Marshall, Illinois, just across the Indiana border from Terre Haute, and was subject to its own notoriety in the area. One of Laura's in-laws, Fred Grabbe, was twice convicted for the murder of his wife Charlotte, who disappeared in 1981 in a case that was featured in the *Forensic Files* television series. Grabbe's daughter Jennie later married Laura's father, Everett "Darrell" Livvix, and their son Adam (Laura's half brother) spent eight months in an Israeli mental facility after he was indicted in a plot to blow up the famous Dome of the Rock shrine. Adam was extradited to the U.S. in 2015, where he faced a litany of less serious criminal charges in Illinois and Indiana.

Under Cloutier's leadership through the 1980s, IMS (and by extension, USAC) appeared to be satisfied with the staus quo, allowing CART to operate and market the Indy car championship series while retaining sanction and control of the Indianapolis 500. Tony George, on the other hand, was not pleased with the way Indy car racing had developed in the dozen years since his grandfather's death and vowed to take a more active role in what he often called the stewardship of the sport.

Despite record growth in terms of attendance and sponsorship revenue, George believed substantial changes were necessary for Indy car racing to achieve its true potential. He viewed the increasing number of road and street course races as a threat to IMS and oval racing in general, and he expressed concern over the lack of American Indy car drivers brought up through USAC midget and sprint car racing.

George also believed the Indianapolis Motor Speedway deserved a greater role in the overall governance of Indy car racing, and like his predecessors in the 1970s, he was convinced that the car owners had far too much control of the sport under CART's leadership model. He was convinced that the cost of Indy car racing could be made much cheaper with simpler cars and engines that didn't require controversial lease programs.

CART also underwent a series of personnel changes in the late 1980s. John Frasco, chairman since 1980, along with recently installed president John Caponigro, were ousted in late '89, largely because many of the team owners (and shareholders) believed that Pat Patrick and Roger Penske wielded too much influence—a reputation Penske would never lose. Frasco was also accused of multiple conflicts of interest, given his additional roles as promoter of CART races at the Meadowlands, Vancouver, and Miami. His troubles started in '87 when he created a nonchampionship race called the Marlboro Challenge to be run on the same weekend as his Miami event, which was the CART season finale. The $730,000 purse for the Marlboro Challenge far exceeded every other race on the CART schedule outside of the Indianapolis 500, and its inclusion as a high-profile sideshow to the title decider infuriated CART's longtime title sponsor PPG Industries.

PPG had poured more than $80 million in prize money and promotion into CART since 1979, and the company's racing director Jim Chapman expressed his unhappiness to the *Indianapolis Star* in April 1987. "PPG is a conservative company and we've never been in any controversy," Chapman told Robin Miller. "In the eight years PPG has sponsored CART, we have never tried to influence any part of CART's operation. But I felt it necessary to express our reservations to John Frasco in this case.

"We don't want to make a federal case out of this," Chapman added. "I told him we didn't object to the event, but we do object to the timing. A race of this type has the potential to divert from the official race at Miami and the year-end battle for the championship. We are also concerned about priorities that permit the prize money to exceed not only the purse for the official Miami race, but for any other official race on the CART schedule."

CART's internal woes were stoked by Andy Kenopensky, the owner of the Machinist's Union team, who wrote a strongly worded letter calling for the company's reorganization in September 1989. Although his was one of the smaller teams (with a best result of second place achieved by Josele Garza at the '86 Michigan 500), Kenopensky took his CART board duties seriously, and he emerged as a vocal advocate for the "little guy" teams fighting the might of the Penske, Patrick, and Newman/Haas organizations.

Kenopensky had already made the decision to withdraw the Machinst's Union team in 1990 (he died later that year), but his parting shot made waves. Without naming names, he called out several team owners for not making decisions in the best interest of CART because of significant conflicts of interest, including track ownership, race promotion, and supply of cars or key components.

"It appears clear that the current concept of an elected CART Board of Directors has failed to meet the needs and desires of a majority of CART owners," Kenopensky wrote. "The personal business bonds and individual competitive ego/goals of certain Board members go well beyond a sound overall perspective for our sport. Those individuals are continually placed in important decision-making roles where, in a number of critical instances, they cannot and have not functioned in an unbiased fashion. Some of our Board members have to sell cars and engines to maintain their market shares, while others actively participate in the awarding of CART track sanction arrangements."

Kenopensky questioned CART's ability to attract major sponsors and pointed out a lack of talented young drivers in the pipeline beyond Michael Andretti and Al Unser Jr. He also criticized CART's poor relationship with the media and lack of coverage compared to NASCAR.

"Certainly some of the aloofness I have observed from CART management to the press ultimately affects the sponsorship/involvement balance," he wrote. "The NASCAR/Formula One partnership with the media is a thousand times more fertile and productive than our CART management's 'above-it-all' arrogance. Have you ever tried to find hometown newspaper coverage of a CART event? Does the general public have any idea what CART is? Try telling somebody what you do without mentioning the word 'Indy.'"

Kenopensky's letter and a subsequent meeting at Laguna Seca ultimately resulted in changes to CART's management structure. At a board meeting in Chicago on October 31, 1989, Frasco was removed as chairman, and the CART board was expanded from nine members to twenty-four, or one from each team owner or Championship Properties Inc. franchise holder. Frasco was paid a $3 million settlement and Caponigro took over as CART's front man, but his reign lasted just six weeks. After making some critical remarks about PPG, his contract was not renewed and former chief mechanic/team manager John Capels took over on an interim basis until a permanent replacement could be found.

To the outside world, CART appeared to be in a state of turmoil. "Championship Auto Racing Team, Inc., founded twelve years ago by Indy car owners who rebelled at being ruled by a twenty-one-man United States Auto Club board of directors and what they believed was a weak president, will open its winter meeting today with a twenty-four-man board and no president," wrote Shav Glick in the *Los Angeles Times*. "As might be expected, the Indy car family—despite record crowds and an excellent 1989 season—is in something of a state of disarray."

After a four-month search that produced more than seventy candidates, the twenty-four-man board unanimously approved the hiring of former Playboy Enterprises Licensing and Merchandise Group President William Stokkan as its new chairman in April 1990. CART hoped that the forty-year-old Norwegian's marketing expertise would help the series grow at an even faster rate than it had under Frasco.

"It surprised me that so few American companies seemed to have any form of awareness for how powerful Indy car racing could be as a marketing tool," Stokkan said when his nomination was confirmed at the CART race at Phoenix International Raceway. "As I got to learn more about the sport, I realized the problem probably laid within some of the organizational issues within CART. This is a sport that had started out almost as a hobby foundation, and it's just grown so big and they've been a little late in putting together the marketing side of the infrastructure. It seemed like they had been so busy taking care of the technical side and most of the controversy surrounding the changes of the cars that they almost forgot to sell the product."

Stokkan was the the first CART leader to publicly note dissatisfaction with the name of the organization. "To the uninitiated, it sounds like we are either doing go-kart or shopping cart races," he told the *New York Times*. Meanwhile, he hatched a plan to officially lease the rights to the IndyCar brand from IMS.

Stokkan inherited the Australia race from the Frasco regime, and he vowed that any additional international expansion for CART would occur only on oval tracks. "Our idea is not to compete with Formula 1 on a worldwide basis," he remarked to Shav Glick. "Oval racing is distinctive to Indy cars, and with the way the auto industry is moving, it would be difficult for us to grow without a presence in Japan. It would also be important to have one in Europe, one in South America, one in Australia, and the rest in North America. All but Australia would be on ovals. We definitely want a balance between road courses and ovals, and if we export our brand of racing, it should be on ovals. Formula 1 has already filled the foreign appetite for road racing."

Stokkan's first call upon assuming the CART position was to Tony George, and the two men held a series of meetings over the next year, sometimes bringing in CART team owners, including Patrick, Penske, and Jim Hall. The CART chairman noted that improving relations with George and the Indianapolis Motor Speedway was critical for the success of the company and the PPG IndyCar World Series. "[George] has a problem with the CART structure," Stokkan said. "Our board meetings are sometimes what I call an exercise in ego pinball."

In the background, George and his legal team spent six months preparing a proposal to reorganize the government of Indy car racing, and he and a small entourage presented their plan to the twenty-four-man CART board in Houston on November 5, 1991. George proposed a new company to be known as IndyCar, Inc., to be governed by a vastly reduced board consisting of himself, Kears Pollock of PPG, two car owners to be nominated by IMS, a driver, and an at-large member (with George's preference being IMS Chief Steward Tom Binford), along with Goodyear's Leo Mehl as commissioner. The at-large and commissioner nominations were reportedly nonnegotiable.

By all accounts, the meeting went poorly. Several CART board members noted that George, a shy man and notoriously poor public speaker, appeared unprepared for the meeting. They viewed the IMS proposal as surprisingly sparse and unprofessional. "Compared to the one we heard from the Cleveland Grand Prix that morning, the Speedway's was Mickey Mouse," an unnamed CART board member told the *Star's* Miller. "Considering the importance, it was very unimpressive," added another. "It was weak, uncertain, and didn't even have a format." The CART board was also wary of the notion of Mehl as commissioner ("Leo is not perceived by everyone as a straight shooter," said one owner) and pushed for the appointment of Stokkan instead.

George, on the other hand, felt he and the Speedway were shown a shocking lack of respect by the CART board. "For all intents and purposes, my proposal was rejected," the IMS president told media when he got back home to Indianapolis. "I'm disappointed because I feel we had a positive proposal that presented representation, balance, and unity. We're all looking to make sure the sport is properly represented so we can take it to the next level. Maybe this is just a question of dancing with your partner before you become emotionally attached.

"Obviously, a lot of issues are very important to the owners, and I'm still interested in coming up with some common ground," he added. "I'm trying to be optimistic, but I can't deny I'm disappointed."

A day later, he was even less happy about the way he and his proposal were treated. "From talking to a couple car owners, what they are proposing is so far from what we have and closer to what we have now," he noted to the *Indianapolis News*. "If that is the case, I would be very, very disappointed. I'm disappointed now. It's only going to hurt racing. I guess I expected more from these guys, but they have a hard time relinquishing control. They're only looking at their own interests."

Stokkan made it sound like the two sides were not that far apart. "Tony's proposal was quite well received," he said. "It needs a little bit of clarification on a few issues, but it's a good plan. It just didn't make it all the way to home base." Added team owner Dale Coyne: "I'm sure Tony wanted a one-day decision, but let's be honest, that's expecting a bit much in three hours, isn't it? A lot of us never saw the proposal until [two days earlier]. There are some good things about it, but business is business and we're not going to make any hasty decisions we might regret later."

George may not have actually expected CART to make a decision on his proposal that day, but he was clearly demanding a response in fairly rapid order. When he got it, he didn't like what he saw. CART countered with a plan to form a committee of five car owners, George, and two IMS-appointed representatives, chaired by Stokkan, which would work throughout 1992 to put a new form of government in place prior to the '93 season.

Three weeks after the ill-fated Houston meeting, George pulled the plug on talks between the two sides. "As far as I'm concerned, it's over," George declared on November 28. "CART agreed to respond with the issues of our proposal that were acceptable and unacceptable, but they didn't," George commented. "Instead, they came back with a proposal to continue to dance. They had the ball in their court and they dropped it. So I see no reason to waste any more of my time. The car owners are blinded by power and greed and they feel their board is balanced. We made a good-faith attempt, and they didn't want to hear it. They made it clear that they don't want Leo Mehl to be the commissioner and that kills the deal for me."

George then issued a thinly veiled threat to CART. "No matter what we choose to do, I don't think CART is going to like the alternatives," he stated. "We will fall back and go on in 1992, but I will continue to pursue all our options. It's no secret I've been talking to Bill France [Junior, NASCAR president], Bernie Ecclestone, and Max Mosley [leaders of the Formula One Constructors' Association]. CART can run its sixteen races, and who knows, some day that race in New York City might be the biggest one on its schedule."

In the meantime, George carried on the Hulman family tradition by making extensive upgrades to the Speedway facilities. New garages had been constructed in 1986, and the oval was fully repaved in '89, before George treated the track to the biggest round of changes in nearly a century. Prior to the '93 Indianapolis 500, the inner lane, known as the apron, inside the four corners was replaced by a grass verge with new separate warm-up lanes in the infield for pit lane entry and exit. This change tightened the racing line and caused the pole speed to drop by nearly nine mph. The pit lane itself was widened, and the area where the cars were serviced was resurfaced in concrete. New concrete walls built to the international standard height of one meter (an increase of a little more than three inches) were erected around the track, topped by a taller, stronger catchfence. The following year, a new victory lane featuring an elevated rotating platform was introduced, a new scoring pylon was constructed, and the IMS administrative offices were moved from the Hall of Fame Museum to a new building constructed outside the track at the corner of 16th Street and Georgetown Road.

The IMS golf course also got a major makeover in 1993, with the twenty-seven existing holes reduced to eighteen, including four in the track's infield; the newly christened Brickyard Crossing Golf Course hosted a round of the PGA Champions (Senior) Tour from 1994 to 2000. The premium nature of the golf course, which was designed by noted Indiana architect Pete Dye, resulted in a substantial reduction in infield parking, part of George's plan to eliminate the Speedway's notorious "Snakepit" party area to create a more family-friendly atmosphere at the 500.

The Speedway (with an assist from PPG) had also responded in a big way to complaints from competitors about prize money not keeping up with the rising cost of racing. The Indianapolis 500 purse increased by nearly 400 percent in the 1980s, from $1.5 million to $5.72 million, with the winner's share more than tripling. Emerson Fittipaldi became the first $1 million winner in '89.

CART also continued its impressive growth in the early 1990s. Next-generation stars Al Unser Jr. and Michael Andretti came of age, winning consecutive PPG IndyCar World Series championships in 1990 and '91. But the sport arguably reached its peak in '93, thanks to another foreign import. Having reached an impasse in his contract negotiations with Williams Grand Prix Engineering, and with no other acceptably competitive F1 rides available, reigning F1 World Champion Nigel Mansell succumbed to longtime overtures from Newman/Haas Racing owner Carl Haas to join his team to race in the CART series. Mansell effectively switched places with Michael Andretti, who switched to F1 for the '93 campaign with the Marlboro McLaren team.

The two men experienced remarkably different fortunes. Andretti struggled to adapt to the more nimble F1 cars and the intimidating presence of his teammate Ayrton Senna, who produced some of the most memorable performances of his storied career in 1993. Andretti's F1 career lasted less than a full year; after he finished a season-best third in the Italian Grand Prix, Michael was replaced by McLaren's reserve driver, Mika Häkkinen.

Interestingly, Senna had entered the 1993 season out of contract, and as a form of leverage, he accepted an offer from his friend and countryman Fittipaldi to test a Penske Indy car at Firebird Raceway in December 1992. Kitted up in his Marlboro F1 uniform, Senna looked right at home climbing into the Marlboro-sponsored Penske PC21.

"The track was really slow, and the car behaves in a very particular way, but the sensation, the feeling, is great," Senna commented in a Brazilian television interview. "I'm very happy for finally being able to actually experience an Indy car. One day, I will drive this car—it's just a matter of time. I have to wait for the right moment to compete in the U.S." Sadly, the three-time F1 World Champion and his legion of fans would be denied that scenario, as Senna was killed on May 1, 1994, in the San Marino Grand Prix.

Mansell, meanwhile, stepped into the dominant Newman/Haas Lola that Andretti had vacated and picked up right where Michael left off. Mansell won his CART debut at Surfers Paradise Australia, benefiting from a lucky break when a black-flag infraction for passing Fittipaldi under yellow coincided with the need for him to make his first pit stop for fuel. CART subsequently changed its rules to mandate a separate stop for any black-flag penalty, but not before Mansell claimed an impressive and hugely popular first win.

Mansell and his family settled in Clearwater, Florida, and the worldwide media attention his move to America and the IndyCar Series attracted was simply staggering. More than one hundred media members from around the globe showed up for his first oval test at Phoenix, and Newman/Haas public relations manager Michael Knight was compelled to issue special media credentials for the event. Knight eventually resorted to using a megaphone and a cattle prod to control the chaos surrounding his new driver. "Carl Haas whispered to me, 'This thing might be bigger than we thought,'" recalled Knight.

Interest in Mansell's move to America reached a fever pitch when he suffered a spectacular crash in practice during the Phoenix race weekend that left a huge hole in the concrete wall. He sustained a concussion and severe bruising to his back and was unable to make the start, but he returned two weeks later to finish third at Long Beach. International media interest continued to grow, to the point where the Indianapolis Motor Speedway had to nearly double the size of its media center to accommodate the press from around the world. But some observers were convinced that the additional coverage focused on a foreign road racer actually upset George and IMS officials; they believed the Speedway was more interested in making the papers in Edinburgh, Indiana, than Edinburgh, Scotland. In any case, domestic and international media coverage continued to peak throughout 1993 as Mansell went on to win four additional races (all on ovals) to claim the CART championship at his first attempt. For a few weeks in September 1993 when he held both the F1 and IndyCar titles, Mansell took to calling himself a "Double World Champion."

By every measure other than the percentage of drivers from a midget and sprint car background, Indy car racing was more stable and commercially successful in the early 1990s than at any other point in the sport's ninety-year history. But the path that CART had taken to get to that position concerned the Indianapolis Motor Speedway and Tony George, who was convinced that despite a considerable amount of tangible evidence, the sport was going in the wrong direction. George viewed CART's increasingly higher profile in America and around the world as a threat to his track and family business, and before long, he took steps to protect what he perceived was a dwindling power base.

Since the collapse of the Championship Racing League in 1980, CART had based its series around the Indianapolis 500 while operating in relative peace without outside interference from the Indianapolis Motor Speedway. That was about to change in dramatic fashion.

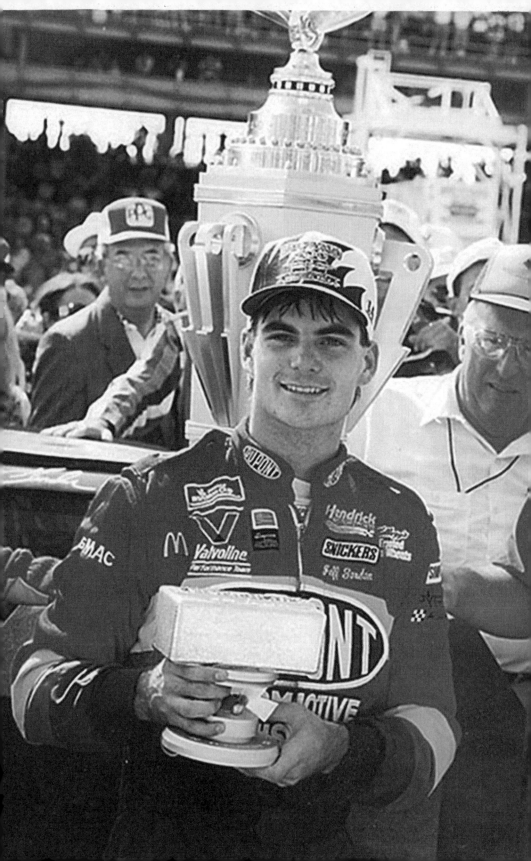

CHAPTER 9

THE SPEEDWAY FLEXES ITS MUSCLE

In September 1991, occasional NASCAR competitor A.J. Foyt brought one of his stock cars to the Indianapolis Motor Speedway to film a television commercial for Craftsman Tools. Foyt's godson, IMS President Tony George, who casually raced throughout the '80s, stopped by and hopped into the car to run a few laps of the Hulman family racetrack.

This occurred just a few weeks before the Houston meeting where the CART board rejected George's proposal to reorganize the governance of Indy car racing, and it may have been the final inducement he needed to approach his family about going against tradition by expanding the Speedway's annual schedule to include an additional marquee event alongside the Indianapolis 500. Adding a NASCAR race was a risky move; on one hand, if the event were to prove successful, it could be a significant moneymaker for the Speedway and the Hulman-George family. A healthy NASCAR event could also serve as a bargaining tool (and cash generator) for IMS if the Speedway's relationship with CART continued to deteriorate. However, Indy's reputation was built on the 500, and the danger existed that a NASCAR race at IMS could potentially anger the Indy car fan base and devalue the 500 and/or the month of May.

An exploratory first step toward the diversification of IMS came June 22-23, 1992, when nine NASCAR Winston Cup Series teams conducted an "acclimitazation test" for Goodyear. The likes of Dale Earnhardt,

Bill Elliott, Davey Allison, and Ernie Irvan lapped the 2.5-mile oval at 167 miles per hour, some 60 mph slower than the Indy cars of the era. But that didn't deter around fifty thousand spectators from shelling out five-dollar admission over the course of the two days to experience the novelty of NASCAR at Indy.

"Last December, my family decided to pursue some possible opportunities and investigate the possibilities of having another event here," George remarked. "I've received a lot of mail and people want another race. And anybody that's a race fan knows that NASCAR puts on a good show.

"Like everyone else, I thought [the test] was great and it really doesn't need much explanation. The reaction was just about what I thought it would be, and the crowd was just about what I expected, considering the restrictions we put on them. But I still don't know NASCAR's reaction, and we've got to huddle."

Though respectful in deference to the traditions of the Indianapolis 500, the NASCAR set could barely contain its glee at the prospect of invading Indy car racing's hallowed home turf. "From NASCAR's standpoint, it would be a neat deal to run here someday," said NASCAR CEO Bill France Jr. "The cars looked good out there, they sounded good, the fans liked them and the drivers liked the track. To my knowledge we haven't seen any negatives."

George said any NASCAR race at IMS would likely not take place before 1994, citing the need to finish the major renovation project in progress at the Speedway before any decision was made. When that was completed on schedule in April 1993, George and France jointly announced that the inaugural NASCAR Brickyard 400 was set for Saturday, August 6, 1994. It would be the first race other than the Indianapolis 500 at IMS since the Harvest Day Classic in September 1916.

"I think it's the greatest day in the history of the track since the day my grandfather bought the track in 1945," George said. "My grandfather had a lot of respect for [the late William H.G.] France and I feel very comfortable I'm not making a decision that would cause him to be barrel-rolling in his grave . . . I think Pawpaw and Big Bill are up there smiling and shaking hands right now."

"I think people are going to look back after thirty years and say it was one of the high days in the history of motorsports," added France Jr.

Others were somewhat more skeptical. "It'll be a good show, a lot of people will come and watch, and the Speedway will make a lot of money. But Indy is Indy, and anything else you do there is going to take a little bit away from it," said Indy car champion Rick Mears, who had unexpectedly retired from driving at the end of the 1992 season, barely a year after he joined A.J. Foyt and Al Unser as the only four-time winners of the Indianapolis 500.

Mario Andretti was even more vocal about his concerns. "I hate to see it happen because, to me, Indianapolis has always been sacred ground for open-wheeled, single-seat thoroughbreds," he commented to Robin Miller of the *Indianapolis Star*. "There's always been a mystique to it, and I think a NASCAR race will definitely hurt the Indy crowd. In my opinion, the Speedway has to be very careful playing with something so good and so successful. If the Speedway wants to break tradition, then the Indy 500 should be a four-day event just like NASCAR. That's the way it should be.

"I think NASCAR has everything to lose and nothing to gain coming to Indy," he added. "We can't afford to go to Daytona, and I don't think they can afford to come to Indy."

When the Brickyard 400 was announced, George was nine months into serving as a nonvoting member on a CART board that had been restructured yet again. The slimmed-down version that debuted in July 1992 included five elected team owners along with CART chairman Bill Stokkan (also in a nonvoting role) and George. But Stokkan's power base was eroding, and in August 1993, he announced that he would not seek a contract extension. After arriving with a reputation as a marketing and licensing specialist, Stokkan generally failed in that area, with one notable exception: in October 1992, he obtained a license from the Indianapolis Motor Speedway to use the term "IndyCar" (one of many "Indy"-related trademarks owned by IMS) and from 1993 onward, CART was legally known as IndyCar.

The newly christened company was once again searching for a new leader, and the situation was complicated by yet another restructuring of the board, back to one vote for each of the twenty-four franchises, distributed among sixteen team owners. The re-expansion of the board did not please George. Nor was he impressed by the way the CEO search panned out. Three main contenders emerged: SCCA President Nick Craw, attorney/manager Cary Agajanian (supported by George), and a last-minute candidate who was a complete newcomer to the Indy car scene. Andrew Craig was a Switzerland-based Englishman who since 1983 had worked in senior management for International Sport and Leisure (ISL) Marketing AG, where he developed global initiatives for the FIFA World Cup and the International Olympic Committee. Upon learning about the opening at CART from *Autosport* magazine, Craig aggressively pursued the job, writing letters to all of the selection committee members followed up by phone calls. Agajanian fell out of the running when Craig inserted himself into the mix, a month before Craig and Craw made final presentations to the full CART board in December 1993.

Impressed by his preparation, the team owners chose Craig, and he agreed to a two-year contract. He admitted he had a lot to learn. "It's true that I don't know American racing," he said in his introductory interview. "My experience with Indy car racing consists of attending two Indianapolis 500s and watching races on television. On the other hand, I don't think it will be too difficult to settle into the American racing scene. For example, I already know [IMSA President] John Greenwood through his involvement with the Los Angeles Olympic Games. I got to know Nick Craw during the interviewing process for the CART job, and I intend to meet with the other sanctioning bodies, the promoters and the sponsors, with Tony George number one on the list."

But mere hours before CART revealed Craig's appointment to the public on January 7, 1994, the announcement was upstaged by news that George was quitting his nonvoting role on the CART Board. The move was not unexpected, and like many other pieces of news released by IMS over the next few years, the timing was anything but coincidental.

"My decision is based on continuing dissatisfaction with the decision-making process dictated by the organizational structure of CART," George stated. "CART is an organization of car owners representing their individual and collective needs and desires, rather than an organization that better represents all constituencies within our sport and which has more focus on the long term betterment of the sport. It is my intention to continue to work for the betterment of the sport."

George offered a bit more to the *Star*'s Robin Miller. "I felt very strongly [the CART leader] should be an American with a pretty strong motorsports background," he said. "Nothing personal to Andrew Craig, but I was planning to resign anyway."

George didn't wait long before making his next move. On March 11, 1994, he made an announcement that sent even bigger shock waves through the Indy car community than the establishment of the Brickyard 400 had. "George Plans Series Featuring Indianapolis 500," read the headline of a seven-sentence press release that lacked any real or specific information other than the inclusion of the 500—not even a name for the proposed series.

"I have personally made every effort the past two years to work with the car owner organization currently governing the series in order to hear and be heard with regard to the direction the series is heading," read George's statement. "I have come to the conclusion that the Speedway and the current car owner organization are simply going in different directions.

"The primary purpose of the new series is to maximize the tremendous growth potential of the series surrounding the Indianapolis 500 for the added benefit of the fans, sponsors, promoters, and participants."

In an interview with the *Indianapolis Star*, George stopped short of declaring war on CART. But he also left no doubt that after years of being ignored, he and the Speedway were going on the offensive.

"I was never taken seriously in those [CART] meetings, and this announcement may not be taken seriously," said the IMS president. "Some may say 'He's blowing smoke again.' But I guarantee you one thing is certain: The time for all the talking and positioning is over. It's obvious we are going in different directions.

"This is not going to be a blood bath; that's not our intention," he added. "I'm not trying to do anything on the spur of the moment so people don't have a chance to react. I'm not for causing any great hardship right now. We've got definte ideas of where we're going and hopefully they will work with us and participate."

Leaving aside his dissatisfaction with CART's management structure, George expressed displeasure about several other aspects of how the sport had evolved and stated his worries for the future of oval track racing.

"I think Indianapolis, and Indy car racing, is missing some American flavor," he said. "I'm not opposed to foreign manufacturers and competitors, but it rubs me the wrong way that America's premier series has to look overseas for talent because they have a fat checkbook. Maybe I'm too idealistic to think that guys can still earn their way to Indy on their talent. Jeff Gordon went to NASCAR without any money, and you can't do that here anymore.

"I lean toward oval tracks because it makes sense in terms of more exciting races, easier television production, and higher ratings," he continued. "I don't mind some road courses and street races and I wouldn't want to say they are out of the question. But I'm concerned about the long-term health, because at the rate things are escalating, it's going to take $12 million to field a car capable of winning. I don't know how you can realistically expect to do it immediately, but there's a lot of fat in there."

Once again, the timing of the announcement was clearly calculated, as many of the PPG IndyCar World Series participants were on a charter flight en route to Australia for the 1994 season opener when George faxed his press release. Though he did not officially take over as CART's CEO until March 31, Craig held a press conference upon arrival in Surfers Paradise. "The Indianapolis 500 is immensely important to us," he said. "It is the world's biggest motor race, and we value our involvement with that event. We have differences on our future direction, but we have more common ground than things that divide us."

Against this brewing political backdrop, CART's 1994 season started with a victory on the Gold Coast for Michael Andretti, who was back in Indy cars, but driving for Chip Ganassi instead of Newman/Haas after his short-lived and generally unsuccessful Formula 1 experiment. More significant was the victorious debut for Reynard Racing Cars. With March gone since 1990, Lola had taken over as the dominant Indy car customer chassis, but Reynard would soon surpass Lola in terms of market share. This was also the first win for Chip Ganassi Racing.

A native of Pittsburgh, Ganassi's father, Floyd, ran one of the largest paving and aggregate companies in the region. Chip's promising career as a driver was cut short by a devastating accident during CART's Michigan 500 in 1984; he was lucky to survive. He did return to the cockpit to compete at Indianapolis in 1985 and '86, but soon turned his attention to team ownership. Ganassi took a minority stake in Patrick Racing prior to Emerson Fittipaldi's dominant run to win the Indy 500 and the CART title in '89, before acquiring and rebranding the team as Chip Ganassi Racing in '90. Fittipaldi and his Marlboro sponsorship transferred to Penske Racing, so Ganassi hired Eddie Cheever, an American with ten years of Formula 1 experience, as his driver. He also inked what would prove to be a long and mutually beneficial sponsorship from Target, a rapidly growing chain of discount department stores.

On the engine side, CART featured some good old fashioned Chevrolet vs. Ford competition in the early 1990s as Cosworth Engineering produced a new engine—this time with official Ford involvement—that set new standards in terms of power and packaging. After five years of Chevrolet/Ilmor domination, Michael Andretti won five races with the Ford-Cosworth XB in '92, and the engine powered Nigel Mansell to his '93 PPG IndyCar World Series title. The rapid advent of the Ford-Cosworth, along with Ilmor's desire to respond with an accelerated development pace, prompted Chevrolet to withdraw from the CART series at the end of the '93 season. General Motors's 25 percent stake in Ilmor Engineering was picked up by Mercedes-Benz as the German firm worked to create an in-house engine supply for its return to Formula 1.

Ilmor's fourth-generation Indy car engine was campaigned without manufacturer branding in 1994, but it proved remarkably successful. Roger Penske created a three-car Marlboro Team Penske superteam, featuring Al Unser Jr., Emerson Fittipaldi, and Paul Tracy that won eleven of fifteen CART-sanctioned races, with Unser claiming his second PPG Cup trophy. But Ilmor made an even bigger mark at the Indianapolis 500.

For more than a decade, Ilmor principals Paul Morgan and Mario Illien had casually talked with Penske about what some perceived as a loophole in USAC's Indy 500 engine regulations that tried to give turbocharged "stock-block" engines a fighting chance against the more exotic (and more expensive) pure racing designs. Engines with simpler overhead valve engine technology were viewed as an avenue for less well-funded teams to compete at Indianapolis, and those engines were granted significantly more turbo boost than the more sophisticated Ilmor and Cosworth purebred racing engines featuring overhead cams—fifty-five inches versus forty-five. That, along with 29 percent greater capacity (209 cubic inches versus 161), gave the Buicks a significant power advantage.

The Buick engine was effective for Indianapolis qualifying, and it powered the pole winner in 1985 and '92. But it was difficult to drive and unreliable, and it was not until Al Unser finished third at Indianapolis in '92—some ten years into the program—that a Buick actually completed the full five hundred miles. The Buick was viewed as a good way to secure pole at Indy, but one that offered little realistic chance of winning the race.

What resparked Illien's interest in designing a bespoke pushrod engine was a 1992 modification to the USAC rulebook that no longer made it a requirement for an Indianapolis 500 engine to actually have a production car base. USAC bulletin 1107 read:

Turbocharged four-cycle single non-overhead camshaft (camshaft in block) engines with pushrod operated valve mechanisms, two valves per cylinder, will be limited to a maximum piston displacement of 209.3 cubic inches (3,430 cc) and a maximum of eight (8) cylinders.

Since the advent of superior overhead cam technology, nobody had created a clean-sheet, pushrod-actuated, overhead-valve engine for racing purposes. CART didn't allow the ten inches of extra turbo boost that USAC allowed for Indianapolis, so there was no incentive to develop a pushrod engine for other races. John Menard, the home improvement store magnate who began sponsoring Indy 500 entries in the 1980s, absorbed the cost of creating a lighter version of the Buick engine by commissioning the design of an aluminum block. But Roger Penske revered the Indianapolis 500 like no other race, and he was willing (and financially able) to do almost anything possible to win it. Having constructed his own chassis since '77, Penske now sought out an additional unfair advantage with his own engine.

In great secrecy, Ilmor designed and built a 209-cubic-inch pushrod V8 to the letter of the USAC rules. After initially offering badging rights to Chevrolet, Penske convinced Mercedes-Benz to fund the Indianapolis 500 program and enticed his employees to keep the program underground. "We had to let our people know what was going on," he said. "I sat down with them in different groups and said, 'Guys, it's just like cutting a piece of your paycheck off.'" Snowplows were employed as Tracy accumulated test miles throughout the winter at the Penske-owned Nazareth and Michigan Speedways prior to the engine's debut to a stunned public on April 13. The engine finally completed a 500-mile endurance run at Michigan on May 8, the opening day of Indianapolis 500 practice.

Although slightly taller and heavier than the standard Ilmor "D" engine, the Mercedes-Benz 500I was designed to fit the 1994 Penske PC23 chassis, requiring few modifications other than strengthening the clutch, transmission, and driveshafts to withstand the pushrod engine's immense torque. Penske topped the slightly bulbous engine cover with a soon-to-be-copied fin. Engine and gearbox reliability was a constant concern, but the engine's prodiguous power (later confirmed as 1,024 horsepower at a time when the Ford-Cosworth was making about 800) guaranteed that the Penske team would dominate the month of May.

"You have to get used to it," said Fittipaldi. "It's very easy to over-rev the engine, and in traffic, if the revs drop by 1,000, a lot of the power is gone. So it's a very narrow window. But we have worked hard to get the same throttle response as our regular engine, and in reality, it's much less advantage than people realize—the other drivers are also reaching 240 miles per hour on the straights."

Still, there was clearly a lot of sandbagging going on in the Penske camp. Unser, never known as a great qualifier, took pole position at 228.011 mph and was the only driver capable of keeping up with Fittipaldi on race day. The Brazilian led 145 laps and looked set to win his third 500 since 1989, but he got greedy and crashed while trying to lap teammate Unser with just sixteen laps remaining. That set Al Jr. up to cruise to an easy win over rookie Jacques Villeneuve's Reynard/Ford-Cosworth.

The Mercedes-Benz 500I engine was a remarkable triumph for Penske and Ilmor. Significantly, it also marked the last time that one team or manufacturer was able to create a unique, innovative alternative to the norm that created a significant advantage. In many ways, the 500I was the last hurrah for technical creativity at Indianapolis.

"We felt it was more than likely with the increasing interest from major manufacturers, such as Honda, Toyota, and Ford, all becoming very interested in the Speedway, that one of them would go and build a pushrod engine for the USAC rules," said Ilmor coprincipal Paul Morgan. "We felt like rather than talking about it, it would be the best thing to go and actually build one.

"This engine went from the discussion stage to drawings, to castings, and onto dyno in twenty-five weeks," he added. "Even for a small, agile company like Ilmor, that is a remarkably short cycle time to take an engine from general concept to working prototype. It was also quite likely that the engine would be eligible for only one race—the 1994 Indianapolis 500—since we rather expected the equivalency formula to be banned immediately after that race. Therefore, it was absolutely essential that it worked correctly the first time—it was a unique opportunity, almost do-or-die, if you like."

The Penske/Mercedes domination of the 1994 Indianapolis 500 infuriated George and the USAC faithful. To them, it was just the latest example of the rich getting richer, not a clever group of engineers who had the brains and the technical (and financial) capability to build a faster and more powerful car to a loosely defined set of rules. As Morgan predicted, USAC quickly worked to minimize the Mercedes engine's advantage, declaring in June that its boost would be restricted to fifty-two inches in '95. But Ilmor calculated that the engine would still be competitive at that boost level, so thirty sets of heads, blocks, and camshafts were machined in preparation for the '95 Indianapolis 500, when the engine would be made available to all Ilmor customers.

On July 8, 1994, George announced his new series would debut in '96 and revealed a red-white-and-blue logo that mimicked that of Major League Baseball, along with a name: Indy Racing League. The IRL's governing board was filled with familiar faces, including USAC CEO Dick King, former IMS president John Cooper, True Value Hardware CEO Dan Cotter, and longtime short-track race promoter Don Smith. The press release also stated that USAC would sanction all IRL races, and vaguely noted that IRL participants would be rewarded with financial incentives and guaranteed starting positions for each league race.

This news created little in the way of response from the CART camp. But the August 10 announcement of the proposed engine rules for the IRL got their attention. To the surprise of almost everyone, the IRL cast aside rampant talk of stock blocks and equivalency formulas and decreed a turbocharged 2.2-liter overhead cam V8 with forty-five inches of boost—essentially a downsized version of the 2.65-liter formula that had been the standard for Indy car competition under USAC and CART sanction since 1969. This was viewed as a positive step in terms of cooperation between the two groups. "We told them reducing capacity was the best way to reduce horsepower, and thankfully for many of us, that's exactly what they did," commented Ilmor's U.S. Vice President Paul Ray.

However, the IMS announcement also noted a rule change for the 209-cubic-inch Mercedes for the 1995 Indianapolis 500: it would be restricted to forty-eight inches of boost, a level that would likely render the engine uncompetitive. If the '96 IRL regulations were to Ilmor's liking, the rule aimed specifically at handicapping the pushrod program the company had invested so much in (remember those thirty engines already in production for '95?) incensed Roger Penske.

"The '95 rules were in place, so why does USAC change them without talking to me or gathering any technical data?" mused Penske. "Number one, you can tell it was politically motivated. There was no science involved. Sixty days ago the boost was at fifty-two inches and now the boost for the Buick is still fifty-five inches. Nobody ever asked us about what kind of power we were getting or what rpm's we were turning. How can they expect to be an organization to run any series?"

In July, IMS announced the hiring of Jerry Hauer, then the executive director of the Indiana State Emergency Management Agency, as director of New Series Development. With the IRL lacking credibility even in Indianapolis, the *Indianapolis News* quipped: "There's plenty of joke potential in wondering why George would hire a disaster expert for that task, but that's another story." Hauer, with zero previous auto racing experience, was named IRL commissioner just forty-five days into his IMS employment. Yet by the end of the year, there were already rumors of his demise; on January 4, 1995, his departure was confirmed and longtime auto racing marketing figure Jack Long was appointed the league's executive director.

As the calendar turned to 1995, CART was still riding high, and what existed of Tony George's proposed new Indy car series was in considerable disarray. Still, no one on either side recognized how close relations between the sanctioning body and the Indianapolis Motor Speedway were to finally reaching a breaking point.

CHAPTER 10

THE SECOND SPLIT: IRL VS. CART

Just prior to Christmas 1994, the Indy Racing League issued guidelines for its '96 chassis rules, featuring higher sidepods, smaller wings, and reduced underbody tunnels. The aerodynamic modifications were aimed at reducing speeds on one-mile ovals like Phoenix and Milwaukee. The most notable aspect of the regulations was a substantially wider tub and cockpit—to fit A.J. Foyt in case the IRL needed him to come out of retirement, so the joke went. Foyt was the only CART team owner who at that point had committed to entering the IRL.

Newly instituted IRL executive director Jack Long's cocky, gun-slinger persona rubbed many in the CART community the wrong way. But Long soon had more news to promote. On January 10, 1995, ABC revealed that it would produce live broadcasts for all IRL races, naturally including the Indianapolis 500. On the twenty-eighth, the IRL announced its first event outside of the Indianapolis 500: the Walt Disney World 200 was scheduled for January 27, 1996, on a 1.1-mile tri-oval to be built by a new company called IMS Events in a parking lot at the sprawling Florida amusement park. IMS Events would also promote the race and bring in temporary grandstands. "This will undoubtedly become one of the largest sporting events in the state of Florida," predicted Al Weiss, president of the Walt Disney World Resort.

The Disney announcement made barely a ripple within CART, whose members resolutely declared no interest in entering an IRL race, even with a guaranteed purse of $1 million. The lack of interest (or cooperation) from the CART community toward the IRL extended to the league's engine and chassis package. None of CART's existing chassis or engine suppliers would commit to building products to IRL specifications, causing the league to announce on March 10 that it would use 1995 CART-spec cars and engines for its '96 inaugural season while leaving the question of '97 and beyond unanswered.

This was portrayed in the media as a victory for CART and an embarrassing retreat for the IRL, but many of the CART team owners made a critical mistake by selling their 1995 and older cars for pennies on the dollar to teams intending to compete in the IRL. Ford-Cosworth provisionally agreed to provide engines to IRL competitors, something that Honda, Mercedes-Benz, and new CART entrant Toyota refused to do. Allowing its teams and one of its engine manufacturers to supply the low-cost equipment the IRL needed to get off the ground was a crucial error that CART would come to regret.

George remained bullish on his league. "This is not about control," he reiterated. "I don't want to run a car owner's organization. I want to get away from that circus atmosphere and get back to traditional racing. There's no question it will be a challenge, but I think there are enough fans to go around and I think two series can survive. I'm going to do whatever it takes to make this one work.

"We're definitely not going away. We're going to have a schedule of races, no matter what, and it's going to get all of my attention from now on. It may take ten years, maybe fifteen [prescient, in retrospect], but I'll be perfectly happy to give this thing the opportunity to be successful. If it is, I'll be ecstatic. If it isn't, I'll be disappointed."

George continued to talk about the IRL in terms of enhancing or adding value to the sport of Indy car racing by working with CART rather than going into competition with the existing series. CART CEO Andrew Craig, on the other hand, sounded much more defiant in a February 1995 interview with *RACER* magazine.

"I know what Tony wants very clearly is to see this sport develop for the future, and he is very committed—probably more committed than almost anybody in our sport—to see Indy car racing develop," Craig said. "And I must say, quite frankly, I think I'd rather have Tony as a partner than as a rival.

"Let me say very clearly that our preferred scenario is that we reach a resolution with the Speedway and we put the series back together as one series. We continue to work with that aim in mind. I guess the one scenario that doesn't seem to be talked about very much is: What happens to Championship Auto Racing Teams if we don't reach an accomodation?

"I want to be very clear about this: We are not going to go away," Craig added. "We will continue to run our race series, we will continue to promote our race series, and we'll market the hell out of it and make it into an extremely strong series."

In early April 1995, the IRL issued a four-race '96 schedule, featuring two-hundred-mile races at Walt Disney World, Phoenix International Raceway (PIR), and the new Las Vegas Motor Speedway that was under construction at the time. The announcement was delayed until after CART raced at Phoenix; promoter Buddy Jobe had an uneasy relationship with CART, and he feared reprisal if PIR's move to the IRL was announced prior to CART's race weekend. A fifth race set for August 18 at New Hampshire International Speedway (Phoenix and New Hampshire being the only CART venues to switch allegiance to the IRL) was added in late May.

"It would not behoove any of us if we started scheduling races against one another to try to make a political statement," George said. "I think that everybody is going to keep a level head and work at trying to maintain the good relationship that we've fostered through the years. We may have disagreements about certain issues, but that doesn't mean we're not friends and don't have personal, social, and business relationships with people in [CART]. I think we'll all be working for what's in the best interest of Indy car racing."

Also in April, Bill France instigated a meeting in New York that included George and Long from the IRL, along with Craig, Roger Penske, Les Richter, and John Cooper. CART's proposal of a governing board consisting of three car owners, three race promoter directors, and three at-large directors was curtly refused.

George perhaps underestimated CART's resolve and was therefore stunned when what he frequently called "the car owner run organization" announced 1996 chassis rules that, with the exception of the wide-body tub, were broadly similar to those proposed and withdrawn by the IRL. Also revealed was a '96 schedule that featured a pair of seemingly avoidable conflicts. Dates for the CART race in Australia and a new event being added on a modified oval near Rio de Janeiro, Brazil, bookended those of the IRL race at Phoenix, making participation there virtually impossible. And CART's race at Road America was slated for the same weekend as the IRL at New Hampshire.

The month of May was left open, and the CART team owners vowed to compete at the Indianapolis 500. "There's not even a question of boycotting Indianapolis," remarked Carl Haas on a number of occasions. But Roger Penske sounded less optimistic. "I don't anticipate any problems from our side," Penske said. "Of course, we still don't know what the rules are for next year, or if we'll be welcome there."

The reason for Penske's skepticism became clear on July 3 when the IRL confirmed something that had been expected since George made his original breakaway announcement in March 1994. Three-quarters of the starting spots in the field for every IRL race—including the Indianapolis 500—would be reserved for IRL points leaders. In other words, twenty-five of the thirty-three grid positions for the Indianapolis 500 would be reserved for IRL regulars as long as they showed the ability to meet minimum speed parameters. In theory, this meant that significant bumping would only occur for the eight "at large" qualifying berths available for the 500, and a CART driver who ran 225 miles per hour could lose out to an IRL regular stuck at 219.

"It's obvious leverage to entice teams to run the Indy Racing League events at Orlando and Phoenix and the first major offensive in what promises to be a nasty war between George's group and Championship Auto Racing Teams," wrote Robin Miller in an *Indianapolis Star* column titled "George's IRL Plans Will Damage Indy's Respectability." "Besides being high-speed extortion, it's also a terrible idea that could seriously damage the credibility of this race.

"This whole confrontation figures to get real mean," Miller concluded. "But desperate moves, more often than not, turn out to be dumb ones. Four laps should decide your fate at Indianapolis, not politics."

George fueled the flames by uttering what came across as a flippant quip during an appearance on ESPN's SpeedWeek program to defend the IRL's starting field guarantee. "Tradition is a consideration, but it's not a priority," he said.

The grid seeding, or "25/8 Rule," as it became known, had been part of the IRL plan dating to the very first March 1994 press release. But the reality of the situation still came as a shock to the competitors in the CART series, who faced the very real possibility of sitting out the biggest race of the year.

"I think it means Tony's series does not have much support," said Andrew Craig. "Most successful things do not have things forced down people's throat. Never, in any form of motorsport, is there a situation where the fastest don't make the grid."

Bobby Rahal, a three-time CART series champion and winner of the 1986 Indianapolis 500, was incensed by the IRL's actions. "I have to ask, where were these people in the 1980s when CART was building the series back up?" he asked. "They were MIA in the '80s. Now, because of the success of Indy car racing, they want to take it over.

"I'm a believer in fair and open competition," Rahal continued. "I don't care if it's a midget, a stock car, or a Formula 1 car, the drivers and teams should have to prove themselves. There are no gimmes, no exceptions. This special seeding at the Indy 500 is a heavy-handed approach to something that is unneeded. You can ask Al Unser Jr., Emerson Fittipaldi or myself . . . we've all won the Indy 500 and we've all sat on the sidelines and watched the Indy 500."

Rahal spoke from experience. He failed to qualify at Indianapolis in 1993, and he came perilously close to missing the show again a year later. In '95, both Team Penske cars couldn't muster the speed to make the field after crushing the competition just twelve months earlier.

"That's what makes Indy so great," Rahal said. "Even the champions can be bumped. You hope reason will prevail, but these rules are totally contrary to what the sport is all about. And this idea that Americans are not getting rides and drivers are buying rides isn't correct. The buying rides goes back to Indy many years ago. If I were Jimmy Vasser, Robby Gordon, or Bryan Herta, I'd be pretty upset with people saying there are no good young American drivers. But there are good young international drivers too, like Gil de Ferran, Christian Fittipaldi, Jacques Villeneuve, and Paul Tracy. I just want to drive against the best drivers—not ones that are hand-picked because they drove in selected races before the Indy 500."

The IRL spun the reservation of 75 percent of the grid for league points leaders as a tool of inclusion, rather than exclusion. "It is anything but exclusionary," argued Long. "It's an exemption based on participation and performance. The incentive is designed to reward those entrants who compete in our series. The opportunity is there for any and all cars to enter our events under our rules.

"I don't get the exclusion part," he added. "We sent invitations to every team in the sport. How is that a lockout?"

Long seemed unconcerned that the 1996 Indianapolis 500 might not include the established stars of Indy car racing. "The Indy 500 makes stars, stars don't make the Indy 500," he said. "We'll have great new drivers and the cars will be the same."

Long's comments and similar remarks from the likes of A.J. Foyt were perceived by many as arrogant and ignorant. "What made this race so great was the strong tradition that it enjoyed over the years," said Mario Andretti. "Indianapolis would not be Indianapolis if you didn't have the greatest drivers in the past that competed here. To say that the facility itself is the only thing that will create stars, that's ludicrous. I think it goes hand in hand. Jimmy Clark was not created by Indianapolis, but when he came to Indianapolis, he brought something to Indianapolis. I think credit where credit is due."

Bruce McCaw began supporting Indy 500 entries in the early 1990s before he formed PacWest Racing to contest the PPG IndyCar World Series on a full-time basis in '94. McCaw ultimately became one of CART's strongest proponents. But not before he offered George a chance to communicate what the IRL had to offer.

"I wrote him a letter in probably early June '94, because I was not at all committed to CART," McCaw said. "I didn't know much about CART, and I said in the letter, 'I've been reading about your new series; I've just joined CART, I'm not a franchise holder, I'm interested in what you are doing.' He never responded to that letter, which is very interesting."

McCaw increased his commitment to CART in 1995 and wrote a memo to his team and its partners explaining his rationale. "While the proposed series [the IRL] has published a schedule and discussed a few seemingly lofty goals, in my mind they have proposed little of substance and nothing beneficial," he said. "Indy car racing in its present format has become the United States' racing 'export' to the world. A unique blend of ovals, superspeedways and road courses is our formula for success. It appeals to a broad spectrum of fans with its diversity of racing, challenging teams, and drivers to expand on their talents and to be most adaptable.

"The Indianapolis 500 is a wonderful event and an important and traditional part of our racing heritage," he added. "We hope and expect that the Indy 500 will remain part of our calendar, and that the Speedway will not compromise the dignity, importance, or quality of this event by inhibiting the participation of any team due to their affiliation."

In August, Cary Agajanian—George's spurned candidate in the search for the CART CEO that resulted in the appointment of Andrew Craig—was named executive vice president of USAC, in charge of administrating the IRL. The league also revealed a complicated points system that multiplied base points by the number of IRL races the driver entered, and declared that the Indianapolis 500 would serve as the final race in the series championship, meaning the inaugural 1996 series champion would be crowned after only three races.

With head-to-head conflict now looking inevitable, the public posturing continued through the second half of 1995. Yet efforts were still being made behind the scenes by both sides to try to salvage the situation. Les Richter, a former NFL player who transitioned into an executive role in the racing industry with Riverside Raceway and later NASCAR, was brought in as a mediator. He got the IRL and CART to lay out four specific issues for resolution: interim management, schedule of events, term of interim rules and chassis freeze, and sanctioning.

CART proposed adding Orlando, Phoenix, Indianapolis, and New Hampshire to its 1996 schedule, with Orlando running as a non-championship round to '95 rules because upgraded '96 chassis would not yet be ready. More importantly, CART also called for a significant reduction in the number of days on track at Indianapolis during the month of May and was firm in its intent that Andrew Craig would serve as chairman of the board of the combined interim organization.

With those caveats, the unification talks fell apart in September 1995. And perhaps not surprisngly, that's when the first rumblings of CART running a rival race at Roger Penske's Michigan International Speedway surfaced. This only seemed to fuel the IRL's confidence; George and Jack Long were almost boastful in their interactions with the media throughout the autumn. George penned a lengthy and impassioned "Letter to the Editor" of the *Indianapolis Star* in which he tried to state his case to local residents and businesses.

"Let's make this clear before we go any further: There is no lockout," George wrote in the letter published on October 22. "What I believe to be the case is that Championship Auto Racing Teams, following an effort to eliminate the IRL and gain control of the Indianapolis 500, is in the uncomfortable position of having created deliberate and unnecessary conflicts from which it will not extricate itself. . . . Chassis compatibility and schedule conflicts: CART created both these problems after the IRL was on record as sincerely having tried to avoid them.

"The expressed purpose of the IRL is to provide growth, stability, and opportunity for open-wheel, oval track racing. That mission is certainly not intended to harm CART or control CART. In fact, it has nothing to do with CART. We simply do not want the Indianapolis 500 to be controlled by an outside group that does not have as its most important goal the future of Indianapolis-type oval track racing. Not to mention, a group that is based out of state (CART headquarters were located in Bloomfield Hills, Michigan) and is far removed from the significance of the 500 in this community.

"On the subject of power, I can only say it as simply as this: My desire is not now, and never has been, control of CART, IndyCar, or the entire series of whatever cars run in the Indianapolis 500. The payback on that side is simply a peace of mind that comes from maintaining the sovereignty of this wonderful event. We are an oval race track, and we want to ensure our future. It is that simple," he concluded.

Craig's rebuttal appeared on the same letters page one week later. "Tony George's article in the Oct. 22 *Indianapolis Star* presents a one-sided view of the events and motivations that contributed to the current dispute between the Indianapolis Motor Speedway and Championship Auto Racing Teams, Inc. (IndyCar)," he opened, before calling the 25/8 Rule "a lockout in every sense of the word" and defending CART's moves with regard to the schedule and its safety-oriented chassis changes. He also took offense to George's out-of-state blast by observing that while CART was based in Detroit, most Indy car teams operated out of Indianapolis.

"IndyCar is part of the commercial fabric of Indianapolis and an important part of the community," Craig noted. "The actions of the Speedway are not an act of defense against some invading horde but rather an attack against good and hard working people within the racing industry in Indianapolis and an attack against all the traditions and all that is good about the Indy 500.

"What is disappointing about the current dispute between the Indianapolis Motor Speedway and IndyCar is that so much energy is being spent on non-productive tasks as each organization jockeys for position. It is ironic that Tony George states that his prime objective is to protect the future of the Indy 500. While this ambition is appropriate for someone in the important position of president of the Indianapolis Motor Speedway, the actions taken in recent months appear to have the potential to achieve exactly the opposite. The sport is in grave danger of being deeply damaged at a time when its potential for growth is there for all to see. If the sport is damaged, then it follows that the Indy 500 will suffer as a result.

"IndyCar's sincere wish is to be in Indianapolis for the month of May and to be racing in the Indy 500 on Memorial Day weekend," Craig concluded. "We have no reason to wish otherwise and hope that an opportunity for sensible, rational discussion and a resolution of our differences can still be found. It must be understood, however, that confronted with barriers to free and open competition, we have little choice but to reluctantly look for alternatives."

The chasm between the groups only widened as the calendar marched toward 1996. On December 14, the IRL announced it would adopt a 4.0-liter production-based V8 as its sole engine formula for '97 and beyond. No mention was made about chassis regulations or who would supply or build these engines, but it was made clear that CART-style leasing programs would not be permitted. CART teams might be able to use their '95 cars and engines to compete at Indianapolis in '96, but for the future, they were being told they would be required to invest in completely different equipment to run at Indy.

Pat Patrick summarized the challenges that CART faced from George and the IRL in a "Situational Analysis" paper he prepared in late 1995, noting that as recently as November 15, IMS attorney Jack Snyder had engaged him to serve as a mediator between CART and IMS to no avail.

"Basically the problem is that Indianapolis Motor Speedway President Tony George wants to take control of Indy car racing away from Championship Auto Racing Teams (CART), the association of team owners," Patrick wrote. "Through organizations which he controls absolutely, he plans to become the sanctioning body, the promoter, the rulemaker, and the arbiter. Whether, in fact, this is good for the sport is a question anyone who has dealt with the establishment which runs the Indianapolis 500 will have no difficulty in answering.

"The facts are relatively simple," he continued. "George is not happy that under the management of CART, Indy car racing has become an international series with strong foreign competition on a wide variety of road courses and street circuits, many of which represent key markets for teams and sponsors. Instead, he plans to create a series for oval tracks only and is trying to regulate that series back to the low budget, low tech all-American 'backyard-engineering' era of the 1940s and '50s—ignoring the fact that cars built and maintained by such part-time Owner-Driver-Mechanics will certainly be far more dangerous and less reliable than contemporary professionally engineered and maintained vehicles."

Finally, on December 18, what everyone suspected was in the works was officially confirmed: CART announced it had leased Michigan International Speedway from Roger Penske and would stage an inaugural 500-mile race to be called the U.S. 500 on May 26, 1996—the same day as the eightieth Indianapolis 500.

"It's a decision that hardly anybody enjoys or wants," commented Rahal. "But it's life, reality. I would like to be in Indianapolis on May 26, but it takes two to tango and we would look silly dancing alone.

"There is only market support for one or the other. There is not money for both," he added.

Michael Andretti was equally pessimistic. "It seems Tony is pretty much dug in and doesn't want to compromise," he said. "All of us hope deep down inside there is a compromise . . . nobody is going to win. We're not going to win, and the Speedway is not going to win."

Although Rick Mears retired from driving at the end of the 1992 season, he remained involved with the sport as a driver coach and advisor for Penske Racing. The four-time Indianapolis 500 winner (and six-time pole qualifier) hoped things could eventually be worked out between the two factions.

"Indy has always been the best team or the best man wins," Mears remarked. "That's what Indy stands for, and I think when you start trying to regulate who can and who can't run a particular race, such as Indianapolis, it's just not fair. I really don't agree with it. I don't think it should have happened, and I think it is happening for no real reason. Down the road it will be resolved, eventually, but it's a shame that it had to happen to begin with."

After fifteen years of uneasy coexistence between CART and the Indianapolis Motor Speedway, Indy car racing was heading back to 1979, with two philosophically opposed series competing for spectator attention and sponsor dollars. The difference this time is that most of the teams and drivers familiar to fans would not be spending the month of May in central Indiana, a development that would put the Indianapolis 500's credibility and star-making reputation to a serious test.

CHAPTER 11

HEADED FOR A SHOWDOWN

B y the time the Indy Racing League ran its first race at Walt Disney World Speedway in late January 1996, Tony George had a prototype driver in mind: Jeff Gordon. The only problem was that Gordon was already firmly established as a NASCAR Winston Cup Series star.

Gordon was born in August 1971 in Vallejo, California, and he quickly developed into one of the western region's top young kart and quarter-midget drivers. Age restrictions in California prevented him from advancing into bigger, more powerful cars, so in the summer of '86, Gordon's stepfather and manager John Bickford moved the family to Pittsboro, Indiana, a small town fifteen miles west of Indianapolis. In an unprecedented move, the young phenom was granted a USAC competition license on his sixteenth birthday.

Before too long, Gordon was dominating USAC racing, winning the 1990 midget championship and the Silver Crown title the following year. By then, the twenty-year-old driver was already running full-time in the NASCAR Busch Grand National Series, the development tier one rung below Winston Cup, with his career path seemingly set.

Gordon attended schools for both road racing (Skip Barber) and ovals (Buck Baker), and he received NASCAR job offers before he even completed the Baker school. But as late as mid-1990, he still had dreams of racing Indy cars. Linda Conti and her husband Dave ran a racing team out of a shop near Pittsboro not far from where Bickford worked on his stepson's sprint car chassis. The Bickfords and the Contis became acquainted, and in the summer of '90, Conti Racing gave Gordon a test day in a customer's Formula Super Vee car on the Indianapolis Raceway Park road course. A few weeks later, Gordon accompanied the Contis to CART's Cleveland Grand Prix, where they attempted to introduce him to Indy car and Indy Lights team owners. The story of his rejection by the CART glitterati has become an Indy car urban legend.

"Jeff was dressed in his best polo shirt and chinos, and he had prepared a one-page bio," Linda Conti recalled. "Those that would give him a minute of their time only wanted to know how much money he could bring. I remember John Andretti trying to get Jim Hall to take a minute to talk to Jeff, but he could have cared less. A.J. Foyt was the only one that spent any amount of time talking with him, and I don't think Carl Haas even said hello. Jeff was pretty dejected on the ride home. He thought teams might actually want to hire him because he had talent, but he said Foyt told him, 'Get the hell away from these assholes and go NASCAR racing. They actually want a driver, not a check.' I never heard Jeff mention the Indy 500 after that."

Gordon doesn't have specific memories about his introduction to the CART community, but he believes his die was already cast long before the unproductive trip to Cleveland with the Contis.

"It's not like there were ten offers on the table and it was like, 'Hmm, which one of these do we take? Oh, let's bypass Indy cars and go NASCAR racing,'" Gordon told *Autoweek*. "I was evolving as a sprint-car driver, racing midgets, and doing the TV series"—the successful USAC 'Thursday Night Thunder' that ran from 1988 to 2002—"on ESPN. That brought some opportunities.

"Like all drivers, I wanted to race and do well enough to turn that into something else up the ladder. We pursued Indy car racing, but not too heavily. I might have gotten more consideration if I'd had talent and an open-wheel, rear-engine, road-racing background. But I'd been on dirt and paved ovals most of my life. I wasn't a road racer."

The flow of drivers from USAC into Indy car racing had slowed long before Jeff Gordon arrived on the scene, but his rapid, rags-to-riches ascension into stock car stardom created a blueprint that many drivers were determined to follow. By the late 1990s, despite the hopes and best efforts of Tony George and the IRL, USAC was very much viewed as NASCAR's premier training ground. A series of prominent young oval trackers, including Ryan Newman, Kasey Kahne, Kenny Irwin, and Mike Bliss went straight from USAC to NASCAR without even considering the Indy car option, whether through CART or IRL.

"My goals have always been NASCAR-oriented," said Newman, who claimed eighteen Cup Series wins in a lengthy stock car career. "I think it takes a little bit of a different kind of driver to run CART, not so much because of the road courses, but the street courses. I think the biggest difference between [USAC Silver Crown] cars versus Champ Cars is that we can slide ours. If they slide their cars, they're looking at white paint. They have to make up or visualize their edge. We can feel our edge. There are theories about creating a balanced, four-wheel race car that apply no matter what kind of car it is. A good driver can drive anything, which is why I admire people like Mario Andretti, A.J. Foyt, and Parnelli Jones. They did it all."

Gordon refuses to accept credit for being the driver who legitimized USAC racing to the NASCAR world. "I've been told that maybe I opened the door for Midwestern-based, short-track, dirt-track, open-wheel guys, that maybe some drivers wouldn't be here if I hadn't come down and had some success," he said. "I'm not sure that's a fair assessment, but I appreciate it. I look at it like I pursued NASCAR and got an opportunity because someone recognized a talent. Maybe I can take some credit for them not being narrow-minded just to the Southeast or stock-car drivers or Late Model racers—for them to say, 'Hey, let's reach outside more.'"

Gordon never raced in the Indianapolis 500, but his name will be forever linked with the Indianapolis Motor Speedway, because on August 6, 1994, he won the inaugural Brickyard 400. It was one of those too-good-to-be-true stories that so frequently seem to happen for NASCAR. Despite his California roots, Gordon's successful stint in USAC made him famous in his early NASCAR years as "Jeff Gordon from Pittsboro, Indiana." As his star rose, IMS and Indianapolis media naturally maximized Gordon's tenuous links to the area, and the Brickyard win was spun as the ultimate "Indiana hometown boy makes good" story.

The victory also brought out all kinds of conspiracy theories that Gordon had gotten "The Call" from NASCAR as the designated winner, the most popular being that his car was significantly underweight.

Suspicious as that triumph may have been, Gordon backed it up by developing into one of the greatest NASCAR drivers of all time, winning ninety-three Cup Series races and four championships in a stock car career that lasted until 2016.

More importantly for George in the short term, the inaugural Brickyard 400 was a smash success, with grandstands sold out long in advance and a massive wave of positive publicity. The IMS president was also fortunate because another young driver was already rewriting the oval track USAC records that Gordon had so recently set before his ascension to stock cars. And this kid was an Indiana-born Hoosier who was desperate to race Indy cars.

In 1995, twenty-four-year-old Columbus native Tony Stewart created United States Auto Club history by winning the Triple Crown of sprint car, midget, and Silver Crown championships in the same season. A.J. Foyt gave Stewart a multiday Indy car test at Phoenix in late '95, but Foyt balked at Stewart splitting his time between the IRL and Busch Grand National stock cars, where Stewart had already inked a deal to run eleven races in a partial season for Harry Ranier.

Then John Menard entered the picture. Menard made his fortune with a chain of hardware and home improvement stores throughout the Midwest that he promoted with a folksy jingle that became a staple of radio and cable television. He began sponsoring fellow Wisconsinite Herm Johnson in the Indianapolis 500 in 1980 and quickly got much more serious. Menard invested a considerable amount of money in developing the Buick V6 engine; Menard's driver Al Unser achieved the Buick's best Indianapolis result with third place in '93, and he eventually commissioned and produced a lighter aluminum version of the block. He also started to hire established Indy car veteran drivers, including Unser, Gary Bettenhausen, Scott Brayton, and Arie Luyendyk. In '92 and '93, Menard also entered a car for three-time Formula 1 World Champion Nelson Piquet; the Brazilian badly broke both of his legs in a '92 practice accident. For '96 he was set to run Brayton and Eddie Cheever, but his team manager Larry Curry convinced him to test Stewart. Benefiting from his earlier track time with Foyt, Stewart was highly impressive in his test, and he was offered a third Menard entry into the IRL opener at Walt Disney World.

"This is an absolute dream come true, but I seriously never thought it would happen until Tony George came up with the IRL," Stewart said. "I hate the politics of racing, and I figured maybe I'd get lucky and follow Jeff down south. Then I heard Larry wanted a young driver and this thing fell into place. This has been like an extended Christmas. John and Harry are willing to work with me to make both programs work and it's so nice. What a dream . . . an Indy car and stock car ride. I feel like I've hit the jackpot.

"Jeff would be running Indy cars if somebody had given him a chance, and I'm thrilled with the way things have gone so far," Stewart continued. "These are big momentum cars like sprinters. I learned how to keep the momentum up by driving sprinters at Winchester and this is similar. I feel if I can get a top-ten finish without any testing, that would be good."

The IRL put together a preliminary twenty-seven-car entry for Walt Disney World, though two were withdrawn before the weekend even started and only twenty cars ultimately took the green flag. Prior to the race, George talked with Knight Ridder News Service writer Steve Crowe about the challenges his new league had overcome to make it to the starting line.

"We're trying our best to put on the best possible show we can, but it's going to be a challenge at each and every event," George said. "Cosworth stepped up, thinking they weren't going to be the only [engine supplier], and they've done everything they could to help the IRL teams. Plus, they've taken a lot of flak from the other side of the ledger. I appreciate everything they've done. But we're still faced with an equipment shortage.

"There's no support at all from the local newspaper [the *Indianapolis Star*]," he noted. "The media really escalated this and incited a lot of fear, I think, early on. And I've been trying to get out personally and talk to a lot of the folks around town. That's really been pretty well received. Despite what the paper may say, things look pretty good right now. I'm proud of the guys we have running, proud of the new guys we have coming up. At the very least, they're fervent in their commitment."

Stewart was the star of the show at Disney. He outqualified his more experienced Menard teammates Cheever and Brayton, and quickly moved from eighth on the grid to the lead in just twenty-nine laps. But he was no match on the day for Buzz Calkins, a veteran of three years of Indy Lights who hadn't won a race in a rear-engine car since he earned a regional Formula Ford championship in 1990. Calkins, whose father's chain of convenience stores served as his sponsor, led 130 of the 200 laps to beat Stewart by 0.866 second, with Robbie Buhl two laps back in third place.

The victory at Orlando helped Calkins land a sponsorship for the Indy 500 from the State of Indiana's Hoosier Lottery. Local musician Jimmy Ryser penned a radio jingle with the lines "Buzz Calkins / The driver that's got ev'rybody talkin' / Yeah, Buzz Calkins / Keep on winning, never be forgotten!" But Disney proved to be the peak of Calkins's career; he achieved only one other IRL podium finish and quietly retired at the end of 2001.

Meanwhile, USAC's competence was once again called into question by a scary incident late in the Orlando race. Responding to an accident involving Cheever and Scott Sharp, a USAC safety vehicle drove onto the track before the racing cars had slowed—in fact, right into the path of a still-at-speed Stewart, who had to drive over debris and nearly hit the wall in avoidance. "Who were the rookies—the drivers or the safety crew?" snarled the already cocky young driver.

George was happy with what he saw, grading the event "A-plus-plus." He added: "It was fun watching these guys trying to take advantage of opportunities. I'm so proud of these guys. They're such professionals."

With his USAC background and brash, trash-talking personality, Stewart was the toast of the IRL after just one race. "I told John Menard that Tony had talent and the same attributes as Jeff Gordon," said manager Cary Agajanian to *Indianapolis Star* writer Curt Cavin. "After the race, he said, 'Where did you find him?' I said, 'I've got ten more like him who just need a chance.'"

Even if he had not finished the Orlando race, Stewart's performance still would have drawn attention. And he backed it up in the next IRL event at Phoenix, again leading laps before the unreliable Menard engine let him down.

"We knew Tony would be good, but nobody expected him to be so spectacular," raved his team owner. "In traffic, he looks like Tom Sneva in his finest hour, and he's arguably the best driver in this series. I'm not sure we couldn't go to CART with him and run up front and we might even look at that. I believe if Tony had a Ford he would have won that race at Orlando and maybe Phoenix too. I know he could win Indianapolis if I leased a Cosworth."

One reason why the Menard Buick cars peformed better than expected at Orlando was revealed seven weeks later in the run-up to the IRL race at Phoenix. To equalize competition, the Buicks had quietly been allowed to run sixty inches of boost instead of the fifty-five prescribed in the rulebook. Unexpected and arbitrary rule changes were nothing new for USAC, but not informing Ford-Cosworth and the two-thirds of the IRL field using the Cosworth engine was a new tactic that not surprisingly didn't go over well with the non-Buick teams.

"I received a letter last week that told me the rules had been changed, and at the bottom, there was a paragraph informing me this rule had been in effect since Orlando. It was like, 'Oh by the way, we've been letting the Buicks run sixty inches since January,'" fumed team owner John Della Penna, who entered a Cosworth-powered car for defending Formula Atlantic champion Richie Hearn in the IRL and selected CART races. "I got screwed and didn't even know I was getting screwed. They say they're doing it in the interest of competition, but it's not fair and it's not right."

CART, meanwhile, opened its 1996 season on March 3 and packed five races into March and April, including the PPG IndyCar World Series's first trip to Brazil, where André Ribeiro was a popular native winner. By the time teams arrived at Michigan International Speedway in May for two weeks of U.S. 500 activity, Jimmy Vasser had won three races for Target/Chip Ganassi Racing and enjoyed a comfortable lead in the point standings.

Off the track, the Indianapolis Motor Speedway's business practices continued to anger key sponsors, an important factor that was crucial to their loyalty to the CART series. In 1995, IMS decreed that teams would no longer be allowed to cook their own meals for their crews and hospitality guests, insisting that food and beverages must be purchased at inflated prices from approved caterers. Imagine a sponsor like Miller Brewing or Budweiser being told it must buy its own product from an outside vendor for $48 per case! Paul Newman was furious, and despite the threat of a $5,000 fine from USAC, he defiantly delivered food prepared by Newman/Haas Racing hospitality chefs Peter and Mary-Lin Murphy to the NHR crew in the garage on a golf cart.

In the spring of 1996, Miller ended its long-term sponsorship of the popular Carburetion Day pit stop competition with IMS because the Speedway demanded similar buys at all IRL races, and were charging premium rates for what sponsors saw as a devalued product. Coors Light quickly stepped in to take over naming rights for the pit stop championship.

"We were told eight to ten of CART's franchise holders would be at Orlando, 40 percent of last year's Indy lineup would be at Indianapolis, and the U.S. 500 was nothing but smoke and mirrors," said Valvoline's racing sponsorship manager Mark Coughlin. "After Orlando, it became apparent a lot of those things were undeliverable, so we asked to renegotiate at a lower price because, obviously, the value of the Indianapolis 500 has changed. Clearly, the 1996 Indy 500 will not be what it was in 1995."

At the same time, the Brown & Williamson Tobacco Corporation reentered racing in a lucrative partnership with CART team owner Barry Green, with plans to groom American drivers for Indy cars. Despite the IRL's overt recruitment of American participation, B&W chose to back a pair of Indy Lights entries in 1996 for Greg Ray and Chris Simmons under the Team KOOL Green banner, with the goal of advancing at least one of the young American drivers into the CART series in '97.

"There doesn't seem to be a lot of opportunity for financial support for American drivers, and we wanted to provide opportunities for deserving Americans," said B&W sponsorship manager Bert Kremer. "We rely heavily on Barry and Kim Green to assess talent and our only stipulation is the drivers are Americans. Obviously Indy is the crown jewel and we would prefer to be there, but it was not the breaking point of this program. We're in this for sixteen races a year, all over the world." By 1998, Team Kool Green's drivers were a Scotsman (Dario Franchitti) and a Canadian (Paul Tracy).

In the summer of 1996, the Speedway terminated its suite lease agreements with just about everyone who had remained loyal to CART, including Mario Andretti, who unloaded his frustration to the *Indianapolis Star*'s Robin Miller. "It's so small-sighted, so petty," Andretti said. "Tony is being vindictive because some of us don't agree with his way of doing business and we expressed our feelings . . . I guess I could have been a hypoocrite like a lot of people and not ruffled any feathers, but you have to stand up for what you believe in. I revere Indy and always will, but Tony goes against the principles of the Speedway and his agenda is a hidden agenda. Tony is taking this personally and that's his business. But it's my living and he's disrupting it. That's my strong feeling. Myself and a lot of guys like Roger [Penske] and Pat [Patrick] were here long before he was."

It's difficult to describe the acrimonious state of Indy car racing in the mid-nineties. In a much smaller and closely knit community, it was similar to the overall political climate in America twenty years later, when distrust and dislike between the two major parties became so intense that the pursuit of common goals and a desire to benefit the greater good often fell completely by the wayside. Battle lines were drawn, affiliations were determined, and disdain for what the other side represented was deep-seated and non-negotiable.

CART backers poked fun at the IRL's sometimes scruffy older race cars and inexperienced, less pedigreed drivers; for the respective 1996 season openers, the IRL field totaled 797 Indy car starts and six race wins, half of which were achieved by Arie Luyendyk. The CART grid featured 1,616 starts and 124 wins. Meanwhile, IRL fans lamented the greed-fueled budgets of the CART series, the "Mickey Mouse" street courses, the demographics of the "wine-and-cheese" fan base, and the overall foreign flavor of the field.

George fueled the flames by publicly denigrating the very drivers who had made up the majority of the Indianapolis 500 field for the last decade. He contended that the field that would comprise the 1996 Indianapolis 500 was every bit as qualified as the men who would be racing at Michigan the same day.

"They're race drivers," George said. "They've competed and won at other levels, and there's no magic to competing at this level."

The reality is that all of the drivers were used as pawns in a dangerous game of chicken between Indianapolis Motor Speedway management and the CART team owners, with the Indianapolis 500 used as the ultimate bargaining tool.

"It's not the driver's choice—it's the owner's," observed Menard Racing IRL driver Scott Brayton. "All I know is that it's the Indianapolis 500. I don't care who's there. I want to be there and I know that's where everybody else really wants to be. It's still the one race that counts."

"Obviously it's a losing situation for everybody," remarked two-time Indianapolis winner Emerson Fittipaldi, who angered many IMS fans when he drank orange juice in addition to the traditional milk after his victory in the 1993 Indy 500. "Who's winning this? Nobody. Why do we have this situation? Someone has to answer that question. We [CART] have the most competitive open-wheeled series in the world, yet we're going to be in Michigan in May, not Indianapolis. It's a shame for our sport and so hard on my heart."

The prospect of missing at least one attempt at winning Indianapolis during the prime of his career was particularly hard on Michael Andretti. "Not going to Indy is disappointing to everyone, and for somebody who's never won it, this is just one more chance I won't have," remarked Andretti, who was coming off a win at his home track of Nazareth Speedway and would have been a favorite at IMS. "It's going to be strange not spending May in Indianapolis because it's been such a big part of my life. But I haven't let it take away from my enthusiasm."

Not everyone was upset that they would not be spending a month at the Brickyard. The argument to condense Indy 500 activity to a shorter period of time had waged for years, and some drivers and team owners were resolute in their belief that spending less time at Indianapolis would be cost beneficial and open up other opportunites to grow the CART series.

"It's going to be great because you're going to be able to live like a normal human being," said Bobby Rahal. "We'll go racing once or twice instead of pounding around someplace for twenty-one days, taking tremendous risks and spending a hell of a lot of money."

The relative lack of sponsorship dollars at Indianapolis in 1996 was reflected in the number of practice laps—down 53 percent from a year earlier. On one memorable day, not a single car was seen on track during ESPN's daily hour of live practice coverage from IMS, despite perfect conditions. Attendance was down throughout the month, though not as dramatically as it would be later in the '90s after the public had the opportunity to assess what the IRL had to offer.

Up in Michigan, CART assembed a $3.6 million purse and attracted twenty-seven entries to its U.S. 500. Almost everything was designed to have an Indianapolis-tinged feel to it, from the use of a Silver Badge credential to a multiple-day qualifying format to a grid comprised of rows of three. Adrian Fernandez ran a 235.608-mph lap in practice, and the Mexican star qualified second behind Vasser, who achieved a pole speed of 232.025 mph. Bryan Herta completed the front row.

The first weekend of Indianapolis qualifying was also May 11-12, and thanks to a freshly repaved track and the use of faster 1995 and older specification cars (not to mention Firestone's rapidly developing tires), speeds were even higher. Arie Luyendyk ran a 239.260-mph lap in practice and established the official IMS one- and four-lap records at 237.498 and 236.986 mph respectively. But those eye-popping speeds did not earn Luyendyk pole position; his car was found underweight on Pole Day, so his qualification run came on Day Two and he therefore lined up twentieth through Indy's unique qualifying rules. For the second year in a row, Scott Brayton earned pole at 233.718 mph, this time after withdrawing his original speed and making a dramatic second attempt.

"With all those guys at Michigan, it's quite a bit different and obviously not the competition it's been in years past," Luyendyk commented after his record-setting run. "There are less people that we have to beat and not as much sense of urgency. A lot of teams don't have the overall knowledge and not a lot of depth, but there are still a lot of qualified people here and I really think the race is going to surprise people."

On May 17, tragedy visited IMS. Brayton, making a shakedown run in a spare Menard entry, cut a right rear tire and crashed in Turn One with a flush left-side impact. He was transported directly to Indianapolis Methodist Hospital, but was declared dead around thirty minutes later. It was the first fatality at IMS since rookie driver Jovy Marcelo perished in a practice crash in 1992, and a bruising blow for Indy car racing as a whole. Although he never won a race in CART or IRL competition, Brayton was a fan favorite who was often viewed as the heart of the Buick engine program. He was also one of the IRL's top draws, an American driver with pedigree in the CART series, where he made 147 starts with a best finish of third.

Brayton's accident had nothing to do with the CART-IRL rivalry, but it served as a sobering reminder of the ever-present danger that exists in auto racing. In the long term, it inspired Tony George to work even harder on soft wall protection for oval tracks, eventually resulting in the development of the SAFER Barrier that was put into universal use at all Indy car and NASCAR speedways by 2006.

But in the context of late May 1996, it meant that Indy car racing headed into the most contentious weekend in the history of the sport already under a dark cloud.

CHAPTER 12

MAY 26, 1996: INDY CAR RACING'S DAY OF INFAMY

The dawn was gray and wet in both Indianapolis and Brooklyn, Michigan, on May 26, 1996, but the traditional 11:00 a.m. start of the Indianapolis 500 was delayed by only about five minutes. Meanwhile, CART set the start time of the U.S. 500 for around 2:00 p.m., allowing the television audience to view the majority of both 500-mile races if they desired.

The familiar voice of lead announcer Paul Page greeted fans tuning in to ABC's Indianapolis 500 broadcast. "Today's winner may be unfamiliar to you now, but tomorrow, his name will be in headlines in every newspaper in America," Page declared. "Like others before him, he will drink cold milk from a bottle in Victory Lane. His likeness will go on the famous Borg-Warner Trophy, and he will join Harroun, Foyt, Mears, the Unsers, and Mario Andretti as a champion of the Indianapolis 500."

The IRL was out of the gate first, and to its credit, it staged a race that—on the surface, anyway—looked a lot like the Indianapolis 500 that fans were accustomed to. And the first half of the 1990s set a high bar.

Arie Luyendyk smashed the race record for average speed in 1990; his new mark of 185.981 miles per hour bested the old standard by more than 15 mph and would endure for nearly twenty-five years. May 1991 included the heart-warming story of Willy T. Ribbs battling to become the first African American to race in the Indy 500, a race that included a thrilling shootout finish between Rick Mears and Michael Andretti.

Nineteen ninety-two produced the coldest conditions and the closest finish in the long history of the event. Pole man Roberto Guerrero spun off on the pace lap, Michael Andretti dominated but broke, and his father, Mario, and brother, Jeff, ended the day in Methodist Hospital. Al Unser Jr. held off a charging Scott Goodyear by 0.043 second at the line in the closest finish in Indianapolis 500 history. "You just don't know what Indy means!" exclaimed an emotional Unser. "Mansellmania" arrived in 1993, and Nigel rose to the occasion and contended for the win before losing out to Emerson Fittipaldi and Luyendyk on a late restart.

The 1995 edition was perhaps the craziest Indy 500 of all. It was a race that nobody seemed to want to win, allowing Jacques Villeneuve to make up a two-lap penalty he incurred early in the race. Mauricio Gugelmin led the most laps but faded, and Scott Pruett and Jimmy Vasser both crashed while leading. On the final restart, leader Goodyear passed the pace car, which appeared to enter the pits much slower than usual. Goodyear crossed the line miles in the lead, but USAC stopped scoring him with six laps remaining, leaving a shocked Villeneuve as the victor.

So even without the tradition of eight prior decades, the 1996 Indianapolis 500 had a lot to live up to just based on the recent history of the event. And it generally delivered. The start was comically slow and spread out, but the comparatively inexperienced field soon settled in. The race contained ten cautions (there were thirteen just four years earlier in the inordinately cold '92 Indy 500) and though just nine cars were running at the finish, there was only one major crash, a last-lap melee triggered by Guerrero which resulted in Alessandro Zampedri suffering severe leg injuries when his car got up into the Turn Four fence.

Tony Stewart, who was elevated to pole position following Scott Brayton's death, was again the star. He led forty-four of the first fifty-four laps, but engine problems eliminated him prior to half distance. "That's one of those USAC junk pop-off valves," Stewart told reporters, though subsequent investigation showed that the Menard V6 burned an intake valve. "If we had a malfunction with the car or something went wrong with the motor that we had done, I could understand. But to have a pop-off valve issued by USAC go bad, that's a very frustrating thing. It makes you sick to your stomach. At least next year in the IRL when we go to normally aspirated motors we don't have to worry about that."

The race came down to a battle between Davy Jones and Buddy Lazier—Americans from road-racing backgrounds rather than the IRL's preferred USAC bullrings. Jones finished third in the 1983 British Formula 3 championship behind Ayrton Senna and Martin Brundle before moving on to a successful stint racing sports cars with the TWR Jaguar team. Lazier, meanwhile, stayed at home in the U.S. and scratched out a career at the back of the CART grid, making a total of fifty-five starts for eight different teams between '89 and '95 with a best finish of seventh place.

The IRL afforded Lazier the opportunity to run up-to-date equipment for the first time, and he made the most of it. He teamed up with Ron Hemelgarn, who began fielding cars in the CART series in the mid-eighties, often running pedigreed drivers on a shoestring budget. Hemelgarn Racing was a minnow in CART, but in the IRL, it ranked with Menard Racing and Treadway Racing (Luyendyk's entrant) among the league's big fish. Driving an ex-Ganassi Reynard/Ford-Cosworth, Lazier was fastest in winter testing at Walt Disney World Speedway, and he earned pole position for the IRL's inaugural race by more than three mph.

But Lazier crashed heavily in practice at Phoenix International Raceway in March 1996 when a rear wing end plate fell off his car. He sustained two fractures of a vertebra, multiple fractures to his pelvis, and a concussion, putting his participation at Indianapolis very much in doubt. Throughout May, Lazier walked with the aid of a cane, frequently flew back and forth to his native Colorado on a medical jet for therapy, and simply getting into and out of the car was a painful ordeal for the twenty-nine-year-old.

On race day, Lazier turned in one of the gutsiest performances in the long history of the Indianapolis 500. Still battling severe back pain, Lazier stayed in contention all day, flexing his hands during caution periods to relieve the stress on the rest of his body. He moved from third to first in the closing stages, passing Jones for the lead on Lap 193. When he arrived at Victory Lane, it was difficult to ascertain whether his flowing tears were the product of joy or pain.

"I had given up a lot of hope for this event," Lazier said. "At the beginning of the month, my bones were not healed. They were like taffy.

So this is extra sweet coming back from the injury. I'm going back to Vail and lay in bed for a week. That's what I desperately need.

"I gave it everything I had—heart and soul—and everybody else did," he added. "It is the Indianapolis 500. As many years as I've raced and been around here, this field would have equaled any other field in the past. I'd love to be out here with everybody, but at the same time, there's some great drivers here. And judging by the way the whole race went, showed there's some real ability and some talent. Take a look at the speeds. Take a look at the start of the race."

Lazier's last remark may have been pointed toward what was happening 225 miles to the north in Michigan, because in the closing stages of the Indianapolis 500, word began filtering through that CART's U.S. 500 had gotten off to a very embarrassing start. Or more accurately, hadn't gotten started at all.

On the ESPN television broadcast, lead announcer Bob Varsha tried to build up the drama. "At the controls of the pace car, actor/racer Paul Newman—eminently qualified to pace the field for this important race," Varsha remarked. "So much at stake . . . a crowd of over 120,000 on hand (the actual announced attendance was 110,879), and all of the familiar teams of Indy car racing. Each individual in this great racing plant has their own reason for being here, but make no mistake: history will be made here today at Michigan. The field is perhaps the most qualified in Indy car history, with World Championships in both Formula 1 cars and sports cars. Seven championships, 131 total Indy car victories between them . . ."

And one very embarrassing twelve-car crash before the green flag even waved.

Starting three abreast at Michigan for the first time for no other obvious reason than to copy Indianapolis 500 tradition, the cars of pole winner Jimmy Vasser and second qualifier Adrian Fernandez touched, shoving outside front row starter Bryan Herta into the wall and creating mayhem behind as ten or more other entries were swept in.

It didn't matter who was out of position or didn't give his fellow drivers enough room. After months of build-up and hype, it had taken just a few seconds for CART to embarrass itself in the biggest possible way. The "Stars and Cars" had publicly blown it, and for many, this was the credibility-shattering moment that the karma and the momentum in the long fight between CART and the Indianapolis Motor Speedway shifted very much in the Speedway's favor—even if it took years to become apparent.

A.J. Foyt led the gloating at Indianapolis. "For the world's greatest professional drivers, they sure have made a lot of mistakes," he scoffed. "The rookies over there have outshone every one of the regular drivers. I'm sick and tired of them running their mouths off about how great they are. Almost every race they've had, there's been an accident on the first lap. And it wasn't the rookies."

"In some ways, I think the pressure is more on the CART drivers because of all the talk about their ability," added Tony George. "When they make a mistake, it's unexpected. Unfortunately, they've made a few this year that weren't expected. But our boys did a good job."

In Michigan, they regrouped. Crews went to work rebuilding race cars, or wheeled out and prepared spares, and all but Fernandez were able to restart the race an hour later. From there, the U.S. 500 was a typical Michigan Indy car race, with only a couple wrecks but extremely high attrition. There were ten retirements as a result of engine failure and only eleven cars running at the finish. Vasser won by eleven seconds over Gugelmin, the only other driver on the lead lap, and the Ganassi driver ramped up the CART-IRL rivalry by declaring "Who needs milk?" in Victory Lane. He collected $1.145 million for the win, in the ballpark with the $1.368 million Lazier earned at Indianapolis.

Media reaction to the dueling 500s was mixed. "Both sides in the bitter war for control of Indy car racing in America claimed a moral victory after the first showdown between the Indy 500 and the rival U.S. 500—and the struggle between the two rival series shows no sign of dying down," wrote Andrew Benson in *Autosport*. "The one definitive conclusion that can be drawn is that neither side is going to back down. For now, neither side has won. The split looks set to continue. And the animosity caused by comments from both sides in the past few weeks has probably widened it."

The star of the U.S. 500—in fact, the star of the rest of the 1996 CART season and two spectacular years to follow—was Vasser's team-mate Alex Zanardi. Championed by Reynard, the twenty-nine-year-old

Italian was a former Formula 3000 champion who had failed to make an impression in F1. Zanardi led 134 of the first 175 laps at Michigan before his Honda engine blew up in the most spectacular smoky fashion. Apart from winning three Indy car races in impressive style as a rookie, the charismatic driver captivated American race fans with his dynamic and outgoing personality, something CART failed to completely capitalize on during his time in the series.

After the buildup to the dueling Memorial Day 500s, the IRL took a two-and-a-half-month break. The Indianapolis 500 had marked the conclusion of the league's first three-race championship season, and it ended in a tie between Disney winner Buzz Calkins and Scott Sharp, who didn't win a race but scored the same number of points and was generally publicized as the champion. The IRL also staged the first two races of its ten-race 1996-97 championship later in '96, with Sharp and Calkins finishing 1-2 at New Hampshire International Speedway in August and Richie Hearn triumphing for still-disgruntled team owner John Della Penna at Las Vegas Motor Speedway in September. The Las Vegas race was notable for a number of hard crashes, including one that left Stewart spending the winter on the couch at his mother's home in Dayton, Indiana, recovering from fractures to his hip, pelvis, collarbone, and left shoulder.

After the disastrous start at Michigan, CART spent the rest of 1996 in damage control mode. The U.S. 500 proved to be Vasser's fourth and last win of the season, but he held on down the stretch to secure the series championship. Michael Andretti won five races and had the last truly competitive season of his career, but a mid-season stretch of three consecutive DNFs prevented him from challenging Vasser for the title.

The biggest on-track story in 1996 was the emergence of the Reynard-Honda-Firestone "package." In '95 Firestone returned to Indy car racing after a twenty-one-year absence, with Scott Pruett claiming the tire company's first modern-era win in July at Michigan Speedway after a thrilling last lap shootout with Al Unser Jr. Firestone was also the winning tire when André Ribeiro drove Tasman Motorsports's Reynard to Honda's first CART series victory at New Hampshire International Speedway just three weeks later. Led by Ganassi, team after team began switching their allegience from Goodyear, and Firestone soon dominated

Indy car racing to the extent that Goodyear completely withdrew from both IRL and CART after the '99 season.

CART also experienced a tragedy in 1996; driver Jeff Krosnoff was killed in July when his car locked wheels with a car driven by Stefan Johansson on the curving back straight of the Toronto street course and was launched over the catchfence into a tree and a lamp post. Track marshall Gary Avrin was fatally swept into the incident.

At the end of 1996, CART looked on the surface to have a significant advantage over the IRL, with record attendance at many venues and sponsorship and manufacturer involvement at historic levels. The IRL was miles behind by those measures. Of concern to CART was the series's shrinking television audience; Nielsen ratings in '95 for most races dropped from the 2.5 to 3.0 range to the 1.7 to 2.5 range. The U.S. 500 drew a 2.8 rating on ESPN, a substantial decline from the 4.0 rating that CART's '95 Marlboro 500 at Michigan achieved on ABC. The IRL averaged a 2.2 rating for its '96 races outside of Indianapolis, with the Indianapolis 500 declining from an 8.4 rating in '95 to 6.6 in '96.

With the Indy Racing League set to adopt completely different engine and chassis specifications for 1997 and beyond, two things were becoming obvious: the relationship between CART and the Indianapolis Motor Speedway was beyond immediate repair. And with the IRL slowly getting up to speed, the IMS was clearly prepared to chart its own course.

The IRL had mapped out its vision for the future of Indy car racing with a set of 1997 chassis regulations announced on April 2, 1996, to accompany previously revealed normally aspirated 4.0-liter V8 engines. With the goal of creating a simpler, less expensive chassis that would reduce speeds to around 225 mph at Indianapolis, the IRL decreed that the new-look cars for '97 would be built by production racing car specialist Dallara Automobili of Italy and G-Force Precision Engineering, a five-year-old firm based in England (and originally co-formed by Chip Ganassi) that had never constructed a full car. At the same time, General Motors's Oldsmobile brand and Nissan's Infiniti division confirmed their intention to create IRL spec engines, which were to be sold in kit form to league-approved builders for $75,000. The chassis price was capped at $263,000, including gearbox, drive axles, and fuel cell, compared to around $450,000 at the time for a CART-specification Reynard or Lola.

"The whole concept is a delicate balance between sport, entertainment, and technology," explained IRL founder Tony George, who said his goal was to reduce the average cost of running an Indy car from $300 per mile to $125. "We're not allowing any one of those things to drive it. This announcement gives us an opportunity to control our own destiny."

While G-Force was an unproven entity, Gian Paolo Dallara worked for most of the great Italian sports car marques in the 1960s, spending his formative years at Ferrari and Maserati before he moved to Lamborghini and contributed to the design and development of the 350 GT and the Miura. Dallara finally settled at de Tomaso, where in addition to being the lead designer for the Pantera, he designed Formula 2 and Formula 1 cars that competed in the late '60s and early '70s.

After establishing his own firm in 1972, Dallara created a series of successful racing cars for Fiat and Lancia as well as F1 chassis campaigned by the Scuderia Italia team, all while using Formula 3 as the platform for his company to develop into Europe's dominant constructor of production racing cars. In '94, Piero Ferrari commissioned Dallara to create a Ferrari branded sports prototype for competition in the American IMSA SportsCar Championship, where one of his main customers was Scandia Racing owner Andy Evans. The Ferrari 333SP turned out to be Dallara's entry into the American market.

"Andy was a 333SP client and he wanted to compete at Indianapolis," Dallara recalled. "We had never built a car for the Indy. Evans came to meet with me with Tony George, who also wanted some cars for the new IRL series. It all happened as quickly as it did casually. We talked, and at a certain point, Tony George said, 'If you agree to design a car for my series, I'll buy fifteen from you immediately and I will also give you an advance.' I obviously could not say no to that, and George ordered fifteen cars from us and fifteen from G-Force in Britain."

The most obvious visual difference between the first IRL cars and Indy cars of the past was the inclusion of an air induction opening integrated into the roll hoop behind the driver's helmet, molded into a higher engine cover. In basic terms, an IRL car looked like a simpler, bulkier Indy car with an airbox.

"Safety aspects of the rules package—a wider and higher tub and enhanced features inside the cockpit to protect the driver—represent the latest technology and thought in the racing world's ongoing efforts in that area," stated IRL executive director Jack Long. "And competitive parity should be achieved through the various design talents and engine programs as they combine with the creativity of our race teams. Contrary to the beliefs and questions of some, the IRL is not, and never will be, a 'spec series' in any form."

With choices available to competitors for chassis, engine, and tires, the IRL was certainly not a spec series by definition. But the rules were much more highly restrictive than at any time in the history of Indy car racing, with an emphasis on cost-cutting and little scope for teams to improve upon league-mandated components. And the cars were, to be polite, very much crude, dumbed-down versions of what during the CART era had become increasingly sophisticated Indy cars. Formula 1 technology generally took about five years to migrate into CART, but the technology level of 1997 IRL cars was five to ten years behind what was by then common in CART. The first generation of IRL cars were built to a price point, and it showed. CART star Paul Tracy dubbed them "Crapwagons."

Dan Gurney, who reentered the CART series as a team owner and made-in-America chassis constructor in 1996 after a ten-year absence, was livid with the Speedway's plans. "You've got to realize you are dealing with a bunch of liars who don't care about U.S. investment. They don't care about anybody but themselves," Gurney told writer Robin Miller. "I see between the lines and it's got nothing to do with what's good for this sport. It's all about control, and you've got scoundrels masquerading as saviors. It's not the kind of army I want to join because I don't like spec racing or contrived racing. We [CART] are on the verge of whipping the world in open-wheel racing, and now they want to turn it back to the lowest common denominator."

The other jarring aspect of the new IRL cars was the sound of the normally aspirated engines—a NASCAR-like deep roar that was incongruous with the high-pitched scream of smaller turbocharged V8s that dated to the late 1970s and the Cosworth DFX. While George abandoned his hopes for true stock-block engines, the IRL still attempted to incorporate tangible links to road cars by mandating common cylinder bore and stroke measurements. This created a fundamental problem, because the small bore/long stroke architechture favored by road car engines was at odds with the specialized requirements of racing—especially oval racing, where engines are run at constant high rpm's much of the time. The layout created extremely high piston speeds, which despite imposed rev limits, league-mandated steel connecting rods simply could not handle.

As a result, the early IRL engines blew up with alarming regularity, often in a catastrophic manner that oiled down racetracks and frequently led to crashes. With engines in short supply and rarely lasting long, the IRL was fortunate that rain ended the 1997 season opener at Walt Disney World after 149 of the scheduled 200 laps because there were only nine cars still running. Eddie Cheever was credited with his first major open-wheel victory since he won a Formula 2 race at Zandvoort in '79, a span that included 132 winless starts in F1 and another 82 in CART.

Cheever claimed five race wins in seventy-seven IRL starts, topped by victory in the 1998 Indianapolis 500. He emerged as one of the IRL's staunchest proponents.

"When I left Formula 1 and came to race in the states, my objective was to win the Indy 500," Cheever said. "When the 500 was no longer part of the calendar, the CART series as a whole didn't excite me like it had before. It's a very exciting series, very eclectic, and there are some great drivers there, but it has a hard time defining itself now. The American public and the world public understand the Indy 500. I don't mean this in a demeaning way, and I'm probably one of the few people in the world who can say it because I have driven Formula 1 for so long . . . but when you take the Indy 500 out, it runs the risk of becoming a 'Formula 1 Lite.' Having done the real thing, I'm not really interested in doing the 'Lite' version."

The irony to Cheever's remarks is that the IRL was often referred to as "CART Lite." And things got worse for the IRL before they got better. At the next round at Phoenix nearly two months later, the IRL staged one of the most embarrassing contests in more than a century of Indy-style racing. It took two hours and fourteen minutes to complete two hundred miles; with nine cautions totaling eighty-six laps, some 70 percent of that time was spent at pace car speed. The 89-mph race average was the lowest at Phoenix in thirty years.

"I certainly don't know what to say; we're not stretching the car, yet we keep blowing motors," observed defending IRL series champion Scott Sharp, whose A.J. Foyt Racing entry went through three Oldsmobile powerplants in less than one hundred laps over the course of the weekend.

In his weekly *RaceFax* briefing, Forrest Bond wrote, "It was a sad testament to the inept planning of the Indy Racing League, and proof anew that, contrary to what Oldsmobile, Nissan, and Tony George believed, you can't go oval racing on a shoestring budget . . . suddenly the cost of a CART engine lease looked like the only bargain in big-bore auto racing."

Despite the embarrassing haze of oil smoke, the IRL was saved at Phoenix by one of the biggest "David-defeats-Goliath" stories in the history of motorsports. Jim Guthrie, a thirty-five-year-old journeyman who operated an Albuquerque body shop and relied on friends and family to fund and staff his Blueprint Racing team, took advantage of the unique circumstances to beat Tony Stewart and the richest team in the IRL to the checkered flag. "I hate to lose, but if I had to get beat by somebody, it's kinda neat to see a low-buck guy get a win," said Stewart. "But this wasn't a fluke; Jim was fast all day." It was highly improbable and never repeated. Guthrie made a total of nine more starts in IRL competition through 2001, managing a pair of top tens.

Carl Haas, co-owner of the Newman/Haas Racing team that competed in the CART series, closely followed what was happening in the IRL, and the veteran Indy car campaigner remained unimpressed. "Having viewed the Phoenix IRL race this past Sunday, it is quite obvious that CART has nothing to fear," Haas wrote in a March 24, 1997, letter to CART CEO Andrew Craig. "It was a terrible event—the cars were slow, with a high number of engine failures, crashes, and long yellows. It was also apparent the race had a very low spectator turnout. The only real concern I have about this race is that the public continues to associate the CART series with the IRL."

To be fair, there was also an engine manufacturer in CART that was struggling in a very public way in the Spring of 1997, despite a seemingly unlimited budget. Toyota entered Indy car competition in '96 in partnership with Gurney's All American Racers, and results were even poorer than Honda's shaky arrival in '94 with Bobby Rahal and his team.

The early Honda engines were underpowered, overweight, and unreliable, prompting Rahal to lease a pair of Ilmor-powered cars from Roger Penske when he faced the prospect of his team failing to qualify for the Indianapolis 500 for the second year in a row.

While Honda improved substantially and won a race in its second season, the Toyota program seemed to regress, and the situation reached a crisis point in April 1997 when Toyota lost twenty-one engines during the course of the Long Beach and Nazareth race weekends. At Nazareth, Hiro Matsushita blew two Toyota engines in the thirty-minute pre-race practice, including one that lived less than four minutes. The race ended under caution because Juan Fangio's Toyota erupted, denying a potentially classic shootout for the win between Paul Tracy and Michael Andretti.

After meeting with CART Chief Steward Wally Dallenbach to consider the Toyota problem, Craig sent Toyota a strongly worded letter on April 30 that was leaked to some members of the media. With Toyota not only just an engine supplier but an increasingly important corporate partner for CART itself—Toyota was the title or presenting sponsor for six of the seventeen races on the schedule—the company was very sensitive to what Craig called "speculative and misleading" coverage.

The memo Craig subsequently wrote on May 13 to the CART Board of Directors gave the first hint of the kind of clout possessed by Toyota and the other participating engine manufacturers. "I wrote to Toyota on April 30 setting out our concerns and offering to work with Toyota to find practical ways in which the sanctioning body might be able to help Toyota get its engine program to a more competitive level . . . I know that everyone would agree that the sensible course is to do everything we can to help Toyota achieve a more competitive level of performance at the earliest possible stage."

Craig's actions helped Toyota save face, but it also emboldened the manufacturer to throw unprecedented amounts of money at its Indy car engine program—and eventually toward teams and drivers. Within the next few years, the power base within CART shifted from the team owners to the engine manufacturers, generally with disastrous results.

CHAPTER 13

BUMPY RIDE FOR THE IRL

After the PR disaster of the 1996 U.S. 500, CART elected to not go head-to-head again with the Indianapolis 500. The Motorola 300 was scheduled for Saturday, May 24, 1997, at Gateway International Raceway, an oblong 1.25-mile oval in western Illinois near St. Louis. The track was conceived by Long Beach Grand Prix founder Chris Pook as part of Dover Motorsports's expansion into additional racetrack development. Slowed by intermittent rain, the Motorola 300 played out to a sellout crowd of 48,500, with Paul Tracy moving from fifth to first in the final twenty-five laps to score Penske Racing's ninety-ninth Indy car race win.

Given the month of May that unfolded at Indianapolis, CART could be satisfied with staging a nondescript race that didn't generate any negative headlines. While engine problems were fewer than expected after the oil-soaked opening two races of the 1997 IRL season, the three weeks of track activity at the Indianapolis Motor Speedway featured no fewer than twenty-four accidents, resulting in serious injuries to four drivers. It was becoming increasingly clear that the IRL's new breed of normally aspirated Indy car was indeed slower (Arie Luyendyk's Indy pole speed of 218.263 mph was more than eighteen miles per hour down on the IMS track record he established in '96), but decidedly not safer.

The IRL announced the elimination of the controversial "25/8" grid seeding for 1998 on May 16, but the reopening of the Indy 500 field failed to make an impression on the absent CART teams and drivers. "We believe these changes signal that the Speedway and IRL recognize

Indianapolis Motor Speedway

167

the importance of having the teams and drivers that race in the CART/ PPG Series as part of the Indy 500," stated CART CEO Andrew Craig. "But there remain many major issues that separate CART and the Speedway. We hope motor racing fans everywhere are not misled into believing this announcement guarantees the teams and drivers that comprise CART will be racing at Indianapolis in 1998."

Meanwhile in 1997, only twenty-three of the protected twenty-five contenders from the early rounds of the championship made a qualifying attempt. That created a Bump Day scenario where unprotected 210-mph cars were locked out of the field in favor of 206-mph cars that had earned guaranteed starting spots. Sometime during Bump Day, the IRL made the decision to expand the field to accommodate any extra entries that met the minimum speed criteria, but it failed to inform the competitors until ninety minutes after qualifying ended. By then, Alessandro Zampedri (the same driver who nearly lost his feet at Indianapolis the year before) had bravely requalified in a light rain shower, and Scott Harrington had crashed, leaving the field seemingly set with Johnny Unser and Lyn St. James bumped out despite posting speeds more than three mph faster than slowest qualifier Fermin Velez. Shortly after qualifying ended, the IRL used a promoter's option to reinstate St. James and Unser, most likely as a way to add two more Infiniti-powered cars to the field, bringing the total to six in a field dominated by Oldsmobile. As in 1979, thirty-five cars were permitted to start the Indianapolis 500.

The race was postponed until Monday by rain, and six cars quickly dropped out in the fifteen laps that were completed prior to yet another rain delay. But once again, the IRL competitors rose to the big stage of Indianapolis and waged a competitive and entertaining race on Tuesday. Luyendyk triumphed over his Treadway Racing teammate Scott Goodyear, who suffered his third heartbreaking Indianapolis 500 loss in the space of six years.

An underappreciated champion who made the transition from CART to IRL with dignity and grace, Luyendyk became the only driver to win Indy in both CART- and IRL-specification cars. Until his 1990 winning race average was finally eclipsed in 2013, he held the one-, four-, and two-hundred-lap speed records at IMS; his qualifying records may never be beaten.

"Some people don't regard 1997 as a true win because all the teams were not there, and I can totally understand that," Luyendyk reflected. "On the other hand, that was a hard fought win. It wasn't easy at all. Those cars were not easy to drive. They had too much weight in the back and the back end never felt great. It was nothing like my 1990 car or my 1996 car. So you were always a little bit on edge and it was a nerve-wracking deal. I was nursing or babying it a little bit and with about forty laps to go, I said to the guys, 'Can I run it in fifth gear with higher rpm?' And they said go for it, the engine is good. So then I used it a little bit harder and it worked out."

But most of the goodwill Luyendyk's win could have generated was negated by the way USAC bungled the finish of the race. The Dutchman seized the lead from Goodyear with a thrilling outside pass in Turn Three on Lap 194, only for the caution to wave for debris two laps later. Racing briefly resumed until Tony Stewart soon brushed the wall and the racers were again greeted by the yellow flag at the end of the 198th lap. It appeared that the race would end under caution, but as Luyendyk led the field to take the white flag, the green flag was also displayed. Adding to the confusion, the yellow caution lights remained illuminated around the track until the leaders had exited Turn Two. It transpired that the USAC official in charge of changing the track lights from yellow to green had failed to hear the radio call.

"It was crazy because I had no indication at all and neither did Scott," said Luyendyk. "I thought we would cruise to the end, but then I saw the green flag so I said, 'The hell with it. If they don't know what they're doing, I know I do,' and I gassed it."

Goodyear lost the 1992 Indy 500 to Al Unser Jr. in a photo finish, then had the '95 race in the bag until he was disqualified for passing the pace car—which appeared to be moving much slower than usual on a late restart, something many observers contend was a blatant example of USAC incompetence. Still sore about '95, the '97 incident was almost too much for Goodyear to take. "I'm not feeling good at all," he said. "I saw the yellow in Turn One and in Turn Two. I was on the gas, but I didn't know what the hell to do. What if I get a run on him? Should I pass him? It was yellow."

USAC and Luyendyk were again the center of attention at the very next IRL race, held June 7 at the new Texas Motor Speedway near

Fort Worth. This was an important event for the IRL on many levels, starting with establishing a foothold in one of America's largest and most prominent sporting markets. The 500-kilometer contest would be the first night race in the history of Indy car racing, and it would also mark the first time in many years that Indy cars would attempt to race on a high-banked oval. The one and only time USAC Championship cars raced at the then-new Daytona International Speedway in 1959, George Amick flew out of the park and died in an accident; open-wheel cars never returned to Daytona or any of the few other high-banked speedways that existed prior to the oval track building boom of the '90s.

CART Chief Steward Wally Dallenbach had visited the 1.5-mile Texas facility and determined that the twenty-four-degree banking was unsuitable for the cars of the PPG IndyCar World Series. The IRL, with cars featuring considerably less power and greater downforce, had no such concerns; in fact, the IRL cars were so stable and planted, the drivers were able to constantly run flat-out, racing in close proximity in packs similar to a NASCAR restrictor plate race. This was uncharted territory for open-wheel cars running 210 miles per hour.

During the practice sessions at Texas, USAC noticed a few anomalies with its timing and scoring when several cars failed to trigger the system as they entered the pits. The sanctioning body thought it had the problem diagnosed and fixed prior to the race, but that proved incorrect. Laps completed by Luyendyk and four other drivers failed to register at times when they pitted during the race, and despite Treadway Racing's legitimate complaints while the race was running that Luyendyk was the leader, USAC ignored their pleas. With the scoring error going unverified until after the race, Stewart, still winless in IRL competition, was shown as the leader as the laps wound down. Then his Oldsmobile engine blew and he crashed with two laps to go. USAC midget ace Billy Boat, driving for A.J. Foyt, led the field to the checkered flag under caution.

Correctly believing he had won the race by a full lap, Luyendyk did not take this news well. He stalked down to Victory Lane to confront USAC officials, but was intercepted by Foyt, who lunged at Luyendyk and knocked him into a flower bed with a back-handed slap. Caught on live television, the incident quickly made national headlines, including a merciless mocking from Keith Olbermann on ESPN SportsCenter.

Several hours after the race, USAC Chief Steward Keith Ward and Timing and Scoring Director Art Graham admitted that the race officials had erred and that Luyendyk was the actual victor. "We were wrong; we are embarrassed," said Ward. Though Foyt subsequently and unsuccessfully appealed the reversal, he called Luyendyk to apologize. But he never did return the trophy. "I know it looked awful bad on TV from my part, which was shown throughout the world, I guess," Foyt said. "It was one of those misfortunate things. I guess you have to say, 'That's A.J.'"

Coming so soon after the last-lap gaffe at Indianapolis, USAC's fundamental failure at Texas was a serious black eye for the IRL. "I've been on the phone for two days and all I do is talk about what happened after the race," commented Luyendyk. "Nobody wants to talk about the race itself. Indy was a good race and there was some real good racing at Texas. But both times, USAC put a cloud on it."

Tony George acted swiftly. Nine days after the Texas debacle, the Indy Racing League terminated USAC's sanctioning duties, announcing June 16 that it would bring key sanction and officiating responsibilities in-house. The decision impacted sixty-five people who traveled to all IRL races, including six full-time staff—though many were subsequently employed by the IRL. USAC's sanction of sprint car, Silver Crown, and midget racing was not affected.

USAC's snafus at Indianapolis and Texas temporarily diverted attention away from the IRL's much more serious issues involving safety. By the summer of 1997, the league's vaunted new cars were landing drivers in the hospital at an unprecedented rate. After the Texas race in early June, IRL cars had been involved in at least sixty accidents in half a season, in which fourteen drivers incurred serious injuries. Particularly disturbing was a trend of spinal and neck injuries, along with a quantity of concussions not seen in the past.

The first generation of IRL cars clearly had serious safety flaws, starting with the league-mandated spec gearbox. As was common throughout the car, the gearbox, produced by EMCO, was built to a strict cost limit. Though not close to the level of technology seen in Formula 1,

CART gearboxes had grown increasingly compact and sophisticated—and by extension, expensive. The IRL identified the gearbox as a key area for cost savings, but the resulting budget-driven product carried unintended consequences. The earliest EMCO gearboxes were as much as fifty pounds overweight—weight at the very back of the car, which is the absolute worst place in terms of balancing the handling of a racing car. The heavy gearbox not only created a pendulum effect that made it easier for the car to spin and crash tail end first, but the over-rigid structure of the gearbox casing and rear bulkhead transferred all of the force of a rearward impact directly to the driver's spine and neck, even at extremely low speeds.

Eliseo Salazar was the first driver to crash an IRL car, and he sustained a spinal fracture despite what he estimated was no more than a 50-mph impact speed at Walt Disney World Speedway. Davy Jones, who had finished second to Buddy Lazier in the 1996 Indianapolis 500, was not so lucky; his crash at Orlando caused serious neurological damage and effectively ended his racing career. Scott Sharp missed the Indianapolis 500 after suffering a cerebral hemorrhage in a practice accident; starting from pole position upon his return at Pikes Peak International Raceway six weeks later, Sharp spun on the opening lap and hit the wall backwards barely hard enough to knock the rear wing of his G-Force/Oldsmobile askew. But the driver was unconscious after sustaining another cerebral hemorrhage. In all, more than three-quarters of the nineteen accidents that hospitalized drivers during the IRL's eight-race '97 season involved spine or head injuries.

CART did not achieve a perfect safety record in 1997, but it was much cleaner than the IRL's. With a new chassis that featured a wider cockpit with a removable padded horseshoe around the driver's shoulders, CART incurred seven accident-related injuries over the course of its seventeen-race campaign, including three concussions at the season finale at Roger Penske's new California Speedway.

Built on the site of a fomer steel mill in Fontana, about an hour east of Los Angeles and within three miles of the old Ontario Motor Speedway, California Speedway was a near copy of Penske's two-mile Michigan Speedway. Because of its D-shaped layout and higher banked turns, Michigan produced slightly higher speeds than Indianapolis, and

California was faster still. Mauricio Gugelmin turned an unofficial lap of 242.333 mph in practice and backed it up with a 240.942 mph run to pole position.

Breaking the 240-mph barrier was exciting, but it was also a cause for concern. With a pair of driver fatalaties in 1996 and the IRL racking up injuries at an unprecedented rate throughout '97, safety in Indy car racing was a hot topic and some fans began asking, "How fast is too fast?"

"Two-forty is a magic number, but everybody is a bit nervous," Gugelmin admitted. "Nobody is comfortable; I'm not. I think sometimes we push the laws of physics too far. At that speed, every single input had to be minute because it's very easy to lose control. It's almost like another planet because you have to have your mind so far ahead of the car. You're basically on a wire and it's like flying a jet. You had to be as smooth as you could and just hold your breath for a couple laps. But it was a great feeling."

CART Director of Medical Affairs Dr. Stephen Olvey believed it was important to address the issue with the drivers, which he did in an October 22, 1997, briefing. "It is easy to assume that one is safer going at a slower average speed on any given racetrack. Unfortunately, that is not the case," he wrote. Olvey went on to explain that while CART crashes at Fontana were taking place at very high speeds, the angle of impact was such that the change of velocity relative to the wall was in the area of thirty-five mph, which was no different than what occurs at a substantially lower average speed such as Milwaukee.

"In general, the IRL average speeds are twenty to thirty miles per hour less than our speeds on the same tracks," he noted. "The only difference is the average change in velocity in the crashes involving the IRL is higher than the average change in velocity involving our cars, which are traveling at substantially higher speeds. It is the angle of impact with the wall and the resulting change in velocity that causes injury. Therefore, to simply slow the cars down with regard to average speeds is not the answer to making the sport safer. It is imperative that this concept be understood by everyone discussing safety in motorsports."

Fearing a public outcry, CART did take action to reduce speeds on the Michigan and California Speedways by implementing a new rear wing for 1998 known as the Handford Device. This was essentially a standard rear wing, with a massive four-inch reverse wicker (angled down toward the track) that created a huge amount of drag to slow the cars down. It also created an enormous draft effect, making it almost comically easy to tow along and slingshot past the car ahead. The first Handford race (the '98 U.S. 500 at Michigan) unofficially had a record sixty-three lead changes, with Greg Moore triumphing over the Ganassi Racing duo of Jimmy Vasser and Alex Zanardi in an exciting finish. But the drivers were less than thrilled, believing the passing was artificial and the increased closing speeds over cars with a standard rear wing created a different kind of danger.

"The show was great," remarked Zanardi. "But I don't think what you saw today was racing."

The U.S. 500 was negative for CART in another regard. The right-front wheel from Adrian Fernandez's crashed car flew into the grand-stands, killing three spectators and injuring six others. CART came under scrutiny for not halting the race, but the unfortunate accident immediately led to the development of wheel tethers, which CART mandated from the start of 1999. Tethers were mandated in the IRL beginning with the '99 Indianapolis 500, but unfortunately that move came one race too late. Three spectators were killed and eight more injured at an IRL race at Charlotte Motor Speedway on May 1, 1999, after a fiery multicar accident launched a wheel into the grandstands.

Increasingly reliable engines and the addition of a foam block "attenuator" to the gearbox of IRL cars helped the league dramatically improve its safety record in 1998 and '99, with a total of ten drivers incurring serious injuries. CART had a mostly clean '98, but '99 was one of the most tragic years of the modern era. In September, rookie driver Gonzalo Rodriguez failed to negotiate Laguna Seca Raceway's famous Corkscrew turn and was killed instantly due to basilar skull fracture when his Team Penske Lola flipped over an earth bank.

Far more devastating to the sport was the death of Greg Moore in the 1999 CART finale at California Speedway. Starting from the back of the pack after missing qualifying (Moore fractured his wrist when a spectator backed a car into the scooter he was riding in the paddock), the emerging Canadian star was cutting through the field when he spun to the inside of Turn Two. Upon hitting the transition from grass to a paved track access road, Moore's car was flipped onto its side, with the top of the cockpit smashing an inside wall. He was killed instantly. CART Chief Steward Wally Dallenbach determined that Moore's death was caused by angle of impact, not speed. Moore's accident led to widespread paving of grass areas at Fontana and many other oval tracks to prevent similar incidents.

"When a car jumps out at 220 miles per hour, nothing can help a driver until they make contact," said CART Chief Stewart Wally Dallenbach. "All the advantages leave when a car enters the grass, and the surface road was six inches lower than the grass. Greg's car tripped because it was like a flat rock skipping across a still pond. It dug in and inverted itself."

Just twenty-four years old, Moore was predicted by many to be Indy car racing's next great star. He won only five races during his four-year CART career, but three of those victories came with a Mercedes-Benz engine that was extremely down on power and unreliable. In fact, Moore was the only driver who ever won races with the unloved "E" and "F" variants of the Ilmor/Mercedes engines in 1998 and '99. His performances caught the eye of Roger Penske, who signed Moore and Brazilian Gil de Ferran (the last man to win an Indy car race on Goodyear tires) as his drivers for 2000. Penske quickly tabbed twenty-four-year-old Hélio Castroneves to fill the seat intended for Moore.

No one man was capable of saving Indy car racing from destroying itself, but if anyone stood a chance, it was arguably Moore. He had already captivated millions of fans and conquered the drivers he fought against on the track in the CART series. But perhaps more important was the way the young Canadian triumphed over his rivals—with a huge smile on his face and a contagious energy that created strong, lifelong friendships among his competitors. In the spirit of Moore, camaraderie among competitors has become a hallmark of modern Indy car racing.

"Greg showed us that we didn't have to hate each other, but when we got on the track, trust me, he was as hard as anybody," recalled friend and rival Dario Franchitti. "I don't know how many races, championships or 500s he would have won, but it would have been a lot. It would have been quite something, and I think he would have re-written the record books. That talent in those Penske cars would have been something special. And it would have been lovely to see it."

Despite the rash of deaths in the second half of the 1990s, Indy car racing as a whole continued to be a leader and instigator for improvements to safety. The Indianapolis Motor Speedway pioneered the use of a staffed, on-site medical center and in the mid-sixties, a young man named Stephen Olvey served as a staff resident. By '75, Dr. Olvey was asked by USAC to put together a traveling medical program that would provide care to drivers similar to what they receive at Indianapolis. Along with Indianapolis-based orthopedic surgen Dr. Terry Trammell, Olvey then organized the CART Safety Team, which developed into a motorsports industry leader.

On-site care was provided at first in a fifth-wheel trailer, which was expanded in 1995 into CART's Mobile Medical Unit, with 850 square feet of space, four beds, and advanced trauma and life support equipment. By the late '90s, the CART Safety Team included a fleet of rescue vehicles equipped with medical supplies and state-of-the-art extrication equipment and a staff of forty. The IRL employed its own Safety Team with a staff of thirty-three under the leadership of longtime IMS Medical Director Dr. Henry Bock. NASCAR, however, maintained a system that utilized local doctors and accident response teams until 2017 despite frequent criticism from leading Cup Series drivers about safety issues.

In his "day job" outside of racing, Olvey was a renowned neurological surgeon who headed the Neuroscience Intensive Care Unit at the University of Miami's Jackson Memorial Hospital. He and Trammell compiled detailed accident reports and medical records for the drivers they treated, and they wrote a pair of academic papers published in *Physician and Sports Medicine* that charted the transition of driver injuries from mostly orthopedic in the 1980s to skull and spinal related in the '90s.

Some key safety developments at the outset of the twenty-first century dramatically reduced the number of driver injuries. The first was the invention of the Head and Neck Support (HANS) Device, a U-shaped composite collar that sits on a driver's shoulders around the back of the neck tethered to the helmet that minimizes the whiplash effect that causes basilar skull fractures. CART was the first major sanctioning body to mandate the HANS Device, beginning with oval tracks at the start of 2001 and all tracks later that year. The HANS, or a simlar neck restraint system, is now compulsory in all forms of racing, as much a part of a driver's safety kit as helmet, fireproof overalls, and gloves.

In terms of track safety, efforts to develop a "soft wall" for oval tracks finally began to gain traction. After Mark Blundell survived a huge accident in 1996 when his car's brakes failed, organizers of the CART race in Brazil restrained bundles of banded tires behind a rubber conveyor belt, a system that was generally effective from 1997 to 2000. Meanwhile, the Indianapolis Motor Speedway installed compressed foam padding it called PEDS (Polyethylene Energy Dissipating System) to the inside wall near the pit entrance in 1998, but the system's shortcomings were immediately exposed when Arie Luyendyk had a hard crash in an IROC stock car. The car slammed into the test wall during the Brickyard 400 weekend, and the foam exploded into thousands of pieces, creating an unmanageable debris field.

George and IMS persevered. He contracted Dr. Dean Sicking, a civil engineering professor at the University of Nebraska and director of the Midwest Roadside Safety Facility to begin development of what became known as the SAFER Barrier system. NASCAR soon contributed its support to the project. This time, the crushable foam was placed behind a series of square steel tubes, preventing the snagging of cars that resulted in the Brazilian system and the shower of foam debris from PEDS.

Now in universal use, the SAFER Barrier is without question the most important safety development in the history of oval track auto racing. Every driver who competes on ovals owes a gratitude of thanks to Dr. Sicking, as well as Tony George, IMS, and NASCAR for their investment in simple but important technology that has undoubtedly saved many lives.

Through all the hostility and friction over the years between CART and the various IMS/USAC/IRL factions, making safety the number one priority for participants and spectators was something that the two sides could always agree on.

CHAPTER 14

CART GOES PUBLIC

As if staging a 500-mile Indy car race in direct competition with the Indianapolis 500 in May 1996 didn't create enough confusion, CART was soon cast into an identity crisis when the Indianapolis Motor Speedway forced the company to drop the brand name "IndyCar," which it had licensed from IMS since '92.

The term "Indy car" became popular in the 1970s when USAC dropped dirt races from the Championship Trail and the cars used at Indianapolis were tailored to race on all paved ovals and road courses. By the time of CART's inception, top-level American open-wheel competition had generically become known as Indy car racing due to the obvious connection to the Indianapolis 500 and IMS. Even so, the rebranding of Championship Auto Racing Teams as IndyCar in the early '90s was done as much to distance the company from a long-perceived negative association with go-karts as much as it was to formalize the link to the Indy 500.

From the Speedway's standpoint, CART's use of the trademarked name was all fine and well as long as the participants of the PPG Indy-Car World Series formed the majority of the Indianapolis 500 field, as they had since 1979. But when CART committed to the '96 U.S. 500, that was no longer the case. IMS President Tony George reacted by informing CART in writing on March 18, 1996, that the "IndyCar" license agreement would be terminated in thirty days.

"IMS believes that CART has changed its business purpose in a material or substantive manner and has engaged in or permitted conduct which casts IMS in an unfavorable light," George wrote, citing a series of media quotes attributed to CART CEO Andrew Craig. "There have been efforts to discuss and resolve our differences, but that has not happened. Even after CART added the U.S. 500 to its schedule and created the direct conflict with the Indy 500, there were discussions about expanding the field at Indianapolis to include the CART team. That was also rejected by CART, and it is apparent the common ground on which the License Agreement was based no longer exists. . . . CART's decision to schedule a race that competes directly with the Indy 500, together with the announced intention of the CART teams to not compete at Indianapolis, makes it clear that continued use of the IndyCar mark by CART no longer makes any sense."

Through a separate license from PPG, CART was permitted to maintain the name "PPG IndyCar World Series" through the end of the 1996 season. Bizarrely, IMS and the IRL also agreed not to use the term "IndyCar" through December 31, 2002, but retained the rights to the designation "Racing League," while CART was granted use of the term "World Series." From 1997 to 2002, Indy car racing therefore technically ceased to exist.

When the IRL introduced its new chassis and engine formula for 1997, the cars that raced at the Indianapolis 500 suddenly looked and sounded considerably different than the cars that made up the field for the last twenty-five years. The "Indy cars" that had evolved over decades for racing at Indianapolis were no longer part of the 500, and they could not legally be called Indy cars. Nor could the IRL cars that took over as the mandated cars at Indianapolis. This fundamental question about what constituted an Indy car in the late '90s created a considerable amount of confusion and dissent among fans, sponsors, and media. The bigger, simpler cars being raced at Indianapolis were never really thought of as Indy cars, and even after the ban on the term "IndyCar" ended, longtime participants in the sport continued to refer to them as IRL cars.

"We don't see a need to use the term 'IndyCar,'" remarked IMS Communications Director Fred Nation, adding that the Speedway had "invested a lot of money and time" in the IRL nomenclature.

CART's championship became known as the PPG CART World Series in 1997, and when PPG announced its intention to reduce its involvement, CART was successful in landing a new title sponsor with much greater name brand recognition: Federal Express, the widely known overnight air freight company. From 1998 to 2002, CART's product was marketed as the FedEx Championship Series, with the cars reverting to the "Champ Car" terminology used up through the early 1970s.

"Clearly the name change is an issue," admitted Carl Cohen, CART's executive vice president of marketing from 1997-99. "There's an awareness challenge, both for the drivers and for the sport as a whole. There are two sanctioning bodies out there pushing open-wheel racing, which causes confusion and leads to a lack of awareness. We need to build an emotional link to the drivers—that's missing in CART. It's there in NASCAR and other sports, and it's a big element of their success. And I think as a business, NASCAR took advantage of the split in open-wheel racing. Until recently—until the growth of NASCAR—a Champ Car was what a race car was all about."

While FedEx was a much more recognizable consumer brand than PPG, the title sponsorship was not especially lucrative. In fact, FedEx reportedly profited handsomely from transporting the CART series's cars and equipment to overseas races in Japan, Australia, and Brazil.

"We looked at all our sports sponsorships and identified a gap," said Jim Lyski, U.S. vice president of marketing for Federal Express. "It came down to shared attributes such as speed, technology, teamwork, and precision, as well as the amount of ownership we could have. Internationally, our brand is not as strong as it is in the U.S., so as the series explores other countries and continents, it's good for us. The opportunity to generate some revenue from the sport propelled CART right up to the top."

Meanwhile, the IRL acquired a title sponsor at the same time, signing a five-year pact with Pep Boys, a Philadelphia-based auto parts retailer. But the Pep Boys Indy Racing League lasted just two years until the partnership dissolved in a series of lawsuits. Pep Boys fell into financial difficulty and withdrew by claiming that the IRL failed to meet television audience targets. The IRL sought around $18 million in damages from Pep Boys for money not spent in 1999 and the remaining three years of the contract.

With FedEx on board, CART then took a major step to solidify itself as a business by becoming one of the first major sports leagues to operate as a public company. Formula 1 had considered a global public offering around the same time that CART was completing its stock sale. But Bernie Ecclestone failed to get unanimous support from the F1 teams, and antitrust concerns raised by the European Community ultimately forced underwriters to shelve the plan.

Pat Patrick sparked CART's movement to go public, with an initial public offering price set at sixteen dollars per share. With about one-third of the shares (4.7 million out of 14.7 million) sold to the public, CART was making itself accountable to shareholders other than racing team owners for the first time. Existing CART team owners received 400,000 shares for each of the twenty-four franchises. Now those team owners could place a value on their property and their participation—$6.4 million. But what was a stock buyer actually getting when acquiring a piece of CART? In theory, it was not just shares in a company that operated auto races, but a share of all of the participating teams—Penske Racing, Newman/Haas Racing, Dale Coyne Racing, etc.

Going public also opened CART's finances for outside scrutiny. The prospectus showed that attendance climbed on the CART circuit from 1.8 million in 1991 to 2.4 million in '96. Sanction fees that promoters paid CART to host races were expected to grow from $24.4 million in '97 to $30.4 million in '98, and the company's direct sponsorship revenue was expected to jump to $12.1 million in '98, from $7.2 million in '97.

CART expected the Initial Public Offering (IPO) to generate $63 million after brokerage fees, from which the company planned to spend $10.5 million to acquire the Indy Lights series and the Formula Atlantic championship from their owners (Pat Patrick and Gerald Forsythe), with the goal of bringing the open-wheel development "ladder system" (the road-racing version of USAC's midgets and sprint cars) in house. Another $9.5 million was used to pay obligations owed to existing race teams.

"To be a member of the New York Stock Exchange puts us in the same league as our sponsors," remarked Patrick. "I think it lends tremendous credibility to the sport. Sponsors know we're liquid, solvent, and capable of carrying out our commitments."

"I think the IPO is very positive for the whole sport," Craig added. "It's helping to change the perception of CART within the business world. Obviously, it has been very beneficial for the shareholders because it has given these teams some long-term security. They have a vested interest to see the business grow and see it be successful. And it has given us capital, which the company never really had before. It literally lived off its workings, its cash flow. The IPO was the culmination of a five-year process, because now clearly and unequivocally, it is a business."

As part of the restructuring, CART created a two-board structure. The existing Franchise Board remained in place, with each of the twenty-four stakeholders maintaining their votes on rules and racing activities. A corporate "Delaware" Board, named for the state in which the company was incorporated due to favorable tax laws, was formed to manage the company itself. That board of directors consisted of seven team owners and Craig, along with a pair of veteran corporate leaders—NBC television executive Don Ohlmeyer and former Textron CEO James Hardymon.

Heading into 1999, Craig was bullish about CART's prospects. "If you look at the championship today, pretty well every parameter by which you measure it is very positive except for one—television," he told reporters. "We have strong audiences, increasing newspaper coverage, greater presence, much more promotional activity in the marketplace, $435 million worth of corporate support, and more races. Frankly, if we could fit them all in, we could expand to twenty-four or twenty-five races."

But as always, the elephant not present in the room was the Indianapolis 500. "The popular wisdom was that without the Indy 500, there would be no fans, no drivers, no sponsors, and no race teams," Craig said. "None of that seemed to happen. The series actually got stronger than it's ever been before. But we still face some very major challenges, including having special events that attract a broader group of fans. If you really want to kick-start the sport, you need some high-profile events. But mega-events aren't created; they evolve. They become cultural icons. So you don't set out to create one from scratch, although the Super Bowl is an example of how that can successfully happen. We can say something is a mega-event, but until the consumer agrees, it isn't.

"There's no secret that we think the Indianapolis 500 is a really big event, and big events are becoming more and more important from a television perspective than ever before," Craig added. "There's no question the Indy 500 would be very attractive in that regard, but I've got to develop the sport, promote the sport, and build the sport as if the Indy

500 didn't exist. Yet at the same time, it does exist. It's an important event and I have to look for every opportunity to get it back on board."

Perhaps driven by the need to create such an event, Craig revealed on January 25, 1999, that CART had entered into an agreement to participate in a $10 million nonchampionship race to be known as the Hawaiian Super Prix (HSP). Proposed for November 13, two weeks after the FedEx Championship Series season finale at California Speedway, the HSP would run on a 1.8-mile airport road course at the Barbers Point Naval Air Station in Leeward, Oahu. The event would consist of two sixty-minute heats, split by a sixty-minute celebrity-filled halftime show, with the overall result based on points, not time. Drivers could earn points for laps led, fastest lap, passes made, and qualifying position, and the second heat would feature a grid inverted from the first heat finishing order.

Significantly, organizers announced that the race would be broadcast on a live, pay-per-view basis on the Showtime network, as well as internationally in over 195 countries, reaching a potential worldwide audience of approximately 300 million viewers. Adding to the incentive for fans to pay a reported $19.95 for the telecast was the chance for them to grab their own share of the pie, with one lucky viewer scoring a $1 million prize of his or her own for phoning in the correct answers to contest questions.

Local organizers calculated the inaugural race would cost $20 million to stage, including the purse, sanctioning fees, transportation of cars and barriers (something FedEx would have no doubt been pleased to support), and administrative costs, and said they had taken out a performance bond from Frontier Insurance.

It turned out they needed the insurance policy. Despite the recruitment of Mario Andretti as a spokesman, the Hawaiian Super Prix never stood a chance. The announcement of the event came far too late for sponsors and engine manufacturers to include it in their 1999 budgets, and it failed to gain the corporate support necessary to get off the ground. Mauricio Gugelmin ran a few laps around the proposed course in the summer to drum up some positive PR, but that was the closest Hawaii came to hosting an Indy car race. Original promoter Dick Rutherford was replaced by Phil Heard, the former general manager of the Molson Indy Vancouver, and despite eleventh-hour efforts by Don Panoz to help as a silent partner, CART announced the cancellation of the event on October 19. Under terms of the agreement, CART collected the $5 million surety bond that was posted in February.

"I can't remember the exact conditions, but we couldn't cancel the race," Craig later explained. "It had to get to a certain point in time before we could say no. Even though it was clear to me quite early on that Rutherford wasn't going to make it happen, I couldn't stop it without invalidating the insurance policy. I had two or three people on the board that were very keen to do this, but I can't judge what their motivations were. Putting aside the economics, the general idea was okay. On a very basic concept level, it had some attractions, definitely. But the business model didn't make sense and Rutherford didn't have the ability to put it together. I was the CEO and I allowed it to happen, so I take full responsibility."

Craig had other more pressing issues to contend with in the spring of 1999. For starters, CART's relationship with its television partners at ESPN had reached an all-time low, as evidenced by a series of letters exchanged between Craig and ESPN Executive Vice President of Programming Dick Glover.

From the very start in 1979, television had been a sore point for CART. The company committed very early to a time-buy strategy, and while other sports began to cash in on lucrative rights fees paid by networks, CART got left behind. When CART became a public company, one of Craig's tasks was to increase television revenue to a more representative level for an organization of CART's history and stature, and he predicted that "an increasingly unhappy partner in ESPN" was likely "an inevitable consequence of pushing for change."

The conflict in 1999 was triggered by an audit conducted by Deloitte and Touche of the financial aspects of the CART/ESPN relationship from which CART requested a $6 million adjustment. That, along with the unexpected announcement of the Hawaiian Super Prix and the Showtime pay-per-view broadcast, disagreements over international rights, and the last-minute cancellation of a series of "Inside CART" thirty-minute news/feature programs, prompted Glover to communicate ESPN's displeasure to Craig and the CART board.

"Some of these issues involve infringement of our contractual rights and others entail the violation of the spirit of an economic partnership that we have invested enormous amounts of time and money to develop," wrote Glover on March 31. "We have stood with CART through the very bad times since your split with the Indianapolis Motor Speedway. In doing so, we have jeopardized our ability to retain marquee properties like the Indianapolis 500 and the Brickyard 400. Since the split, CART's ratings have plummeted. This has caused a serious under-delivery of rating points to our advertisers and your sponsors. To solve this problem, over the last two years, we have donated over 5 million dollars worth [sic] of ESPN commercial inventory and other programming to make good the ratings shortfall.

"We remain committed to CART, its teams, promoters, and sponsors, but we feel that despite our being good partners for many years, we are being misrepresented and shabbily mistreated," he concluded. "If you no longer value ESPN and ABC as partners, we should discuss mutually agreeable steps to end the relationship. If you want to work together with us to grow CART, then we must find a more productive way of communicating and conducting business."

But despite the contentious relationship with ESPN, the partnership continued into 2000, boasting the most broadcast time in CART's history—a record 128 hours, with ten of the series's twenty races to be televised on ABC. Nine of the remaining ten were scheduled for ESPN, and most races enjoyed the benefit of longer two-and-a-half-hour broadcasts, which CART hoped would boost sagging ratings.

"Obviously the television numbers concern us," Craig said. "Although sponsorship is really a more sophisticated tool than just having the cars get on television, the fact is, television is how most people judge the health of the sport. It is an important measure. The fact of the matter is when your TV ratings are weak, it suggests the sport is weak."

On April 12, 1999, CART reported to the Securities and Exchange Commission that several key shareholders announced their intention to sell approximately 12 percent of the company's stock, including All American Racers Inc. (selling 100,000 of its 420,000 shares), Team Green Inc. (256,000 of 360,000) and Patrick Racing (400,000 of 800,000). But the real eye-opener was Roger Penske's intention to sell 87.5 percent of his CART stock, or 720,000 of his 800,000 shares.

Patrick said his sale was part of a reorganization of his estate, while Penske followed his registration with the announcement that Penske Capital Partners was making an $83 million investment in United Auto Group. He netted about $19 million from his CART stock sale, at a share price of $27.50. But Penske also claimed he wanted to divest himself from CART because he was concerned about a personal conflict of interest due to his simultaneous major shareholding in Penske Motorsports, the company that owned and operated Michigan, California, Nazareth, and Rockingham Speedways, along with controlling interest in Homestead-Miami Speedway.

That's why it was such a surprise on May 10 when Penske Motorsports announced a merger with International Speedway Corporation (ISC), the racetrack company owned by the same France family that owned and operated NASCAR. This really wasn't a merger; ISC simply absorbed the Penske tracks, creating what would eventually become a thirteen-track empire that hosted more than half the races on the NASCAR schedule.

Penske's sale of his CART stock was widely viewed as a vote of no-confidence in the company he had cofounded, especially when coupled with the fact that Penske refused to accept a seat on the CART "Delaware" board. At the announcement of the Penske/ISC merger, both Penske and Bill France Jr. said that with NASCAR in a very healthy state, the biggest key for success for the ISC tracks was a unified open-wheel series.

By the time the Penske/ISC deal was announced, it was widely known that CART CEO Craig had been meeting informally with Tony George in the latest attempt to find common ground. The reunification rumors were boosted by a wildly speculative May 11 "Research Note" by J.C. Bradford & Co. analyst E. Breck Wheeler that made it seem like the end of the Indy car split was imminent. By the next morning, demand for CART stock accelerated to the point where demand was so much greater than the available supply that the New York Stock Exchange briefly suspended trading, with the share price exceeding thirty dollars.

George met again with Craig on Indy 500 pole weekend, and the rumor mill peaked a few days later when the IMS president met with France, purportedly discussing only the duo's partnership in a track being built near Joliet, Illinois, that would become Chicagoland Speedway. But during a series of impromptu chats with the media at IMS on May 27, George poured cold water on the notion that CART and the IRL were anywhere close to working together in the future. He also, for the first time, floated the idea that the recent attempt at reunification (and the apparent leaks of the meetings from the CART side) were made in an effort to boost CART's stock share price.

"Nothing substantive was addressed," George said. "There is still a very big gap where we are philosophically and no indication that we are any closer. I can't say I'm encouraged by anything I've heard so far. The media, in this case, tends to jump to conclusions.

"I think we can continue to have talks, but I don't think they will be substantive," he added. "It's a distraction, and all this does is fuel one's real goal, and that is, in this case, to manage the stock price. They are trying to shift some of the attention onto themselves and they continue to need to give some glimmer of hope that something is in the offing to keep their stock price where they want it to be. They are struggling, at this point, to keep their sponsors." On May 27, the day of George's remarks, CART stock reached a record high of $32.94 per share.

"They have been welcome to come back and run here, but all I can say is it's going to be under the rules that are in place," George said. "I'm committed to our philosophies, principles, and values. Those are things you don't compromise, and I'm not going to compromise ours to get them back here. It's about as simple as that. We have proven we don't need CART to run successful events.

"I think both sides can go on, but whether we can flourish, I don't know that," George concluded. "It will eventually have to be one series, but I don't have a crystal ball and I can't predict what the outcome of that will be."

Roger Penske was among many who were confused and frustrated by George's denial that CART and the IRL were close to reaching an agreement. "I was disappointed in that comment, because I think that the conversations that have taken place—and I'm sure there have been many by car owners and other people at Indianapolis—they're genuine and they're positive. I can tell you from Marlboro Team Penske's perspective that we firmly support a transition and some opportunity to combine the open-wheel racing into one sport and one enterprise. I think that it's obvious to everyone.

"We need to think positively, and there's no question in my mind that we can pull this back together. But I think one man's got to make that decision," Penske added. "I think our group is poised and ready to sit down and put it together. But Tony is the guy that could close it. I think he can close it on terms that everyone is a winner—not just Andrew Craig or CART or IRL, but the whole industry, the fans, and the press."

The unification efforts initiated by CART in 1999 may not have borne fruit, but they did result in change: on November 5, CART announced a twenty-race 2000 schedule that, for the first time since the split occurred in 1996, left the month of May open for CART teams to participate in the Indianapolis 500.

"It is widely known that we made significant efforts to secure a resolution to the issues that have divided CART and the IRL," Craig stated. "When it became apparent in early October that our efforts were not going to result in a resolution of those issues, CART and its team owners examined whether it would be feasible to compete in the Indy 500. Many of the specific issues relative to Indy, which precluded CART teams from participating in recent years, have been resolved. Also, the management of IMS has repeatedly stated that the Indy 500 is an event fully and completely open to any race teams, including those in CART, and that teams from anywhere are welcome to participate. Our teams have decided it is in their best interest, as well as that of the sport, to return to the Speedway to compete for the title of Indianapolis 500 champion."

No mention was made of which, if any teams, were planning to participate at Indianapolis in May 2000. But IRL Executive Director Leo Mehl believed there would be a large influx of return competitors. Mehl, the former head of Goodyear's worldwide racing operations and a longtime favorite of Tony George, took over as point man for the IRL after Jack Long departed in late 1996 and held the position through the end of '99.

"We will have a number of CART teams running at the Speedway for the year 2000," Mehl predicted. "There's been a flurry of activity, and I think for sure we're going to have ten or twelve cars. I'm pleased that they're willing to come here and buy our cars and run these engines, and we'll see what happens after that."

The level of on-track professionalism in the IRL increased considerably in the latter part of the 1990s. John Menard's team had the budget and the personnel to match any major CART effort, taking Tony Stewart to the 1996-97 IRL championship. Kenny Brack, a European Formula 3000 frontrunner from Sweden, crossed over to America and won the '98 IRL championship and the '99 Indianapolis 500 for car owner A.J. Foyt, finally giving Foyt that elusive fifth Indy win. The often tongue-tied Foyt declared, "I'm so wonderful!" in a post-race television interview.

Greg Ray, whose background included stints in the CART-sanctioned Formula Atlantic and Indy Lights series, was the league's 1999 champion for Menard Racing. And Buddy Lazier and Hemelgarn Racing proved their victory in the '96 Indy 500 was no fluke. Lazier won seven more races in an Indy car career that continued through 2017, capped by the 2000 IRL championship.

Despite the softening of its hard line on the month of May, CART still appeared to hold the upper hand heading into 2000. Aside from losing the Pep Boys title sponsorship, the IRL was forced to step in and take over promotion of its races at Las Vegas Motor Speedway and Atlanta Motor Speedway after track operator Speedway Motorsports Inc. reported a $3 million loss it directly attributed to IRL events.

For 2000, the league signed a new title sponsor—Northern Light, an internet search engine and competitor to the likes of Lycos, Infoseek, Excite, and Yahoo. The IRL failed in an attempt to take over CART's Cleveland Grand Prix, leaving it with a nine-race 2000 schedule, down from eleven in 1999. More importantly, the IRL also pressed ahead with a second generation of cars, with slightly sleeker new chassis from Dallara and G-Force and normally aspirated V8 engines downsized from 4.0 to 3.5-liters capacity in an effort to reduce power. For the foreseeable future, potential Indy car competitors would still be forced to decide between investing in CART or IRL specification cars and engines, with very few able to acquire both.

"They're asking us to change our equipment, but I don't see a good reason to change," George told reporters at the IRL's 1999 season finale at Las Vegas. "The IRL doesn't need to compromise. We're happy with what we have. We don't have to change and we won't change. There's nothing imminent that's going to happen. We're not the ones that feel an urgency to get back together. They're the ones who need Indy."

By opening up the month of May on its schedule, CART seemed to admit as much. And while Andrew Craig remained high on the FedEx Championship Series's many positive aspects, it was increasingly clear that CART's long-term prospects were dependent upon the state of its relationship with the Indianapolis Motor Speedway.

"CART is the second largest racing series in the world, second only to Formula 1, with over a billion viewers cumulatively," Craig said. "So I think we find ourselves in an attractive position. We're part of the second largest sport in the world, second only to soccer, and we're the second largest series in the second largest sport. That's an attractive position to be in if you're a global player. Our TV ratings were up very slightly, and that's the first time that has happened since the split with Indianapolis. While it's a very small rise, we can take some comfort in that—it's a move in the right direction. We're not short of fans, but we need to make them more active and more involved in the sport.

"I think without question the most critical issue CART still faces is its relationship with the Indianapolis 500," he continued. "We do a lot of research, and it shows clearly and consistently that the division in the sport is a major impediment to future progress. It's as simple as that. I think one of the great achievements of CART in the last few years, is despite that impediment, it continued to build its business.

"The split with Indianapolis is not appreciated by the fans at all," Craig concluded. "They haven't gone away, but their interest has declined. About 20 percent of people who were avid fans five years ago will tell you today, 'Well, I'm still a fan, but not as much as I used to be.' At the same time, a large number of people will say, 'I'm still a CART fan, but I'm also a fan of NASCAR.' Those things cause a significant swing in your sport, and they have been driven by the split."

Four years into the latest and most damaging phase of the split, the chances of unification between CART and the Indy Racing League seemed more distant than ever. And although CART would never return to the Indianapolis 500 en masse, a slow trickle that would turn into a tide was about to begin.

CHAPTER 15

UNITY LOST

After CART left the month of May open on its 2000 schedule, Leo Mehl's prediction that up to a dozen CART teams would enter the Indianapolis 500 proved to be wildly optimistic. In the end, only one organization chose to step up to the sporting and financial challenge. Perhaps surprisingly, it was not Penske Racing.

Target/Chip Ganassi Racing had dominated the CART series since the split, winning the championship in each of the four years with three different drivers. Heading into the 2000 season, 1996 PPG Cup (and U.S. 500) champion Jimmy Vasser continued to anchor the team, while Alex Zanardi returned to Formula 1 after earning the FedEx Championship Series title in '97 and '98. Zanardi's young replacement achieved success even faster; Juan Pablo Montoya won seven races and the CART series crown as a twenty-three-year-old rookie in '99, edging Dario Franchitti, another emerging star, on a tiebreaker.

Michael Andretti scored CGR's (Chip Ganassi Racing) first win in the 1994 season opener in Australia, and since switching to the effective Reynard-Honda-Firestone "package" in '96, Ganassi had overtaken Roger Penske as Indy car racing's most successful team owner. Disadvantaged by increasingly uncompetitive Goodyear tires and a radical Ilmor-designed engine that adversely affected all the Mercedes-contracted teams from '98 onward, Team Penske won just three CART races between '96 and '99, a period when Ganassi won twenty-nine times.

The IRL's alternate chassis and engine rules meant a two-car CART team faced a logistical nightmare as well as a minimum expenditure of

$1.5–2 million just to try to make the show at Indy. That high price, along with some unresolved corporate entertainment and catering issues that remained from when CART last raced at Indianapolis in 1995, meant most sponsors weren't willing to make that kind of commitment.

But on February 28, 2000, Target and Ganassi did. They announced that the team's CART drivers—Vasser and defending FedEx Series champion Montoya—would run the Indianapolis 500 in a pair of G-Force/Oldsmobiles. The cars would run in the familiar Target livery, but with significant support from Budweiser.

It was no small task. In the ninety days from when the project was announced until Indianapolis 500 race day, CART staged five races, including trips to Japan and Brazil. Making things tougher physically, psychologically, and logistically, CART's April 9 race at Nazareth Speedway was *snowed* out and rescheduled for Saturday, May 27—the day before the Indy 500.

Montoya, who had never been around the Brickyard in a racing car, raised a few eyebrows with his apparent indifference toward the historic venue after hitting 217 miles per hour on his fourth flying lap during an April test. "When I thought of racing in the United States, I thought of CART—not the Indianapolis 500," he commented. "So far, it's been very simple to get around here. Everyone said it was really smooth, and the fact that it's a bit bumpy surprised me."

By the time the Ganassi team's attack on the month began in earnest on Monday, May 15, rivals had already put in two days of practice on top of the three years of IRL car development experience they possessed. By contrast, Ganassi had a total of four days of testing—less than a thousand miles for each driver, according to Team Manager Mike Hull—when Vasser and Montoya went directly to IMS for a shakedown run after the twenty-hour trip from Japan. Montoya had dominated the CART race at Twin Ring Motegi before a bizarre mishap during a pit stop dropped him to seventh place and gifted the victory to Michael Andretti, who kept Ford-Cosworth's perfect winning record in Japan intact.

The Ganassi team publicly downplayed the pressure that was on them and insisted that CART/IRL politics were not on their agenda. "As far as flying any CART flags or any other things, it's not like that," said Vasser. "I don't feel like I'm representing the CART guys. We just came in here to race, simple as that. We're racing for ourselves, and unless Chip tells me different, I'm doing it for my race team."

Montoya was edged for pole position at Indianapolis by defending IRL champion Greg Ray, who was the class of the series in 1999 with three wins for John Menard's team. Montoya was then comfortably fastest on Carb Day. Chip Ganassi rented the Milwaukee Bucks' Douglas DC-9 to fly the pit crews to and from Pennsylvania for the rescheduled CART race at Nazareth, where Gil de Ferran ended Penske's three-year victory drought with the team's one hundredth Indy car race win.

Having run a race in Pennsylvania the day before, the Ganassi team was actually grateful that rain delayed the Indianapolis start by three hours. Once the 500 got going, Montoya was content to cruise behind Ray until they got into backmarker traffic. On Lap 27, Montoya snatched the lead for the first time, and extended it when he made his first routine pit stop. Ganassi's superior stops were a hallmark throughout the day. Ray crashed out at the halfway point, and Vasser's alternate pit stop sequence didn't pan out, leaving 1996 Indianapolis winner Buddy Lazier as Montoya's only real challenger.

By the time the checkered flag fell, Montoya was ahead of Lazier by 7.184 seconds after leading 167 of the 200 laps. He became the first rookie since Graham Hill in 1966 to win the Memorial Day classic. It was also the most dominant Indy performance since '87, when Mario Andretti led 170 laps but failed to finish.

"I think it will take time to realize what I just won," Montoya admitted. "It's so exciting, I can't believe it. It's not only a win for me, or for Chip, or for Jimmy, but for every person on the team."

Vasser praised the level of competition from the IRL regulars and thanked Ganassi for "putting it all on the line," while Ganassi called it the best day of his life. "It's huge," he said. "It's hitting me now. Everyone is interested in the political side of things, and I'm not. This is still the biggest race in the world, and this is the biggest win in the world. And it will get bigger as time passes."

In some ways, the manner in which Ganassi's team turned the Indianapolis 500 on its head was more impressive than when Penske commissioned the infamous Mercedes-Benz 500I pushrod engine that powered his team to victory at the Brickyard in 1994. Rather than exploiting a unique technological avenue to gain a performance advantage, Ganassi beat the IRL regulars at their own game with the same off-the-shelf equipment available to anyone.

"They raised the level of competition to a whole new level," noted two-time IRL champion car owner John Menard. "It's certainly going to raise some questions about the ability of IRL teams to compete with CART. But they were the best of the best, a very powerful and organized team."

Ganassi team members were finally able to admit the weight of high expectations. "Anything short of winning would have been a failure," remarked Managing Director Tom Anderson, acknowledging what CART fans had been thinking all month long. "We always had enough money and talent to do the job. It was just a matter of time. I'm still in awe that it's been pulled off. My biggest relief is that we'll be able to show our faces in the [CART] Milwaukee paddock and hold our heads high."

The first part of the 2000 CART season was notable for the ascension of Toyota's engine program. Rising from laughingstock status, the Toyota engine finally started producing some decent results in 1999 with Cal Wells's PPI Racing team. Scott Pruett earned Toyota's first pole position in the season finale, and young Brazilian Cristiano da Matta, the '98 Indy Lights champion, produced several top-five finishes. For 2000, perhaps hoping lightning would strike twice, Chip Ganassi changed up his "package" by replacing Honda with Toyota and switching chassis supplier to Lola, which was rebounding from several uncompetitive years with a new design.

Once again, Ganassi appeared to be ahead of the curve, because in his team's hands, the Lola-Toyota was fast. But it wasn't reliable; Montoya led 305 laps but had only a pair of top-seven finishes on the board in CART prior to his win at the IRL-sanctioned Indianapolis 500. That turned around in early June at Milwaukee, when the Colombian followed up his Indy triumph with Toyota's first CART series win. It had been a long, hard, expensive, and sometimes embarrassing road to victory for the Japanese giant. Having finally tasted success, Toyota really started to wield its muscle.

Driven by Toyota, the shift in the balance of power within CART from the team owners to the engine manufacturers was beginning to accelerate. And CART seemed powerless to stop it. In fact, by the time

Montoya led the field to the green flag at Detroit just a week after his Milwaukee breakthrough, CART had a new leader—or more accurately, a new interim leader. In a move surprising only for its timing, Andrew Craig abruptly resigned his position as chairman and chief executive officer of Championship Auto Racing Teams at a board meeting on the Friday morning of the Detroit weekend. A subsequent board vote resulted in Bobby Rahal being named interim CEO, with board member James Hardymon nominated as chairman.

Six years into his employment with CART, and with his contract set to expire at the end of 2000, Craig had come under increasing pressure from all directions when CART's performance in the American sports marketplace declined as the Indy car split dragged on. Somewhat unfairly, Craig was made the scapegoat.

"The board was in agreement that Andrew wasn't going to go any further on his contract," stated Hardymon. "It just seemed like a good thing to do it now rather than wait until the end of the year. This is a company that has not been out of the IPO phase for very long, and sometimes you go through that with one type of manager and one type of person who is very adept at doing that, and I think Andrew did a great job. Now we have someone [Rahal] that is well known in the sport, can represent the sport to the media, to the promoters, to the owners, the drivers and to the fans."

Craig certainly had his share of backers, including PacWest Racing founder and CART Delaware Board member Bruce McCaw. "Overall, I think Andrew put together and ran a pretty effective organization," McCaw said. "One of the challenges that CART had was that it never let the management manage. I think we should have controlled the board better. The way the world works in a democracy is the majority make the decision and the rest really need to go along with the decision that got made. In CART, that really didn't happen. The minute somebody didn't agree with something, they would be down in the pit lane talking to certain people in the media. I think that hurt the organization in a lot of ways because it allowed the integrity of the organization to be compromised."

Gerald Forsythe was one CART team owner and board member who increasingly began to make waves. Forsythe formed a team in 1982 that fielded Danny Sullivan's first Indianapolis 500 entry. Later that year, Forsythe scored one of the most bizarre and unlikely wins in the history of Indy car racing with ex–F1 pilot Hector Rebaque at Road America. In '83, rookie Teo Fabi claimed pole position at Indianapolis and four wins in the CART series, but Fabi left to chase a ride in Formula 1 and Forsythe withdrew from racing after the '85 season to focus on his businesses.

He then returned to team ownership partnered with Barry Green in 1993 as Forsythe-Green Racing landed a lucrative sponsorship from Player's cigarettes to create a Canadian driver development program and advance the career of Jacques Villeneuve, the son of legendary Formula 1 driver Gilles Villeneuve. In '95, Forsythe and Green split, with Green maintaining the Player's sponsorship and Villeneuve, who won the Indianapolis 500 and the CART championship that year. The revived Forsythe Racing ran the '95 season with Fabi, then took over the Player's sponsorship in '96 to field a car for rising Canadian star Greg Moore. Player's funded a second CART car beginning in '98, and in '99, Forsythe created a satellite team to run a third car in the CART series for driver Tony Kanaan with sponsorship from McDonald's under the Forsythe Championship Racing (FCR) banner. Forsythe also campaigned cars in Indy Lights and Formula Atlantic to keep a supply of capable Canadian drivers in the pipeline.

Forsythe wanted a third CART franchise for his FCR operation, but CART's longstanding bylaws limited any individual from holding more than two. Forsythe took his case to CART's Delaware Board, who granted unanimous approval for a third franchise. But CART's Franchise Board—still comprised of twenty-four votes from the sixteen team owners—refused Forsythe's request. He was livid, because his satellite team would therefore not receive paid travel to CART's overseas races in Brazil, Japan, and Australia and other benefits. He subsequently withdrew the entry before the 2000 season.

"It doesn't make sense to anybody," Forsythe said. "I told the CART Board and I told the Franchise Board in meetings I've attended, 'Hey, if I can find sponsors to run five cars, I'll run them.' That's to the benefit of CART. But they all got tunnel vision. It's very short-sighted, and most of the team owners out there are just that way. They're all very protective about their own team. They aren't looking at the big picture. If they want to play hardball with me, I'll play hardball with them. Obviously, they think they have plenty of cars out there and they don't need me. That's what they told me by not giving me a franchise.

"I'm tired of fighting with the establishment there," he added. "They're only interested in their own little kingdom. They're not interested in CART as a whole. It's unfortunate. But they're racers. They can't see the big picture. None of those guys can see to the end of their nose."

Interim CEO Rahal defended the decision, along with CART's management structure. "The CART system may be unwieldy and frustrating at times because there are many different opinions," he said. "But I believe that, ultimately, if you look at the quality of the racing, it works pretty well. It's not for the impatient, believe me, and it doesn't make a lot of sense sometimes. But I think that, generally, a democracy is still the way to go."

Ganassi's return to the Indianapolis 500 naturally opened up a discussion about whether or when other participants in the CART series would do the same thing. The focus shifted to the possibility of creating some commonalities in equipment between the CART and the IRL, whether through engines or chassis, that would make it easier and less expensive for CART teams to enter the Indianapolis 500.

Carl Haas was one of the strongest opponents of switching to the IRL formula, particularly if it was not tied to an agreement for CART and the IRL to come together to compete as a single series. In a ten-point memo to the CART Board of Directors, Haas declared that installing CART-specification engines in an IRL chassis would be "next to impossible" and warned that the company risked losing engine suppliers Honda, Toyota, Ford, and Mercedes-Benz, whom he called CART's largest advertisers.

"I could understand the chassis change if CART and the IRL were getting together," wrote Haas. "However, I do not see this happening, and therefore the change would only help the IRL, not CART. . . capitulating to the IRL rules without getting together gives the IRL a tremendous advantage.

"We are doing all of this at a time when CART should be working from strength, not weakness, especially after the results of the Indy 500 and the favorable press CART has received throughout the country," he concluded.

CART's interim CEO Bobby Rahal also targeted engine commonality as a path back to Indianapolis. For years, CART had struggled to come up with an engine formula to supersede the 2.65-liter turbocharged V8s used since the USAC era in 1969. As far back as '97, the CART Engine Committee recommended switching to a downsized version of that engine with a capacity of 1.8 liters and boost initially set to fifty-five inches. Intended as a ten-year formula, the boost would be reduced on a yearly basis to keep power and speeds in check. CART's unwillingness to commit to the new long-term formula frustrated the manufacturers.

"We've tried to push in that direction, but that advice obviously is not being taken on board," remarked Ilmor Engineering Vice President Paul Ray.

"It's been three years, and nobody's come back to us to say why that's unacceptable," added Ford Racing Program Director Bruce Wood. "Maybe the attempts to get back to Indy could have been a fly in the ointment. But it does seem that nobody wanted to hear that answer. From Ford's point of view, we're involved in NASCAR as a low technology series, so we want to see CART retain that high technology. It's very important to us."

Rahal defended CART's deliberation on such an important technical building block. "The amazing thing is that today's engine formula is more than twenty years old in its basis," he said. "That's probably the most continuous engine specification in any current formula, so whatever we do in the future, we have to be responsible about the costs to the manufacturers. We'd like to get that same kind of longevity for it, and that's why you don't just haphazardly come up with ideas.

"There are pros and cons for normally aspirated and turbocharged engines," he added. "You could probably make a very strong case either way. They each present different challenges to the manufacturers and different challenges to us as a sanctioning body. For example, normally aspirated engines would be extremely loud, and I think that would be an issue on the many street circuits we visit. A turbocharger is an excellent muffler in many respects."

CART's engine manufacturers participated in the behind-the-scenes reunification attempts that occurred in 1999 and accepted that some compromise would be necessary on their part if an accord was to be reached with the IRL.

"Here's an analogy we've used: If you assume that the technology in Formula 1 is a ten on a scale of one to ten, NASCAR is probably more like a two or a three, maybe a three and a half in terms of its technology for people who really know about it," said Toyota Racing Development President Lee White. "CART is maybe an eight. We're hoping that somewhere between a five and a seven is where we end up, and I think the other side [the IRL] is probably hoping for something between a three and a five."

In September 2000 at Laguna Seca Raceway, CART announced further reductions to turbo boost for the existing 2.65-liter engines, down to thirty-seven inches in '01 and thirty-four inches in '02, with possible additional cuts to control speeds on superspeedways. The engine development battle of the late 1990s was so intense that by 2000, Gil de Ferran broke Mauricio Gugelmin's three-year-old closed-course speed record at California Speedway, upping the mark to 241.028 mph in a Penske Reynard-Honda despite lower boost and the addition of the drag-inducing Hanford Device rear wing. CART also announced that it planned to completely change its engine formula from '03 onward, though the specification was still not determined.

The engine manufacturers believed they were being assigned the brunt of the blame for the declining quality of racing in the FedEx Championship Series, especially on short ovals where CART struggled to achieve the right balance of mechanical and aerodynamic grip to suit the more powerful engines of the era. Goodyear's departure from open-wheel racing at the end of the 1999 season didn't help matters. Once Firestone (and parent brand Bridgestone, which took over branding of CART's tires in 2002) achieved single-supplier status, tires were made much more durable, taking tire management out of a driver's strategy playbook.

The single-file nature of many of CART's oval races was in marked contrast with the IRL, which by 2000 had become famous for closely bunched "pack" races on 1.5- and 2-mile superspeedways. Similar to

NASCAR restrictor plate races at Daytona and Talladega, these IRL pack races were often thrilling to watch, but they were also exceedingly dangerous. With about three hundred less horsepower than the CART cars of the era and much more downforce, it was relatively simple for IRL drivers to run foot-to-the-floor, side-by-side for lap after lap. The closeness was artificial because of the restrictions on the cars, but it was a closeness that was often missing from CART races, which CART believed was a factor in its poor television ratings.

"Nobody likes to change, and certainly no one likes to spend money, although there are always funds used for engine development," said Rahal. "But I think there is a higher calling or higher goal here than anyone's narrow self-interests and that is to produce the best racing that we can. We don't need to be going 240 miles an hour to prove we're the fastest series in the world. We had some of our best racing when we had 725 or 750 horsepower back in 1992. At places like Milwaukee we had two and three abreast because it was the right formula, the right relationship between power and downforce compared to what we have now.

"The reality is that we have aerodynamically tried to govern the speeds over the years," he continued. "In some cases it's been successful—if we didn't have the Hanford Device at Michigan and Fontana, we'd be going 250 miles an hour and maybe even faster. But on the short ovals, that solution has not been successful. Our obligation is to produce the best racing that we can. That will drive the fan base, that will drive the TV ratings, and that will drive all the issues that seem to confront us."

While Rahal helped push through the 2001 and '02 engine specifications, he did not stick around to orchestrate CART's long-term plans. In September 2000, the Ford Motor Company hired Rahal to move to England to take over as CEO of the Formula 1 team it had purchased from Jackie and Paul Stewart and rebranded as Jaguar Racing. Rahal's tenure in F1 would last just nine months; in August 2001, he was ousted in a boardroom coup that saw F1 legend Niki Lauda assume Rahal's duties, with little more success than the American enjoyed.

By the time he returned to the U.S., Rahal was even more aware of CART's problems and the urgency to determine its future path in terms of engines. He began to push for adopting the normally aspirated IRL formula. Among the engine manufacturers, Toyota was the most willing to pursue that avenue and Honda the least. Mercedes was no longer a factor, having announced its withdrawal from the CART series with shockingly little notice in September 2000, leaving its teams other that Penske Racing (which had already switched to Honda for 2000) in a very difficult position. The Mercedes pullout was especially destructive to PacWest Racing, which ceased operations at the end of '01.

As a team owner, Rahal believed the economies of scale that could be gleaned from having the flexibility to compete in CART or the IRL—or both—was becoming a necessity.

"We need to come up with some sort of mechanism to allow teams to compete across borders between the IRL and CART," Rahal said in 2001. "More and more teams will go to Indy; [Team Rahal] is going to be going to Indy next year. That's only going to increase the need for a solution, and I think you need to have that for open-wheel racing to take its rightful place.

"I think we ought to adopt the IRL engine spec, even if you bump the rev limiter up a bit to get more power," he added. "There's always going to be a segment that says that high tech is the draw. But our audience doesn't really care whether you have three valves per cylinder or four. What they care about is the show, is their heroes, and whether the sport is being merchandised by the sponsors that participate. So I'm less inclined to get hung up by the mechanical aspects. The Can-Am was the most free mechanical series in the world, and if that was the draw, why did it disappear a long time ago?"

But the engine conundrum wasn't Rahal's problem to solve. The task fell to Joe Heitzler, who was hired as CART's new president and CEO on December 4, 2000. Heitzler, who boasted a varied resume in the broadcast communication industry, impressed the nine-man CART Delaware Board and signed a multi-year contract.

Heitzler's name was one of the last submitted to CART's search committee, but he overcame stern opposition from Long Beach Grand Prix creator Chris Pook and Rick Welts, the executive vice president and chief marketing officer of the National Basketball Association. Pook withdrew from the running, citing a conflict of interest with his employer Dover Downs Entertainment, while CART reportedly came close to a deal with Welts but they were ultimately unable to come to terms. In

2011, Welts, then president of the NBA's Phoenix Suns franchise, was the first major sports executive to come out as gay.

"The opportunity to merge a passion for open-wheel racing with my business experience fulfills a life-long dream," Heitzler stated. "I am extremely honored to have been chosen by dedicated leaders of this industry to lead the CART team into its entertainment sports future. I will strive to have all of our key groups—from investors, team owners, and drivers to sponsors, track promoters, and our management staff—to work as a team with the singular goal of providing an enhanced sports entertainment product to our dedicated fans. With our fans' dedicated participation, we will continue to grow and prosper among the rapidly changing and new sports entertainment mediums."

Before taking the reins at CART, Heitzler worked for National Mobile Television Productions Inc., where he served as president and chief operating officer since 1998. His hire was driven by what was reported as very strong links to the television industry, which remained a major hot-button topic for CART at the turn of the century. Attendance also started to slip noticeably in the late '90s, especially at oval tracks, though CART's spectator count was still much larger than that of the IRL.

"I don't see an emergency situation here," Heitzler told reporters on his first conference call. "The main weakness is a lack of visibility to the public, but mainly it will come down to dramatic tweaking of a successful product. Our drivers are a commodity, and we need to enhance their visibility and acknowledge the great drivers that built the sport. We need to include them in going forward. I'm well aware of the marketing decline, but we have a wonderful core product. No one knows that product like the team owners and our track partners and sponsors, and I believe my ability to build coalitions was what the board was after when they unanimously voted for my skill set.

"In CART, I saw a company that was looking for leadership," Heitzler added. "Everybody seemed particularly focused about making CART change. I think the issue of leadership was resolved when a unanimous board vote was asked for and received. That request, plus the granting of it, made me realize that leadership is no longer just a talking point, it's a point of action. The tone of the board is that they don't want this to be a board-driven company. They want it to be corporate-driven. And to me, development and articulation of the business plan is the sole responsibility of the CEO of CART."

Despite the turmoil that affected the second half of 2000, CART still appeared to hold the upper hand over the IRL five years into the split. But cracks in the foundation were becoming more readily apparent. Without question, the period between 2000 and '03 is when the tide turned in the Indy car split and the momentum and power shifted squarely from CART to the IRL. Target/Chip Ganassi Racing's victory in the 2000 Indianapolis 500 may have demonstrated the superiority of CART's best team on the race track, but it also revealed many of the weaknesses of the CART organization as a whole. If anything, Ganassi's Indianapolis victory somehow gave the IRL a much-needed boost. And while CART was able to keep the magnitude of its issues shielded from the public throughout 2000, the following year under Heitzler's command was nothing short of a disaster, putting the company in serious peril and allowing the IRL to seize the lead in the bitter fight for control of the sport.

CHAPTER 16

A RAPID DOWNHILL SLIDE

C ART supporters were flying high on May 27, 2001. Three high-profile CART teams—Penske Racing, Target/Chip Ganassi Racing, and Team Green—fielded entries in the IRL-sanctioned Indianapolis 500 and swept the top-six finishing positions. Leading the CART charge was Marlboro Team Penske, although federal regulations stripped the cars driven by Hélio Castroneves and Gil de Ferran of their tobacco branding on race day when they scored Roger Penske's eleventh victory (and first 1-2 finish) at Indianapolis. CART star Michael Andretti also returned to Indy and finished third for Team Green, while Ganassi's Jimmy Vasser, Bruno Junqueira, and Tony Stewart (who left the IRL after the 1998 season to embark on a NASCAR Cup Series career that netted forty-nine race wins, three championships, and enshrinement in the NASCAR Hall of Fame) finished 4-5-6. Seventh place for Eliseo Salazar in an A.J. Foyt Racing entry was the top result for an IRL regular.

But despite the clear demonstration of superiority, Roger Penske and the other CART participants refused to gloat. "This feels terrific," said Penske. "It's a great day for us and a great day for our team. Helio is something else, and I can't say enough about both of our drivers. We were strong in '94, and then we didn't make the field in '95, so we knew nothing could be taken for granted here this year."

Pressed on whether the CART drivers and teams were superior to their IRL counterparts, Penske didn't take the bait. "I don't think we need to look at the statistics to say it was a CART win over the IRL," he

LAT Images

207

said. "There's a number of fellows in the IRL who could come over and drive one of our cars, I'll tell you that.

"We came here to run the Indy 500," Penske added. "If this helps us get back together, that's important to me. One open-wheel league with Gil, Juan Montoya (who moved from CART to Formula 1 in 2001), Tony Stewart, everybody. That way we can take open-wheel to where it needs to be. Because right now we need to move it up to where it needs to be."

IRL founder Tony George also refuted the idea that his league was inferior to the CART series. "I don't look at it that way, but what the media does and how they spin it could be another thing," George commented. "Some of it was self-inflicted [pole winner Scott Sharp's first-lap crash], some of it was bad luck. Sooner or later, I'm sure all the teams will examine this day and the events of this day."

Even with the results of the Indianapolis 500 to brag about, CART backers had to keep their hubris in check because just about anything else that could go wrong for the FedEx Championship Series in 2001 did go wrong. Joe Heitzler's single year on the job (December 2000 to December 2001) was a study in crisis management from the very beginning, starting with the February cancellation of CART's race in Brazil scheduled for March 25.

CART President and CEO Heitzler angrily placed the blame squarely on the newly elected mayor of the city of Rio de Janeiro, Cesar Maia. CART had raced in Brazil since 1996, but promoter Jorge Cintra suffered severe financial difficulty in the run-up to the '98 event and was bailed out at the eleventh hour by a $2.5 million loan from CART. That debt was essentially passed on to former Formula 1 and Indy car champion Emerson Fittipaldi, who took over as the promoter of the Rio CART event from Cintra. Under Fittipaldi's promotion in 2000, the Rio race attracted its largest crowd to date of about fifty-five thousand.

"We had come to a point in our preparations for the race where we were not receiving any responsible responses from the Rio mayor's office," stated Heitzler. "In my thirty-odd years in the sports and entertainment broadcast industry, this is one of the most immature activities of this nature I have ever dealt with—unprofessional and bordering on illegal."

CART's inability to determine a long-term plan for engines was given a jolt the same month when Toyota revealed that it would start to build normally aspirated engines to IRL specifications in 2003. The announcement was viewed as a political move to force CART to adopt a similar engine to allow greater crossover between the two American open-wheel series.

But the engine negotiations were put on hold by what happened when CART attempted to make its debut at Texas Motor Speedway near Fort Worth. Texas had already gained fame for its ultra-close IRL pack races, and a significant portion of the CART community expressed concerns about the ability of the faster cars of the FedEx Championship Series to race safely on the high-banked track. Those concerns turned out to be justified, though for different reasons than anticipated.

Confirmed in late 2000 during Bobby Rahal's tenure as interim CEO, the CART race at Texas resulted from the close friendship that developed between Rahal and TMS President Eddie Gossage, who had been the PR manager for Team Rahal's longtime sponsor, Miller Brewing. Outgoing CART Chief Steward Wally Dallenbach put his doubts on record, and rumors about cancellation were widespread in the months leading up to the April 29 event.

Fears were allayed when Team Rahal driver Kenny Brack, the 1999 IRL champion, tested a CART car at Texas, running just a few miles per hour faster than IRL cars. Trying to quell fears of a driver boycott, Championship Drivers Association President Mauricio Gugelmin said reports of the race being in jeopardy were blown out of proportion.

"The truth is that the cars are already too fast at some of the places we go, and there is the potential for even more speed at Texas," Gugelmin said. "But we're going to find a solution to race there."

But CART never did actually race at Texas. Speeds were much higher than expected in practice and qualifying, as Brack claimed pole position at 233.447 mph and Paul Tracy ran a practice lap at 236.678 mph (which calculated to 239.2 mph using the IRL's longer track measurement). There were a couple of major accidents involving Cristiano da Matta and Gugelmin, whose crash was spread over more than half a mile from Turn Two to Turn Three. The experienced Brazilian was unable to explain how the accident happened. Bruised but otherwise uninjured, he credited the recently mandated HANS Device for saving his life.

Crashes at Texas were nothing new, but these crashes carried an unusual element. Neither Gugelmin nor da Matta could comprehend what happened. A series of meetings took place on Saturday afternoon into Sunday morning after twenty-one of the twenty-five drivers admitted that long runs on the twenty-four-degree banked oval caused them to experience dizziness, nausea, or visual distortion.

CART Medical Affairs Director Dr. Steve Olvey said the extent of the problem was not fully known until the regular drivers meeting Saturday afternoon. He explained that the intense vertical and lateral G-loads the CART drivers experienced when lapping the 1.482-mile superspeedway were uncharted territory for racing drivers.

"A situation developed Friday afternoon that, in my twenty-five years of being involved in motorsports, I have never heard of or never seen at any other racing venue," Olvey commented. "It came to my attention that two drivers pulled off the racetrack after long stints at over 230 miles per hour, and they pulled in because they were experiencing rather severe dizziness and light-headedness and felt that they could no longer safely control the race car. Then on Saturday, a driver who came into our medical unit for another reason said something really funny had happened to him that day when he got out of the race car. He said he couldn't stand straight or walk for four to five minutes. This led me to think that we were possibly having a problem with too high G-loading with our drivers in these cars at these speeds at this particular type of racetrack."

Tony Kanaan explained what the drivers were experiencing. "I did a long run and after a while things got kind of fuzzy," he said. "I had trouble focusing and when I slowed down for a lap it got better. Then when I got out of the car I was dizzy and I had to sit down on the pit wall. I thought it was something I ate, but then Patrick Carpentier and a couple other guys came up right then and said the same thing."

Olvey consulted with Dr. Richard Jennings, a former flight director at NASA (the American aerospace program) who then specialized in aerospace medicine at the University of Texas. "Dr. Jennings said that the human tolerance in a sitting position, whether in a boat, an airplane, or a car, in terms of vertical loading is somewhere between four and five G, depending on the person," Olvey remarked. "He also said that because we experience high lateral Gs due to the cornering of these cars, that effect is additive and actually can be worsened by that situation, and all those things can be aggravated by dehydration, heat, and by the duration of the exposure to those Gs.

"I then got a telemetry printout from one of our teams, because none of us knew what the vertical G-loads were because in testing, none of the speeds approached the numbers that were produced this weekend. The maximum instantaneous G-loading over a lap was 4.33 Gs, and a force of 3.36 Gs was sustained throughout the banking at either end of the track. Our lateral Gs are somewhat over 5 in different cars in particular situations. I notified key officials and we brought all the drivers together to discuss this. Dr. Jennings related that when Gs are 4 or higher, like in a fighter plane, pilots are required to wear a G-suit.

"I don't know of another instance, and neither did Dr. Jennings, of any incident when this was a problem in racing cars on closed course tracks," Olvey concluded. "We know at this particular racetrack that you can relatively safely run a race in the realm of around 225 miles per hour and below. Over 225 I cannot give you an exact figure, but there appears to be a threshold somewhere around 230 and above where it becomes an issue. The combination of vertical and lateral Gs is unusual, and it's never been an issue at any other racetrack. There is an edge we don't want to go beyond."

Several solutions were discussed in a hastily convened owners meeting, including cutting turbo boost, building a chicane to slow the cars, or utilizing the TMS infield road course. But all were deemed impossible, impractical, or laden with legal issues, and two hours before the scheduled start of the race, CART CEO Heitzler delivered the news that the event was canceled due to safety concerns.

"I am confident that we have exhausted every available option to find a solution," Heitzler said. "This decision has the full support of Firestone and the engine manufacturers. Once we processed the data we gathered over the last eighteen hours, we concluded that there was no alternative."

Although they were aware of the public relations implications for themselves and the CART series, the drivers backed the cancellation.

"All in all, we found the limit of our bodies," noted Gugelmin, whose Friday accident featured impacts measured at 66 and 113 G. "The speed was not a surprise, but the physical effects were. It's all about safety, and I'm very impressed with the way Joe handled the situation and the way he stood behind the drivers. The track did what it could to improve things and they did a fantastic job, but these cars are just too fast. I only felt dizzy after a twenty-five-lap run, but it wasn't a factor in my accident."

Not surprisingly, fans were not impressed, creating signs with slogans like "Cowards Aren't Racing Today." TMS President Gossage was also extremely upset.

"The bottom line point is CART should have known," Gossage stated. "We questioned the speed in meetings, in letters. We even offered some of our own suggestions about what to do to the cars. On April 21, I got a letter from Joe Heitzler saying, 'CART is ready, willing, and able to run the race.' That was in response to some of the questions that we were still raising as recently as ten days ago about the cars and the speeds.

"There's a credibility issue between CART and Texas Motor Speedway, and between CART and the fans, and that won't make it easy," he added. "I think everyone had the best intentions, it just didn't come off. I think the world of Joe Heitzler. He's a first-class guy, and I hope he has the strength, literally, to carry this thing and right this ship and push it forward every day. I personally wouldn't have that job for a million dollars. They have a great, great product and great talent. They need to find a way to go forward and have their races and not have things like this and Brazil occur. Fans don't believe you after a while, and that's unfortunate."

Michael Andretti had a bitter rivalry with Rahal throughout his career, finishing second in the standings after all three of Rahal's CART championship seasons. Reflecting on the aborted Texas weekend, Andretti was unusually outspoken.

"It was Rahal's fault," Andretti said. "It was done for the wrong reasons, because he's friends with Eddie Gossage and because this is the biggest market for his sponsor, Miller Beer. We said the track wasn't safe for years, but when Rahal quit driving and became the CEO, suddenly it was safe. The test was a joke. Wally didn't want to run here but it got put on the schedule. Not racing was the right thing to do.

"It wasn't the speed, it was the G-forces," Andretti added. "For a long time everyone always wondered when we would find the limit, and on that weekend, we did. Joe did a good job with the situation and he took the driver's side. I got blamed and I took a lot of heat for that. Ever since then, people said I was trying to kill CART."

TMS ultimately brought suit against CART and several CART officials in the 393rd District Court in Denton County, Texas. "We wanted to avoid this suit, but CART has not been very responsive regarding the losses and damages suffered by Texas Motor Speedway and its fans," said Gossage. "The Speedway has begun the process of refunding millions of dollars worth of tickets held by fans. Unfortunately, CART has refused to refund the purse and sanction fee paid by the Speedway. Our fans deserve to get their money back, and the Speedway deserves to get its money back as well." The Texas lawsuit was settled out of court in October 2001 for a reported $3.5 million.

Dallenbach, the respected chief steward of the CART series from 1979-2004, has no regrets about standing his ground and insisting on the cancellation. "I said I'm not going to ignore the fact that we could kill somebody here—it's not worth it," he reflected to author Gordon Kirby. "I said we should cancel or postpone the race until we could figure out a way to come back and put on a safe race. By then, twenty thousand fans were on the way into the track. It was a tough situation, but I said I wasn't going to put these guys on death row. Some people called us names and inevitably there was a lawsuit, but I wasn't going to let that race happen with the cars we had in those days."

By the time the CART series arrived in Michigan for the Detroit Grand Prix in mid-June, the spectre of the cancellation still somewhat overshadowed the dominant performance by CART teams in the Indianapolis 500. Then an even bigger political problem for CART developed during the Detroit weekend. "Valvegate" was the latest and most public indication of the intense multimillion dollar corporate war that simmered between Honda and Toyota.

Over the off-season, a Honda engineer moved over to the Toyota camp. The new Toyota man informed his superiors that Honda (and, as it transpires, Ford-Cosworth) had designed a plenum chamber that aerodynamically created a low-pressure area near a measuring sensor that manipulated the CART-issued pop-off valve into allowing an extra two to three inches of turbo boost—worth up to seventy-five horsepower. As a key area of engine development, the plenum chamber was regulated closely by CART, and all manufacturers were required to submit their designs for approval from the sanctioning body in advance. Honda claims it followed that procedure to the letter.

"Were we cheating? In my mind no, because we had everything approved," stated Honda Performance Development (HPD) President Robert Clarke. "Was there some advantage to our design? I hope so, because that is what racing is all about."

Toyota believed that even if Honda's plenum had been declared legal, its function violated the spirit of the rules. Faced with a significant horsepower deficit, Toyota had two options. It could embark on a hasty and expensive redesign of its plenum. Or it could find another way to negate Honda's advantage, which had been brought to light most graphically at Twin Ring Motegi, where most of the Toyota cars were clustered at the back of the grid for the annual battle between the Japanese titans on home ground. Ironically, Ford-Cosworth beat them both for the fourth consecutive year. So Toyota brought the matter to CART's attention. Since Honda technically wasn't cheating, there wasn't much CART could do to address Toyota's concerns. But Toyota had a bargaining chip to play with: its previously announced intention to build IRL-specification engines in 2003, with the unspoken implication that the company would also leave CART.

During the five-week gap in the FedEx Championship Series schedule while the focus was on Indianapolis, Toyota took its evidence about Honda's plenum advantage to CART. "I can't prove that anyone cheats," said Lee White, manager of Toyota Racing Development. "But we proved in theory that it could be done. There's a Bernoulli effect you can achieve by very carefully crafting your plenum design. It's within the rules, but since Motegi a year ago, a huge engineering and corporate effort has gone into this. It's been refined to a high level. We showed our data to [CART's technical bosses] Kirk Russell and Jeff Horton and suggested some things so that everybody was playing on the same field, not at opposite ends of the continent."

Not only did Toyota inform CART that it believed Honda was cheating, it provided a suggestion for how to stop it: A three-quarter-inch spacer mounted at the base of the pop-off valve where it connects to the plenum was found to negate the aerodynamic effect that Honda and

Ford were achieving within the plenum. Neither Honda, Ford, nor their drivers teams or engineers knew anything about the spacer until it was introduced at a CART-sanctioned aerodynamic test session at Michigan Speedway on the Tuesday prior to the Detroit race weekend. CART had already asked Honda and Ford to tune their engines to thirty-six inches of boost for the test (rather than the normal thirty-seven) in an experimental effort to reduce speeds. Toyota also was issued the modified valve for a rookie test at Mid-Ohio the same day.

Penske was one of the teams testing at Michigan, and Tim Cindric recalled his shock at being issued the modified pop-off valve. "Gil de Ferran ran a few laps at 196 miles per hour and reported terrible boost fluctuations," Cindric said. "We removed the spacer so we could begin to accurately evaluate the items that we were told in advance that we were there to evaluate for CART. A couple days later at the Franchise Board meeting, they talked about their 'intent' to implement it, and said they 'wanted' to. But everything was directed at slowing the cars at Michigan. Nothing was ever said about running it at Detroit in the board meeting. Nothing was decided or finalized."

Despite a lack of formal approval from the Franchise Board, on Friday morning at Detroit, CART issued Competition Bulletin 22.1, which stated, "All race cars must be fitted with the extended housing manifold pressure relief valve during all practice, qualifying, and race on-track activities." The Honda entries were held out of the morning practice, and by Friday evening, Ford-Cosworth and Honda both filed protests with CART.

"Since the Michigan test there were hints that CART might like us to run the spacer in the future," said Cosworth USA President Ian Bisco. "But there was nothing about mandating it in Detroit. We are challenging the way this new piece of equipment was introduced without adequate time to evaluate and test the way it would affect our engines. This is a protest based on the principle of the way it was introduced more than a protest of the piece itself. We tried to get CART to delay the introduction of the spacer for a couple of races in order to enable us to properly evaluate it, but they didn't want to play ball."

On Friday night, Honda's six-point official protest was unanimously denied by a CART board of three judges. CART said in a statement that it informed the teams present at Michigan and Mid-Ohio that it would use the modified valve beginning at Detroit. Kirk Russell, CART's vice president of competition, added: "As the sanctioning body, CART has the obligation to implement any changes it deems necessary to ensure the integrity of the sport as well as for the best interest of all competitors. The valves are the property of CART and maintained by the sanctioning body to ensure the operation of all valves is as identical as possible."

Despite its belief that the extended pop-off valve had more of an adverse effect on its engine compared to the competition, Honda finished 1-2 at Detroit. But the events of the Detroit weekend, along with the eventual resolution to the conflict (a July 2 appeal ruled in Honda's favor and required the standard, pre-Detroit pop-off valve for Toronto and the next two races on the Michigan and Chicago ovals, but Toyota immediately appealed and the spacer valve was mandated for the rest of the 2001 season) proved immensely damaging to CART.

"This is extremely frustrating for Honda," said HPD President Clarke. "The relationship between CART and the manufacturers is based on trust and I feel CART has totally violated that relationship. This was totally in the wrong direction as far as building relationships and trust that can lure manufacturers to the series and keep them in the series. The biggest issue is that one manufacturer had prior knowledge of this and was given an opportunity to test and evaluate the new valve. The actual decision statement by the appellate judges, combined with quotes and comments that came out in the press before that, show that there was clear indication of collusion between CART and Toyota. CART and Toyota admitted that Toyota tested the spacer on the dyno. They knew exactly the effect it would have on their engine. They tested other ideas as well and ultimately decided on the spacer."

American Honda Executive Vice President Tom Elliott was even more upset. "I'm very unhappy," Elliott said. "CART approved our plenum chamber. They approved every aspect of the engine. In the eight years we've been in CART, I've never seen anything handled as poorly, and to do it in collusion with one of the engine suppliers causes us great concern. It really does make me question why we're here. I seriously question the value of our long-term interest in CART."

Barry Green, a Honda-affiliated team owner, said the way CART handled the pop-off valve controversy was something it could not overcome. But Green thinks CART also failed to provide Heitzler the required guidance and advice he needed to make the decision. "I think that was perhaps one of the biggest messes CART ever made," Green said. "I begged the board to step in, and the board should have stepped in and insisted on understanding what was going on. I don't think Joe Heitzler had any idea how damaging this argument could get. Nothing against Toyota; if Toyota thought one of the engine manufacturers was pushing the envelope, they should take it to CART. I'm not sure really how, why, or what went wrong.

"Perhaps Joe just didn't understand what the argument was really all about," Green continued. "Certainly the way it was handled politically was devastating. But I would go on record as saying that CART's engine manufacturer problems started two or three years before that. The Franchise Board couldn't decide on a direction, for whatever reason, and CART could not provide good direction for the company on the engine side. This went on and on while everybody was busy trying to win races, we never paid enough attention to it and we never got a reasonable direction and a comfort level for the manufacturers."

Honda was already unhappy with the way Toyota altered the fundamental relationship between engine manufacturers and teams. It was no accident that Chip Ganassi, Carl Haas, and Pat Patrick all joined the Toyota camp within a short period of time; Toyota started offering those team owners considerable financial inducement.

"When we first found out about Ganassi and the actual numbers that Toyota was throwing, I met with Andrew Craig in 1999 and said, 'A bad thing is starting to happen here and you really need to get a handle on it,'" related HPD's Clarke. "I said, 'They're going to ruin the series. It's easy to imagine what's going to happen now because every team in the paddock is going to want that kind of a deal.' Andrew's reaction was, 'That's great! The teams are going to be well-supported. It's not going to be a problem.'

"I told him: 'The problem now is that the teams are now dependent upon the engine manufacturers at a level that they have never been before,'" Clarke continued. "When we first got into the program, the relationship between the teams and the engine manufacturers was such that the teams didn't trust the engine manufacturers because the engines were leased, and they weren't allowed to see what was going on and to work on the engines. I said that relationship was going in a direction where the manufacturers were going to have even more control, not only of the teams but ultimately of the series. And that's what happened."

Heitzler's circumstances got even more difficult when a Steve Mayer-penned story in *National Speed Sport News* revealed that the CART CEO's résumé was deceptive. Still, he managed to hang on in spite of his critics and was even voted chairman of the board in July 2001.

In September 2001, Toyota flexed its power to an even greater extent. It announced that the only racing engines it would build for '03 and beyond would be to the IRL's already announced specifications. CART had still not committed to *any* future engine platform, and Toyota's move seemed to force the sanctioning body's hand. On October 4, within days of Toyota's IRL-only statement, the CART team owners voted to introduce an IRL-like normally aspirated engine formula in '03. Only Gerald Forsythe voted against the move, and Mo Nunn abstained. Forsythe, the largest shareholder among CART's team owners, was incensed by the decision. He insisted the team owners were not empowered to make a major rule change and said he would resort to all legal means to reverse the decision.

"I question whether the Franchise Board can make a decision that affects the future of CART," Forsythe declared. "I believe the [Delaware] board of directors is the only group who can make a decision like that. I don't consider what they did valid. The Franchise Board is mandated to determine rules, regulations, and venues. It's not their mandate to make long-term decisions that affect CART, and this is certainly a decision of that type. That decision, or whatever they want to call it, is not going to hold up."

Forsythe had emerged as one of CART's strongest proponents. He was the company's largest individual shareholder, with holdings just under the federal 10 percent threshold, and he vowed to take on a greater leadership role. "We don't need to be associated with the IRL," he said. "We're a separate series that is very different technically and as far as venues and so forth that has so much to offer the race fan. And you and

I know that the merger of the two series will never happen. What we have to do is focus on the business of our company. One of the reasons I've been successful in business is to differentiate my product from my competition and that's what CART has to do. We are a very different product from the IRL and must maintain that difference. I have absolutely no doubts about that. I believe in the future of CART and I want to do everything I can to make sure it's a bright future. It's not as bleak as it might appear on the surface."

But shortly after Forsythe uttered those words at the 2001 Houston Grand Prix, things did get worse for CART. Eight days after the announcement of the normally aspirated engine formula for '03, Honda revealed its intention to withdraw from CART competition at the end of '02. Along with Team Penske and driver Gil de Ferran, Honda won the CART championship for the second year in a row in '01, and Honda had actually powered every champion driver in the series dating to 1996. But the company's lack of confidence in CART as an organization put it in a position where departure was the only option.

"CART's problems have been ongoing, and this year, there was the cancellation of the Rio race, the Texas situation, then the (pop-off valve) spacer," said HPD's Robert Clarke. "We had growing concerns about CART, but when the spacer issue hit, it brought it to a whole new level. Things came out of that process that were very disturbing to Honda, and in our minds, CART was basically on notice. We were waiting to see if CART was able to conduct itself in a professional and consistent manner as an organization."

Honda publicly maintained that the IRL's heavily regulated low-tech 3.5-liter package held no interest to the company. "For an engineer, it's an act of frustration and we are opposed to what would be a spec engine," Clarke affirmed. "If you want us to build an Aurora engine and put a Honda badge on it, we're not interested. It doesn't meet any of our objectives, which are technology development and people development."

Honda had long made its lack of enthusiasm for an IRL-specification engine well known (in direct opposition to Toyota), and that had contributed heavily to CART missing a March 2001 deadline to set its own '03 engine regulations. But by this stage, Honda's view seemed increasingly in the minority. Many factions within the sport, notably Toyota, believed it made sense for CART to adopt IRL specs to make it easier for CART teams to race in the Indianapolis 500—the only IRL race that really mattered to any of the engine manufacturers or teams. By late '01, the common wisdom was that a single engine formula was the only way CART and the IRL could ever unite to form a single open-wheel championship, which the sport desperately needed as it continued to lose ground to NASCAR in the American sports marketplace.

Behind the scenes, CART was dealing with additional crises. The company's Delaware board had undergone several changes, with its twelve members now split equally between team owners and outside business professionals. A pair of outside investors with holdings just under the 10 percent threshold—Jon Vaninni and newly installed board member James Grosfeld—began to call for Joe Heitzler's ouster, with the idea of replacing him with Long Beach Grand Prix founder Chris Pook.

Gerald Forsythe was extremely unhappy with Grosfeld and Vaninni's attempts to stronghold company management, and Dover Downs Entertainment (DDE) sent CART a strongly worded letter warning the company that individual board members were tortiously interfering with Pook's employment with DDE, where he held a lifetime contract.

"Now there is an effort to oust Joe after less than a year on the job. . . . What are certain people thinking?" queried Forsythe in a November 28, 2001, letter to CART board members, specifically calling out Grosfeld and Vannini. "This is a foolish course of conduct. I wholly and unequivocally, together with other board members, support Joe. Those of you who have been on the board for a while will recall how in the past CART has been crucified in the press for our 'revolving door' presidency. I have the single largest investment in CART, am a team owner, and own race events. As such, I have more at stake than anyone and will not stand idly by while certain individuals pursue their own agendas to the detriment of CART and its shareholders. . . . I urge each of you to consider your fiduciary obligation to do what is best for CART and its shareholders. Self-interest and individual motivations have no place on this board."

Forsythe's pleas went unheeded. In a nine-hour board meeting on December 4, 2001, Heitzler was forced to resign as CART's CEO just a year and a day into his tenure, agreeing to relinquish day-to-day running of the company as soon as a successor could be found. However, Heitzler remained as the chairman of the board, prompting one board member who asked not to be identified to call it "a nice, civil compromise" and adding that had the matter come to a vote, Heitzler was looking at a vote of ten to one against his remaining.

As if CART's fortunes couldn't get any worse, Penske Racing announced two days later that it was withdrawing from the CART series and switching allegience to the IRL, with immediate effect. "It was a decision made with our principal sponsor based on our collective business interests and objectives for 2002," explained Team President Tim Cindric.

Penske won the 2000 and '01 CART championships with Gil de Ferran and also crossed over to claim a 1-2 finish in the '01 Indianapolis 500, where Hélio Castroneves scored the victory. But the team was not allowed to run full Marlboro livery on the cars on race day at Indy due to stricter U.S. tobacco advertising laws that allowed only one sport series sponsorship. Philip Morris USA was also unhappy with the increasingly international slant of the CART schedule, with two more races outside the U.S. to be added in '02, when only ten of nineteen races were set to run in the United States. The IRL still ran exclusively on ovals in the USA, with an expanded fifteen-race '02 schedule.

"We have enjoyed Marlboro Team Penske's tremendous successes in the CART series over the years and we have developed special relationships with the CART community," said Ina Broeman, who headed the Marlboro Racing program for Philip Morris USA. "However, since Philip Morris USA only markets its products within the United States and its territories and our intent is to communicate with adult smokers who attend races in the United States, we believe that the IRL is more closely aligned with our business interests and objectives for 2002."

With Heitzler ousted as CART CEO, attention quickly turned to Pook, who came close to landing CART's top job in late 2000, before his withdrawal from the search process opened the door for Heitzler. Second chances rarely come around in the corporate business world, but Pook's contract obligations to DDE were quickly resolved and he was elected as CART's president and chief executive officer in the company's December 18 board meeting.

Heitzler's tenure as chairman was short-lived, and not without drama. In March 2002, CART sued Heitzler, accusing him of fraud and unauthorized expenditures. Heitzler countersued, and he filed another suit seeking $20 million from team owners Carl Haas and Pat Patrick for character defamation. The suits were settled out of court in '03.

Pook was CART's fourth chief executive in the last eighteen months, and the eleventh in the company's twenty-three-year history. "The board believes that Mr. Pook has the experience in the motor racing industry necessary to guide CART during these critical times," stated Grosfeld, who was the second-largest individual shareholder behind Forsythe in the race-sanctioning organization. "His reputation in the industry, significant shareholder support, and outstanding business accomplishments made Mr. Pook the logical candidate for this position. We believe Mr. Pook has the necessary skills and contacts to immediately make a positive impact on the Company and our sport. We expect and will demand results from Chris, and similarly, he expects and will receive our support as he leads this company forward."

Certainly Chris Pook commanded respect around the industry, but he joined CART one year later than many observers had expected or hoped. The question moving forward was whether the man who many predicted could be the organization's savior had arrived a year too late.

CHAPTER 17

BEYOND HOPE

C hris Pook arrived at Championship Auto Racing Teams in December 2001 with quite a reputation. For twenty-five years, the Long Beach Grand Prix (LBGP), which Pook created in the mid-seventies to host Formula 1 before switching to the PPG CART IndyCar World Series in 1984, had formed a blueprint for the kind of street races in urban areas that CART grew to embrace throughout the '80s and '90s. The LBGP spawned more than a dozen copycat events and was frequently credited with sparking the redevelopment of the City of Long Beach. But its sustained popularity over the years was undoubtedly also linked to Southern California's fundamental love of cars and car culture, and the LBGP's success was generally the exception to the rule. The vast majority of CART's street course events went bust within a few years. Still, as the Godfather of Long Beach and arguably the man responsible for creating the modern-era rush to street courses, Pook carried a great deal of credibility as CART's new leader.

His appointment was met with enthusiasm by the CART community. "I supported it 300 percent, and this is the best Christmas gift CART could have dreamed of," said Mario Andretti. "Finally, the owners made a decent decision."

"I think he is the only guy that can generate the confidence among all the constituents that the decisions and plans that he makes will grow the sport and make it better," noted Bobby Rahal. "So I think it's a good day for CART. I think Joe Heitzler walked into a snake's nest. I think some of the things he did were quite good, but if you don't have the confidence

John Orecwicz

of the constituents, it's hard to rule. Unfortunately, he did not have that confidence."

The early signs were promising. Within six weeks, Pook and his staff were able to do something that his predecessors—Joe Heitzler, Rahal, and Andrew Craig—were unable to do in six years: they announced details of CART's new technical formula for the future. Purists were dismayed to learn that despite a compelling offer from Ford-Cosworth for a less expensive, more durable version of the longstanding 2.65-liter V8 turbocharged package, CART essentially adopted the Indy Racing League's 3.5-litre normally aspirated engines and corresponding chassis. The plan called for common tubs that would utilize CART's aerodynamic package, including the Hanford Device on superspeedways, but with less restrictive engine regulations compared to the IRL that would include traction control and a 12,000 rpm rev limit (the IRL limit was 10,500). The CART cars would also use a proprietary gearbox, replacing a known problem component in the IRL.

CART believed the rationale behind embracing the IRL spec was obvious: The simpler equipment would theoretically cut costs and make it easier for CART teams to cross over and race at the Indianapolis 500, the only IRL event that they cared about. To that end, CART instituted a series of price caps ($2.7 million for an annual engine lease, $60,000 for a semi-spec gearbox) that were expected to cut the era's $10 million per car budgets in half. The new rules were set to run from 2003–06.

With the loss of Penske Racing for the 2002 season, CART's car count was down to twenty. The legendary team's move to the Indy Racing League also created an intriguing storyline for the IRL. Penske, the most successful team in the history of Indy car racing, and coming off two consecutive CART championships with Gil de Ferran, would provide the first major challenge to Sam Hornish Jr., the IRL's hot, young, American star. A race winner in Formula Atlantic and a product of the CART ladder system, Ohio native Hornish took over the Panther Racing IRL entry from the retiring Scott Goodyear in '01 and immediately emerged as the class of the league. Hornish won six of thirteen races in '01 and easily claimed the IRL championship as American drivers finished first through fourth in the standings.

Tony Hulman and Wilbur Shaw, the men credited with saving the Indianapolis Motor Speedway from potential redevelopment. *Indianapolis Motor Speedway*

Tony Hulman is seen with his grandson, Tony George, circa 1961. *Indianapolis Motor Speedway*

A.J. Foyt won the Indy 500 for the first of four times in 1961 in this Trevis roadster. *Indianapolis Motor Speedway*

Crew Chief Jim McGee pushes Mario Andretti out to qualify in 1969.
Dave Friedman/LAT Images

The front row for the 1972 Indianapolis 500 (left to right): Mark Donohue, Peter Revson, and pole winner Bobby Unser. *Indianapolis Motor Speedway*

Tony Hulman took a victory lap with A.J. Foyt after the 1977 Indy 500. Hulman died five months later. *Indianapolis Motor Speedway*

Rick Mears was the brightest star to emerge from Indy cars in the 1970s.
Indianapolis Motor Speedway

During his short tenure as IMS President, John Cooper helped create and abolish the Championship Racing League. *Indianapolis Motor Speedway*

First raced in 1979, the Chaparral 2K set the blueprint for every Indy car since. *John Oreovicz*

U.E. "Pat" Patrick was key in the formation of CART in 1978. He also sparked the company's public offering in 1998. *Championship Auto Racing Teams*

Dan Gurney (left) and Roger Penske (right) were the other key figures in CART's creation. *Michael Levitt/LAT Images*

The rapid evolution of the Indy car can be seen in Bobby Unser's three 500 winning cars from 1968, 1975, and 1981. *John Oreovicz*

A new wave of road racing trained stars emerged in the 1980s, including (left to right) Michael Andretti, Bobby Rahal, and Al Unser Jr. *Paul Webb*

The Long Beach Grand Prix's switch from Formula 1 to Indy cars in 1984 gave CART a boost. Mario Andretti leads the field in 1985. *Paul Webb*

The Unser family (left to right: Al Jr., Bobby, and Al) have combined to win nine Indy 500s and seven season championships. *Indianapolis Motor Speedway*

Named president of the Indianapolis Motor Speedway when he turned 30, Tony George was often in conflict with "the car owner group" known as CART. *INDYCAR*

Al Unser Jr. leads Scott Goodyear across the Yard of Bricks by 0.043 second in the closest Indy 500 finish on record. *Indianapolis Motor Speedway*

Driving for Newman/Haas Racing, Nigel Mansell made a huge impact on the CART series in 1993 and '94. *LAT Images*

Andrew Craig (right, with Roger Penske) led CART from 1994-2000, but had the bad luck to be in charge when Tony George formed the IRL. *LAT Images*

Andrew Craig (left) and Formula 1 head Bernie Ecclestone (right) walk through the Long Beach pits. LBGP founder Chris Pook can be seen between them. *LAT Images*

The Penske-commissioned Mercedes-Benz 500I engine won the 1994 Indianapolis 500, to the displeasure of Tony George and USAC. *Illustration by Tony Matthews*

Alex Zanardi was a two-time CART series champion, but he never raced in the Indianapolis 500. *LAT Images*

Arie Luyendyk (seen here in 1997) is the only driver to win the Indy 500 in CART- and IRL-spec cars. His speed records may never be broken. *Indianapolis Motor Speedway*

The IRL was a great springboard for Tony Stewart, who won the 1997 championship prior to embarking on a successful career in NASCAR. *Indianapolis Motor Speedway*

Rising star Greg Moore was killed in 1999 before he had a chance to truly demonstrate his talent for Team Penske. *Paul Webb*

Defending CART champion Juan Pablo Montoya made winning the 2000 Indy 500 against IRL competition look easy. *Phil Abbott/ LAT Images*

Joe Heitzler's year on the job as CART CEO was a study in crisis management. *LAT Images*

Paul Tracy was not the only one who believed IRL/CART politics denied him a rightful victory in the 2002 Indianapolis 500. *Indianapolis Motor Speedway*

Earning three series titles between 2001-06, Sam Hornish Jr. gave the IRL a young American champion to promote. *INDYCAR*

Long Beach Grand Prix founder Chris Pook joined CART a year too late to save the company. *LAT Images*

Gerald Forsythe fielded Indy cars since the early 1980s, and he eventually became CART's strongest supporter. *Michael Levitt/ LAT Images*

Chris Pook is flanked by Craig Pollock (left) and Kevin Kalkhoven (right) at the PK racing announcement in 2003. Within a year, Kalkhoven was part-owner of Champ Car. *LAT Images*

Carl Haas (left) and Paul Newman (right) remained loyal to Champ Car and won four consecutive championships with driver Sébastien Bourdais. *Paul Webb*

Michael Andretti (left) jumped from CART to the IRL in 2003 when he transitioned to team ownership, winning titles with Tony Kanaan (center) and Dan Wheldon (right). *Indianapolis Motor Speedway*

Mario Andretti and Paul Newman worked tirelessly to help end the Indy car split, and Mario remains a key advocate for the sport. *Joe Skibinski/INDYCAR*

Surrounded by drivers, Tony George (left) and Kevin Kalkhoven (right) announce the amalgamation of Champ Car into the IRL IndyCar Series in February 2008. *LAT Images*

Justin Wilson earned arguably the most popular race win of the modern era when he ended a lengthy Penske/Ganassi winning streak at Watkins Glen in 2009. *John Oreovicz*

Randy Bernard was in many ways a breath of fresh air for INDYCAR. *INDYCAR*

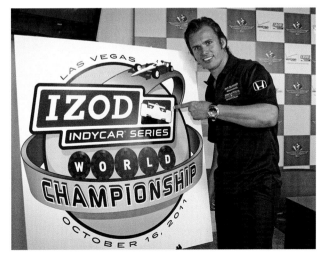

Pack racing finally turned deadly in 2011 when Dan Wheldon was killed at Las Vegas Motor Speedway. *INDYCAR*

Renamed after development driver Dan Wheldon, the Dallara DW12 was difficult to drive in early testing. *John Oreovicz*

Dario Franchitti and Scott Dixon are the sport's top twenty-first-century performers, combining to win ten IndyCar Series championships. *Chris Owens/ INDYCAR*

The 2015-17 "Aero kit" era was a costly dead end. *Honda Racing*

In 2018, Josef Newgarden unveiled the Universal Aero Kit that redressed the basic Dallara chassis that had been in use since 2012. *John Oreovicz*

The Dallara IR18 brough back styling cues common to cars from the CART era. Ed Carpenter is seen here. *Chris Owens/ INDYCAR*

Longtime Hulman & Co. executive Jeff Belskus (left) led the transition from the Tony George era to Mark Miles (right). *Indianapolis Motor Speedway*

On the day the sale of the Speedway to Roger Penske was announced, Tony George became emotional on the dais. *Chris Owens/INDYCAR*

Members of the Hulman-George family pose with Greg and Roger Penske on November 4, 2020. *Indianapolis Motor Speedway*

More than 110 years after its construction, the Indianapolis Motor Speedway continues to thrive as The World's Greatest Race Course. *Indianapolis Motor Speedway*

Hornish started 2002 where he left off by defeating the Penske drivers in a straight fight in the season opener at Homestead-Miami Speedway. He added another win at California Speedway and arrived in Indianapolis for the month of May leading the IRL standings. The big story at Indy from a CART standpoint was that Team Green entered cars for all three of its CART drivers—Paul Tracy and Dario Franchitti, along with Michael Andretti, who had tested the water in '01. But with Team Penske running full-time in the IRL, and Ganassi Racing and Mo Nunn Racing already splitting their efforts with full-time entries in both open-wheel series, the CART-vs.-IRL storyline was not as compelling as it was in 2000 and '01.

Until race day.

As the laps wound down near the end of the 2002 Indianapolis 500, Penske's Hélio Castroneves was in position to win for the second consecutive year—only this time, his victory for Penske would represent the IRL instead of CART. But Castroneves was running low on fuel, and he was being rapidly reeled in by Tracy in a Team Green entry with ties to CART. Tracy embraced his role as Indy car racing's resident villain. He was a vocal opponent of the IRL, famously calling the cars "Crapwagons."

This much is not disputed: Tracy was racing Castroneves for the lead on lap 199 of 200, and he executed a clean pass on the Brazilian in Turn Three. But almost simultaneously, a crash between Laurent Redon and Buddy Lazier occurred behind them in Turn Two. Caution lights were illuminated around the track and on the dash panel of every car, and the yellow and white flags were displayed at the start/finish line. Tracy completed the lap ahead of Castroneves, and the scoring monitors and pylons briefly showed Tracy as the leader after 199 laps.

For a minute or so, it appeared that a CART team had rained on the IRL's parade at Indianapolis for the third consecutive year. But Indy Racing League Chief Steward Brian Barnhart ruled that the caution period for the accident began before Tracy made his pass, and he therefore declared Castroneves the race winner under yellow. Hélio celebrated the victory in his usual fashion by climbing the fence lining the track before heading to Victory Circle for the traditional bottle of milk and the presentation of the Borg-Warner Trophy.

Team Green owner Barry Green believed video evidence and testimony from other drivers (including Hornish, who exclaimed "Tracy just won!" on in-car footage) showed Tracy completed his pass prior to the instant the yellow caution light blinked on. Green filed a protest, which was denied by Barnhart a day later. Green then filed an appeal, which IRL founder Tony George elected to hear himself. Team Green and Team Penske presented evidence on June 17, and George issued his decision on July 3.

George could have asked an independent individual or a panel of experts to rule on the matter. Instead, many industry insiders believe he unnecessarily introduced CART vs. IRL politics into the equation by appointing himself judge and jury. Few objective observers believed George would award the victory to a CART team and driver and take it away from the IRL's flagship organization, no matter how compelling the evidence might be.

So the decision that kept Castroneves and Penske as the winners didn't surprise many people. But no one expected the case behind the decision to be as weak as it was. And George's presentation to the media was shockingly inept. Never known as a great public speaker, the Indy chief panicked when he found the last page of his prepared notes missing. He only regained his composure after a series of frantic hand signals from IRL Communications Director Fred Nation.

An eleven-page decision bearing George's signature based its case on the determination that the order cars are placed in at the commencement of a yellow caution period is a "judgment decision not subject to protest or appeal." However, George said he decided to hear the appeal "because of the unique facts and circumstances of this situation" and the Indianapolis 500's status as "the biggest single day sporting event in the world."

That portion of the decision alone prevented Green from fighting for his cause. But George also claimed the IRL had data (provided by Penske but never released to Green or to the public) that demonstrated Castroneves backed off on the entry to Turn Three because his in-car caution light flashed on for the Redon-Lazier accident.

Barry Green was informed of George's decision by fax a few minutes before George's shaky presentation to the media. Two hours later and about eight miles away from IMS at his northwest Indianapolis race shop, the losing team owner presented his case to the press.

"The only question that I believe we had to answer was whether car number 26"—Tracy—"was past car number 3"—Castroneves—"before the yellow light came on and the caution period began," Green said. "Rule 7.14 in the IRL Rulebook says that racing will cease with the display of the yellow flag or the yellow light. Now I'll read page seven from Tony's decision this morning, which says, 'During a race, a yellow caution period begins when Race Control calls it on the radio.' Folks, that is not what the Rulebook says. Racing does not cease until the display of the yellow flag or yellow light. That is what the Rulebook says."

Green also believed that his team of mathematicians and videographers had accurately reconstructed the sequence of events in Turn Three that took place between the time of the Redon-Lazier accident and the moment the yellow track light came on. By their calculations, using synchronized, time-stamped video, Tracy had just nosed in front of Castroneves when the yellow light flashed on as the pair exited Turn Three.

"Castroneves said in a sworn affadavit that he saw the yellow dash light and lifted off," Green said. "But we can verify that he never lifted off until he got to the exit of Turn Three. That is where the wall light came on, and Paul Tracy is clearly ahead prior to the wall light, after the wall light and after the 3 car lifted off. Our calculations demonstrate that Castroneves could not have lifted until after Paul had passed him."

To many observers, Castroneves's disputed victory at Indy in 2002 was the second of Penske's then-record twelve Indy wins with an asterisk next to it. Bobby Unser was penalized a lap after winning the 1981 race for Penske when postrace video analysis showed that he illegally passed a line of cars under caution while exiting the pits. There was no protest, but when the official race results were announced the following morning (a long-standing Indianapolis tradition), USAC awarded the victory to second-place finisher Mario Andretti and Patrick Racing. Penske appealed the decision, and some four months later, the win was given back to Unser, who was fined $40,000. The friendship between the drivers was seriously impacted, and to this day, Andretti often wears the '81 Indy 500 winner's ring that he was presented at the Victory Banquet.

"I guess you could just say that I am very disappointed in Tony George and the IRL," said Green. "I believe Tony lost his way here. I have to feel sorry for Mr. Penske, really, because I think this race is not going to sit well with him. It cannot after he saw the evidence we had."

Even though Castroneves was allowed to keep the win, Tracy is frequently hailed as the moral victor of the 2002 Indianapolis 500 by everyone from Mario Andretti to Alex Zanardi. But the sometimes controversial Canadian has always handled the disappointment on missing out on what would have been the biggest win of his career with class.

"It's frustrating because this is a sport and it started out as a sport to race head-to-head against other guys," Tracy remarked. "We raced head-to-head on the track, and I feel that I won the race, but we weren't able to win the political side of it. That's frustrating for Barry, and I think it's frustrating for a lot of the fans that it has come down to politics. It's sad for the sport and it's sad for open-wheel racing. I think this just shows how deep the gap is between IRL and CART. It's so wide now that it's frustrating."

The way the IRL handled the finish of the 2002 Indy 500 had to concern Honda, which shocked the racing community on Indy's Carb Day by announcing that it had entered into a partnership with Ilmor USA to build normally aspirated engines to IRL specifications for the '03 season. Just three weeks earlier at the CART race at Motegi, Japan, Honda executives flat-out denied that they were working on an IRL program. But the presence at Motegi of George, Barnhart, and other IRL officials gave away the game.

Two days before the Japanese race, American Honda Executive Vice President Tom Elliott tried to quash the rumor that Honda was headed to the IRL to reporters at Motegi. "I think people heard that Tony George was going to be here and they put two and two together to get six," said Elliott. "It's no secret that Tony is talking to Motegi about holding an IRL race here and that's no surprise. The track needs more races to become profitable. We want to have an American racing program, but Honda won't have an engine for any American racing series in 2003.

"Certainly in 2004, for sure we want to be racing again," Elliott added. "With CART's rules for next year [the slightly higher-tech 3.5-liter normally aspirated engine based on IRL architechture], neither series really meets our goals of racing in a technologically challenging environment. Of course, it would take eighteen months to design and build an engine for either series, and at the moment we have nothing on paper, let alone ready for development."

Given how economical the Honda executives were with the truth at Motegi, perhaps it was not surprising that Honda Performance Development President Robert Clarke was sweating profusely when he confirmed news of the HPD/Ilmor partnership to the media at IMS on May 24. "Competing in the IRL series, with its rules to intentionally limit the use of high-cost technology and thus provide more parity in the racing field, will give Honda a new competitive experience and the fans more exciting racing," said Clarke. "This new direction builds on a foundation of nearly ten years of CART racing and will serve to elevate HPD's capability from engine assembly to engine design and development and reflects a new commitment to American racing." To its credit, over the next decade, HPD did make the transformation from being essentially a build shop into a facility capable of creating an engine from scratch.

With Honda and Toyota committed to the IRL in 2003 and Ford-Cosworth less than enthusiastic about building an engine to IRL specifications, CART made an about-face on its move to normally aspirated engines. On June 17, citing heritage but driven by economics, CART approved a plan that locked in a modified version of the FedEx Championship Series's existing 2.65-liter turbocharged engine formula for the '03 and '04 seasons. CART planned to purchase a pool of one hundred engines that would be maintained and supplied to all teams by Cosworth Racing for a lease cost of just $1.125 million per season. The plan was announced in conjunction with CART's creation of an Entrant Support Program, which provided twenty Champ Car teams with $1.5 million in cost savings and benefits. CART also dropped its plans to adopt IRL chassis specs. Lola had rebounded from a dry period in the late 1990s to reclaim almost 100 percent of the CART chassis market by '02, a key factor in Reynard falling into bankruptcy.

"My administration decided to create a common chassis with the IRL to try and give our teams flexibility and good economics to be able to run in both series, and to give the manufacturers involved a greater quantity of clients, so that in turn would bring the cost down," said CART CEO

Chris Pook. "We were summarily rejected on that. We put it out as an olive branch to try to form some type of compatibility with the other side to bring us closer together to see if we could merge the two together. But the olive branch was broken off in two pieces and we were slapped around the face with it and told to get out of town."

The rest of the 2002 season went off without incident or controversy. Driving a Toyota-powered Lola for Newman/Haas Racing, Cristiano da Matta easily won the CART championship in a Brazilian 1-2 over Ganassi's Bruno Junqueira by winning seven of nineteen races. The IRL had a distinct Brazilian flavor as well, as Castroneves and de Ferran battled Hornish for the championship. Hornish, the driver who was becoming known as the IRL's American poster child prevailed by winning the last two races of the season at Chicagoland Speedway (the new 1.5-mile oval co-owned by the Indianapolis Motor Speedway and International Speedway Corp. before ISC assumed full ownership) and Texas Motor Speedway.

As was becoming the norm, CART's biggest drama was happening off the track. After signing a four-year contract extension as the series' title sponsor in 2001, Federal Express took advantage of an out clause and pulled its $5 million of annual support at the end of '02. Pook negotiated commercial partnerships with engine supplier Ford and tire supplier Bridgestone, resulting in the clunky new title for the CART championship of "Bridgestone Presents the Champ Car World Series Powered By Ford."

The IRL was having even more difficulty maintaining a title sponsor. Following Pep Boys's short-lived run in 1998 and '99, the IRL's five-year, $50 million deal with internet search engine Northern Light was also terminated after just two years when Northern Light declared bankruptcy in 2002 after being run out of business by a rapidly growing new search engine competitor called Google. But with the IRL maintaining slow but steady growth, series officials were content to be patient in their search for a replacement. The league claimed a 9 percent increase in attendance from '01 to '02, while television ratings rose 17 percent on ABC and 31 percent on ESPN.

"Strengthened partnerships with General Motors, Firestone, Infiniti and the fact Marlboro, Red Bull, and Hollywood (a Brazilian tobacco brand) have recently chosen the Indy Racing League as a marketing platform proves interest in the series has never been higher," said Tony George. "But it is more important for the series to find the right long-term partner than it is to simply have a title sponsor for next season. We're set to continue moving forward."

The IRL was strengthened in 2003 by another wave of transfers from the CART series. Three weeks after he lost his appeal over the Indianapolis 500, Barry Green announced he was selling Team Green to a consortium led by Michael Andretti. Michael simultaneously announced Andretti Green Racing's (AGR) move to the IRL, a move many believe was motivated by a truckload of Honda cash. Andretti retained Franchitti, hired Tony Kanaan, and revealed plans to retire as a driver after the '03 Indy 500, with his place to be taken by CART Ladder System graduate Dan Wheldon.

Chip Ganassi switched his operation 100 percent to the IRL after running three cars in CART and one in the IRL in 2002. Ganassi's driver lineup included twenty-two-year-old Scott Dixon, who became the youngest-ever winner of an Indy car race when he triumphed in CART for PacWest Racing at Nazareth Speedway in '01. And 1998 IRL champion Kenny Brack returned to the all-oval series in a full-time Team Rahal entry after three years in CART.

"We enter the 2003 season with unprecedented growth, momentum, and competition," remarked George in the IRL's "State of the Series" address in February 2003. From that point, series management minimized usage of the IRL nomenclature and reverted to the term IndyCar Series. "A game plan was put into place just two years ago, and with a lot of hard work, the results are that we're all here today gathered eagerly awaiting the 2003 season. When the league had its first race in January 1996, it was a realization of a vision to create a series where competition is close, costs are controlled, and the same quality of equipment is available to all where the teams and sponsors can afford to compete. Eight years later, we are realizing that vision."

But that progress came at a symbolic cost. With manufacturer engine lease programs and most of the field consisting of drivers and teams formerly associated with CART, the 2003 version of the IRL bore little physical or philosophical resemblance to the IRL of 1996. Indy car racing's minnows instead found their place in CART, which struggled to put together an eighteen-car field for its 2003 championship. Only two marquee teams remained: Newman/Haas Racing (with Junqueira and French newcomer Sébastien Bourdais) and Player's/Forsythe Racing, with Tracy staying loyal to CART to chase his first series title. Tracy dominated the action, winning seven of the scheduled nineteen races (the finale at California Speedway was canceled due to nearby wildfires), but Bourdais won three times and served notice that he was a star of the future—not to mention an obvious rival to Tracy.

The IRL continued its pattern of introducing a new engine and chassis package on a three-year cycle. Infiniti withdrew from competition, but the Japanese company's absence was more than made up for by the arrival of Honda and Toyota. G-Force and Dallara introduced new chassis for 2003, with Dallara employing pullrod front suspension that created a much smaller frontal area with a low, dart-like nose. The Dallara IR-03 and mildly upgraded IR-07 would faithfully serve the IRL for the next nine years.

However, the needle-nose Dallara had a fundamental design flaw that the IRL never was able to satisfactorily fix. With the slightest provocation, the car had an alarming tendency to take flight. The first and perhaps the scariest airborne incident occurred at Indianapolis in April 2003, when sixty-three-year-old retired legend Mario Andretti took a wild ride while shaking down a car for the injured Kanaan. The Brazilian had sustained a broken arm during a violent IndyCar Series weekend at Twin Ring Motegi that sent three drivers to the hospital. The plan for Mario to test was sparked by an April Fool's column in his local newspaper, but it quickly turned serious and it was certainly not a publicity stunt. In fact, had Kanaan not healed quickly and been ready for the start of Indy 500 practice, Andretti Green Racing intended for Mario to qualify Kanaan's car for the race.

What started out as a feel-good story nearly took a tragic turn when Andretti hit a piece of debris after Kenny Bräck blew an engine and crashed in front of him. That launched his Dallara-Honda into an aerial loop that was amazingly captured live by an Indianapolis television station covering the test by helicopter. Once it caught air, the outside retaining fence tipped Andretti's car into a corkscrewing barrel roll, three times in all, before it crashed down upright on its one wheel. It slid backwards into Turn Two, where Mario clambered out nursing nothing worse than a cut chin.

During the Indianapolis 500, another AGR car driven by Wheldon flipped upside down in what was otherwise not a very violent crash. Then just five days later, Castroneves collided with Kanaan's slowing car during a test session at Richmond Raceway and the Penske Dallara was launched into the fence before landing upside down and catching fire. "I was in the wrong place at the wrong time," Castroneves recounted, before joking: "It was like lighting a match in a barbecue, whoosh!"

Those IRL crashes were temporarily forgotten when another storyline came to the fore in the summer. To the surprise of no one, Toyota and Honda brought costly innovations developed in CART-like qualifying engines and "push to pass" fuel enrichment controls previously frowned upon by the IRL. Both Japanese marques destroyed the previously dominant Chevrolet engine throughout the first half of 2003. Despite its best efforts to control costs and ensure parity, the IRL was unable to put an end to the free-spending engine "arms war" mentality that Toyota and Honda carried over from their last few years in CART.

At the Texas race in June, it was revealed that Chevrolet had turned to Cosworth Engineering for help with its struggling program. Though owned by the Ford Motor Company, Cosworth did contract work for several major manufacturers, including Audi. Hedging its bets, Cosworth had a 3.5-liter normally aspirated IRL engine in the planning stage before it committed to completely take over the engine supply for the CART series with its 2.65-liter turbo engines. The Cosworth IRL design was quickly put into production when General Motors came calling. Hornish tested the Cosworth prototype in early July at Kansas Speedway and immediately went five miles per hour faster than he managed in his Chevy.

"Chevrolet has not been competitive," noted Roger Penske, whose team switched from Chevy to Toyota for 2003. "As I understand it, you can make at least one change by applying to the sanctioning body. It's getting like NASCAR where they give a little spoiler or take it away."

Hornish was the only driver to receive the so-called Chevrolet Gen IV engine (quickly dubbed "Gen Ford" or "Cosworth Vega" by cynics) at first, and he proceeded to dominate on the motor's debut at Michigan Speedway, leading 126 of 200 laps before finishing second to the Toyota of Alex Barron. Second time out, the hastily developed Cosworth/Chevy powered Hornish to a crushing victory at Kentucky Speedway. He pulled a twenty-second gap on the field and lapped everyone but Dixon and Bryan Herta, cruising to an easy triumph in what at the time was the fastest race in IRL history. The race was interrupted by only one full-course caution—for Brack's engine fire on pit road—leading to an average speed of 197.897 mph for the 300 miles. That was just fractionally slower than Jimmy Vasser's CART record of 197.995 mph established in 2002 over 500 miles at California Speedway. Hornish broke the magic 200-mph barrier when he won later in '03, also at California, averaging 207.151 mph over 400 miles. That record still stands.

While Honda and Toyota were generally supportive of allowing Chevrolet some help, the two Japanese manufacturers' history in CART suggested they would not stay happy if the IRL continued to use aggressive means to level the technical playing field.

"We're faced with unprecedented circumstances," responded Brian Barnhart, the IRL's top technical man. "Toyota and Honda have raised the level of competition. Chevrolet's request for a change in specification is in the best interest of all parties involved—Toyota and Honda as well as GM."

Suspicions about the "Chevworth" engines persisted. At Michigan, Hornish benefited from a timely caution for debris when it was obvious that his powerful but fuel-hungry powerplant would require him to make an extra pit stop. IRL officials also seemingly turned a blind eye when several teams claimed they caught the twenty-three-year-old American star speeding on pit road during the race. At Kentucky, Hornish didn't need any overt help from the IRL, such was his pace. But several observers reported that Hornish's engine had a higher exhaust note than the rest of the field and no discernable rev limiter. The magnitude of his dominance at Kentucky had Honda, Toyota, and their drivers hopping mad.

"Sam's always had a good car, but how fair is the game when they allow a new engine halfway through the season?" asked Kanaan. "Somebody sits there for six months, sees everybody's weakness, and builds a new engine? I don't want to complain but Honda and Toyota should."

"We understand the IRL wanted Sam and GM to win a race," said Toyota Racing Development Vice President Lee White. "But my feeling is that they need to work just as hard as we do and whatever steps were taken to make him competitive obviously were successful. We expect to be given equal consideration. I think I'll send the IRL a letter requesting that we be allowed to bring in a new motor—immediately."

He added, "The IRL was worried about keeping General Motors, but maybe they should worry about keeping Toyota in the series."

Hornish naturally rubbished talk that he was being favored by the league. "Nobody has complained directly to me, but I've heard some of it," he said. "We didn't sit there and whine when I was sixty horsepower down at the beginning of the year. I don't know what their problem is. It is about as equal as it can get right now. We were running equal to them while sixty horsepower down at six races this year. They have to expect that when we get that sixty horsepower, we are going to be a little quicker than they are. I'm sure there will be a lot of people that have a problem with this, but we have worked so hard this year. I feel bad that they feel that way, but I don't feel bad about winning."

Dixon, who was the IndyCar Series's most consistently successful driver in 2003 and ultimately won the first of his multiple Indy car championships, was perplexed by Hornish and the new engine. "I don't know where that Cosworth came from, but it sure was impressive," Dixon said. "I think it's good for the competition but I also think it's not fair."

Dixon won the title for Ganassi in the most across-the-board competitive season the IRL had staged since its inception. But he spoke for most of the ex-CART drivers when he said that the enforced move to the IRL left him conflicted. "I probably wouldn't have picked it and it was a hard move to come over to the IRL, with the all-oval experience," he said. "But it's one of those things, and with motorsport, it's hard to determine what you are going to do from one day to the next. I was definitely surprised, but I totally and thoroughly enjoyed this year. Life takes different steps, and I am sure if you asked Tony and Hélio they would say they didn't expect to be here either. But it has been a lot of fun so far."

During the Texas race, Brack's car locked wheels with another driven by Tomas Scheckter and got pitched sideways. Brack's Team Rahal G-Force/Honda was then knocked in the air by Scheckter's car, mowing down several hundred yards of catchfence protecting a bank of thankfully empty grandstands on the backstretch. A front wheel remained embedded on a fence post next to a gaping hole, caused when the car hit a gate with an impact measured at nearly two hundred G. Miraculously, Brack was not killed, but he suffered a broken sternum, three fractured vertebrae (including a crushed C-3 vertebra), a broken right thigh, and two badly fractured ankles. His career was effectively ended, though he showed plenty of speed in a one-off run in the 2005 Indianapolis 500.

Brack was notable as one of the few drivers who went from the IRL to CART rather than vice versa. The Swede won the 1998 IRL championship and '99 Indianapolis 500 while driving for A.J. Foyt before taking five wins in the CART series for Rahal and Chip Ganassi.

Recuperating in Indianapolis a few weeks after the accident, Brack offered his assessment. "People complain about Formula 1 and other type of racing where they say, 'There's never any overtaking, it's dull, it's boring, one car wins everything,'" he said. "Then you have the IRL, where you have a really, really extremely competitive show, but the downside to it is that you're running close, running wheel-to-wheel. The slightest mistake or technical malfunction, you have yourself a wild ride to look forward to before you stop. Most of the time you walk out of there uninjured. Sometimes you have a few bruises. But there's the one chance that you get hurt real seriously, too. It really hasn't changed my perspective on it. I'm as aware of the risks now as I was before my accident. I think all the drivers knows the risks that this type of racing means."

In 2003, only twelve of the IRL's twenty-two regular drivers competed in every race and ten of those twenty-two suffered broken bones or were hospitalized at some point during the season. In the eighty-seven IRL races staged from 1996-2003, seventy-six drivers were hospitalized with major injuries. CART tallied thirty-two significant injuries in 147 races during that same timespan.

The IRL cars often looked like power boats during this era, racing in a nose-up attitude in an effort to "hide" the oversized rear wing from the air flow. Mauricio Gugelmin, one of the top superspeedway racers of the period who unofficially turned the fastest Indy car lap in history (242.333 mph) at the CART event at California Speedway in 1997, gave his analysis of the IRL's flying car phenomenon.

"The problem is when you get a bunch of talented people together with a racing car, they want to make it work better than anyone else," Gugelmin remarked. "The hardest thing in this business is to slow cars down, especially when you have talented engineers trying to make them go faster. You have highly restricted cars and you're running them at places that aren't really suitable. I'm sure the IRL chassis regulations contributed to these accidents where cars got in the air. Certainly they have to look very carefully at how they are limiting ride heights and other factors that are contributing to the conditions the cars are being subjected to that are causing them to take off from the ground.

"Clearly in open-wheel racing, when you have an over-downforced car the easiest thing to do is to keep raising the ride height, especially the front end," he continued. "That creates some lift, and they run negative degrees of front wing to make the front kind of 'hide' that big rear wing. You're basically pushing your luck—you're running a lethal weapon at that stage. In ideal circumstances on your own, you'll probably get away with that. But like an airplane accident, a racing crash usually doesn't happen unless there are a number of factors involved. Somebody takes their air, they drop a wheel on the grass, and there they go. The cars are too much on the edge.

"I had an enormous wreck in a CART car at Texas Motor Speedway, and the reason it was so big is that I crashed at a place that our cars were not made to run," Gugelmin concluded. "I remember when we ran the 240-mile-per-hour laps at Fontana, people were saying, 'You're crazy to drive at that speed!' But we had a car that was designed to run at those speeds that was well-balanced with small wings. We didn't hurt people. Yes, maybe it wasn't as close as some people would like to see. But we still had some very good racing, and I think people may have forgotten a little bit about what racing is all about. It has gone completely the other way and now in every series all they talk about is passing. Even Formula 1 got into that, and in America it's even worse. They want to see that last-lap dash to the line, but when you get highly competitive people that close together in open-wheel cars, you're going to run into trouble."

Any joy Dixon derived from his championship faded just ten days after the 2003 season ended when his '04 Ganassi teammate-to-be Tony Renna was killed in a one-car crash while testing at the Indianapolis Motor Speedway. Renna had just landed his big break and was embarking on his first test for the team. As it was a private test, details are sketchy and no video of the accident ever surfaced, but it appears that Renna entered Turn Three on a low line for his first hot lap (after warming up at 227 mph) and the car spun. Somehow, the G-Force/Toyota was launched into the air, flying over the wall and directly into the catchfence. Some reports suggested that the chassis carrying Renna's lifeless body actually landed in the grandstands, something the IRL refused to confirm other than to say "small pieces of debris" ended in a spectator area. Sources familiar with the accident estimated that multiple spectators would have been killed and dozens more injured had the accident occurred on Indianapolis 500 race day with fans in the grandstands. Renna's was the fifth IRL accident in '03 in which a car became airborne.

The IRL and its competing manufacturers worked together to respond quickly, with a series of changes introduced prior to the 2004 season. The cars carried a vertical wicker on the outer edges of the rear wing end plates and a "monocoque center wicker," a 3/8-inch vertical strip that bisected the chassis from the tip of the nose to the cockpit opening and carried on down the profile of the roll hoop and engine cover. The series also mandated a slot in the engine air intake as a temporary means to cut power and announced plans to decrease engine displacement from 3.5 to 3.0 liters beginning at the '04 Indianapolis 500.

"The way the season ended probably accelerated this program by about six months," said IRL Senior Vice President of Operations Brian Barnhart. "We anticipated making this change in 2005, but with the competitive nature of Honda and Toyota joining Chevrolet as our manufacturers, the R&D and the acceleration of technology into the series probably was more than we anticipated. Speeds started going quicker more rapidly than we thought they would."

The IRL attempted to ease the cost burden on Toyota, Honda, and Chevrolet by mandating the existing engine block and heads. The manufacturers could meet the required displacement adjustment with a shorter engine stroke, which required new pistons, connecting rods, and crankshaft. The half-liter displacement cut was expected to reduce power by approximately seventy-five horsepower and knock back speeds to the 220-mph range at Indianapolis and other superspeedways. Fuel capacity was reduced from thirty-five gallons to thirty.

"We think it's without question the right direction for the IRL," noted Toyota's Lee White. "We pushed for this idea two years ago when we prepared to join the IRL and brought the issue back up last year at Kentucky when there were concerns about speeds."

While the IRL's problems in 2003 were mainly safety related on track and in full view for all to see, CART had a clean season of competition but a myriad of business-related issues. Chris Pook's vision to change the conception of CART as a race-sanctioning organization into, as he put it, "a marketing company that will position its open-wheel motor racing series as a 'delivery' mechanism for national and multi-national corporations in which to conduct business" came at a high cost as CART entered into promotion or copromotion of several races on its schedule.

CART also attempted to embrace a concept it called "MotoRock" that would combine its urban events with A-list concerts and other car-related activities aimed at a younger audience. "I've been turning money into noise for the last thirty years," said Trans-Am and Champ Car team owner Paul Gentilozzi. "Now we're going to make a different kind of noise. This is the beginning of a concept that will turn into an entertainment company that changes the way we look at racing on the track. The whole MotoRock idea is going to be much more significant than you think." But after staging shows by Kid Rock and Elton John at CART's Miami Grand Prix in 2003, MotoRock was never heard from again.

In fact, by the end of 2003, CART was bankrupt and teetering on the brink of elimination.

CHAPTER 18

THE END OF CART

In September 2002, Michael Andretti didn't mince any words as he explained why he was taking the recently acquired (and renamed) Andretti Green Racing out of CART and into the Indy Racing League. Since the IRL was formed in 1994, Andretti had been one of its most vocal critics, but when it came time to put his own money on the line, Michael made a choice he admitted that he never expected to make.

"It's a total business decision," he remarked. "We feel that the IRL has a lot of momentum going for it, and in the end, there was nothing going for the CART side. We had no interest from any of our sponsors in continuing in CART. It wasn't done with our hearts, it was done with our heads. If it had been a decision made with our hearts we probably would have made a different decision, but that's not going to feed the eighty families we're responsible to."

"The main thing we wanted going back to April was a guarantee of eighteen cars [on the CART grid in 2003]," he added. "Everybody can say whatever they want that there's going to be eighteen cars, but the reality of the situation is we don't see it. There's no guarantee that there's going to be a field next year."

Andretti's decision was fueled by the loss of Team Green's major sponsor, Brown & Williamson Tobacco and its KOOL brand. After evaluating its options prior to the 2001 and '02 seasons with an eye toward switching from CART to the IRL, sponsorship manager Bert Kremer decided to completely terminate the company's auto racing sponsorship at the end of '02.

Dan R. Boyd

"Until the last couple of years we haven't had serious doubts or concerns about CART, and we've been pretty comfortable where we were," Kremer said. "It's really the evolution of the last several years in CART that has taken us in a direction where, quite frankly, we see our return from this program going down every year. I tell Chris Pook that it's nothing against them, but we've been through four CEOs in seven years, and quite frankly, we hear a lot of the same things. And they just haven't happened. There hasn't been enough time to see any change. We haven't evolved to more of a U.S. schedule. In my view, there just haven't been that many concrete positive developments to do away with the concerns I've had in the past."

Motorola also ended its Indy car program after more than a decade with several teams, but with support from Honda, Andretti was able to assemble sufficient sponsorship for his three-car IRL attack from 7-Eleven convenience stores, Jim Beam whiskey, and Alpine Car Stereo. More significantly, Andretti did not believe CART had enough money in the bank to fund enough teams to make up the numbers for a full season.

"It takes a lot of money to do it, and even if they spend the $90 million they have, that's not enough to do it with the television package that they have to buy and everything else," he said. "They're running out of money. Is [Gerald] Forsythe going to pay for the whole field? Nobody's got that much money."

CART supporters argued that until the mass migration of CART manufacturers, sponsors, and teams to the IRL that started in 2001, Tony George had been financially propping up his league in a similar fashion, with some observers estimating that George had blown through as much as half a billion dollars of the Hulman family fortune. Since coming to power in December 1989, in addition to founding and supporting the IRL, George had undertaken a massive renovation of the Indianapolis Motor Speedway golf course. He contracted renowned architect Pete Dye to transform the Speedway's scruffy twenty-seven-hole municipal layout into a premium eighteen-hole championship track called Brickyard Crossing that hosted a PGA Senior Tour tournament from 1994-2000. Brickyard Crossing also staged an LPGA Tour event from 2017-19.

An even more expensive project was the construction of an FIA (Fédération Internationale de l'Automobile)-grade road course in the Speedway infield, something George envisioned from the day he stepped into the top job at IMS. The goal, successfully achieved in 2000, was to bring Formula 1 racing back to the United States after a lengthy absence. After F1 ended a twenty-year run with Watkins Glen in 1980 and lost the Long Beach Grand Prix to CART in '84, the most popular form of motorsport in the world had struggled for traction in America, running at a series of unsatisfactory (and unsuccessful) street course events in Detroit, Dallas, and Phoenix. In 1991, the third and final year for the Phoenix Grand Prix, the nearby Chandler Ostrich Festival drew a larger crowd.

Bringing F1 to IMS not only gave the international series an American facility with history and the permanent infrastructure it desired, it also strengthened the Speedway's hand. IMS now boasted well-attended NASCAR and Formula 1 races that injected a healthy chunk of revenue during a time period when the Indianapolis 500 was not at peak strength. As an added bonus, CART loyalists were furious that George went to the trouble and expense of building an IMS road course to embrace Formula 1, while continuing to maintain that road racing offered little value to Indy car racing.

George was in a position of increasing power. By 2002-03, when CART's problems were becoming publicly evident, the Indy 500 had started to reverse its attendance slide and was in the early phases of a long, slow comeback. In May 2002, Roger Penske said a merger between CART and the IRL was unlikely, but predicted that the next twelve to eighteen months would determine which series would survive. George was certain that would be the IRL. "We've made a lot of progress in the last eighteen months, and I think it's important to stay consistent," he said. "Sooner or later, people will connect with who we are."

CART netted approximately $64 million from its initial public offering in March 1998, and thirteen months later, an additional 1.8 million shares of stock were offered and snapped up at a price of $28 per share, a substantial increase from the $16 that the stock originally sold for. The share price peaked at $35.63 on June 8, 1999, shortly after that year's reunification furor. Along with received sanctioning fees and sponsorship income, CART put together a war chest of cash reserves of close to $100 million by the turn of the century.

As a public company, CART was required to share financial information on a quarterly basis, so evidence of the organization's rapid decline was on display for all to see. Bolstered by the addition of overseas races that commanded sanction fees of up to $5 million, the company's annual revenues increased to a peak of $75 million in 2000 and remained over $70 million a year later. But the termination of CART's $200 million guaranteed sponsorship contract with Andrew Craig's former employer ISL Worldwide (and that company's subsequent bankruptcy) forced CART to create an in-house sales and marketing department, contributing to significantly higher operating expenses. CART incurred a modest $1.5 million loss in '01, but the numbers were significantly worse in '02, when revenues down by 20 percent (from $70.3 to $57.2 million) combined with $81.9 million in expenses (nearly double the figures posted in 1998 and '99) led to a record $21 million loss.

The numbers for 2003 were simply catastrophic. After spending $9.7 million to self-promote three races in '02, CART spent nearly $21 million in '03 to facilitiate domestic events at Cleveland, Portland, Miami, and Mid-Ohio as well as a two-race international swing that took the series to Germany and England during the month of May. CART spent $14.9 million on television in '03, through production costs and airtime buys, and also paid a $3.5 million settlement to Texas Motor Speedway for the '01 event that was canceled at the last minute. CART also paid a $2.2 million settlement to former CEO Joe Heitzler.

But all of that paled in comparison to the money CART spent just to assemble and maintain a field of twenty cars, even when leases on the pool of one hundred Ford-Cosworth engines that CART bought for $4 million were going for the sweetheart rate of $100,000 per car per season. CART's Entrant Support Program paid out $13.8 million in benefits in lieu of prize money, and an eye-popping $30 million—$1.5 million per car—was distributed as "team assistance."

By the time it finally issued delayed financial guidance for 2003 in June, CART acknowledged that at its current rate of spending, it would not have the necessary funds to stage the '04 season. At the same time, CART announced that it had retained the investment firm of Bear Stearns & Co. to explore strategic alternatives, including the possible sale of the company.

"We've just got to keep going down the road like we've said we would to re-establish the series," said CART CEO Chris Pook following the company's annual meeting in July. "We've got to give it a little stability first. You've got to remember we've come from absolute doom and gloom. Last year people were asking whether we would be able to race, if we would have enough cars on the grid, and so on. Now in the last six months we've been in kind of a quiet period, and people have been saying maybe this thing is going to work. We're in a period where we've got to go ask for the order. We're making our sales pitches."

Despite CART's precipitous decline to penny stock status (the stock was delisted by the New York Stock Exchange in October 2003), one man never stopped buying shares: Gerald Forsythe. Acting on an invitation from the CART Board of Directors in an August 11 letter, Forsythe formed a group of investors, which on August 15 tendered an offer to buy all outstanding shares of CART stock as well as the attached rights to the company, including the Bridgestone Presents the Champ Car World Series Powered by Ford and the CART Toyota Atlantic Championship.

Forsythe, along with fellow Champ Car team owners Paul Gentilozzi and Kevin Kalkhoven, formed a holding company called Open Wheel Racing Series (OWRS), and tendered a bid of $7.4 million in cash, or approximately fifty cents per share for the 14,718,134 shares of CART stock in circulation.

Forsythe, who was CART's largest individual shareholder, with 3,377,400 shares (22.95 percent) of stock, contributed those shares to OWRS, while Kalkhoven and Gentilozzi pledged cash, committing an initial $15 million after the proposed acquisition. OWRS filed a Schedule 13D form with the U.S. Securities and Exchange Commission that described the company as "a specially-formed entity whose principal business interest is to acquire all outstanding capital stock and attached rights of CART."

The filing went on to report: "OWRS believe that an Acquisition presents the best opportunity to continue the CART racing series, including the support series. [We] would like CART to continue to provide a forum for open-wheel racing in North America and worldwide. . . . [We] believe that CART's format, which features racing events on superspeedways, ovals, temporary street courses in urban settings, and permanent road courses, can be successful with the proper organization and capital structure."

The OWRS filing also said the company expected to change the present board of directors and management of CART and might make changes to CART's bylaws that would impede future acquisition of CART. The completion of the acquisition would make the stock eligible for delisting from the New York Stock Exchange.

"The offer price is less than the market price of Common Stock on the date of the offer letter," read the filing. "The offer price reflects the fact that CART will require significant additional capital to maintain its ongoing operations. [We] believe that if such capital was raised through an equity financing, even if such equity financing was available, CART shareholders would likely suffer sufficient dilution to reduce the market price of the Common Stock to less than the offer price. If a third party, which intends to continue to operate the business of CART makes a superior offer, [we] at present intend to support that superior offer."

Beginning in May 2003, Bear Stearns contacted or was contacted by forty-five potential strategic and financial investors, including Kalkhoven and the men who eventually joined him in the OWRS partnership— Gentilozzi and Forsythe. Kalkhoven executed a confidentiality agreement with Bear Stearns on May 14, and by the time the OWRS acquisition attempt was announced on September 10, twenty-five such confidentiality agreements were signed by potential investors.

The most interesting potential buyer for CART was Formula 1 impresario Bernie Ecclestone, who had a longtime personal relationship with Pook. But it's likely that was just a ruse fueled by Pook to take the heat off of CART during a period of intense scrutiny. Another potential suitor with F1 ties was Craig Pollock, a Scotsman who served as 1995 CART (and '97 Formula 1) champion Jacques Villeneuve's manager. After negotiating Villeneuve's move from Indy cars to F1 with the dominant Williams-Renault team, he helped create the BAR (British American Racing) F1 team in partnership with British American Tobacco and Reynard Racing principals Adrian Reynard and Rick Gorne.

Pollock then split with BAR and attempted to buy the Arrows F1 team, only to have the deal fall through at the last minute. During his attempt to acquire Arrows, Pollock met Kalkhoven, who made his reputation and fortune in Silicon Valley as the former CEO of JDS Uniphase. Born in Adelaide, Australia, and educated in Great Britain, Kalkhoven moved to California in 1985 looking for business opportunities. He joined Uniphase, a manufacturer of optical scanning devices in '92, took the company public on the NASDAQ exchange, and created a merger with Canadian competitor JDS Fidel. By the time Kalkhoven left JDS Uniphase in May 2001, the company was a world leader in optical devices and Kalkhoven had been named one of America's fifty top CEOs by *Worth* magazine. His departure came just before the technology stock bubble burst, prompting profiles from *Forbes* and *The Motley Fool* that labeled him as someone who got out in the nick of time. Kalkhoven's financial dealings underwent close scrutiny, and in 2008, he was one of four individuals named in a tax evasion suit that ended with the accounting firm that designed the shelter (EY, formerly Ernst & Young) paying the U.S. government a $123 million fine to avoid prosecution.

Kalkhoven cofounded the venture capital firm KPLJ Ventures, and he and Pollock formed PK Racing out of the ashes of PacWest Racing to field a car in the CART series. "Venture capitalists invest in start-ups, and to me, some significant proportion of this team is that it is a start-up," Kalkhoven said at the PK Racing launch in January 2003. "It's at a time when the market is down, which is always a good time to get in, and I believe it's going to be successful and make money. It's not entirely for altruistic reasons—it's for business reasons. But I believe it will be a successful business, among other things."

Pook, Pollock, and Kalkhoven said they had all individually engaged in informal talks with Ecclestone about getting him involved in a buyout and privatization of CART, but the F1 king was never a serious player. The constant rumors and speculation did serve as a delaying mechanism while Kalkhoven teamed with Forsythe to launch the OWRS bid in association with minority partner Paul Gentilozzi.

"I'm optimistic," Forsythe said. "Certainly I'm willing to spend money to make CART a viable sanctioning body for the future. That's basically all I can tell you. I'm very optimistic and confident. I've been very, very positive on CART for the past several years. There isn't anybody who has been more positive on CART than me. I want to see it survive, and I want to see it succeed."

On August 24, the OWRS offer was upped to $0.56 per share, and at a key meeting in Chicago on September 4, Bear Stearns presented liquidation scenarios that convinced the CART board that accepting the OWRS offer was the company's best alternative. After receiving a second outside opinion from Ernst & Young, the CART board voted on September 10 to accept and recommend the OWRS offer to shareholders, with a special shareholder meeting set for December 19.

But early in December 2003, OWRS pulled out of the acquisition agreement, citing doubts about CART's ability to meet at least one of the terms set forth. Instead, the group proposed that they buy the company's key assets—mainly, the race contracts and sanction of the CART Champ Car World Series and Toyota Atlantic Series. With approximately $7 million in cash to distribute, CART's shareholders would also receive something in the area of the fifty-six cents per share that they would have gotten had they voted for the original proposal at the special shareholder meeting. The new proposal also called for CART to immediately file for Chapter 11 bankruptcy relief, which under federal regulations protected the company from creditors while it reorganized and tried to work out a plan to pay its debts. OWRS nominated Richard P. Eidswick, cofounder and managing director of Michigan-based venture capital firm Arbor Partners, to manage the organization through the Chapter 11 proceedings.

Kalkhoven said he was prepared for the long haul and was willing to finance the initial running of the reorganized company. "We had to get the issues out there and get this thing sorted out very quickly," he remarked. "There's certainly no lack of commitment on the part of the principles. I personally have guaranteed a large amount of money to keep CART running independently for the next sixty days. This is an industry and there are a couple of thousand jobs on the line as well as a form of racing. There are a lot of people who want to see this thing succeed, including a huge number of fans. The board still has to vote on it, but next week will determine where it's all going."

Kalkhoven verified that the way that CART was structured, his group would take over the assets of the operating company, allowing the funds still held by the parent company to be distributed to the shareholders.

"The bankruptcy is declared by the company that holds the assets and the contracts and that is what the judge will rule on," he said. "The public company, or Delaware corporation, will still exist, with all its liabilities and issues. We're just trying make sure that the assets are acquired as quickly as possible to make sure the series can run next year. The costs of acquiring those assets are incredibly small compared to what it will take to keep it up and running, but we're prepared to undertake that."

The case was assigned to Judge Frank J. Otte in the U.S. Bankruptcy Court's Southern Indiana district. Judge Otte scheduled a hearing to auction CART's key assets for January 28, 2004, with a January 23 deadline to submit bids. On January 8, an element of intrigue was added to the ongoing saga when CART and Tony George signed a nondisclosure agreement that allowed IRL attorneys and personnel to examine CART's assets with an eye toward possibly bidding on selected items at the January 28 auction. A team of IRL attorneys and representatives, including IRL Senior Vice President of Racing Brian Barnhart and Vice President of Business Affairs Ken Unger, toured CART's headquarters on Indianapolis's northwest side on January 9. IRL founder and CEO George himself followed three days later.

OWRS had already submitted an asset offer of $1.6 million, to include race event contracts, timing and scoring equipment, pace and rescue vehicles, and CART's state-of-the-art mobile medical unit. OWRS also pledged to pay prize money and other liabilities, bringing the total compensation to around $3 million. Under the OWRS plan, principals Gentilozzi, Forsythe, and Kalkhoven pledged to run at least fifteen races and guaranteed a minimum of eighteen cars. The OWRS offer was structured in a way that alternate bidders were required to make a good faith effort to continue running the CART series, which was something that Indianapolis Motor Speedway Vice President of Communications Fred Nation said the IRL would be unable to do. Nation said that the earliest the IRL could consider absorbing the most desirable events on the CART schedule would be 2005.

Kalkhoven hosted a reception for the remaining CART team owners at Morton's Steakhouse in Indianapolis on January 15, and he remained confident that Judge Otte would rule in favor of the OWRS package on the table. A small group of Indy car beat reporters staked out the restaurant; Robin Miller donned a bow tie and apron and humorously crashed the owners meeting in a private room.

"[The IRL] can come in if they like, but I doubt they will put a bid in to continue the series," Kalkhoven told the media. "The difference is that they want to kill the series whereas we want to build it. Anything else would put hundreds of Americans out of work, and it would also deny millions of fans the opportunity to follow a great American racing series." He also noted that if the IRL were to jettison events after a full acqusition of the CART assets, it would likely bring a significant amount of litigation.

The IRL finally tendered what it called a "substantial" bid for selected assets of the bankrupt CART organization less than twenty-four hours prior to the January 23 deadline. The IRL did not reveal details about its bid, but claimed it was in the best interest to unify open-wheel racing. Sources familiar with the bid said the IRL offered an initial bid of $3.3 million, more than double the $1.63 million offer on the table from OWRS. However, the IRL only bid on the Grand Prix of Long Beach contract, the pool of Ford-Cosworth engines used to power the Champ Car field, and unspecified equipment.

George explained his reasons for bidding on the selected CART assets in an open letter on the IRL website. Calling the Indianapolis Motor Speedway "the primary steward of open-wheel racing in America" since 1909, he said the IRL was founded in response to CART's management of the sport during the '80s and '90s. "Many of you have advocated a single, unified open-wheel series as a goal for some time," he wrote. "If we are successful with our bid, our intention is to work quickly and effectively to create a unified, market-driven North American open-wheel series. We believe there is a window of opportunity right now to accomplish this." The IMS president added that road racing had always been on the IRL agenda and affirmed his commitment to "preserve and protect key traditional road and street races in North America, since CART is no longer able to do so."

Gentilozzi said that OWRS was prepared to significantly up the ante in the asset auction and that he would not be surprised to see the price bumped up to more than $15 million. "It's clear what the IRL's intentions are when you look at which assets they want to purchase," he remarked. "They want to kill the series, yet they hide that fact under the pretext of unification. They're not fooling anyone. Tony told me months ago that he wasn't going to get involved, so these actions don't seem very honorable.

"Obviously he wants to kill off the competition," Gentilozzi added. "But we've put thousands of hours into this and it's up to us to win the auction. We're not going to be intimidated or scared away because he wants to buy some equipment. We will do whatever it takes to save the Champ Car series and ensure its success into the future. Last-minute posturing and provocation by George and his organization will only strengthen our commitment and dedication to do what's right for motorsports. Failure is not an option."

In the seven days between when the IRL submitted a bid to Judge Otte's court and the January 28 hearing and auction, OWRS and the IRL engaged in a war of words in the press. Both sides used the *Indianapolis Star* as a mouthpiece.

"We're not going to convince everybody that we have the best intentions for open-wheel racing at heart," George told his local paper. "There will always be those [fans] who won't be dragged along without kicking and screaming. But our actions will speak for themselves, and in two or three years that will be obvious to any reasonable person."

George told the *Star* that it is the judge's responsibility to get the most money for CART's creditors. But in a Chapter 11 bankruptcy, the highest cash bid is not necessarily the best bid. Unless amended, George's plan would put an end to several successful street racing events, such as those in Toronto and Surfers Paradise, Australia, as well as affect the business of half a dozen permanent road courses across North America.

Long Beach was one of three tracks to file objections to Judge Otte's court regarding the transfer of its event contract to OWRS. In a sharply worded letter to OWRS lawyers, counsel for the Grand Prix Association of Long Beach slammed OWRS for failing to provide basic information like budgets, financial statements, and business plans and called the group "a shell entity that has virtually no assets, no other businesses, no track record, and no management team beyond its Board."

Conversely, organizers of the Surfers Paradise Australia race filed a motion with the court objecting to the IRL's bid, saying that it favored the OWRS plan because it offered to continue the majority of the CART series rather than just one race. The Australian motion revealed that the loss of the Surfers race would result in a claim of $13 million for damages and stated that similar claims could be expected from other tracks dropped by the IRL plan.

The hearing was moved to the largest available courtroom, where around 120 people crowded in on January 28. Another hundred or so people followed the proceedings via a closed-circuit video feed elsewhere in the courthouse in downtown Indianapolis as testimony dragged out over seven hours. The matter was complicated when the IRL increased its offer by $10 million after the lunch break. But James Knauer, counsel for the Creditor's Committee, still strongly believed the OWRS bid would have fewer negative implications.

Finally, encouraged by three key factors, Judge Otte ruled in favor of OWRS in the hopes that the Champ Car series could carry on. He believed significant damages and litigation would have resulted from scrapped CART promoter contracts, the fact that CART's public company planned to waive a $63 million loan it made to CART's operating company in order to stage the 2003 season, and the loss of jobs in the CART community, which Judge Otte projected at 300 to 460.

"I believe based on the information I have heard and based on the report I got from the Creditors Committee—Mr. Knauer did an excellent job—and knowing full well that there is another side to this, I find the best business judgement is to approve the sale agreement and asset transfer to Open Wheel Racing Series," remarked Judge Otte. "Having said that, I recognize that significant differences in opinion exist between strong personalities in this courtroom. I realize we are talking about an organization that has had difficulty. We're breathing new life into an organization to compete with the IRL. The IRL doesn't believe it can do so.

"There is a vast difference between $13.5 million versus $3.3 million, but I must consider the race contracts, and it is almost impossible to determine that value," Otte continued. "We know for certain that they would bring damages and litigation. To litigate would take longer than any racing organization could survive—at least two to three years. We have a group [OWRS] willing to put the money up. I recognize there are no guarantees here, but I also recognize that there are such things as second chances, and that's what we're all about. I hope this provides a new spark of light for the new group and it will be successful. I know it is important because there are 150 or 200 people sitting here."

Reaction was euphoric on the Champ Car side and muted from the IRL. "Obviously we're disappointed," George remarked. "We thought it was an opportunity to unify open-wheel racing. By not being successful today our work will continue. With the economy the way it is, I don't see they have much of a chance of being successful in the environment we're all working in right now. It's going to be difficult to continue with two series."

Defending Champ Car series champion Paul Tracy summarized what many Champ Car supporters were thinking: "All of the fans who followed this battle and asked why CART can't get together with Tony George now know the answer to that question. It's because he never wanted to get together. People didn't want to believe that, but now they know the truth. Tony George wanted to kill CART. He wanted to be king. That's what this was all about."

OWRS claimed its five-year business plan included no intention of unification with the IRL. "Our plan is about building the Champ Car World Series and nothing else," Gentilozzi said. "We're not involved in conflicts or issues with the Speedway. We're moving forward. We're not besieged, but we're busy with calls about the future. We know where we're going. We're going to race on weekends appropriate for us to race, and we can't afford any kind of distraction."

Gentilozzi said the OWRS business plan was engineered to avoid the mistakes made by CART, which lost $92 million in 2003, including some $45 million in subsidies to keep teams afloat.

"We analyzed that in great detail and Kevin brought in experts in the field who told us exactly how they lost it," he noted. "They didn't lose it—somebody found it and spent it. We know how that happened and have the advantage of seeing that lesson in black and white so it doesn't happen again. Our entrant support program will be guaranteed prize money for the entire season. There will not be direct team support.

"We're businessmen who happen to race, not team owners who make racing their business," Gentilozzi continued. "Our complete objective as we've looked at this has been, 'How can we turn around this business?' It wouldn't matter if we were selling tennis shoes. We would have looked at this in the same objective formula. Is there a customer? Is there a need? Are there enough assets to make the turn? And if we put money into this, can it be a self-sustaining business?"

Added Kalkhoven: "As a businessman, I would not have been involved in this decision out of pure emotion. I can't begin to count the number of business plans I've done in my life and this is among the best that we've done. We're very confident about the business aspects of being able to put this series together and grow it as the Champ Car World Series."

But OWRS was not in the clear yet. The Champ Car World Series was contractually required to put at least eighteen cars on the grid for the April 18 season opener at Long Beach, but when the series held its 2004 media preview days in early March, only eleven car and driver combinations were confirmed. Within a few days, that number dropped by two more as Champ Car stalwarts Bobby Rahal and Adrian Fernandez took their teams to the IRL full time, followed by mutterings that they had been lured by a trail of cash from Honda (though Honda Performance Development General Manager Robert Clarke denied those allegations).

"Adrian was not pressured to leave or lured away from CART by Honda," Clarke said. "The team initiated the contact and Adrian and the team's switch was truly their own decision. I can say that HPD does not do any free engine deals, but American Honda offers performance incentives to our teams and drivers based on race results."

Clarke said that HPD's agreements with its IRL teams are confidential. But during the latter years of its participation in the CART series, Honda was known to pay a $200,000 bonus for each race win, with descending incentives for finishing in the top four. A series championship would have netted a Honda team $1 million, with second place worth $500,000 and third place $250,000. In addition, Honda paid some of its teams sponsorship equivalent to the engine lease and rebuild costs for the season, which was potentially upwards of $4 million for a two-car team.

"This was a very difficult decision emotionally for many of us," said Rahal. "But this is a business that we run, and this decision was based on those kinds of considerations. Of course finances are certainly a part of that. But it was also done for sporting reasons. As I've made clear on a number of occasions this year, I truly believe for open-wheel racing to regain the popularity that it had, there really needs to be a focus on one series."

Yet like most of the nucleus of team owners who formed the basis of the CART series when it was at its peak in the 1980s and '90s, by 2004 Rahal had decided the Indy Racing League was a better place to do business.

"I have no doubt I won't be included on a lot of people's Christmas card lists this year, but I might pick up a few new ones," he said. "I don't mean to make light of it, because I don't think anyone quite appreciates how difficult this decision was for me personally, given everything that I had given CART over the years and given everything that CART had given me over the years. But we have sixty-five families to support, and hundreds of people, therefore. While the fans are a very important aspect of all this, the people that work with me are extremely important. I don't treat their futures lightly at all. Sometimes you've got to make the tough calls, and this is certainly one of them."

March 2004 marked exactly ten years since Tony George announced the formation of the Indy Racing League. But even though Championship Auto Racing Teams had been symbolically laid to rest, Indy car racing was still very much a divided sport, with two distinct series battling for a dwindling pool of sponsor dollars and fan and media attention. With a defiant new group running the Champ Car World Series and vowing to extend the fight, the open-wheel split appeared to be wider and deeper than ever.

CHAPTER 19

THE THIRD SPLIT:
CHAMP CAR VS. IRL

Within a few months of Open Wheel Racing Series's January 2004 acqusition of the Champ Car World Series via U.S. Bankruptcy Court, rumors bubbled of a unification or merger with the Indy Racing League. By July, the possibility had already been shot down.

What started out as a throwaway remark by Roger Penske in a May 30 *New York Times* interview advanced within a couple of weeks into a reasonably honest effort to unify American open-wheel racing. But on July 16, Champ Car and the Indy Racing League jointly issued a statement confirming that while talks had taken place, both series would continue down separate paths in 2005 and beyond.

"Following on the initiative of Roger Penske to explore a unification of open-wheel racing, ownership representatives of Champ Car World Series and the Indy Racing League have met with Mr. Penske to consider the issues," read the statement. "While ownership representatives from both series agree that one open-wheel series is the optimal situation, it is the belief of all involved that the time is not right for further discussion of unification. Both parties appreciate the efforts of Mr. Penske, and both parties believe that each has a better understanding of where common ground exists. No more meetings are planned and both series are moving forward with their future plans."

When news of a meeting between Penske and Champ Car's three principal owners leaked out at the Richmond IRL race in late June, it was hoped that common sense would finally prevail and the two

LAT Images

feuding open-wheel series could resolve their differences. Most of the top drivers, sponsors, teams, and manufacturers affiliated with CART when the split occurred in 1996 had switched allegiance to the IRL, leaving Champ Car with a depleted field. Apart from a couple of key teams (Newman/Haas Racing and Forsythe Racing) and drivers (chiefly Paul Tracy and emerging star Sébastien Bourdais), Champ Car's main selling point was the core of loyal fans that continued to support the series's internationally flavored road course and street races.

Kalkhoven and Forsythe strengthened their hand in late 2004 when they acquired Cosworth Engineering and Pi Electronics from the Ford Motor Company, a vital move in terms of protecting Champ Car's engine supply. At the same time, Ford sold the Jaguar Formula 1 team to Red Bull.

"We focused our attention in securing the best future for those businesses, and in brokering a deal that minimizes the impact or fallout on the sport," said Richard Parry-Jones, Ford's group vice president and chief technical officer. "We have worked very hard to sell the businesses to reputable buyers who can provide the most secure future. It was quite a complex deal, but we were able to broker the best feasible outcome."

While Red Bull was soon identified as the only realistic buyer for the Jaguar F1 operation, Cosworth attracted more than sixty bids, of which five merited serious consideration. "Kevin and Jerry moved quickly and were able to complete the deal on time, which was important because Formula 1 had a deadline of November 15 for registration for the championship," Parry-Jones said. "We expected Cosworth would generate quite a lot of interest, but a majority had an unclear idea of what they wanted to do with the company. Out of all the people we talked to, the Kalkhoven/Forsythe bid was clearly the most defined, and in the company's best interest. Our judgment was validated by the way they conducted themselves during the finalization of the deal. It was exemplary."

Kalkhoven and Forsythe also moved to secure the future of Champ Car's most prestigious event by acquiring the Grand Prix Association of Long Beach from Dover Motorsports in May 2005. The IRL claimed it had no interest. "When Dover decided to sell, we decided not to bid," said IRL Communications Director Fred Nation. "It's the Indy Racing

League's policy to deal with professional race promoters, not to own and promote our own events."

Meanwhile, the influx of star names and sponsor and manufacturer dollars increased the level of professionalism in the IRL, but it didn't significantly boost interest in the series. Small crowds of fewer than twenty thousand were the norm at venues outside of Indianapolis (with the exception of Texas Motor Speedway, which in its IRL heyday attracted crowds of seventy to eighty thousand), and despite boasts of recent ratings gains, the Indianapolis 500's U.S television audience was 55 percent down on the last pre-split race in 1995. In short, both sides had few strengths and lots of weaknesses, yet still believed they were better off without the other.

"There are two strong groups," said Penske, who seemed almost amused by how his *New York Times* article snowballed. "[Champ Car owners Kevin Kalkhoven, Gerald Forsythe, and Paul Gentilozzi] put the money down to sustain the open-wheel series. Tony has kept his course. I've worked with Tony for four years; I see a good product and I see progress. Most important is that we all agreed that everyone would be better off with one series, and I intend to do everything I can to do support unification."

George remained aloof throughout the reunification talk. He told the *Indianapolis Star* he was "out of the loop on this one." During the meetings between the two groups and after the nonunification statement was released, he said, "I was never quite sure what to make of it."

By this stage, the lengthy Champ Car–IRL war polarized people on both sides to the point where many lost touch with reality. Everyone agreed that American open-wheel racing would be better off as one entity pulling together, but a common theme from any era of the split is that every key protagonist zealously guarded their own self-interests.

"It would definitely be better for sponsorship and everybody involved to be pulling in one direction in single-seat open-wheel racing in America," noted two-time Indianapolis 500 winner Al Unser Jr., who took three IRL race wins in the twilight of a career that had netted thirty-one CART victories as well as a pair of series championships. "But I don't feel Tony needs to yield. He's yielded as much as he possibly can. I don't know what goes on behind closed doors, but from what I have heard, Tony has done what he can to unify or bring the two series together. He's come to the table every time with an open mind. The proof of it is sitting in this paddock—Ganassi, Patrick, Penske, Rahal, Fernandez . . . I could keep going down the list. That's proof enough that this is where you need to be in America."

Paul Newman, the co-owner of Newman/Haas Racing, was one of Champ Car's most loyal and visible advocates. "I think if open-wheel racing was reunified it would gather strength," Newman said. "But if it's not reunified, Champ Car will gather more strength than the IRL will. I think we have a better chance of getting stronger than [George] does, and this is certainly a hell of a lot more fun. I would much rather go to a race with sixty thousand or seventy thousand people in the stands and watch a good road race than to stand around where there are more people in the pits than there are in the stands."

"Everybody is willing to talk except Tony George," Newman added. "That's clear and it's public. It's not as though I'm throwing something out on the table that is a bad hand. Everybody is willing to talk, but nobody is willing to join with Tony George as the chief operating officer. That would be like sticking a rifle in your mouth. We have made mistakes, but we didn't make as many mistakes as he did. If Tony George were $200 million less rich, this whole thing might come together very quickly."

Instead, the IRL and Champ Car continued to operate as separate entities, with propped-up eighteen to twenty car fields the norm. For the first time in history, the Indianapolis 500 struggled to attract enough entries to create meaningful bumping in qualifying, and the ability to assemble enough cars to fill the traditional "Field of 33" began to be questioned annually.

After the flying car drama of 2003, the IRL's on-track product was far safer in '04 as minor aerodynamic changes and a reduction in engine capacity from 3.5 to 3.0 liters did the intended job of slowing and stabilizing the cars. Tony Kanaan won three races, completed every lap of competition, and finished outside the top five only once in sixteen races to claim the series championship with relative ease for Andretti Green Racing and Honda.

The IRL celebrated its milestone one hundredth race at Nazareth Speedway in August 2004, and a confident Tony George shared his thoughts on the state of the series: "Right now, it's easy to say I would have envisioned the league being where it is today four or five years ago, but hindsight is 20/20. We're pleased with where we're at and just stay focused on where we are today and where we want to be tomorrow, not worry about what could have been. I think we have to do a better job of telling our story and getting connected with the public. That's our biggest challenge today."

The big news was the IRL's decision to incorporate road racing with three events in 2005, including a street race in downtown St. Petersburg to open the season. The St. Pete event was actually a product of Chris Pook, who conceived of it as an East Coast version of the Long Beach Grand Prix during his time at Dover Motorsports. CART opened its final season at St. Pete in February 2003, and while the race had a successful debut by street course standards, it fell by the wayside for '04 in the wake of CART's collapse. The event was revived by a group consisting of Michael Andretti and the Green brothers (Barry and Kim) under the Andretti Green Promotions banner.

George revealed that he watched the 2003 St. Petersburg CART race on television and liked what he saw in the venue. "My impression at the time is that it was a great facility that showcased street racing in a great light," George said. "I hope we can put on an event that is equal to or better than that.

"I think the addition of road courses to our schedule sort of ushers in a new era for the League," he added. "We'll try to continue to provide close exciting racing on track and see what opportunities going into a new discipline and new markets will present us. When we started the League in '94, it was with the hopes that we would encourage more oval tracks to be built, and in a small way, I think we have been able to play a part in that renaissance of being able to build and develop new tracks. All the while, we said we would be interested in running road courses as part of our schedule. We always said that if and when the right opportunity presented itself we would consider it. Fortunately or unfortunately, I don't know, it has taken us until now until we could work out a deal and add them in 2005."

Not only did Michael Andretti serve as the promoter of the revived St. Pete GP, he opened the 2005 season with one of the best weekends of his career as a team owner. First, his eighteen-year-old son Marco won the Indy Lights support race. In the main event, Andretti's cars finished 1-2-3-4, led by rapidly rising star (and local resident) Dan Wheldon.

The top-four sweep was huge for Andretti. But he made an even bigger statement by delivering a successful road-racing debut to the IndyCar Series. Andretti and his partners at Honda were the strongest proponents for the IRL's adoption of road racing, and by 2005, Michael had emerged as one of the few players in the industry capable of influencing IRL founder George. His sudden switch from CART to the IRL also made him extremely unpopular with Champ Car fans.

"I hope that this event would show this is the direction this series needs to go," Andretti said. "I think Tony is sold on it. I think he knows we need to be at places like St. Petersburg, and I'm sure you're going to see some in the future. That's why I felt it was so important to be here and to show what we can do. It couldn't have been any better for what's needed in this series right now."

"We were hoping for fifty to seventy thousand over the three days and we exceeded our expectations," added AGP's Barry Green. "I think it's wonderful for open-wheel racing in this country. It's the kind of event we need to see more of, and the IRL seems to believe that too."

The drivers—nineteen of twenty-one came from a road-racing background, with A.J. Foyt IV and Ed Carpenter (Tony George's adopted son) the only exceptions—were solidly on board with adding road racing to the IndyCar Series schedule.

"Dario [Franchitti] and I rode around in the back of a truck on the parade lap and wondered what was the last time we had done this," said Tony Kanaan, who put on an entertaining show on the way to second place. "It was almost three years since our last street race in CART and it felt great to hear the people screaming again. It felt like we were back in the old days. I think the IRL realizes that and hopefully there will be more events like this. We set the standard for a street race."

Once a hero to CART fans, Andretti emerged as a prominent voice for the IRL, and after the successful show at St. Petersburg, he wasn't shy about confronting critics who vilified him for switching sides in the American open-wheel war. "Those people were ignorant about the product that we have here," Michael said. "Had they been following they would have seen that these cars were good right away on a road course. They're just people who want to say something negative about the IRL and now they've been shut up. The show today was as good as I've ever seen in a street race. There was passing, there was excitement . . . we had everything this weekend and I think it will shut up a lot of our critics."

Wheldon went on to dominate the 2005 IRL championship, winning six of seventeen races, including the Indianapolis 500, to cruise to the title over his AGR teammate Kanaan. Although he came from a road-racing background, Wheldon developed into an oval specialist, and nobody was braver in a wheel-to-wheel pack race on a high-banked speedway. He had a brash, outgoing personality and he enjoyed interacting with fans, giving him an approachable quality that is rare in champion athletes.

The problem was that while Wheldon should have been basking in the limelight of the most fruitful period of his career, his 2005 championship season was almost completely overshadowed by the arrival of Danica Patrick and the pop culture phenomenon that engulfed her.

As a child in Roscoe, Illinois, Patrick was encouraged by her father when she showed promise in go-karts. By the time she was eighteen, Danica was racing small formula cars in England in 2000, which happened to coincide with Bobby Rahal's brief tenure with the Jaguar Formula 1 team. She finished second in the annual Formula Ford Festival at Brands Hatch, matching Danny Sullivan's achievement from 1972 as the best result for an American in the famous annual gathering of young drivers.

Rahal was impressed with Patrick's skill and self-confidence, and he signed her to a long-term contract. She came back to America to compete in a handful of Barber Dodge Pro Series races in 2002 before spending two years in the CART-sanctioned Atlantic Championship. Although she never won a Formula Atlantic race, Patrick acquitted herself well and earned five podium finishes against some reasonably stout competition, including A.J. Allmendinger, Jon Fogarty, Ryan Dalziel, and Joey Hand.

The plan had been to take Patrick into the Champ Car series, but that changed when Rahal made his wholsesale switch to the IRL. So for 2005, the twenty-three-year-old found herself competing for Rookie of the Year honors in the IRL IndyCar Series against the likes of Ryan

Briscoe and Tomas Enge. Whether she was ready or not, Danica Patrick had hit the big time.

Her Indy car career got off to a jarring start. When another driver spun in front of her in the season opener at Homestead Speedway, she misjudged the closing speed and clouted a slower car, leaving her woozy with a concussion. At the Phoenix mile, she was off the pace and finished three laps down.

Then at Motegi, Japan, at one of the trickiest ovals in the world, things turned around. Patrick was quick in practice and narrowly missed out on pole position to two-time IRL series champion Sam Hornish Jr. In the race, she passed Hornish for the lead and ran all day near the front, finishing in fourth place after pacing thirty-two laps. That set the stage for Indianapolis, where her star really took off.

Patrick was fastest in Indy practice on three days; in fact, she turned the fastest lap of the month at 229.880 mph. But she made a critical mistake and nearly crashed on her first of four qualifying laps; a masterful save salvaged a run that was good enough for fourth on the grid. By race weekend, the national media had discovered racing's latest female phenom and was out in force at IMS. They got quite a show. Danica dropped to the tail of the lead lap when she stalled her engine during a pit stop. Later, on a restart, she spun and crashed out Panther Racing teammates Enge and Tomas Scheckter, with the only damage to her car a broken front wing, which was fixed in the pits during the caution period she caused. "No harm, no foul," quipped Rahal on TV.

With thirty laps to go, the rest of the field pitted for fuel. Rahal left Patrick on the track and in the lead, gambling that the race would again be slowed by an accident, which would allow Danica to stretch her fuel to the end. It almost worked, but alas, Wheldon passed a slowing Patrick with six laps to go and went on to take the win. His accomplishment went almost unnoticed. With ABC's lead announcer Todd Harris acting like a cheerleader, more than 50 percent of the television coverage of the race focused on Danica and arguably the most charmed fourth-place finish in the history of the Indianapolis Motor Speedway. Without question, it was the most famous. By recent standards, the TV ratings were spectacular, up 59 percent to a 6.5—the highest since the split in

1996. The Indy 500 beat NASCAR's same-day Coca-Cola 600 in the ratings for the first time in nearly a decade.

Finishing fourth in the Indianapolis 500 landed Danica on the cover of *Sports Illustrated*—the first time Indy car racing had made the cover since Sullivan's famous "Spin to Win" victory over Mario Andretti in 1985. By the time the IRL went to Texas Motor Speedway two weeks later, Danicamania had exploded. She made the front page of the local papers every day; the *Dallas Morning News* featured a minute-by-minute "Danica Watch" and the *Fort Worth Star Telegram* called her "the most important female athlete to visit the area since Annika Sorenstam competed in the 2003 Colonial PGA tournament." The media contingent at Texas was three times larger than usual, and the growth didn't come from small-town newspapers and obscure racing websites. Instead, Danica brought out the heavy hitters, including national magazines like *TV Guide* and *People*, not to mention television producers from the CBS and HBO networks.

While the IndyCar Series as a whole basked in the increased level of attention Danica suddenly brought, the change didn't go over well with everyone. By 2005, female drivers were no longer a novelty, or at least they shouldn't have been; women had been successfully competing at the Indianapolis 500 since Janet Guthrie qualified for the 1977 race. But despite Guthrie posting a ninth-place finish at Indianapolis in '78, more than two decades would pass before a female driver would have the opportunity to compete full time in an Indy car championship.

Desiré Wilson, who won a non-championship Formula 1 race in England in 1980, raced in the CART series in the early '80s without success, and it was not until '91 that another woman competed at Indy: sports car champion Lyn St. James, who actually out-qualified defending CART champion Nigel Mansell at the Speedway in '94.

Both Guthrie and St. James were roughly forty years old when they debuted in Indy cars; on the other hand, Sarah Fisher was only nineteen when she got her chance in 2000. Pushed along quickly by the IRL, USAC racer Fisher claimed a pole position at Kentucky Speedway and earned a pair of podium finishes in an Indy car career that spread eighty-one starts over more than a decade.

Patrick's IndyCar Series rivals mostly kept their frustration private, but a few popped off. "There are guys out there other than Danica, probably some better," snapped Wheldon, who appeared wearing a T-shirt reading "ACTUALLY WON THE INDY 500" at Texas. Shirts worn by Buddy Rice, the 2004 Indianapolis winner, and fellow Rahal Letterman Racing driver Vitor Meira displayed the messages "DANICA'S TEAMMATE" and "DANICA'S OTHER TEAMMATE."

"It wasn't just Danica pushing up the television ratings, it was all thirty-three drivers," Wheldon commented. "I keep telling the IRL that we need to be pushing all the personalities more in front of different people. She's not the only driver that has a fan base."

Meanwhile, Champ Car had a driver that was rewriting the record books, but garnering limited respect because it was against such a depleted field. Sébastien Bourdais picked up where he left off from his impressive rookie campaign to claim seven of the fourteen events in 2004, but he was made to work hard for the title by his Newman/Haas Racing teammate Bruno Junqueira. The Brazilian's hopes of challenging Bourdais for the Champ Car crown in '05 ended when he broke his back in an accident triggered by A.J. Foyt IV while Newman/Haas was competing in the Indianapolis 500 for the first time since 1995. NHR still finished 1-2 in the 2005 Champ Car championship, with Junqueira's replacement Oriol Servia the runner-up to repeat champion Bourdais. Justin Wilson, a former Formula 1 driver from England in his second year racing in America, broke through to score his first two Indy car race wins for the new start-up RuSPORT Racing team.

Champ Car showcased RuSPORT owner Carl Russo as the kind of new breed of entrant the series hoped to attract. Russo held a variety of executive jobs in the rapidly expanding Silicon Valley technology industry before settling in as CEO of Calix, a provider of cloud-based communications platforms. Russo raced Formula Atlantic cars before deciding he was better suited to team ownership. He formed RuSPORT in 2002 and the team guided young Californian A.J. Allmendinger to the '03 Atlantic championship before graduating together to the Champ Car series in '04.

Bourdais continued his mastery of Champ Car in 2006, notching another seven wins on the way to becoming the first driver to win three consective top-level American open-wheel championships since Ted Horn completed the feat in 1948. Wilson became the Frenchman's main competition, though Allmendinger suddenly exploded into prominence mid-season after he was unexpectedly fired by RuSPORT and signed by Gerald Forsythe. Allmendinger notched up five quick wins for Forsythe Racing and looked destined to be the next great American Indy car star, but at the end of 2006, he accepted a lucrative offer from Red Bull to begin what turned into a long but mostly unsuccessful career in NASCAR.

The IRL's biggest issue as 2005 came to a close was the departure of Chevrolet and Toyota. Although Honda got off to a slow start in '03, the Honda engine (and the company's aero and chassis development led by Nick Wirth for Andretti Green Racing) was demonstrably superior in '04 and '05. Like it had done in CART in 1994, General Motors simply withdrew from the IRL when the competition got more serious and expensive; Toyota's exit from open-wheel racing after a ten-year run was driven in part by its desire to strengthen its ties to NASCAR. Toyota entered the NASCAR Truck Series in 2004 and joined the higher-level Xfinity and Cup Series in '07 as American stock car racing's first foreign manufacturer.

Toyota tested an early prototype engine at Indianapolis as early as 1994, but it entered the CART series in '96 and didn't race in the Indy 500 until 2003. By then, the sport's landscape was very different. Toyota may never have made the move into stock cars had Indy car racing not been in such a state of disarray during its decade of participation.

"In 2003, we won the Indy 500 and we won the race in Japan. We won eleven out of sixteen races that year, and that fall, we still had to sell our management to stay in the sport," said David Wilson, who succeeded Lee White in 2013 as president of Toyota Racing Development. "As much as we loved it from an engineering standpoint, we also started realizing that there were a lot of empty seats. Open-wheel racing in the United States was not exactly catching fire, so that started our relationship with NASCAR."

In the three years where engine competition was at its peak in the IRL from 2003-05, Honda scored twenty-eight race wins, twenty-one poles, and two championships; Toyota's record was seventeen wins, twenty-two poles, and one title (in '03, for Dixon and Ganassi); while Chevrolet managed just four wins and five poles, and those came only after GM bought into the Cosworth IRL engine project.

By 2005, longtime IRL stalwart Eddie Cheever grew disllusioned by how the league appeared to morph into something very similar to mid-nineties CART. He placed the onus of blame on Toyota and Honda. "[The IRL] are at the old CART, which is not healthy," Cheever said. "We have to find some formula that works here. I think having Toyota and Honda has done a lot of good technically in this series. They have pushed the limit to look for perfection and made us dig deeper. But the sad thing is that has escalated our costs at a higher rate than we have been able to attract new fans. So we're out-pricing ourselves in the market. Now we have to re-evaluate what we are doing and come up with a paradigm that works. When we started the IRL, I beat Menard's, who had ten times our budget, because we were just better at it. You could compete with small amounts of money because I could buy the pieces and shuffle them together.

"The managers of the Chevy IRL program thought they could rep-licate what they had in the '90s," Cheever added. "That was over the minute the Japanese manufacturers knocked on the door and said they were coming. GM should have immediately ramped up what they were doing, both technically and financially, and they didn't. GM has some incredibly talented engineers. They just never understood the dynamics of Honda and Toyota coming into the IRL."

The IRL was fortunate that Honda elected to remain involved as the sole engine supplier for 2006 and beyond. By switching to a single engine supplier model, Honda and the IRL were able to follow the CART/Champ Car model and cut costs considerably; engines were now prepared to run two thousand miles between rebuilds and the price of an annual engine lease dropped to around $700,000. Improved engine reliability was another benefit for the IRL; during the Honda single-supply era from 2006–11, there was not a single engine failure in the Indianapolis 500. During the '10 season, the Honda engines completed a cumulative 220,000 miles of racing without an engine-related retire-ment. It was very similar to the way the Cosworth XFE engine program transformed the Champ Car series both on and off the track.

"Providing engines for the entire IndyCar field is a dramatically differ-ent role for Honda from that as one competitor in a multi-manufacturer championship," said HPD President Robert Clarke. "It is an opportunity that provides numerous new challenges, not only for HPD, but for several departments at American Honda as well. Certainly, manufacturing and preparing sufficient primary and backup engines for all thirty-three starters at the Indianapolis 500 will be a major effort, and it is vitally important, given our new circumstances, that we treat and care for all IndyCar competitors equally."

Also in 2006, the Rahal and Ganassi teams were the last holdouts to switch from G-Force to the dominant Dallara chassis, officially making the IRL IndyCar Series into a spec series, with all competitors using the same Dallara-Honda-Firestone chassis-engine-tire combination. For the portion of the fan base that viewed the Indianapolis 500 and Indy car racing as a crucible of free-thinking technical development and open competition, this was an unforgivable sin. By 2006, Champ Car was also a Lola/Ford-Cosworth/Bridgestone spec series, Reynard having succumbed to receivership (the British equivalent of bankruptcy) in 2002.

Another difficult pill for racing purists to swallow was the recruitment of KISS front man Gene Simmons and Simmons Abramson Marketing, the Hollywood-based agency he co-owned with former Pee Wee Herman manager Richard Abramson. Simmons attended numerous races serving as a spokesman for the rebranded IRL IndyCar Series.

"This is unique and aggressive, and I think that's a stance we have to take," commented Brian Barnhart, the IRL's president and chief operating officer. "We're really excited to see Gene and Rich bring their entertainment sense and marketing ideas and what they bring in terms of connections to the IndyCar Series at a point in time where we need to be thinking outside of the box. It's very aggressive, and I think it's exactly what the IndyCar Series needs."

Simmons called the Indy car drivers "gladiators" on a conference call with reporters and said he was as "serious as a heart attack" about building the IRL's brand.

"Our job is to be the missionaries of Indy," Simmons remarked. "We're going to make sure people around the world—especially in America—recognize the coolest of the cool is Indy because it *is* America. It's multi-national, it spreads across all lives. We don't want to tell you too much too soon, but as soon as we are ready with specifics, you'll be blown away."

Simmons soon debuted what he called an "anthem" titled "I Am Indy" that was blared nonstop on racetrack PA speakers. The IRL claimed it was the first official theme song commissioned for a professional sport and compared it to Queen's now-generic sports anthem "We Will Rock You/We Are the Champions."

"With 'I Am Indy,' you're making a pledge of allegiance to the United Nations of Indy," Simmons explained. "The phrase knows no bounds—racial, sexual, or otherwise. It applies to drivers, fans, sponsors. You've got to personalize the experience. These are individual, personalized rocket ships streaking at 220 miles per hour!"

On the track, the 2006 IRL season started on a difficult note. Paul Dana, a Northwestern graduate who raced occasionally while covering the CART series for *AutoWeek* magazine prior to embarking on a professional driving career, was killed in a crash prior to the season opener at Homestead-Miami Speedway. Dana crafted a lucrative sponsorship package from a consortium of American ethanol producers and used it to compete in Indy Lights before landing an Indy car drive with Hemelgarn Racing. He fractured his back after crashing in practice at Indianapolis in May 2005 and missed the rest of the season. Dana then took his Ethanol sponsorship to Rahal Letterman Racing for '06. When Ed Carpenter cut down a tire and crashed in the pre-race warmup, the inexperienced Dana appeared to not react in time and smashed into Carpenter's car.

With a spec car, the competition usually tightens up because everyone has the same equipment, and in that regard, the 2006 IndyCar Series championship couldn't have been any closer. It marked the first time that the sport's two most successful teams—Penske Racing and Ganassi Racing—had the same equipment, and the four drivers for those organizations put on quite a show, winning twelve of fourteen races. After 2,510 laps of competition, a Penske and a Ganassi driver actually tied on points. Penske's Sam Hornish claimed the title over Wheldon (now driving for Ganassi) on a four wins to two tiebreaker, with their respective teammates Hélio Castroneves and Scott Dixon in title contention right down to the last lap of the season finale at Chicagoland Speedway. Led by Wheldon, the Penske and Ganassi drivers were in front of the field for 83 percent of all laps.

The IndyCar championship went right down to the wire again in 2007. Dixon looked like he was in control and headed toward a second IRL crown until he ran out of fuel while leading into Turn Three on the last lap of the last race, again at Chicagoland, handing the race win and the title to Indianapolis 500 winner Dario Franchitti and Andretti Green Racing. It was a fraught campaign for the Scotsman; while he won four events, he was lucky to escape injury after being involved in a pair of scary airborne accidents within the space of seven days.

In Champ Car, the Lola chassis that dated to the year 2000 was finally retired after the '06 season, replaced by a new spec chassis designed and manufactured in Georgia by Elan Technology and named Panoz DP01 to honor company founder Don Panoz. Billed as "The Future of Racing," the DP01 combined some classic Champ Car styling cues with a bit of Formula 1 influence like a raised, "single-keel" nose into a smaller, lighter package. The 750-horsepower Ford-Cosworth powerplant carried over essentially unchanged, as did the internals of the Lola-based seven-speed sequential gearbox, but with F1-style steering wheel paddle activation. Designed by Simon Marshall, the 1,460-pound DP-01 was 105 pounds lighter than the outgoing Lola and about nine inches shorter, depending on configuration. Although there were no oval races on the '07 Champ Car World Series schedule, the DP01 was engineered to meet FIA crash standards more stringent than those used by the IRL.

Champ Car set the price of a rolling chassis with gearbox at $295,000, representing about a 35-percent reduction on the estimated $450K that a new Lola commanded. Spare parts were priced about 30 percent cheaper as well. A gearbox was reduced to $45,000, as opposed to nearly $110,000, while the price of a nose assembly was slashed from $33,000 to $16,000.

It was no coincidence that the car was unveiled at a July 2006 gala in Champ Car coprincipal Kevin Kalkhoven's adopted hometown, as part of the second annual Grand Prix of San Jose. Kalkhoven was beaming as the wraps were pulled from the car, as proud of the sleek new design as he was of the upgrades made to the temporary street course after a very bumpy first year. In '05, race cars literally flew over light rail tracks that crossed what was a very makeshift circuit. Urban street races were Champ Car's bread and butter, with new events planned to bookend the

'07 season in Las Vegas and Phoenix, and Kalkhoven was bullish about the future of the series.

But behind the scenes, negotiations were once again taking place with the IRL in an effort to consolidate Indy car racing as one series. Kalkhoven and Tony George found they enjoyed each other's company socially and had forged an unlikely friendship. Urged on by the likes of Honda's Robert Clarke, Firestone's Al Speyer, and Mario Andretti, the business of trying to negotiate an amicable settlement crept along slowly throughout 2006 and into '07.

In a February 2006 interview with the *Los Angeles Times*, George stated that he believed Indy car racing would be better served with a single series. He confirmed informal talks with Kalkhoven a few weeks later at the IndyCar Series opener at Homestead-Miami Speedway, but he cautioned media members and the public from getting too excited about the possibility of imminent unification.

"I think Kevin and I agree on many of the big issues," George commented. "I think we both appreciate diversity in the schedule and agree about a combination of road and street circuits and ovals. We want to operate profitably, we want to keep all of our partners involved, and we want them to have a return on their investment. But it's a delicate balance between sport, business, entertainment, and technology.

"I'm very excited about where the IRL is today, but it's safe to say there is room for improvement," he added. "Over the last ten years, I have worked on relationships that were strained during that time. It has often been challenging, but it's getting better every day."

However, George stopped short of saying he was optimistic that unification could be achieved quickly and cast doubt over whether it could be done in time for the 2007 season, when Champ Car was scheduled to introduce the new spec Panoz chassis.

"Optimistic?" asked George. "It's certainly possible, but we're a long way from there at the moment. Everyone would like to see it happen sooner or later. The most important thing is that we have an orderly transition that will allow us to look to the future together. I believe it is something that is achievable.

"I suppose if all the stars, moons, and planets aligned, 2007 is possible," George added. "There is reason to be hopeful, but I'd caution everyone from getting their hopes too high. It's going to be very difficult, and if the media makes it a big issue every weekend, it's going to be even more of a challenge."

Kalkhoven was slightly more forthcoming in an April 2006 interview with *National Speed Sport News*. "My most important desire is to get it done right," he said. "The history of mergers and acquisitions in general doesn't have a high success rate, and the worst thing that could happen is that we merge and it doesn't work. That would be horrific for everybody. So both our intentions in discussing this is to make sure it's right. As a result, we haven't put a time limit on it. If it happens next year, that's great. If it takes longer to get it right, that's fine too.

"At the moment we've got two series that are doing okay," he continued. "I'm proud of what we're doing here in Champ Car, but throwing that away in pursuit of something that would fail I think would be a huge mistake for American open-wheel racing. I would characterize it very simply as we're continuing to hold discussions with the best intent between us in trying to get it done in the best way possible."

On June 25, the *Indianapolis Star* ran a front page story claiming that open-wheel unification was imminent, quoting George as saying that the two groups had "agreed conceptually" to share ownership. "Now we have to agree on how we would go about resolving differences that might come up," he said.

But on the grid at the Grand Prix of Cleveland, Champ Car co-principal Kalkhoven said that there was much work to be done before American open-wheel racing moved forward as a single unified series. "The story was accurate, but the headline ('Champ Car, IRL Nearing Merger') was a bit misleading," Kalkhoven said. "But we are still talking—and in good faith. You go into either paddock and everybody wants to see it done. The fact that it hasn't been done in ten years is indicative of how difficult it is."

By the end of the summer, the negotiations were again on the back burner as both series planned to move ahead individually in 2007. "That whole thing got blown out of proportion," Kalkhoven said. "Tony George and I have gone a long way to resolving all sorts of issues, but our concentration is on Champ Car, which is going really well now. It would be nice to do a merger in some respects, but culturally, the two organizations are very far apart. It is a completely dead issue, and I don't think I can summarize it any further than that. There was a lot of progress made while the talks were quiet. The moment that it got leaked out, an awful lot of influences came into play who might not have benefited directly from such a unification. A lot of factors came into play, but basically, you can assume that now and for the foreseeable future, it's dead."

After a decade of being denied the opportunity to compete against all the top Indy car drivers in a single series, the drivers began to express their frustration over the constant cycle of rumors, raised hopes, and subsequent disappointment. "It would be lovely," said Dixon. "Everybody wants it to happen. It's so frustrating. You'd think they could just talk and work things out, but they have been trying for years so I think everyone can quite clearly see that it's never going to happen. From my side of the fence it looks like Champ Car is struggling a bit at the moment, and if they just sort of went away, I think everybody would be happy with that. You'd have more cars and more teams heading for one series and trying to make that series better. The depth of drivers and depth of teams would improve and you'd have a lot more fans watching. I don't care which one it is as long as it's one."

If the fans, the drivers, and Indy car racing's other main constituents were frustrated about the continued inability to put the fractured sport back together, that paled in comparison to the men who were on the front line trying to lead the peacemaking efforts. Al Speyer, head of Bridgestone/Firestone's American racing tire development program, was a key player in terms of trying to move the process along. And American Honda President Koichi Amemiya appealed to HPD leader Robert Clarke to devote every means possible into trying to end the decades-long conflict, a responsibility Clarke took very seriously.

"I've put significant time and effort in the past two years into trying to do what I can to try and save open-wheel racing in America," Clarke told journalist Gordon Kirby in early 2007. "Unfortunately, I didn't get any further than anybody else. I put everything I had into it. I approached saving open-wheel racing with the same effort I do everything else, and frankly, I wore myself out. Together with Mario Andretti's efforts, I thought we were making some progress in getting the two groups together. There were a number of meetings and things seemed to be headed in a generally good direction, and then it all fell apart in August. It got so close and I was totally convinced that if it could get that far and not happen, it was never going to happen."

Although he was a vocal opponent of the IRL in its early years, no individual tried harder to unify America's divergent pair of open-wheel racing championships than Andretti. But for years, even Mario's wisdom, clout, and common sense couldn't convince George and Kalkhoven of the need to come together for the greater good of a sport that continued to struggle for media impact, sponsor dollars, and fan interest.

Like Clarke, Andretti believed the two groups were close to an agreement in the summer of 2006 until a key meeting was canceled at the last minute, leaving the gulf between the two sanctioning organizations as wide as ever. "I almost cried," Andretti admitted. "I had a situation put together where a really comprehensive meeting was set to take place and it got derailed."

Andretti declined to say why his potential open-wheel summit never took place. But he did reveal his frustration over how he was getting increasingly fed up with both sides' inability to see the need to move forward into the future as a single entity. "They are all in denial—that's the problem," he commented. "They all have these little victories. Champ Car says things like 'the crowd was up 10 percent at Cleveland,' but give me a break. I was at Portland and the weekend was like going to a funeral. And it's the same thing on the other side in the IRL. They keep thinking things are getting better.

"That's what I fight all the time when I'm reasoning with them," Mario continued. "I'm like a broken record trying to make the point. Then they say they agree, but when it comes down to trying to negotiate through a little bit of give and take, some of the major issues are pulled off the table. I got them to the altar more than once; I just can't get them to say 'I do.'"

While Indy car racing continued to struggle for traction and attention, NASCAR reached its commercial peak in 2005 in terms of attendance and television ratings. This, coupled with the on-again, off-again saga of the open-wheel split, created a sudden wave of Indy car drivers who tried to make the transition into stock cars. Outside of Allmendinger, '07 IndyCar Series champion and Indy 500 winner Franchitti attempted to make the switch with Chip Ganassi's NASCAR team in '08, and three-time IRL champion Hornish transferred to the stock car side of Roger Penske's organization. The exodus of open-wheel drivers rankled Andretti.

"It's a shame that they are looking at that only because of the money factor, and that's all due to the fact that the two Indy car series need to wake up and come together," Andretti commented. "Today the top drivers in either series, IRL or Champ Car, they just don't have the opportunity to earn at the level that we used to be earning in our sport. The top guys don't earn the money that I used to make in the late '70s, for God's sake! That's criminal. That's the travesty of it all, and that's why I keep preaching these things to both sides. Both sides need to wake up because the responsibility is so huge—not only to the fans and to the sport, but to careers.

"Look at A.J. Allmendinger—do you think he's happy where he is? He only went there for the money. But they all have a very narrow sort of timeline to earn to the point of being secure for the rest of their life. And it seems like the discipline of the sport that they really love is not giving them that opportunity. That's a shame, and to me, it's all the responsibility of the powers that be. They should take that into consideration, because if there was one series, things would change dramatically for the better. That's my take on it, and I have to get that out because I so believe in it."

The year 2007 therefore ended with open-wheel unification looking as unlikely as ever, and despite Kevin Kalkhoven's protestations, with Champ Car hanging by a thread.

CHAPTER 20

UNIFICATION AND RECESSION

In Aesop's fable "The Boy Who Cried Wolf," a group of villagers stopped believing that a wolf was actually attacking their flock of sheep after the boy assigned to watch over them issued a series of false alarms. By February 2008, after nearly a decade of having their hopes raised by the prospect of American open-wheel unification only to be disappointed again and again, fans of Indy car racing could certainly relate to that centuries-old tale.

In the four years since Gerald Forsythe and Kevin Kalkhoven acquired the assets of CART, negotiations to combine the best elements of the IRL IndyCar Series and the Champ Car World Series dragged on, but every time the parties got close, leaks to the media and others set back the process. This time, the talks advanced far enough that even when the story broke in late January, IRL founder Tony George and Champ Car co-principal Kevin Kalkhoven privately confirmed that they had finally reached a basic agreement to move forward together as a single entity. It would be called a merger, a takeover, a unification, an acquisition, and a bankruptcy, but whatever the label, the important thing was that it appeared American open-wheel racing would run as a single, unified series in 2008 and beyond under the Indy Racing League umbrella.

Even though the basics for a deal were in place by late January, the process crept along slowly for several weeks as Kalkhoven and George traveled on international business. Both series officially confirmed February 8 that negotiations had taken place toward folding elements of

LAT Images

Champ Car into the IRL, but the ongoing saga took one final turn later that day when Champ Car issued a statement claiming that the talks had stalled.

"Unfortunately, leaks and media reports about a possible unification of Champ Car and the Indy Racing League have significantly hampered discussions," stated series co-principals Forsythe and Kalkhoven. "Over the past three years, we have fielded and offered several proposals regarding unification of the two premier U.S.-based open-wheel racing series, but we have been unable to reach an acceptable solution. Discussions currently are at a standstill, and we therefore are proceeding with plans to continue as Champ Car."

Kalkhoven reiterated those sentiments in an interview with ESPN. com. "If people really want to see unification, the best thing to do is to leave it alone," he said. "It frustrates me because the parties are operating in good faith, and external influences prevent the transaction from taking place. You cannot do a business transaction in the public eye. When you do a normal business merger, the principals agree to the transaction, then you make an announcement, and then you take it to the stakeholders for comment. When there is a leak like this, everyone and their opinions gets involved and it becomes a complete stalemate. This has happened several times before. It's not helping the process."

"Things are progressing, but [the process is] delicate and complicated," affirmed George.

In the latest proposal, several Champ Car races, including the Long Beach Grand Prix, would be added to the existing sixteen-race IndyCar Series schedule, and Champ Car teams committing to run the full slate would receive assistance from the IRL in obtaining Dallara chassis and Honda engines. The Panoz DP01, which enjoyed a successful debut season in 2007 (Sébastien Bourdais won his fourth consecutive Champ Car title; Will Power, Robert Doornbos, Paul Tracy, and Justin Wilson also won races) was essentially tossed into the scrap heap.

The final hang-up centered around a schedule conflict between the Long Beach Grand Prix and the IRL race in Motegi, Japan, on the weekend of April 19-20. Motegi offered to delay its event to the weekend of April 26-27, but that was impossible because the IRL was scheduled to race in conjunction with the NASCAR Truck Series at Kansas

Speedway that weekend. That meant the Japanese race would have to move to autumn, which brought up additional issues: the IRL was adamant that its championship must end on American soil, and Chicagoland Speedway's contract stipulated that it hosted the IRL finale, set for September 7. Moving Japan to late September or early October (possibly pairing it with another Champ Car–based event at Surfers Paradise, Australia) would require designating it as a non-championship race, something Honda and Motegi officials were keen to avoid.

Along with key administrators Brian Barnhart and Terry Angstadt, IRL founder Tony George flew to Japan with Honda Performance Development Director Robert Clarke to try to to convince high-ranking Honda corporate officials to grant some flexibility to the Motegi event in the interest of helping the overall growth of American open-wheel racing under the IndyCar Series umbrella. The resulting compromise was that Motegi and Long Beach would *both* be run as originally scheduled, on April 19 and 20 respectively, with both awarding points counting toward the IndyCar Series Championship.

Champ Car's majority owners Kalkhoven and Gerald Forsythe had gained control of the Long Beach race on May 24, 2005, when they successfully bid $15 million for selected assets of the Grand Prix Association of Long Beach. Since January 2004, when they emerged from U.S. Bankruptcy Court as the custodians of the Champ Car series, Kalkhoven and Forsythe also acquired the rights to the Toronto street race, as well as engine manufacturer Cosworth Racing and key supplier Pi Electronics. So the Champ Car group was certainly not lacking in assets when it came to the negotiations with the IRL.

The teams that expected to compete in Champ Car in 2008 were stuck in limbo, awaiting confirmation whether they would have to frantically gear up to make the conversion to race in the IndyCar Series. Meanwhile, existing IndyCar Series teams expressed mixed reactions about the possibility of Champ Car being merged into the IRL.

At NASCAR's Daytona 500 in February, Roger Penske said he strongly supported the proposed open-wheel unification and told the *St. Petersburg Times* he would go so far as to provide incoming Champ Car teams with "an extra car or pieces in order to get them going." But perhaps not surprisingly, A.J. Foyt was vehemently opposed to Champ

Car teams receiving assistance from the IRL in order to make the transition between series. Foyt's team had competed in the IRL since its 1996 start-up, and his longstanding ties to the Indianapolis Motor Speedway and the Hulman-George family remained unimpeachable.

"I would throw a damned fit and would want to damn near pack up my bags if that was all true," Foyt fumed during a panel discussion with former Daytona 500 winners. "And I think a lot of people that have been loyal to [the IRL] would do the same thing because it just wouldn't be right for people who had to buy and spend a lot of money."

Finally, on February 22, the news was made official. The ownership group of Champ Car had reached agreement in principle for the IRL to acquire and/or merge key elements of the Champ Car World Series into the IndyCar Series. After the thirty-fourth annual Toyota Grand Prix of Long Beach on April 20—which was billed as a gala send off for the Champ Car formula—the Champ Car World Series would cease to exist, and it was hoped that most, if not all, Champ Car teams would join the IndyCar Series.

Although the 2008 schedule was already set, the IRL picked up Champ Car's July Edmonton date and agreed to run the Surfers Paradise, Australia, race in October as a nonchampionship event. The IRL also confirmed plans to resume racing in Toronto in 2009, and as part of the agreement, acquired Champ Car's pioneering Mobile Medical Center, as well as the intellectual property of the company and historical records dating to 1909.

Flanked by around a dozen drivers from both series, George and Kalkhoven addressed the media in a packed conference room at Homestead-Miami Speedway on February 27, 2008. The two men didn't offer much in the way of new information about the upcoming amalgamation of the Champ Car World Series into the IRL IndyCar Series, but by appearing together, Kalkhoven and George symbolized what they hoped would be a brighter future for American open-wheel racing now that it was unified under IRL leadership. The genuine smiles they wore as they shook hands for the cameras was visual proof that the twelve-year battle between Champ Car and the IRL for control of American open-wheel racing—itself a simmering leftover of the original USAC-vs.-CART fight from 1978-80—could finally be put in the rear-view mirror. In fact, it was hard to find anyone on the grounds of the Florida oval (perhaps other than Foyt) who wasn't sporting an ear-splitting grin.

"It's been a long and hard road to get here, but we are here," said Kalkhoven. "This is something that is still going to require a huge amount of work, but I think the long-term potential is extremely exciting for everyone involved with this. The winners today are the fans, the teams, the drivers, and indeed the potential that we have to grow the sport over the next few years. By uniting the sport, I sincerely hope that everyone— and by that of course I also mean the Champ Car fans—recognizes that this is something that was a very conscious decision that we took to try to develop North American open-wheel motorsport and take it into 2008, '09 and beyond in a very positive way.

"We all have to recognize the biggest challenges lie ahead, and how will we deal with them," he continued. "There won't be a sudden miracle cure. It's going to be a hard slog, and if there is a disappointment, the blame will start again. The real question is: Will open-wheel racing adapt and change to different market conditions, or is it stuck in the past? We'll see."

Although the common perception was that the IRL won the war, George dismissed the notion that he would be the sport's sole leader moving forward. He called the road ahead for the IndyCar Series "daunting," yet it was clear he was excited about the possibilities now that all of the sport's constituents would be working in unison, arguably for the first time since the late 1970s.

"I try to lead by example," George said. "I certainly don't like to take all the blame, so I don't like to take all the credit either. You're only as good as the people you surround yourself with, and I'm fortunate to have a lot of good people that I depend on. I'm going to have a lot more now. There's plenty of wisdom, knowledge, and experience out there to draw from to help lead the sport. I've said all along it's going to be by our actions that we show people or convince people that we are working for the betterment of open-wheel racing. The proof will be in what we are able to develop together now over the course of the next couple of years.

"My goal is to bring everybody together," he added. "We need to make sure that there is good leadership that makes good decisions that are in everybody's best interest, not in any one group's best interest, and collectively try to provide direction and support. We'll do our very best to keep together what has taken us so long to put together. Hopefully, progress will be visible and measurable immediately. Chances are it won't be; it's going to take some time. But it all starts here today."

Suddenly, Indy car racing didn't have any excuses anymore. For more than a decade, open-wheel racing's decline—and NASCAR's simultaneous growth into an American phenomenon—was blamed on the split. There would be no more confusion about what constituted Indy car racing. Now everybody would be racing in the same places, including Indianapolis. Indy was the one word in open-wheel racing that didn't need further explanation to casual sports fans, and yes, Danica and that guy from *Dancing with the Stars* (Hélio Castroneves won season five of the ABC television reality show dance competition in 2007) were part of it all. The on-track product was solid. The challenge was to rebuild Indy car racing's fan base and its financial base, not necessarily in that order, and it wasn't going to happen overnight, especially given the recession that descended upon America at the exact time the Indy car reunification took place. In that regard, the timing of the merger couldn't have been worse.

"This is spectacular news, but we all have to be cautious because the act of unifying open-wheel racing in America is not a cure for all that ails the sport," warned Texas Motor Speedway President Eddie Gossage, promoter of (until the addition of Long Beach to the IRL slate) what was then the second-largest race on the IndyCar schedule. "I hope everyone involved doesn't immediately think that the unification on its own will have Indy car racing challenging NASCAR anytime soon. It is a necessary and huge first step, but there is much work to be done."

As much as the powers that be wanted the absorption of Champ Car into the IRL to be a win-win for everyone involved, certainly there were some losers. "It's a great day for the sport but hard for us," said a former Champ Car staffer who was among around fifty who lost their jobs. Suppliers like Panoz, Hewland, and Carl Haas Auto absorbed financial losses, engine supplier Cosworth USA laid off thirty people, and eleven of the fourteen events on the Champ Car schedule were affected. Most were simply canceled outright.

By the time the 2008 racing season got underway, attorneys representing parent companies for the Champ Car World Series had filed

Chapter 11 paperwork in U.S. Bankruptcy Court, intending to continue in the management and possession of the business and property as a debtor-in-possession. Champ Car World Series LLC estimated debts of less than $10 million, topped by $1.825 million owed to engine manufacturer Cosworth Inc. Company assets were estimated at $10-$50 million. An affidavit from Gene Cottingham, vice president and chief financial officer for Champ Car World Series LLC, stated that the company's four-man board of managers "determined that it is no longer economically feasible to sustain an open-wheel series and that [Champ Car] did not have the funds to operate the series in 2008."

Cottingham further noted that Champ Car believed "it is in the best interests of the sport of open-wheel racing in general to sell certain assets to the IRL and to unify the sport of Indy-style open-wheel racing under the IRL, all before the start of the 2008 season."

The affidavit revealed that the Champ Car board of managers authorized the decision to file bankruptcy on February 14, exactly one week before Kalkhoven and Forsythe executed a Memorandum of Understanding for Champ Car to assign race sanctioning contracts and sell substantially all of its intellectual property and other intangible assets, as well as the Champ Car Mobile Medical Unit, to the IRL for $6 million. Judge Anthony J. Metz III was assigned to preside over Champ Car's bankruptcy case.

Perhaps the biggest surprise was Gerald Forsythe's sudden and complete withdrawal from the sport. Just a day after Kalkhoven and George met the press at Homestead, Paul Tracy, then the most successful active driver in American open-wheel racing with thirty-one wins, learned he would be sidelined for the 2008 season. Blaming a lack of sponsorship, Forsythe elected to disband Forsythe Championship Racing rather than take the team to the IRL. Forsythe had almost single-handedly funded his Champ Car team since late '03, when his longtime sponsor, Player's cigarettes, was forced out of racing by Canadian legislation banning tobacco advertising. While his cars retained the familiar blue and white colors associated with Player's, Indeck Energy, a company owned by Forsythe, was listed as the team's title sponsor from '04 onward.

Forsythe's decision to disband FCR left outside observers baffled. On the surface, it appeared he was willing to spend millions to preserve the way open-wheel racing was, but not the way it was going to be in the future. It seemed incongruous that Forsythe would help bring together open-wheel racing by agreeing to disband Champ Car, yet refuse to support the unified IndyCar Series. Forsythe continued to field a two-car effort in the Formula Atlantic championship, including an entry for rising Canadian star James Hinchcliffe, but that too was shuttered at the end of 2008.

"It's pretty late for this to happen, and I'm hoping I can still find a competitive seat," Tracy said. "I think I could do a good job in the IRL." Sadly, thanks to Forsythe's actions, Tracy's full-time career as an Indy car driver came to an end. After participating in the Champ Car finale at Long Beach, he made only eighteen more starts in IndyCar Series competition over the next four years. In a case where the truth was stranger than fiction, Tracy even ran a race for Tony George's Vision Racing operation, his fourth-place finish at Edmonton in 2008 representing the final top-five result of his career.

The drawn-out process of the unification left Champ Car teams hoping to make the transition to the IRL less than five weeks to prepare for the March 29 season opener at Homestead. "As you can imagine, we are all absolutely flat out," remarked Jimmy Vasser, the 1996 CART champion who was retired as a driver and serving as a minority partner in Kalkhoven's KV Racing Technology team. "It's a huge undertaking, and we're working around the clock seven days a week just to get prepared for the first test at Sebring. It will probably be difficult for all the Champ Car teams that are switching over to be there, and then subsequently on the road for back-to-back races at Homestead and St. Petersburg. But it is what it is, and we're working real hard."

Each Champ Car team making the transition to the IndyCar Series received one used Dallara chassis from their "partner" IndyCar Series team during the first week of March, followed by a new chassis that required ground-up assembly. That left even the most established organizations, including four-time defending Champ Car titlists Newman/ Haas Racing, scrambling to put together a competitive effort with unfamiliar equipment. NHR's task was made tougher when rookie driver Graham Rahal (the nineteen-year-old son of three-time CART champion Bobby Rahal) crashed in testing at Homestead and missed the opening race.

"The timing probably wasn't the best, but we have our heads down and we're looking forward to getting on track," said Vasser. "I think there aren't many people out there that won't agree this is the best thing for the sport of Indy car racing, and for the future. We'd all like to see it get back to where it was in the mid-nineties and it's not going to come quickly, but there are some promising signs there."

"Expect the unexpected" was the catchphrase buzzing around Homestead prior to the unified IndyCar Series opener, and with a handful of drivers in the field with little or no oval experience, what transpired was indeed unexpected—a largely clean and competitive event, won by pole man Scott Dixon over Marco Andretti and Dan Wheldon. KVRT's Oriol Servià topped the eight Champ Car–affiliated additions to the twenty-five-car field, five laps down in twelfth place.

"To me it's like when you have kids that have divorced parents and after twelve years of separation they get together," said Servià. "No matter how you look at it, it's good news. Maybe we were the ones living with the mother, but now we're under the same roof and it will take some adjusting for all of us. And we are the ones that have to adjust the most because we're the ones getting to the house a little late. It's a huge challenge for us drivers and the teams."

At St. Petersburg a week later, Rahal took advantage of changing track conditions in a wet/dry race to claim victory on his IndyCar Series debut, supplanting Dixon and Marco Andretti as the sport's youngest-ever race winner. Rahal and Andretti, who was also nineteen when he scored his first Indy car win at Sonoma Raceway in 2006, gave the unified IndyCar Series a pair of legacy drivers who were expected to emerge as major stars as their careers progressed.

Another highly visible driver that the sport was depending on for publicity also made a major breakthrough. About thirty-six hours before Will Power closed the book on Champ Car on April 20 by winning at Long Beach, Danica Patrick crossed the line first at Twin Ring Motegi to win the last IRL race of the split era. Patrick was one of several drivers put on a fuel-saving strategy, but Hélio Castroneves claimed he didn't hear a radio call and drove hard during the first part of the final stint. When he finally acknowledged strategist Tim Cindric's pleas to save fuel, it was too late. Patrick passed Castroneves to lead the last two laps to claim the first (and to date, the only) Indy car race win for a female driver.

Patrick had moved from Bobby Rahal's team to Andretti Green Racing in 2007, attracting sponsorship from Motorola and Boost Mobile. "She wanted to win so bad," said team owner Michael Andretti. "She's such a competitor, so I think it's more a monkey off her back for herself, not everybody else. That's the type of individual she is. Now that it's off, I think you're going to see a different person. I think this is the first of many."

Champ Car ended up contributing ten full-time entries to the IRL in 2008, bringing the weekly car count to twenty-six, but even with that major influx, the Indianapolis 500 attracted only thirty-six car/driver combinations—despite the fact that for the first time in more than a decade the purse got a substantial 25 percent bump to more than $13 million, with upwards of $2.5 million expected to go to the winner. In fact, Dixon collected $2,988,065 after winning the 500 from pole position. An eight-year Indy car veteran who was still just twenty-eight, Dixon swept the first race, the first Indianapolis 500, and the first championship of the sport's new unified era.

Despite the challenges provided by the slumping U.S. economy, the unification of American open-wheel racing was very positively received. One of the compromises required to make it happen was the late addition of the Edmonton event to the end of a previously scheduled five-week run. Making the situation even more difficult, the IRL insisted that the Edmonton race be run on Saturday, July 26, so it would not clash with the NASCAR Allstate 400 at the Brickyard set for Sunday the 27th at the Indianapolis Motor Speedway.

"It's tough on all the teams, and I'm sure it's tough on the officials and everyone, even the fans," said Rahal Letterman Racing General Manager Scott Roembke. "I'm old enough that I remember the first time we did three in a row in CART in 2001 and it was a huge deal. It was Detroit, Portland, and Cleveland, and I remember wondering 'How are we ever going to do three in a row?'"

Now that workload was doubled to six in a row, with the challenge made greater by the fact that the six-week stretch in 2008 required Indy-Car teams to convert their cars from oval track to road-racing trim or vice versa three times. "If they could minimize the changes from track to track and go from oval to oval and road course to road course, that would help a ton," Roembke noted. "Going from Richmond to Watkins Glen, then back to Nashville, then the road course at Mid-Ohio, that's a ton of work. You've got to take the gearboxes apart, and/or have spare gearboxes, rebuild the whole car, and change out the suspension. They get caught up in this whole NASCAR mentality, but you can't find a NASCAR team out there that doesn't have twelve or fourteen cars. And our cars are just not designed to be run week in and week out without proper maintenance. They are highly sophisticated, technical cars, and when you start slapping races back to back to back to back, someone is going to miss something."

The IndyCar Series issued an eighteen-race schedule for the 2009 season that promised to be less stressful on competitors. The trend toward road racing continued, with ten ovals and eight road or street courses, and series officials said their intention was to eventually achieve a fifty-fifty balance of road races and ovals. Most importantly, the season was stretched out by a full five weeks to end October 10 instead of September 7, with Homestead taking over the finale slot from Chicagoland Speedway. "Extending the season will improve the quality of life for everyone involved in the series," commented Indy Racing League Competition President Brian Barnhart.

In late 2008, IRL officials announced that ABC was awarded the contract to continue to broadcast the Indianapolis 500 for another four years, extending a partnership that started in 1965. However, ABC and ESPN committed to carry only four additional IndyCar Series races annually, with the remainder to be televised on VERSUS, a sports-oriented cable network owned by Comcast that was available in 74 million U.S. households, compared to around 100 million for sports television standard bearer ESPN and 90 million for ESPN2.

Formerly known as the Outdoor Life Network, VERSUS was the main television outlet for the National Hockey League, but the channel's biggest draw was holding the exclusive American broadcast rights for the Tour de France bicycle race. The VERSUS deal was for ten years for a reported total of $67 million. IRL officials presented the new contract as a win-win situation, stressing that the main appeal of going to VERSUS was the opportunity to broadcast qualifying and extend race programming to include pre- and postrace activity. Critics likened it to Champ Car's unsuccessful 2004 package on the Spike network (formerly TNN).

"I encouraged our team in Indianapolis to do everything in our power to maximize the opportunities we have with the new unified series and the centennial celebration of the Indy 500 that kicks off next year," said IRL founder and CEO Tony George. "We wanted to understand what was most important to our constituents. It was consistent with our thoughts, and it was good to get that validation. We've come up with a very exciting opportunity."

But the $67 million VERSUS deal was an albatross for the IRL in many ways. The young network was virtually unknown in terms of brand name recognition, and the money involved was paltry when compared to the television windfall that NASCAR was pulling in. NASCAR split its television rights between Fox, ESPN, and TNT in 2005 for $4.48 billion over eight years, nearly doubling the six-year, $2.4 billion package that covered 2001-06.

Ratings were horrible, averaging 0.25 for the ten races broacast on VERSUS in 2009—less than half the already poor 0.58 the IRL averaged for its ESPN and ESPN2 broadcasts in '08. Ratings on ABC also continued to slip, with the Indy 500 losing half a point to a 4.0 in '09 and the other four races producing an average rating of 0.82. The NASCAR deal was expensive for the involved networks, but it was made worthwhile by the ratings, which peaked with a 5.3 average for the thirty-six Cup Series races in '05.

The IndyCar Series started the 2009 season by welcoming a popular former champion back into the fold. Dario Franchitti returned to open-wheel racing after his attempt to break into NASCAR with Chip Ganassi Racing in '08 was sidelined by financial woes and a jarring wreck. A blown tire at Talladega Superspeedway caused Franchitti to spin, and his left ankle was fractured when his car was T-boned at high speed. Dario's enthusiasm for Indy cars was rekindled when he attended the '08 Detroit Grand Prix as a spectator, and when he expressed a desire to make a comeback, Ganassi quickly signed him to partner with Dixon.

Sam Hornish also moved to NASCAR in 2008, driving for Team Penske, and he too endured a difficult transition to stock car racing. Hornish logged just three top-five finishes in 167 Cup Series starts; he won a total of five Xfinity Series races and almost claimed the Xfinity title in '13 in his last year of full-time competition, narrowly losing out to Austin Dillon.

Hornish explained his reasons for switching to NASCAR after an Indy car career that netted nineteen race wins and reflected on the challenge that he and other open-wheel formula car drivers faced in trying to adapt to stock cars. "It's a hard transition," he observed. "I felt like I was complacent in the IndyCar Series. When I won my first championship over there, people said, 'He won't win when Penske comes in.' I won the championship. 'He won't win when those other guys come in,' or 'He won't be able to do it on the road courses.' I got to the point where I thought within a year, I was going to be winning road course races too, and I just felt it was time to try something different.

"I think if I would have made the commitment earlier to live in North Carolina, it could have helped," Hornish added. "When things weren't going the way they should have been, I should have been at the shop every day. It might have helped, and it might not have. The only thing I really regret about the whole thing is not pushing the people around me hard enough to give me all the tools that it takes to make it in NASCAR. It wasn't until I failed that I figured out how to do the right things."

In fact, the only driver with extensive Indy car ties who achieved notable success in NASCAR during the modern era was Juan Pablo Montoya. After racing in Formula 1 from 2001 to mid-2006, earning seven wins for Williams and McLaren, Montoya shocked the world by making a sudden switch to NASCAR with his old boss, Chip Ganassi. Montoya won Cup Series road course races at Sonoma Raceway and Watkins Glen and should have won the 2010 Brickyard 400.

Meanwhile, another top Indy car star was temporarily missing from the grid when the seventeen-race 2009 campaign opened. In October 2008, Hélio Castroneves was led into U.S. District Court in Miami in handcuffs and leg irons to answer a seven-count indictment for tax evasion and conspiracy to defraud the United States government, charges with the potential to land the Brazilian in jail for up to thirty-five years or at least face a substantial fine and possible deportment. Along with his alleged co-conspirators (his sister and business manager, Katiucia, and lawyer Alan R. Miller), a teary-eyed Castroneves entered a not-guilty plea and was ordered to post a $10 million bond. A Penske Racing spokesman said the team had been cooperating with federal authorities as a witness for several months, and that much of the government's case against the driver was based on claims that he failed to pay tax on $5 million he received as part of a licensing agreement with the team.

Penske replaced Castroneves with Will Power for the 2009 season opener at St. Petersburg, and Power was still in the number 3 car when practice opened for the Long Beach Grand Prix on April 17. Castroneves's tax evasion trial came to an end the same day, with a federal jury acquitting the driver on six of seven counts. That set into action a contingency plan that saw Hélio back in his race car for Saturday qualifying at Long Beach. Penske rolled out a third entry with Verizon Wireless sponsorship for Power, who duly claimed pole position and finished second to Franchitti in the race. Although he ran only four more races for Penske in '09 (including a win at Edmonton), Power—like Rick Mears had done thirty years earlier—parlayed the part-time opportunity to substitute for Castroneves into a lengthy and successful career with the legendary team.

At Indianapolis a month later, Castroneves won the Indy 500 from pole position, this time with no controversy. Basking in the limelight of becoming a three-time Indianapolis winner, Castroneves pulled the biggest laugh of the night at the annual victory banquet, making light of his recent tax evasion trial just prior to accepting his record prize money check totaling more than $3 million. "Not everything is mine," he said. "You guys know what I'm talking about . . . it's not mine. But it's definitely going to help to pay my attorneys, no question about it."

Castroneves wasn't the only one having financial drama. In the first half of 2009, more than sixty jobs were eliminated at the Indianapolis Motor Speedway, and the IRL and Hulman & Co.'s helicopter and two jets were put up for sale. The IRL reportedly chipped in around $30 million toward the open-wheel unification, and during the month of May, rumors began to circulate that Tony George's CEO roles with Hulman & Co. and the Indianapolis Motor Speedway were in jeopardy. Some reports claimed that George's sisters Kathi, Nancy, and Josie—who represented half of the power on Hulman & Co.'s six-person board— wanted him ousted.

With speculation reaching a fever pitch over Indianapolis 500 race weekend, the Hulman-George family was forced to deny the rumors, stating that the board had asked George to create a business plan that would allow him to focus on the area of the business that needed the most attention—identified by Hulman & Co. chairman Mari Hulman George as the Indy Racing League. "It represents our greatest growth opportunity and therefore deserves the most attention at this point," said Mrs. George.

A defiant Tony George met the media at the Speedway to explain his position. By 2009, in addition to running Hulman & Co., the Speedway, and the IRL, he was fielding a two-car team in the IndyCar Series called Vision Racing that was also enduring hard times. In fact, the Hulman & Co. board cut off funding for Vision's second car (the main entry was driven by George's adopted son, Ed Carpenter) after Indianapolis, leaving driver Ryan Hunter-Reay on the sidelines.

"Contrary to published reports, I continue to serve as CEO of IMS," George said. He didn't deny that the company had made considerable expenditures under his leadership. "This place wakes up every morning and eats money," he said of IMS. "We spend a lot of money keeping it in the condition we do. Certainly the Indy Racing League has in the past required a lot of capital to keep it going when there were two competing series, and a lot of money was spent last year trying to unify. Everybody was hoping to catch a tail wind, and then the economy is in our face."

When George did not come up with a suitable plan, the board acted swiftly. On June 30, it stripped him of his CEO responsibilities for Hulman & Co. and the Indianapolis Motor Speedway, tabbing longtime financial man Jeff Belskus as the new IMS president and CEO while attorney Curt Brighton assumed similar duties at Hulman & Co.

But what happened next stunned the Hulman-George family and the auto racing community as a whole: Tony George abdicated leadership of the Indy Racing League. "He chose not to continue as CEO of the IRL," explained Fred Nation, executive vice president of communications for IMS. "He is no longer active in the management of any of the companies. He is on the board of directors of all the companies, along with the other members of his family. And of course the board is the ultimate decision maker."

"Our board had asked Tony to structure our executive staff to create efficiencies in our business structure and to concentrate his leadership efforts in the Indy Racing League," stated IMS Chairman Mari Hulman George. "He has decided that with the recent unification of open-wheel racing and the experienced management team IMS has cultivated over the years, now would be the time for him to concentrate on his team ownership of Vision Racing with his family and other personal business interests he and his family share. Tony will remain on the Board of Directors of all of our companies, and he will continue to work with the entire board to advance the interests of all of our companies. Our family and the entire racing community are grateful to Tony for the leadership and direction he has provided since 1990. We are pleased that he will continue to be an important part of the Indy Racing League as a team owner and as a member of our Board of Directors, and we wish him every success."

Blessed with a considerable family fortune and granted power at an early age, George created the Indy Racing League and used the inclusion of the Indianapolis 500 as leverage for the Indianapolis Motor Speedway to gain full leadership of the sport of Indy car racing. Now sixteen months after winning what was, in reality, a thirty-year battle to ascend to that leadership role, George appeared to walk away from the responsibility he created.

"I was surprised, and I'm still surprised," Mari Hulman George told *Indianapolis Star* reporter Curt Cavin in the wake of her son's unexpected withdrawal. "I don't really understand. I'm disappointed he didn't want to continue." Cavin's story reported that "financial concerns over the company's shrinking bottom line are believed to be at the core of the power struggle," and quoted Mrs. Hulman as saying that the family squabble was "not that unusual." She added, "We'll keep our fingers crossed that everything goes well. I don't know what is going to happen next."

"It caught us by surprise," admitted Kevin Kalkhoven, who spent a considerable amount of time with George in the year leading up to the amalgamation of Champ Car and the IRL. "What it means, quite frankly, I don't know. It wasn't what I anticipated when we did the merger."

The mood among the IndyCar Series team owners was uncertain. After news of the unrest within the Hulman-George family became public in May, the owners collectively signed a letter of support for George. They met a few days after his bombshell departure in the Watkins

Glen paddock for an informal briefing from IRL management. George appeared to be in escapist mode at The Glen, trading his trademark Segway in favor of a shiny black scooter, which he rode briskly through the paddock. Vision Racing announced that the IRL founder had no plans to address the media, but instead planned to issue a statement on the team's website.

"Almost nothing has changed" was the message communicated by IRL Commercial President Terry Angstadt to the owners, and a short while later to the media. "We received direct assurance from the board that they are pretty pleased with the direction and the management of the company," Angstadt said. "We have taken on the challenge started three years ago to make this a very viable and sustainable entity on its own, and we are well on the way to achieving that. We are going to exceed the plan that was signed off on by our parent organization, and I think you'll see a continually improving financial picture from this year forward. I want to erase from anyone's minds of concerns about not having an Indy Racing League."

For the short term, new IMS CEO Belskus served as the front man for the IRL as well as the Speedway. Like many key members of IMS management, Belskus was a Terre Haute native who became friends with Tony George through high school and into their time at Indiana State University. A certified public accountant by trade, Belskus was known as the financial man in the background of the IMS hierarchy, a role previously played in the Tony Hulman generation by Joe Cloutier. But with George's ouster from IMS and surprise move to distance himself from the IRL, Belskus found himself thrust into the spotlight.

Aside from the symbolic departure of the man who created the IRL, the IMS management shake-up created serious questions about the long-term financial stability of the sport and the Hulman-George family's continued involvement—though the family quickly worked to dispel the notion that they were pulling back.

"These changes underscore our family's commitment going forward to all of our companies, especially our commitment to the growth of the Indy Racing League and the sport of open-wheel racing," Mrs. George stated. "We believe the Hulman-George family's long stewardship of the Indianapolis Motor Speedway, beginning in 1945, and our significant investment in the Speedway and in the IRL demonstrates that we have full confidence in all of our companies and that we intend to grow them in the future."

During that same weekend at Watkins Glen when the future of the IRL was being so fiercely debated, Justin Wilson and Dale Coyne Racing temporarily diverted attention back to the racetrack. Together, they produced one of the biggest feel-good stories the sport of Indy car racing had ever seen in a century of competition under any sanctioning body.

Team Penske and Chip Ganassi Racing won seventy-five of the ninety-nine races during the Honda single-engine-supply era from 2006-11, and in July 2009, the IndyCar Series's two superteams hadn't been beaten in eleven months. It was inevitable that winning streak would come to an end, but it was incredibly unlikely that Coyne would be the team to do it.

But that's exactly what happened at The Glen as Wilson simply sped away from Penske's Ryan Briscoe and Ganassi's Dixon over the last seven laps to claim a remarkable underdog victory for one of the sport's true good guys. Coyne made his CART series debut in 1984 as the owner/driver of a three-year-old March with a tired stock-block engine, and for the next twenty years, his team rarely ran anywhere but at the back and often had to resort to hiring obscure pay drivers to keep the doors open. But Coyne also made a name for himself as a man with business acumen and integrity who stepped in on multiple occasions to serve as CART's interim leader during transitions between chief executives.

Coyne's team gave future "name" drivers, including Scott Pruett and Paul Tracy, their first Indy car opportunity. In more recent years, Dale Coyne Racing provided a second chance for top-line drivers like Servià, Bruno Junqueira, and Wilson, who was cut loose from Newman/Haas/Lanigan Racing at the end of the 2008 season in the wake of co-owner Paul Newman's death. Wilson was also the last non-Penske or Ganassi driver to win an IndyCar Series race, claiming Newman/Haas's final victory at the '08 Detroit Belle Isle GP four weeks before Newman died.

"I was grinning from ear to ear on the last lap," Wilson related with a huge smile at Watkins Glen. "We've been trying to build this team up and we're coming. This is the best and most important win in my career, winning for Dale. It's a fantastic feeling."

A few days later, Indy Racing League founder Tony George finally spoke out about his decision to relinquish leadership of the organization he founded. "At a board meeting last week, I was asked to continue as CEO of the Indy Racing League, reporting to a new President and CEO of IMS," George wrote on the Vision Racing website. "In my view, this would have created an unnecessary bureaucratic layer between the people in the operations of the IRL and the CEO of IMS that had not previously existed. From the perspective of my experience as President and CEO of the Indianapolis Motor Speedway, I am acutely aware that the interests of IndyCar racing as a sport, the IRL as a league, and the most important motorsports race in the world, are mutually dependant and inter-connected, both now and in the future. I did not feel that a subordinate position as 'CEO of the IRL' was a management vehicle which would allow me to accomplish the objectives that the family and the board requested me to pursue. I declined that position."

George maintained that he would continue to have an active role in shaping the future of the IRL and the IndyCar Series. "While my service as CEO has now ended, I consider my stewardship to be a life-long appointment," he said. "Since our May board meeting, as requested, I have offered my advice to the board on management reorganization, but also and perhaps more importantly, a reorganization of our board, which would provide a structure for better governance for generations to come. It is my belief that, with the recent unification of open-wheel racing, the focus should be on the future rather than the past. In the near future, I will be providing a proposal for the board to evaluate.

"There have been many questions raised in the industry and in the media about whether any of these recent changes reflect a reduction in the commitment of our family or the IMS to the IRL or the sport of IndyCar. I have been assured by my mother that no such reduction of support or commitment is intended or anticipated. I can assure teams, sponsors, media, and fans that our family is sincere in its commitment to the Indianapolis 500, the League, and the sport," George concluded.

George's stunningly swift departure from the world of Indy car racing was seemingly completed in January 2010 when he resigned from the board of IMS and announced that Vision Racing was suspending operations until sponsorship could be sourced. The team resurfaced in a revised form two years later as Ed Carpenter Racing, with George staying mostly in the background as an unofficial advisor to his owner/driver stepson.

He refused almost all interview requests, with the exception of a two-part feature by AOL writer Holly Cain in May 2010 that revealed little in the way of detail.

"We should have addressed the need to restructure sooner," he told Cain. "We had gotten fat and complacent."

George did many positive things during his two decades at the helm of IMS, including thoroughly modernizing the historic track while never asking for or taking a penny of taxpayer money. Those improvements included the construction of the infield road course that attracted Formula 1 back to America after a ten-year absence and ultimately carried the Speedway back to its motorcycle racing roots in the form of a Moto GP event than ran from 2008-15. George was also responsible for the decision that brought NASCAR to Indianapolis, a prime example of a double-edged sword if there ever was one. The early success of the Brickyard 400 certainly lined the IMS coffers, but it also detracted from the uniqueness of the Indy 500 and contributed to turning Indianapolis into one of NASCAR's strongest markets.

Perhaps the most important part of George's legacy was the way he served as a driving force behind the research and development of soft walls for oval tracks, culminating in the now universally utilized SAFER Barrier. Every driver in any form of motorsport who walked away from a major oval accident since 2002 can credit George's dogged persistence for helping them survive. He was also known to be personally generous to those in times of need.

But ultimately, Tony George will mostly be remembered for conceiving and creating the Indy Racing League and its controversial place in the overall history of Indy car racing. By the end of 2009, two full seasons into unification, the sport had been stabilized, but it remained a shadow of what it had been up to the mid-nineties prior to the CART-IRL split. Most importantly, the IRL was still grappling with many of the same key issues that ultimately led to CART's demise, including the need to find the right leader who could manage the IndyCar Series and serve as a dynamic front man for the sport.

CHAPTER 21

RANDY BERNARD AND THE SYMBOLIC END OF THE IRL ERA

When the IRL IndyCar Series opened its 2010 season on a street course in São Paulo, Brazil—let that sink in for a minute—series founder Tony George was no longer involved in any direct capacity.

George succeeded in reclaiming the Indianapolis Motor Speedway's authority over all of Indy car racing, but the Indy Racing League of 2010 bore little resemblance to the former IMS and IRL CEO's original vision for the series. Only three of the twenty-two full-time drivers were American, and rising legacy star Graham Rahal was unable to land a seat for all seventeen races. The tenuous links between Indy car racing and USAC short-track competition were all but severed. Entrants were required to use a standardized, Italian-built Dallara chassis. Engines were acquired via lease packages from Honda, the IRL's sole engine supplier, and this was also the last year with a schedule that featured more oval races than road or street course events.

"Our company is healthy and is weathering the economic recession well," noted Hulman & Co. Chairman Mari Hulman George in a statement acknowledging her son Tony's departure from his roles in the family businesses. "Jeff Belskus, president and CEO of the Indianapolis Motor Speedway, and Curt Brighton, president and CEO of Hulman & Company, are both doing excellent jobs in guiding our companies through this difficult time. Many hard decisions have been made, and now our companies are well positioned for the future."

The IndyCar Series had gotten an important commercial boost in November 2009 when apparel manufacturer IZOD signed a multiyear contract for title sponsor rights. Most importantly from Belskus's perspective, the IZOD money would essentially pick up the tab for the Team Enhancement and Allocation Matrix (TEAM) subsidy program that guaranteed full-time participants at least $1.2 million in annual support—roughly equivalent to a second-place finish in every race—in lieu of prize money. The TEAM program was the latest example of the IRL following a prior example set by CART or Champ Car.

"Getting the right title sponsor was important," Belskus said. "We spent a lot of time talking about 'fair value' and what the series is worth. We're very excited about being associated with IZOD, a brand that we feel good about."

Questions about the long-term leadership of the IRL were answered quickly when Randy Bernard was introduced as the league's new CEO in a February 1 press conference at the Indianapolis Motor Speedway. Bernard, forty-three, was credited with almost single-handedly building the Professional Bull Riders (PBR) Series from a county fair novelty act into a semi-mainstream national sport. The Hulman-George family hoped he could make a similar impact to restore Indy car racing's popularity and relevance.

Bernard's initial contact with the Hulmans was through Josie George, the youngest of Tony George's three sisters. His other link to the IRL was via the VERSUS network, which broadcast the majority of PBR events as well as twelve of seventeen IndyCar Series races. During Bernard's tenure at the PBR, television ratings increased substantially on VERSUS, positioning the league to secure a longtime relationship with CBS Sports that started in 2012.

"I had a sponsor summit in mid-December, and there was a rumor that I was going to leave the PBR, which really wasn't true," Bernard related. "I said the rumor was ficticious, and I said I was very happy where I'm at. And of course, three weeks after that I got a phone call asking if I would be interested in a consulting job. So I flew in and met with Josie George and Jeff Belskus. They called me back a few days later and asked if I would be interested in being CEO of the IRL. When I was approached, I really wasn't sure, but then I started my research and due diligence and I found so much history and culture here. If we can come up with a consistent marketing platform and Brian Barnhart can keep up the great racing, I can't see how this sport won't reignite."

Bernard brought a reputation as a tireless worker and a shrewd salesman, but he lacked auto racing experience. He arrived with no preconceived notions, which after decades of mismanagement under so-called industry insiders wasn't necessarily a bad thing. From his outside perspective, Bernard saw a sport rich in tradition and excitement that lacked convincing leadership and a coherent marketing platform, and had lost touch with its grassroots. He laid out six initial goals for the IndyCar Series, including creating a positive environment, developing relationships, and becoming profitable—not by cutting costs, but by increasing revenue.

"I'm not going to try to come here and pretend that I'm going to become an open-wheel racing expert in one or two years," Bernard remarked. "I think the best thing I bring to IndyCar racing right now is that I don't have politics on any side, so it allows me to look at it from forty thousand feet from a completely different perspective. But I'll market the sport the very best we can, and if we can't put more people in the seats and the TV ratings don't go up, then I would say I haven't done my job. It is a complete different genre in the sporting world than what I came from, but that's what excites me about it. I started with nothing at the PBR. I was the only employee in 1995 and to see it grow I had to learn television, merchandising, marketing, and promotion.

"The IRL is so big already and has so much opportunity," he added. "I really see this as a chance just to reignite America on why the Indy Racing League is so exciting."

Bernard recognized and acknowledged the damage the long rift between CART and IMS had left on the sport of Indy car racing. "Unification was very important," he said. "I would never have accepted or wanted this job if it was divided. It wouldn't make any sense. Since 1995 through today, everyone saw this sport lose millions of fans. Some of them went to NASCAR. But I think a lot of them became uninterested as their hero or legend retired or left the sport. So I think what we have to do is build stars, and we have to start from the grass roots."

One thing Bernard grasped very quickly was the IndyCar Series's need to replace the ancient spec Dallara chassis that essentially dated back to 2003. This important decision had been dragging on for the last several years under the leadership of Barnhart, the IRL competition president, and even with fresh impetus from Bernard, the desperately needed new car was already pushed back from '11 to '12. In April, Bernard revealed a seven-member advisory committee to plot the series's technical strategy for the future. He appointed retired four-star United States Air Force General William R. Looney to chair the group, called ICONIC (Innovative, Competitive, Open-Wheel, New, Industry-Relevant, Cost-Effective).

While some observers grumbled about Looney's complete lack of racing experience and knowledge, others applauded the fact that Bernard took quick and decisive action to consult with a man with a reputation for intelligence and integrity. "This is the defining decision of this decade," Bernard observed. "My knowledge in open-wheel racing is very limited, but now that I'm a part of this, the one thing I want to do is make sure we articulate a process and set criteria that we weigh very importantly. The seven advisors will be experts—engine experts, chassis experts—and I'm going to give a vote to the team owners. It's really important that we all work as a team, and the fan is also very important. We need to understand the pulse of the fan and what they want, and we put six thousand surveys out seeking fan input about the new chassis."

Looney admitted that he also was not an open-wheel racing expert, but said his vast and varied experience could be an asset in terms of managing the decision-making process. "It was not the normal request for the consulting I do, which mostly is involved with defense matters, leadership, and management," Looney stated. "Randy needed someone to facilitate, mediate, and chair the discussion that had no agenda, was completely objective, and had no bias with respect to the businesses of racing. I do fit that bill. He wanted someone who had been in that kind of environment where you bring people with different skill sets together, and you're tasked with a mission that needs to be resolved. Together you work through it to come up with an answer that is good for the enterprise that is the Indy Racing League and all its different stakeholders."

The IRL put out a request for proposals, and existing chassis supplier Dallara was the first to go public with its ideas for the future, releasing three renderings of potential future Indy car designs. Dallara pledged if it was selected as a future chassis supplier, the bulk of production would shift to the USA, and the car would be made available for 55 percent of the cost of Dallara's current car. Two of the Dallara concepts were a fairly radical departure from the look of its 2003 design, while a third, more conservative design blended styling cues from Dallara's contemporary Indy car with recent Lola and Reynard Champ Cars.

Former Champ Car chassis manufacturers Lola and Swift also publicly confirmed that they submitted proposals to the IRL. Swift's presentation included three prospective designs; two were fairly standard looking (though they employed retro styling touches like partially exposed engines), while the other had swoopy, futuristic-looking enveloping bodywork. Swift's proposals included aerodynamic appendages below the rear wing called "mushroom busters" intended to clean up the turbulent wake for following cars, as well as some interesting, fan-friendly technical developments like LED displays built into the bodywork.

But in terms of shock value, nothing came close to the DeltaWing, the brainchild of former Lola Champ Car designer Ben Bowlby. Looking more like a land speed record car than a traditional Indy car, the DeltaWing featured a long, slim fuselage that finally resolved into a fairly standard looking open-wheel car cockpit. But there were no sidepods, bar sculpted fairings fore and aft of the rear wheels. Also missing was the rear wing, replaced by a tall fin like an aircraft. The front end of the DeltaWing was even more unusual. Since the 1970s, designers specified the widest possible front track to clear airflow to the sidepod-mounted radiators and the rear wing. The DeltaWing's front wheels were spaced nearly together—the track between wheel centerlines measured twenty-four inches—and while the rims were the standard IndyCar height of fifteen inches, they were a dragster-like four inches wide.

In plan view then, the DeltaWing looked like a triangle, hence the name. Bowlby said he didn't intend to essentially reinvent the wheel, but when he factored in all the performance, cost, and safety parameters that the IRL was looking to meet, the DeltaWing was the result. The prototype created a healthy debate within the racing industry, but was ultimately deemed a step too far as the "Indy car of Tomorrow." A modified version of the DeltaWing was eventually produced by Don Panoz's Elan Technology and raced in the American Le Mans Series.

In June 2010 the IRL announced its future engine formula, calling for turbocharged, ethanol-fueled, internal-combustion engines with up to six cylinders and a maximum capacity of 2.4 liters, later reduced to 2.2 liters. There was talk of adopting a formula similar to the FIA-driven Global Racing Engine, a modular inline four-cylinder designed for widespread application in racing and rallying, but the allowance of six cylinders was viewed as a concession to Honda, which already had a turbo V6 engine in development for ACO (Automobile Club de l'Ouest, the sanctioning body for the 24 Hours of Le Mans) and American Le Mans Series competition.

Officials revealed that the 2012 engine would feature up to one hundred horsepower in the "push-to-pass" function, and that prices for a year-long engine lease would be capped at $690,000 if there was competition between manufacturers and $575,000 if there was a sole supplier. This marked a significant reduction from the '10 Honda engine lease, which ran $935,000 annually.

On July 14 at a gala presentation at the Indianapolis Museum of Art, the IRL didn't unveil its car of the future, but rather its concept for how cars would be distributed and developed. In fact, the theme of the elaborate program wasn't so much about Indy cars as it was about Indy car racing's future role in the economic development of the City of Indianapolis.

To the surprise of few, Dallara Automobili was selected as the sole provider of the "Safety Cell" platform that would form the basis of the 2012 IndyCar, beating out proposals from Lola, Swift, BAT, and DeltaWing. But what really mattered was that the Italian company confirmed plans to build a new production facility on Main Street in Speedway, Indiana, just a few hundred yards away from the Indianapolis Motor Speedway. Dallara's American headquarters was expected to create eighty jobs and ultimately house a multimillion-dollar simulator identical to the one the company developed in Italy, as well as a coffee shop and a number of interactive exhibits for visitors.

"Today is the biggest day by far in our motorsports restoration program in Indiana," said Governor Mitch Daniels. "This sport is coming back to the state where it was born."

"We have tremendously skilled workers here, and we want to show our commitment to the Speedway and the Indy Racing League," added Indianapolis Mayor Greg Ballard.

Dallara landed the IndyCar contract because it agreed to produce the car in Indiana, persuaded by the promise of tax credits and grants that Dallara and city/state officials believed would result in the revival of a cottage industry of component suppliers in central Indiana. In addition, part of the state inducement package allowed Dallara to offer a $150,000 discount on the first twenty-eight cars sold to teams based in Indiana. Ten of the thirteen teams that comprised the full-season IndyCar grid were based in greater Indianapolis, the exceptions being Team Penske (North Carolina), Dale Coyne Racing (Illinois), and A.J. Foyt Racing (Texas). Foyt later established an Indianapolis base directly across the street from the new Dallara facility.

Price was an important factor, and Dallara agreed to supply the rolling chassis with gearbox, electronics, and other key components for $349,000, or $385,000 with Dallara designed and supplied bodywork. That represented a 45-percent reduction from the $700,000 it would cost to acquire similar 2010 equipment from Dallara.

Although there would be only one chassis, the ICONIC committee addressed the cry for variation between cars by revealing a future plan that would allow any team or manufacturer to develop their own approved bodywork—front wings, sidepods, engine cover, and rear wing. The caveat was that those body kits must be made available to all competitors for $70,000. Teams would be allowed to select and utilize two brands of bodywork for any season, with the cars branded after the bodywork supplier. The so-called "aero kits" were initially delayed until 2013 and did not actually come to fruition until '15.

"Today is the result of listening to all of you," said IndyCar CEO Bernard. "The decision we made was not easy. We had to be cognizant about balancing the cost to team owners and the fans' desire to see change. This is one of the most important decisions of the decade for the IndyCar Series, and it's a huge honor to know that in eighteen months this car will be a reality."

Although it didn't appease purists who were hoping for a fully competitive chassis market, the key to overall future cost reduction was the sole supplier concept for the basic chassis. IndyCar hoped that allowing external development of aero packages would create significant diversity between cars, which was identified as a key demand from fans. The future aero kits seemed to be the best possible compromise under the circumstances, allowing a basic platform to be dressed up and branded by anyone willing to take the financial and competitive risk involved with creating an aero package.

"Aerodynamic bodywork is the key differentiating factor in racing car design, both visually and technically," said ICONIC committee member Tony Purnell, the former head of Pi Electronics and the Jaguar F1 team. "Clothing the safety cell can be done with a fraction of the development cost compared to developing an entire vehicle. It's a revolutionary strategy opening the door for many to rise to the challenge. We believe an industry-relevant approach will attract more manufacturers to the series. We want to challenge the auto and aerospace industry. This is an opportunity to test your technical prowess without breaking the piggy bank."

Another key member of the ICONIC board was Tony Cotman, who was instrumental in the cost-effective development of Panoz DP-01 chassis used in the last year of the Champ Car World Series. "Initially it seemed like we were just choosing a car," Cotman observed. "Instead we came up with a concept that seems to have addressed all of our stated goals while achieving the impossible—cost reduction. With this plan, costs will remain under control, but teams will still have access to the latest and greatest. We started out with a simple choice and ended up with a concept that will revolutionize and reenergize the sport."

A few months later, on an unusually warm and sunny November day in Indianapolis, General Motors and its Chevrolet division, in collaboration with Ilmor Engineering, announced their reentry into the IndyCar Series as an engine supplier for 2012. In '05, original company cofounders Roger Penske and Mario Illien purchased Ilmor's Special Projects Group along with the rights to the Ilmor name from Mercedes-Benz, and Penske was the key figure in reestablishing GM's participation in Indy car racing.

The Chevrolet-to-IndyCar deal was significant because it brought engine competition back to Indy car racing for the first time since 2005, ending a period of spec-car racing that was wholly against the grain of the Indy 500's tradition of open innovation. More importantly, the new competition for IndyCar stalwart Honda was a U.S. company, and an iconic one at that. "This reinforces our legacy as an authentic American brand and reinforces our heritage of performance," said Chevrolet Marketing Vice President Chris Perry. "Auto racing produces some of the highest return on investment in any activity we conduct. Indianapolis Motor Speedway has been a proving ground for manufacturers since Louis Chevrolet, our co-founder, raced here in 1909. This is a natural fit for Chevrolet. . . . This is where it all began."

IndyCar Series participants soon learned they would have a choice between three engine manufacturers in 2012 when the Lotus brand announced its entry into American open-wheel competition. Recently acquired by the Proton Group of Malaysia, the legendary marque that made such an impact on the Indianapolis 500 in the 1960s made the announcement at the Los Angeles International Auto Show in November 2010. "Last March I learned really quick that the fans wanted the spec series to go away—that was the number one thing," remarked Bernard. "Lotus is a renowned name in racing, with a long association with some of the greatest names in motorsports. I think the most exciting part for me is that Lotus has never run their own engine at Indy 500."

Meanwhile, the 2011 schedule demonstrated a major change of philosophy—or a serious reality check—for the IndyCar Series. At an event staged at the Milwaukee Mile on the eve of the 107th anniversary of the first-ever race at that historic venue, IndyCar CEO Randy Bernard unveiled a seventeen-event slate that welcomed Milwaukee back to the open-wheel ranks after a year's absence. Although it had an even longer history in open-wheel racing than the Indianapolis Motor Speedway, Milwaukee had fallen on hard times as an Indy car market, even though between '04 and '06, both Champ Car and the IRL staged races at Wisconsin State Fair Park. Milwaukee continued to struggle to draw fans after the unification, even after Michael Andretti's group took over promotion of the event and tried to create a "festival" atmosphere similar to the IndyCar Series's street races.

Bernard also used the occasion to officially confirm that the name "Indy Racing League" was being put to rest. "'IRL' has a negative connotation since the divorce, whereas 'IndyCar' is known around the world," Bernard said. "I just got back from a trip to Europe talking to manufacturers and everyone I had meetings with knew what IndyCar was, whereas some didn't know about IRL. Same thing with Brazil. We want to create perception and we want to welcome back those 15 to 20 million fans that we lost in the mid-nineties. Let's go back to our roots; let's go back to what made IndyCar, and the first thing we need to do is make sure that our brand image is positive."

Also being cast aside—for the short term, at least—was the rebranded INDYCAR's relationship with International Speedway Corporation (ISC), the track operator that provided the IRL with numerous race venues over the last fifteen years. There was a common perception that ISC did a less-than-stellar job in promoting its IndyCar races, thereby ensuring that the France family's other key business—NASCAR—remained America's undisputed number one form of motorsport. Plenty of circumstantial evidence existed to support that theory, with empty seats the norm at ISC's IndyCar races from Homestead to Fontana and everywhere in between. That fact wasn't lost on Bernard, who quickly determined that running IndyCar races in front of sparse crowds at ISC tracks was hurting open-wheel racing's image more than it was helping it.

"We don't want to shut doors with ISC, but we have to go with places that we believe are best for the series," Bernard remarked. "We want to work with promoters that are aggressive at marketing and activating IndyCar. Fortunately, this brings opportunities with new venues and promoters that are fully aligned with our strategy moving forward. We want to be in a position next year where we have twenty-five or twenty-six hungry promoters coming to us trying to secure one of our seventeen or eighteen races."

ISC-owned tracks Michigan Speedway, Phoenix International Raceway, Richmond International Raceway, and Auto Club (California) Speedway had already fallen into open-wheel oblivion. In 2011, Kansas Speedway, Watkins Glen International, Chicagoland Speedway, and Homestead-Miami Speedway were also dropped. Like Milwaukee, most of those tracks enjoyed robust crowds in Indy car racing's glory days, only to go into decline as open-wheel racing lost market share to NASCAR during the CART-IRL split years.

In February 2011, Bernard announced a high-profile addition to the IndyCar Series schedule: The final race of the slate would be run October 16 at Las Vegas Motor Speedway (LVMS), which had been updated into a virtual clone of Texas Motor Speedway under Speedway Motorsports, Inc. ownership. LVMS had not hosted an Indy car race since Champ Car ran there in '04 and '05 and, in addition to now having higher twenty-degree banking, had recently been repaved.

Hoping to attract a few big-name NASCAR or Formula 1 drivers, Bernard upped the ante by offering a $5 million prize to any qualified non–Indy car driver who entered and won the Las Vegas race. "We believe our drivers are the best drivers in the world," Bernard said. "We have to gain credibility for these drivers, and there's not a better way than to throw a challenge out like this. This is a challenge to showcase the sport of IndyCar to other motorsports around the world and try to attract a new audience and some new drivers and showcase how tough it is to be an IndyCar driver."

But the LVMS race was more than just a championship decider with a $5 million twist. INDYCAR rented the track and self-promoted the race, signaling a potential new direction for the series in an era when oval track promoters found it increasingly difficult to entice crowds. Even NASCAR attendance was starting to noticeably slip after peaking in 2005. Las Vegas was viewed as a key market by Bernard, who forged strong links to the City of Sin when he was the head of the Pro Bull Riders tour through early '10.

In the meantime, the 2011 season got up and running. Dario Franchitti picked up right where he left off by winning the now-traditional St. Petersburg season opener over Will Power, resuming the year long '10 championship battle that was resolved in the Scotsman's favor. Since returning to Indy cars in '09 with Chip Ganassi's team, Franchitti was often the man to beat. He bested Ryan Briscoe to the '09 championship, then won Indianapolis in '10 before prevailing over Power down the stretch to claim his second consecutive (and third overall) series title.

While the IndyCar Series as a whole still looked like it was stuck in neutral following the '08 unification, the Indianapolis 500 was enjoying a renaissance. The 500 was boosted by a three-year-long promotional campaign called the Centennial Era that celebrated the one-hundred-year anniversary of the period between when the Indianapolis Motor Speedway opened in 1909 to the first Indy 500 in 1911. Though the

Speedway's estimated 230,000 grandstand seats were still not yet filled on race day, attendance showed solid growth, and moving Carburetion Day (or in modern parlance, Miller Lite Carb Day) from the Thursday to the Friday before the race was an instant hit. The success of the annual Carb Day concert, usually alternating classic rock dinosaurs with more modern artists, eventually led to IMS utilizing the venue for stand alone country and rock music shows.

Indianapolis marked Dan Wheldon's first race of 2011, and his Indy car career was hanging on by a thread. After crushing the competition to win the '05 IRL championship with Michael Andretti's team, Wheldon moved to Chip Ganassi Racing and came within a tiebreaker of defending his title in '06, losing out to Sam Hornish Jr. on win count. Wheldon won four more races for Ganassi in '07 and '08, but he was let go when Franchitti returned to Indy cars after his brief NASCAR experiment. The thirty-three-year-old Englishman then drove for the once-dominant Panther Racing team in '09 and '10, continuing to demonstrate his flair at Indianapolis with a pair of second-place finishes, but failing to score a race win.

For 2011, Wheldon teamed up with his old Andretti Green Racing teammate Bryan Herta, who was testing the waters of team ownership. While he surprised many by qualifying the one-off Bryan Herta Autosport entry sixth, few believed the small team had a shot at winning the race. But as often happens, the 500 turned into a fuel strategy contest, and one by one, drivers peeled into the pits for a splash-and-go as the laps wound down. First to blink was rookie Bertrand Baguette, with three laps to go. That left Franchitti in the lead, but he significantly slowed his pace to make the finish and was passed on the penultimate lap by rookie J.R. Hildebrand in the Panther car vacated by Wheldon. Hildebrand led into the fourth turn of the 200th and final lap, where he encountered Charlie Kimball's slow-moving car trying to coast to the line after running out of fuel. Blocking out pleas over the radio to take it easy because he had a ten-second margin over Wheldon, Hildebrand caught Kimball at the apex of the corner and misjudged the pass. The front of his car ran wide into the marbles of rubber that had collected off-line throughout the race and shot toward an impact with the wall. With his right front suspension deranged, Hildebrand limped toward the finish line, only to be passed on the home straight by an incredulous Wheldon. On the one-hundredth anniversary of the first Indianapolis 500, the grand old event served up one of the most memorable finishes in its history.

Although he didn't have any more 2011 IndyCar Series races lined up, Wheldon wasn't short of work. He gained a new legion of fans with his color commentary on a few VERSUS race broadcasts, and he was tabbed as the development driver for the prototype '12 Dallara that debuted at Indianapolis to mixed reviews. The most controversial aspect of the new design was a floor that stretched to the outside edge of the tires and the almost completely enclosed rear wheels, with bulbous shrouds at the front and protective "bumpers" at the rear. Purists were also upset that while the new car would feature a turbocharged engine, it still featured a roll hoop air intake (or airbox) with a tall engine cover like an IRL car, rather than the sleek, low rear bodywork common to Indy cars of the 1980s and '90s.

Wheldon ran several shakedown tests with the new Dallara in August and September 2011, but before he could finish the development work on the new chassis, he was drafted back into the IndyCar Series as a competitor. Randy Bernard's original plan to offer five non–Indy car drivers the opportunity to compete in the IZOD Indy-Car Series finale at Las Vegas for a $5 million prize if they won the race had been recast as the GoDaddy IndyCar Challenge Bonus. But there just wasn't that much interest in the offer. And where there was interest, logistical or contractual issues prevented those drivers from accepting the challenge.

"We had two dozen inquiries about the opportunity, we had six sign up with applications, and we had many others call and inquire about it," Bernard said. "The only three that we felt had a serious opportunity to help drive millions of new fans to our sport that could be showcased as great, successful drivers were Travis Pastrana, Alex Zanardi, and Kasey Kahne."

But INDYCAR couldn't secure any of the three top choices. NASCAR star Kahne insisted on driving for Team Penske, and paraplegic Zanardi (the popular Italian lost his legs in a crash during a CART-sanctioned race at EuroSpeedway Lausitz in Germany on September 15, 2001) only considered participating if his modified car was fielded by Chip Ganassi

Racing. With Penske and Ganassi in the midst of a heated championship battle with regular drivers Power and Franchitti, neither team wanted to deal with the distraction of an extra entry there purely for publicity.

Pastrana, with very little open-wheel or oval racing experience, was the most intriguing prospect. But the X-Games star broke his ankle during a July 28 Moto X stunt, putting his car racing aspirations on hold for the foreseeable future. "I want to thank all three of them because they all had a lot of interest in this, and we felt that it was a lot of fun just getting to visit with them about this and try to make it happen," Bernard said. "We had a lot of buzz, a lot of interest about this $5 million challenge. So we felt we should try to go on and try a new challenge within the sport."

The semicontrived result was that surprise Indianapolis 500 winner Wheldon was given the opportunity to split the $5 million prize with a fan, provided that Wheldon piloted his Bryan Herta Autosport/Sam Schmidt Motorsports entry from the back of an expanded thirty-four-car field to win the Las Vegas race. "I've been just desperate, period, to get back in a race car since Indianapolis," said Wheldon. "It's going to be hard, though I have actually started last when I got loose in qualifying at Richmond when I was driving for Michael Andretti's team and came through and won. Thank you for the opportunity, but please don't expect any flips like Travis Pastrana does because I'm not into that. I'm going to keep it on all four."

Those words, spoken a few days prior to the event, are haunting in retrospect. After starting from the back of the thirty-four-car field, Wheldon had moved up to twenty-fourth place when carnage unfolded on the eleventh of two hundred laps. Cars driven by James Hinchcliffe and rookie Wade Cunningham touched; Cunningham spun, and all hell broke loose. At least three cars went airborne, and Wheldon had no time to react before his car clouted the back of E.J. Viso's car, launching Wheldon's car into an aerial barrel roll. The car struck the catchfence with enough force to shear the roll hoop cleanly from the top of the Dallara chassis, and Wheldon's helmet struck a 4.5-inch diameter steel post on the track side of the chain link fence, causing what INDYCAR called "unsurvivable injuries."

The morning of the race, Wheldon had signed a contract with Michael Andretti's Andretti Autosport team to return to full-time competition in 2012. "He was a very close friend and we had just literally inked it this morning," said Andretti. "We had great plans to do fun things together. I'm going to miss him. There was a lot of life in that guy. But it's part of our sport. He knew the risks; we all know the risks when we get in the car. It probably touches me a little more because of everything that was going on. It's a terrible thing, but, unfortunately, in our sport we've had a lot of days like these. They suck, but that's the way it is."

INDYCAR issued a 216-page report documenting a two-month long investigation into the fifteen-car accident, concluding it was an unpredictable racing incident with fatal consequences. As the multi-car wreck unfolded in front of him, Wheldon managed to slow his car from 224 to 165 miles per hour before contacting another car and flying through the air for approximately 325 feet. Wheldon's car covered the length of a football field in less than 0.8 second, rotating ninety degrees to the right so that the top of the cockpit was fully exposed to the wall and fence. The expanded field was not considered a factor, and series officials also discounted the notion that Wheldon took additional risks because he was racing for a chance at a $5 million prize. Instead, the report concluded that the cars were too easy to drive on the recently repaved, variable-banked LVMS oval, allowing the drivers to pretty much drive anywhere they wanted on the track, rather than sticking to a racing "groove" limited by the performance of the car.

"Pack racing," a trademark of the early years of the IRL and a style of competition still championed by a small but vocal group of fans, had finally turned deadly.

In terms of what actually killed Wheldon, the design of the fence at Las Vegas Motor Speedway—where the poles were mounted on the track side of the mesh fence, rather than on the grandstand side—came under scrutiny. A similar specification of fence was used at Texas Motor Speedway, where two of the most devastating (but thankfully not fatal) accidents in recent Indy car history left Davey Hamilton (2001) and Kenny Brack (2003) with life-threatening injuries that they survived.

TMS President Eddie Gossage vigorously defended the design of the fence in an interview with *RACER* magazine. "According to our engineers who've studied this for years, the way we have it placed at Texas Motor Speedway—from the racetrack to the grandstand it goes SAFER

Barrier, wall, cables, upright posts, mesh fencing—is the best way, and it won't be changed. It is the safest for the drivers and safest for the fans."

The INDYCAR report attempted to deflect attention and blame away from the fence design. But it cetainly implied that it could have been a factor in Wheldon's death. "The fencing (including post, cables, and fabric) at the Las Vegas Motor Speedway was found to have performed to all expectation in retaining a race car from leaving the track," stated the report. "The only change that would be preferred is for the fence fabric to be on the track side of the post rather [sic] its current configuration. While there is no evidence that placement of the fabric would have changed the consequences of this accident, there are accident scenarios that can be envisioned in which the fabric placement might have some significance. For that reason, the preferred fabric placement at any track hosting an INDYCAR event is on the track side of the fence post."

With a new technical formula set to be introduced in 2012, the Las Vegas race was anticipated as the end of an era. The retirement of the needle-nose Dallara chassis used in the IRL since '03 was the kind of symbolic disconnect from the Indy Racing League identity that Randy Bernard so desperately wanted. Instead, the IRL era ended under a veil of tragedy, with Wheldon's death triggering a massive outpouring of sympathy and grief similar to what accompanied Greg Moore's death at California Speedway in the 1999 CART season finale.

The 2012 Dallara chassis under development was renamed DW12 in honor of Wheldon, but as the calendar turned to the new year, there were serious doubts that the new spec chassis could be transformed into a decent racing car. Conceived by committee and built to a price, the DW12 prompted a considerable number of people involved in the series to grumble that Dallara was "Italian for 'disaster.'" The PR-savvy Wheldon never publicly played up the car's shortcomings, something that became obvious when testing moved on to the engine manufacturer phase and the car scared the likes of Dario Franchitti and Tony Kanaan while resolutely refusing to go faster than 216 mph around the Indianapolis Motor Speedway.

Following another round of oval testing at Auto Club Speedway in Fontana, California, Scott Dixon gave a more honest assessment of the car, calling it "a bit of a pig" with an even more pronounced pendulum effect than the Dallara IR03, which was already a tail-heavy car. The DW12 initially had a weight distribution of 41 percent front, 59 percent rear, as compared to the IR03's 45/55. The DW12's handling improved during the next round of testing at Homestead-Miami Speedway, mainly due to an extreme measure: twenty-six pounds of lead ballast in the nose of the car to balance out the weight distribution. Complicating matters, with the new generation of car, INDYCAR tightened up the rulebook and allowed teams much less leeway to build their own parts and create their own lines of development.

"Working with the car has been a little bit frustrating," Franchitti said. "For me, it's very important that the series allows teams to fix the car and to work with the car and not paint us into too tight a box. The series needs to allow teams the latitude to adjust the car to different driving styles. I would say that's the one thing that's kind of concerning me. Hopefully they can come up with an elegant engineering solution to fixing the problems of the handling imbalance the car's had."

After initially blaming suppliers for suspension and gearbox components that didn't meet target weight goals, Dallara reacted to the crisis. Revised suspension geometry helped shift the weight forward, and a heavily revised new oval track aero package went into development. The car was originally designed for left-foot braking only, so Dallara also belatedly produced a modified brake pedal for drivers like Franchitti and Hélio Castroneves who preferred to brake with their right foot.

The field for the now-traditional IndyCar opener at St. Petersburg was missing one familiar face: Danica Patrick. The saga of her long-term future was finally revealed in August 2011 when she announced that she would leave Indy cars to compete full time in the NASCAR Nationwide Series for JR Motorsport, the team owned by popular star Dale Earnhardt Jr. Patrick was then expected to ascend into NASCAR's top-level Sprint Cup Series in '13 with Stewart-Haas Racing. Although Danica's NASCAR effort would be funded by her long-term sponsor GoDaddy.com, the internet developer maintained a presence in the IndyCar Series with Andretti Green Racing and driver James Hinchcliffe.

Patrick's departure had little or no effect on the IndyCar Series's public perception or television ratings. By the end of her time in open-wheelers, she had as many detractors as fans. Aside from her sole race win at Motegi in 2008, Patrick achieved six other podium finishes in 116 starts, including a pair of competitive second-place finishes and third place in the '09 Indianapolis 500. She also achieved her best IndyCar Series championship result of fifth place in '09.

But after signing a big money contract for Andretti Green Racing in 2007 and later securing her lucrative relationship with GoDaddy, Patrick appeared to be distracted from her primary job as a race car driver. She became most famous for a series of racy Super Bowl advertisments for GoDaddy, and the move to NASCAR did not bring on-track success. In 191 Cup Series starts between '12 and '18, Danica failed to achieve a top-five finish.

"She did unbelievable things for IndyCar, and we'll always be appreciative," Bernard remarked in an interview with *Car and Driver*. "She brings a lot of exposure to NASCAR, and the fact that she came from IndyCar will be part of that exposure. But Danica sort of had this big umbrella that took away some of the light from our current and upcoming stars."

At St. Petersburg, Castroneves scored the first victory of the DW12 era for Team Penske and Chevrolet. Teammate Will Power then took control of the 2012 IndyCar Series Championship with three consecutive victories heading into Indianapolis. Chevy therefore dominated the opening third of the season, but when the first round of Honda engines mileaged out, upgraded replacement units suddenly thrust Chip Ganassi's cars into contention on Carb Day. In the race, Franchitti held off a charging Takuma Sato to claim his third Indy 500 win since '07. In a classic finish, Sato spun and crashed in Turn One while trying to pass Franchitti on the 199th lap. Having also added the '11 IndyCar Series Championship title in come-from-behind fashion over Power to bring his total to four, Franchitti was one of the sport's very best performers in the twenty-first century and an all-time Indy car great. He suffered a severe concussion in a crash at the Houston street course in '13, putting a premature end to his driving career.

In 2012, Power lost out on the title for the third consecutive year in heartbreaking fashion. This time, a crash during the season finale at Auto Club Speedway allowed Ryan Hunter-Reay to make up a seventeen-point deficit in a 500-miler that was won by Ed Carpenter. Surprisingly, INDY-CAR failed to capitalize on the fact that it produced a rare American champion, the first in IRL or IndyCar Series competition since Sam Hornish Jr. in '06. In addition, Hunter-Reay is the only driver who won races under CART, Champ Car, and IRL sanction, and he added a victory in the '14 Indianapolis 500 to the championship he won two years earlier. Yet he remains one of the sport's most underappreciated stars.

Randy Bernard's tenure as the CEO of INDYCAR ended on October 28, 2012, a little under thirty-two months after he took the job. The former head of the Professional Bull Riders series was a slick salesman, and although he had no auto racing experience, it was hoped that his marketing skills would be an asset to a struggling form of motorsports. INDYCAR demonstrated areas of growth during Bernard's first two seasons on the job, but his lack of deep industry knowledge eventually caught up to him, and he never seemed to escape the fallout from Wheldon's fatal accident. Much of his final year was marked by controversy and dissent.

Bernard helped attract two new engine manufacturers to the IndyCar Series (though Lotus's participation was extremely short-lived), and he fast-tracked the new 2012 chassis. While somewhat unattractive, Dallara's IR-12 produced excellent racing and would serve as the series's basic platform for more than ten years. But despite a generally satisfactory performance since he took over in March '10, Bernard's power base weakened throughout '12 as a group of IndyCar Series team owners led by Panther Racing's John Barnes waged a behind-the-scenes campaign for his ouster. He put himself on even shakier ground when he drew attention to his plight on Twitter following the Indianapolis 500. For the next five months, rumors of Bernard's fate dominated Indy car news and even though the dissenting team owners didn't directly orchestrate his departure, once they started their campaign, Bernard's position was in jeopardy.

A conflict over the cost of spare parts for the new car served as the focal point for the unhappiness between the competitors and the INDYCAR CEO. In addition, the IndyCar Series continued to struggle with decreasing television ratings, and some promoters grew unhappy with sweetheart deals Bernard cut to convince some oval tracks to join the schedule. He tried hard to recreate USAC racing's relevance to the IndyCar Series and regrow the sport's oval racing grassroots, but he also recognized that street races brought in bigger crowds and that international events had the potential for bigger profits.

The cancellation of yet another race scheduled to run in China, which resulted in the nonreceipt of a $4 million sanction fee, was a further factor in Bernard's rapid downfall. This was the latest example of Indy car racing, whether under CART, Champ Car, or INDYCAR sanction, failing to follow through on announced plans for a race in a far away foreign land. CART and INDYCAR both had short-lived events in Brazil, but Champ Car failed to get multiple announced events in China and Korea off the ground, bringing embarrassment to the series at a time when it could ill afford it. International events continued to polarize fans, sponsors, and competitors as well, with influential team owners, including Roger Penske and Chip Ganassi, strongly holding the belief that the IndyCar Series needed to concentrate on the North American market.

Bernard's situation was complicated in 2012 when Indy Racing League founder and former CEO Tony George explored the possibility of reacquiring the series he created in the mid-nineties. The IMS board publicly stated that INDYCAR was not for sale, but the board also failed to provide Bernard with a vote of confidence, a clear signal that his tenure was near its end despite having two years remaining on his contract. When George was compelled to resign from the board of directors of Hulman & Company on October 19, citing conflict of interest, it became apparent that his attempts to acquire INDYCAR and Bernard's tenuous employment status were completely separate issues. Nine days later at a special meeting of the Indianapolis Motor Speedway Corp. board, Bernard resigned under pressure after INDYCAR reportedly failed to post a profit for the third consecutive year.

Although his time with INDYCAR was comparatively brief, Bernard was Indy car racing's most visible front man in decades, and he was particularly adept at connecting with race fans, with whom he built a solid rapport. News of his departure was met with shock and disbelief on increasingly important social media platforms, including Twitter and Facebook. "The last three years have produced some exciting times, and some difficult times," Bernard said. "But we have created a foundation for INDYCAR that positions it to grow over the next several years, and I am proud of what everyone at INDYCAR has been able to accomplish since I came on board. With the Hulman-George family's firm commitment to the betterment of the sport and the dedication of our teams, drivers, partners, and fans, INDYCAR is better poised for success than it has been in many years." After his departure from INDYCAR, Bernard became co-manager for his friend, country music star Garth Brooks.

A bitter irony was that George formed the IRL in 1994 to ward off the power base of the team owners, but nearly twenty years later, it remained clear that the owners still wielded as much power than the supposed managers of the series. As a result, Indy car racing continued to fail to achieve its potential. Five years into the unified era, the IndyCar Series was coming off its most competitive and compelling season of racing in several years, yet the focus down the stretch, as the championship was fought out between Hunter-Reay and Power in thrilling fashion on the track, was instead again thrust upon controversy over the management of the sport. A form of motorsport that should have been celebrating its first American champion in a unified series since 1994 was instead dwelling on the latest change in leadership. And the quality of racing that resulted during the 2012 season from the implementation of the Dallara DW12 chassis and turbo engine formula—Randy Bernard's real contribution to the legacy of Indy car racing—pretty much got ignored. Now heading into '13, INDYCAR appeared to be a rudderless ship without a captain.

CHAPTER 22

CONSOLIDATION AND
A SELLOUT 100TH

After Randy Bernard was forced out as INDYCAR's leader, Indianapolis Motor Speedway Corp. CEO Jeff Belskus reassumed his duties on an interim basis. But a more encompassing change soon occurred: six weeks after Bernard's ouster, Mark Miles was named chief executive officer of Hulman & Company. It looked like a smart hire on a number of levels.

As the architect of the 1987 Pan-Am Games, the ambitious track-and-field event that put Indianapolis on the map as a prominent venue for amateur athletics, Miles gained respect in the city's sports and business circles. He then served for fifteen years as president of the Association of Tennis Professionals (ATP) Tour during a period of strong international growth for men's tennis. More recently, Miles served as chairman of the committee that brought Super Bowl XLVI to Indianapolis in 2010, a hugely successful event that caused the National Football League to reassess the possibilities that Super Bowl week offers—even in cold weather cities.

In short, Miles had credibility in Indiana, which was vital to the Hulman-George family and the vast majority of the IndyCar Series's fan base. But he also had national and international sports management experience that could be of critical importance moving forward, because even though his mandate was not specifically to fix Indy car racing, Miles's new role at Hulman & Co. put him in position to have huge influence on the sport. Miles eventually assumed INDYCAR CEO responsibilities later in 2013.

"I think [the IndyCar Series] is vitally important," Miles said in his introductory press conference. "It's important as an economic question financially, and for the board, I think we believe that the destinies of IMS and the Indianapolis 500-Mile Race and the IndyCar Series are inextricably welded, woven together. So we are determined to grow the IndyCar Series as a sport, and that will help the Indianapolis 500-Mile Race in the process."

Much of the ATP Tour's growth was fueled by sponsorships and international expansion, and Miles told a story from his tennis days that demonstrated that he truly understood the international potential of the IMS and INDYCAR brands. "From 1990 to 2005, it happened that Memorial Day coincided with the French Open Championships in Paris," he related. "So I would hurry back from Roland Garros and get to the hotel and turn on the television, never wanting to miss Jim Nabors singing and catching the race on TV. We could follow it wherever we were in the world. During those years, living and traveling outside of the United States more than 50 percent of the time, I can tell you that it's absolutely true: You can't go anywhere in this world and have conversations with any people who have any kind of worldview and not have them know about Indy, INDYCAR, and the Indianapolis Motor Speedway. So I come to this challenge with the perspective that we have a remarkable opportunity with a remarkable, potent, global brand."

Also in late 2012, the Boston Consulting Group (BCG) was retained to help Hulman & Co. develop a revised business plan that essentially encouraged IMS to monetize the facility in any and every way possible. "It's part of our normal business planning cycle as we think about the future and both our near-term and long-term plans," Belskus told *Sports Business Journal Daily*. "It's helpful to have an independent view and fresh eyes on what we're dealing with. What opportunities are there out there? How do we take advantage of those opportunities?

"We're focused on revenue growth, revenue generation, and our cost structure," he added. "What do we do to reduce costs? We're focused on value to partners. We have a lot of external stakeholders, and we want to make sure we're providing value."

A copy of the 115-page BCG report was leaked to Associated Press auto racing writer Jenna Fryer, who revealed that it "offered a wide array of suggestions on how to better position the troubled open-wheel series and historic speedway," most controversially the introduction of a NASCAR-style three-race playoff. BCG also recommended that all television coverage should come from a single network, which they identified as ideally ABC/ESPN, with as many races on ABC as possible. The firm created a fantasy fifteen-race domestic schedule that opened in Houston and concluded with a championship decider on the Indianapolis Motor Speedway road course. Finally, BCG recommended that INDYCAR drop the Entrant Support Program (each full-time team was paid a $1.1-million subsidy plus small bonuses for top-five finishes) in favor of a traditional prize money structure.

As for the Speedway itself, BCG supported changing ticket prices, raising the cost of premium seats for the Indianapolis 500 while reducing most tickets for the Brickyard 400 and the Red Bull GP motorcycle race. BCG claimed that only 21 of the 132 days the track was used in the year studied were considered "major revenue generating events."

Miles put several of the BCG recommendations into action. He led a consolidation of the Hulman-George family's racing industry interests into an umbrella company called Hulman Motorsports in an effort to streamline operations between IMS and INDYCAR. He also made a number of key promotions and hires. Former NASCAR team owner Jay Frye joined Hulman Motorsports as chief revenue officer, but his skills were better utilized on the racing side, and he was named president of competition and operations of INDYCAR in late 2015. C.J. O'Donnell, who oversaw the rebranding of several marques owned by the Ford Motor Company, took over the company's top marketing role and held it through '17.

In addition, Doug Boles was named president of the Indianapolis Motor Speedway in 2013. Boles was a local attorney and minority owner in Panther Racing who had served as the Speedway's vice president of communications since '10. Relations between INDYCAR, the Speedway, and its competitors improved dramatically with this new management team. Brian Barnhart, the controversial chief steward and race director dating to the IRL era, left the series in '16 to return to racing team management.

Although INDYCAR didn't make a profit while Bernard was in charge, he put the company in position to turn the corner. And while the

IndyCar Series did not enjoy anywhere near the popularity of the sport's most commercially successful era in the early 1990s, within the industry, it was in comparatively good shape. While NASCAR and Formula 1 experienced huge declines in attendance, sponsorship, and television ratings over the last decade, the unified IndyCar Series held steady or demonstrated modest growth.

F1's television audience dropped by 40 percent between 2008 and '17, and NASCAR's attendance and television ratings dropped by more than 50 percent after peaking in '05. F1's troubles could be traced to fans' unhappiness over the way one team or driver tended to constantly dominate the action, while NASCAR's problems intensified when it began tinkering with its championship format. Matt Kenseth won the '03 Cup Series title (the last under Winston sponsorship) with only one race win during a season when Ryan Newman won eight races and finished sixth in the standings. That apparent disparity resulted in the introduction in '04 of the "Chase for the Championship," which reset the points among the top-ten drivers two-thirds of the way through the season in an effort to make the final races of the campaign more exciting and meaningful. After originally simply limiting the number of championship-eligible drivers, a series of elimination rounds were added to the Chase (or Playoffs as they were renamed in '17), creating confusion among casual followers and outright animosity within NASCAR's traditional fan base. The adoption of "Stage" racing, in which races were broken into three points-paying segments separated by now customary "competition cautions," confused matters even more and drove off the few remaining traditionalists.

While the Indianapolis Motor Speedway had helped accelerate NASCAR's growth with the addition of the Brickyard 400, IMS was also indirectly responsible for contributing to NASCAR's decline. The term "competition caution" entered the racing lexicon at the 2008 Brickyard 400, when the Speedway's freshly diamond-graded surface played havoc with Goodyear's tires. With the rubber unable to last longer than about fifteen laps, "competition cautions" were called every ten to twelve laps for mandatory pit stops and tire changes. The event turned into a farce. Saddled with the reputation of being an exceptionally boring race, Brickyard 400 attendance was already slipping, but the Goodyear debacle sent the spectator count into freefall. By '15, IMS was barely a quarter full for the Brickyard.

Formula 1 had also encountered tire problems at Indianapolis. In 2005, two cars equipped with Michelin tires suffered blowouts on the road course, which utilized part of the oval and featured the only ultra-high speed banked corner in all of F1. As many as eight Michelin tires failed or were on the verge of failure in practice and qualifying, and Ralf Schumacher crashed heavily but was uninjured.

Michelin advised its teams that the tires would not last more than ten laps, but Formula 1 rules in 2005 prevented changing tires during a race unless it was weather related. Without prior notice, all of the Michelin-equipped cars pulled into the pits at the end of the warm-up lap and withdrew from the race, which was completed with just six cars on Bridgestone tires. The tiny field infuriated spectators and caused great embarrassment to F1, Michelin, and IMS, which offered refunds and distributed twenty thousand free tickets to the '06 USGP at Indianapolis. But the damage was done, and following the '07 event, a Moto GP motorcycle race sponsored by Red Bull replaced F1 as the premier event at the IMS road course.

Unlike Formula 1, NASCAR and IMS maintained their relationship mainly because NASCAR's lucrative television contract allowed the Brickyard 400 to remain profitable for IMS. Still, the swathes of empty grandstands at the most famous racetrack in the world made the Brickyard the most obvious example of NASCAR's difficulties in the twenty-first century. The surreal scene is all the more remarkable given the Brickyard's immense popularity in the late 1990s, when it was arguably the Indianapolis Motor Speedway's strongest event.

In an effort to improve attendance, the Brickyard was granted a September date in 2018 and made the final cutoff race before the NASCAR Playoffs, in the hopes that cooler weather and the perception of greater importance would stimulate attendance. When that tactic failed, the race was moved to Fourth of July weekend. In 2021 and beyond, the race will be staged on the IMS road course.

"The Brickyard 400 is the third largest attended sporting event in the state of Indiana every year," remarked IMS President Boles. "So while it's not the Indianapolis 500, it still is a massive event, and there still are a lot of people here. Economically, it makes sense for us, it makes sense for this community, and it makes sense for NASCAR. Would we love to have more people? Absolutely, and we continue to try to do that every day. But is there any way you can say it's not a success? Absolutely not."

INDYCAR had major commercial news to reveal early in 2014 when Verizon Wireless replaced IZOD as the series's title sponsor. "Circumstances change and now we're seeking new partnerships with brands looking to align with the fastest, most versatile form of racing," stated Mark Miles. "Verizon is the perfect partner to showcase the high level of innovation and technology that is inherent in our sport."

In 2015, work started on what IMS called Project 100: the implementation of a series of improvements intended to modernize the fan experience while honoring and maintaining the tradition and history of the Speedway. Restrooms were upgraded, concession stands (now outsourced to Levy Restaurants, as recommended by the Boston Consulting Group in an effort to make the facility more profitable) were modernized, a new scoring pylon and much larger video boards were erected, and on-site cell phone and WiFi connectivity was enhanced.

For decades, IMS was defined by history and tradition, yet constant change and reinvestment toward facility upgrades were important hallmarks of the Hulman-George family's seven decades of owning the track. What differentiated Project 100 from past enhancements was the fact that it was funded by state money. The Indiana Senate passed a bill that created a special district to capture taxes paid at the track and its golf course while making the money available to the Speedway for the project. IMS was granted a $100 million loan to be repaid over twenty years by proceeds from the new admission tax.

In addition to all of the Project 100 improvements made to the IMS facility, the month of May got a major makeover in 2014 with the addition of an IndyCar Series race on the IMS road course. Traditionalists will likely never warm up to the notion of IMS as a road-racing venue, but the IndyCar Grand Prix quickly proved to be a more effective profit generator for IMS than hosting a few poorly attended days of oval practice. It also offered a chance for hardcore IMS fans to sample the kind of IndyCar Series race weekend that the rest of the world is accustomed to outside of Indianapolis. A polarizing track since it was constructed in 2000 (seven-time Formula 1 World Champion Michael Schumacher famously criticized the initial layout as "Mickey Mouse"), the IMS road course emerged as a consistent moneymaker, hosting track days and driving schools as well as events that include the largest vintage car racing meeting in North America and even the '17 SCCA Runoffs.

"Balancing tradition with investing in and updating the facility is the most important litmus test we go through as we're thinking about projects for the Indianapolis Motor Speedway," said Boles. "It's important that we make investments in the facility to position it for the next century, but we can't forget that the Speedway is special because of what happened in the first century. It's definitely a difficult balancing act, and it creates some interesting debate internally when we start thinking about ways to invest in the facility that allows us to be positioned for growth and at the same time pay respect to what makes the Indianapolis Motor Speedway and the Indianapolis 500 so great."

The rapid decline of the Brickyard 400 was made even more apparent by the slow and steady rebound of the Indianapolis 500, which peaked with the historically significant one hundredth running of the great event in 2016. Although the "Centennial Era" promotion focused on the years 2009-11 to commemorate the time between the opening of IMS and the first 500, the fact that the event was suspended during the two World Wars (the Indianapolis 500 was not contested in 1917 and 1918 and from 1942-45) meant that the actual one-hundredth race didn't occur until five years after the one-hundred-year anniversary of the first.

Since the unification of the sport in 2008, attendance for the Indianapolis 500 increased at a gradual but noticeable pace, and in May 2016, the track announced the first complete sellout of grandstand seats since the first half of the 1990s. Boles also confirmed that general admission (GA) tickets sold at a much faster rate than in recent years, with a claimed increase over '15 GA sales "in excess of the capacity of Lucas Oil Stadium," the 70,000-seat venue that plays home to the Indianapolis Colts. The track also added eighteen temporary suites outside of Turn Two, and IMS and city officials stated that the 33,000 hotel rooms in greater Indianapolis sold out eight weeks earlier than they did in '15. Boles estimated that race-day attendance would approach 350,000, rivaling the track's biggest crowds in the 1960s and '70s.

"Every Indianapolis 500 is special, but the buzz surrounding the one hundredth running has been building for nearly a year," said Boles. "The ability to talk about the one hundredth, and to talk about the year-long project of improvements we're making to the venue has really gotten a lot of support from the community. We've gotten more community support than I can recall in my twenty-five years in the sport."

The Speedway actually completely cut off general admission ticket sales four days before the race and declared a total sellout. The customary local television blackout was lifted, and Indianapolis ABC affiliate WRTV-6 was permitted to broadcast the race live for the first time.

"This unexpected development surprised us," said Hulman & Co. CEO Miles. "It's fair to say a lot of people thought we might sell out the reserved seats. But I don't think people anticipated getting to the place where we would have to say we really should not sell any more infield general admission tickets. There's no event in the world like the Indy 500, and this sellout is a testament to the enduring legacy of the Greatest Spectacle in Racing, the thrilling racing of the Verizon IndyCar Series and the bright future for both. We need to make sure those people have a great experience and make sure they want to come back."

By the time the one hundredth Indianapolis 500 was run on May 29, 2016, the IndyCar Series was a little more than a year into the so-called "aero-kit" era. As promised when the "Indy Car of Tomorrow" concept was revealed by Randy Bernard in '10, engine manufacturers Chevrolet and Honda were permitted to create their own wings, sidepods, engine cover, and other aerodynamic bits to create unique visual identity between the two brands. The results were polarizing, to say the least, with the general consensus that the aero kits took an ugly racing car and made it even uglier. The Honda design, with at least twenty additional winglets and spats hung onto the front and rear wings and sidepods, looked particularly outlandish, but it was not as effective on track as Chevrolet's visually simpler upgrade.

Given that there wasn't much wrong with the actual racing produced by the stock Dallara package from 2012-14 (especially at Indianapolis, where classic races in '13 and '14 were won by Tony Kanaan and Ryan Hunter-Reay), the big question was whether a minor adjustment of the car's looks could make a difference in the overall popularity of the

IndyCar Series. It was billed as a whole new era for Indy car racing, and as such, expectations were high. The biggest gamblers were Honda and Chevrolet, because the engine manufacturers still served as the financial backbone of the sport, as they had since the late-1990s. On top of the millions of dollars they had already invested in the development of the 2.2-liter turbocharged V6 engines that powered the cars, the two manufacturers bankrolled additional millions in wind tunnel research to create the new aero kits. But they were required to sell the kits to teams at a heavily subsidized league-mandated price—$75,000 for the first kit for each car, going up incrementally for additional kits, which represented a substantial loss.

Chevrolet dominated the three-year DW12 era, winning thirty-three of fifty-two races from 2010-12, but the addition of aero kits ensured that being competitive was no longer all about engines. Not only did the new campaign offer either manufacturer the opportunity to catch up where it may be lacking in terms of horsepower, fuel mileage, or drivability, a superior aero package could overcome any potential engine shortcomings. Of course, a bad aero kit could negate the advantage of a superior engine, as Honda would subsequently demonstrate. The other element to this equation was driver and team affiliations, where Chevrolet strongly held the upper hand, with its program anchored by star-studded, multicar efforts from Team Penske and Chip Ganassi Racing. Ganassi actually bounced from Honda to Chevy in '14, then back to Honda in '17. On the other hand, Andretti Autosport started the DW12 era as a Chevy team, but switched to Honda in '14 when Ganassi joined the Chevrolet camp.

The aero-kit era got off to a rough start when a first-corner collision at the 2015 St. Petersburg GP showered debris from the complicated new wings onto the track and beyond. A female spectator who was six months pregnant and standing at a concession stand several hundred feet from the track was struck by a piece of flying carbon fiber, sending her to the hospital for two days with a depressed skull fracture. The race was won by Juan Pablo Montoya, who made a shock return to Indy car racing in '14 with Team Penske following thirteen years in Formula 1 and NASCAR.

Montoya then scored his second Indianapolis 500 triumph in May 2015, and he entered the season finale at Sonoma Raceway with a comfortable thirty-four-point championship cushion. But he collided with teammate Will Power during the race, allowing Scott Dixon to sneak away with his fourth IndyCar Series title. Dixon's task was made easier by the controversial implementation of double points for the last race of the season, a change made in '14. The IndyCar championship battle had been a remarkably close affair every year since '06, and many fans viewed the introduction of double points as an unnecessary gimmick for what was consistently the most exciting title competition in motorsports.

The aero kits also caused problems at Indianapolis. INDYCAR stated that one of its goals for the new components was to create cars capable of breaking Arie Luyendyk's twenty-year-old track record in conjunction with the one hundredth race. But it went badly wrong when five serious crashes occurred during the space of six days in May 2015, including one that seriously injured popular driver James Hinchcliffe. Three of the accidents resulted in Chevrolet-bodied cars driven by Hélio Castroneves, Josef Newgarden, and Ed Carpenter becoming airborne and upside down. All were lucky to escape injury. INDYCAR scrapped its plan to allow extra turbocharger boost for qualifying to chase the speed record and also mandated that all cars qualify in race trim, eliciting loud complaints from the Honda camp, whose cars were slow but did not suffer severe aerodynamic instability like the Chevrolet competition.

Chevrolet won thirty-three out of forty-eight races and powered the IndyCar Series champion during all three years of the aero-kit era, delivering Dixon a fourth championship in 2015, followed by triumphs for Team Penske drivers Simon Pagenaud and Newgarden in '16 and '17. But Honda reigned supreme at Indy, winning in '16 (Alexander Rossi) and '17 (Takuma Sato). And with crowds back above three hundred thousand and majesty fully restored, the Indianapolis 500 continued to produce arguably the most compelling show in auto racing. Following Rossi's dramatic fuel strategy victory in '16, the '17 race was decided by a late-race shootout between Castroneves and Sato, with the Japanese driver denying the Brazilian a record-tying fourth Indianapolis win by 0.2 second.

The big news at Indianapolis in 2017 was the presence of two-time Formula 1 World Champion Fernando Alonso. In the midst of a miserable F1 campaign with uncompetitive Honda engines, recently installed McLaren CEO (and former resident of Indianapolis, where his JMI marketing firm was located) Zak Brown teamed with Andretti Autosport to field a McLaren-branded Honda entry at Indianapolis. Alonso's first test in an Indy car (with a papaya-orange livery evocative of McLaren's 1974 Indianapolis winner) was streamed live by IMS Productions, attracting more than two million viewers from around the world. Alonso lived up to his World Champion title in the race, leading twenty-nine laps before retiring with a blown engine while running in the top five.

Outside of Indianapolis, the aero-kit era did deliver the promised increase in speed, resulting in lap records at many circuits. But it did not pass without tragedy; Justin Wilson was killed in a freak accident during the 2015 Pocono 500 when he was struck in the helmet by a piece of flying debris from a car that Sage Karam had crashed nearly half a mile ahead of Wilson on the track. Wilson's death, along with fatal accidents in Formula 1 (Jules Bianchi) and Formula 2 (Henry Surtees, the son of 1964 F1 World Champion John Surtees) thrust a new focus on driver head protection that ultimately resulted in the '18 introduction of a device called a "halo" that shielded the cockpit of F1 cars. INDYCAR followed suit two years later with a cockpit protection system called the "Aeroscreen"; developed by Red Bull Technology, the Aeroscreen was essentially an F1-style halo surrounded by a tall plexiglass windshield.

By the end of 2017, nobody was sad to see the end of the aero-kit era. In general, the aerodynamic enhancements were viewed as a costly dead end that did not provide the anticipated differentiation between Honda and Chevrolet, and also failed to enhance the quality of the racing. Chevrolet generally dominated the competition, even when Honda was granted special dispensation to try and catch up.

But to INDYCAR's credit, the basic concept that the ICONIC Committee proposed back in 2010 had merit. In '18, the IMSA WeatherTech Sports Car Championship, operated by the France family of NASCAR fame, introduced a category called Daytona Prototype International (DPi) that successfully integrated manufacturer-designed bodywork onto an approved homologated prototype chassis. These cars were much more attractive and popular among fans than the first generations of Daytona Prototypes they replaced, and the class immediately attracted entries from General Motors and its Cadillac brand, along with Honda Performance Development/Acura and Mazda.

CHAPTER 23

BACK TO THE FUTURE

At the same time IMSA rolled out its DPi class, INDYCAR redressed the basic Dallara IR-12 chassis with a standardized spec bodywork and wing package that quickly became known as the Universal Aero Kit. In an attempt to cut costs and bring back parity, all while improving safety and creating more fan appeal, the series managed to give the six-year-old platform a convincing makeover. Overall downforce was reduced by around 20 percent, and as the result of driver input, a greater emphasis was placed on developing that downforce from the redesigned floor rather than complex plus-sized wings. Larger, higher sidepods were moved forward, radiators relocated, and additional anti-intrusion protection was added to the cockpit sides, safety gains derived from information gleaned from accidents in the last few years that injured drivers Justin Wilson, James Hinchcliffe, and Sébastien Bourdais.

The rear wheels still remained heavily shrouded, and the floor still extended to the outer edge of the rear tires. But the rear "bumpers" that were a controversial design element of the DW12 and the aero-kit cars were removed. In addition, the high air intake behind the roll hoop was eliminated in favor of a low engine cover reminiscent of CART-era Indy cars. The resemblance to those cars was very much intentional, and given the IR-12's reputation as a bit of an ugly duckling, whether in DW12 trim or with Chevy or Honda aero add-ons, the designers did a highly effective job of creating a sleek, modern-looking car with evocative retro styling cues.

The Dallara IR-18 redesign was revealed in July 2017 and early development was entrusted to veteran Indy car pilots Juan Pablo Montoya

John Oreovicz

and Oriol Servià. It was a much smoother process than the troubled gestation of the DW12, and Dallara began delivering updated kits to teams in November.

"This has been a year and a half in the making, and the process has finally come to the point where we can get the car on the track, so we're quite excited about that," said Jay Frye, INDYCAR president of competition and operations and the man charged with plotting the IndyCar Series's future direction. "Over the last few months we kept putting out some different things to get reactions from the fans to see what they thought of the project. It helped us a lot because it made us feel like we were certainly going in the right direction, which was great. We took what we thought the car should look like, and that's where we talked about reverse engineering the car to esthetically have the historical feel, but yet have a very forward looking car, and we think we've done that."

The resulting package immediately resonated with drivers and fans. The drivers enjoyed having a less planted car that they could throw around and slide, while fans were just happy to see Indy cars that looked and drove like Indy cars again after the slot car–like handling of the aero-kit cars.

The most obvious visual change was the removal of the rear bumpers. They were introduced as a safety measure in 2012 in reaction to the number of cars that were launched into flight between '03 and '11. But they added weight to the rear of an already tail-heavy design and had the unintended consequence of contributing to the car's tendency to lift when in a state of yaw (sideways) or traveling backwards. Ultimately, they were removed from the '18 car more for safety reasons than aesthetics.

"Some people might question removing the wheel guards as a safety negative, but although well-intentioned when the DW12 came out, they didn't fix the problem," said INDYCAR aerodynamicist Tino Belli. "In Scott Dixon's accident at Indianapolis"—a massive crash during the 2017 race—"there is one frame of film where the wheel guard had gone from being there to being out of the picture. They just did nothing. We've learned that the wheel guards actually considerably helped produce the back flips."

The 2018 season opener at St. Petersburg demonstrated the potential for the new car to shake up the established order, as three rookies qualified in the top six. They were led by Robert Wickens, a twenty-eight-year-old Canadian who was a single-seater standout in North America and Europe prior to a successful six-year stint in the German DTM championship. Teamed with his friend and countryman James Hinchcliffe at Schmidt-Peterson Motorsports, Wickens claimed pole position for his first IndyCar Series race and led 69 of 110 laps. His job was made easier when front row starter Will Power spun on the first lap and faded to a tenth-place finish, leaving Alexander Rossi and wily veteran Sébastien Bourdais as the competition.

After his shock victory in the 2016 Indianapolis 500, Rossi accepted and embraced the fact that his future would lie in Indy cars instead of Formula 1. He developed into a regular frontrunner, beating Scott Dixon in a straight fight to win at Watkins Glen in '17. Then Rossi really came into his own with the low-downforce '18 package. He developed a reputation as a ruthless racer who was all too willing to bang wheels or push rivals beyond the track limits, making him an ideal villain for the series.

At St. Pete, Rossi hounded Wickens all day, but it looked like the Canadian rookie would win his Indy car debut until a pair of late cautions necessitated restarts. Wickens aced the first one, but Rossi got the jump for the second, forced his way to the inside at Turn One, and nudged Wickens's Honda into a gentle spin. Bourdais snuck through the confusion to lead the final two laps to steal the win with Rossi third and Wickens an unrepresentative eighteenth after stealing the show.

On the renamed ISM Raceway oval near Phoenix, Wickens dazzled again in his oval track debut. Bourdais took pole position, another happy milestone in his comeback from injuries sustained in a savage accident during Indianapolis 500 qualifying in May 2017. The Frenchman led sixty laps, and Power another eighty before crashing, leaving the race in the hands of Wickens. The rookie looked in position to score a remarkable win, but again, fate worked against him. Ed Jones crashed with twenty-one laps remaining, and several drivers, including defending series champion Josef Newgarden, pitted for fresh tires. Eight laps remained when the race restarted; Newgarden quickly moved from fifth to second, then spent four laps looking for a way past Wickens before making a risky move around the outside of Turn One on Lap 247 of 250. From there it was an easy cruise to the line for the win. Rossi was third, but he was the star of the race, passing fifty-three cars as he twice worked his way through the field after incurring a penalty.

Rossi's momentum continued a week later when he claimed pole position at Long Beach and converted it into a dominant victory. Newgarden triumphed for the third time in four years at Barber Motorsport Park—a beautifully manicured road course outside of Birmingham, Alabama, that quickly became a surprisingly successful venue for INDYCAR. Then Power swept the month of May at Indianapolis, beating a charging Scott Dixon on the IMS road course before edging local favorite Ed Carpenter in the Indianapolis 500.

The 500 featured thirty lead changes, but it did not produce the late-race shootout for the victory that had become commonplace in the DW12 and aero-kit eras. The race was generally interesting and entertaining, but it lacked the slingshot passing and wheel-to-wheel excitement that was a hallmark of the event since 2012. The overall number of position passes declined by a third, from 641 to 428.

For several years, the drivers and almost everyone else in the sport were clamoring to make the cars more difficult to drive, and that goal was clearly achieved with the IR18. Several high-profile drivers crashed on their own without explanation, including former Indy winners Hélio Castroneves and Tony Kanaan, as well as Danica Patrick, who made a one-off return to Indy cars for the final race of her career. Fuel strategy created drama late in the race, yet ultimately, the two fastest cars of the day—the Chevrolets of Power and pole position starter Carpenter—battled it out for the win. But Power's margin of victory was 3.16 seconds, or the length of a straightaway, which some fans deemed unacceptable after three photo finishes since 2014.

"This was a race you wanted to lead," Power remarked. "At last they have a formula now, where, if you had a good car, the leader could benefit and pull away. I liked it. It definitely made it harder to drive. This was a race like it was from 2008 to 2011. It was about your speed. The tires would degrade. You were never wide open. It put the drivers back into it more, in my opinion."

The level of dissatisfaction expressed over what was in almost every respect a competitive and compelling Indianapolis 500 underscored the unrealistic expectations that many racing fans have developed in the modern era. Not every race can feature a twenty-car pack jostling wheel-to-wheel as they hurtle toward a photo finish. But a growing number of fans complain if that's not what they get, and that puts sanctioning bodies in the tricky position of trying to satisfy a finicky fanbase while maintaining an acceptable level of challenge for the drivers.

The other unintended consequence of spec car racing is safety related. When the equipment is essentially all the same and teams are prevented from developing any kind of speed advantage, it creates the kind of close competition that fans apparently clamor for. But it's an artificial parity that racing purists resent, and while it often provides the wheel-to-wheel competition and photo finishes the public demands, it also forces drivers into taking greater risks, with little or no margin for error. Race starts and restarts are often the only realistic opportunities drivers have to overtake, which results in some aggressive and highly questionable driving tactics. That's especially critical at 220 miles per hour on a superspeedway, where there is no such thing as a small accident.

Such a scenario played out at Pocono Raceway, where a first-lap accident left Wickens badly injured. His car touched Ryan Hunter-Reay's as they raced into Turn Two, launching the Canadian's car nose first into the catchfence. Spinning like a top, the car thankfully came to rest upright, but Wickens sustained numerous fractured bones and a significant spinal cord injury. Though he has been unable to return to racing, Wickens frequently shares details of his progress through social media, in the process building a fan base as large as any active Indy car driver.

In the second half of the 2018 campaign, Dixon repeatedly demonstrated how he has developed into one of the greatest Indy car drivers of all time. He strung together three midseason wins at Detroit, Texas, and Toronto, then protected his points lead down the stretch—most notably at the revived Grand Prix of Portland, where after being forced off track on the first lap, Dixon rallied to finish fifth. That left him in position to cruise to an easy second place in the season finale at Sonoma with the championship out of reach from Rossi, his closest contender.

The path to Dixon's fifth championship was not easy. In his third season in Indy cars, Rossi emerged as a genuine star, with a brash style that sometimes left other drivers fuming. Rossi matched Dixon's three wins in 2018 and was utterly dominant on a couple of occasions. Led by

Rossi, Andretti Autosport reestablished itself as a top team, with Hunter-Reay adding a pair of wins. The Ganassi-Andretti one-two punch helped Honda win the IndyCar Manufacturer's Championship for the first time since engine competition returned to the series in '12.

There was plenty of commercial news off the track. In March 2018, INDYCAR announced it had signed a three-year deal (2019-21) with NBC Sports Group that would broadcast all IndyCar Series events under the same family of networks, with eight races, including the Indianapolis 500, on the flagship NBC network. NBC created a premium "Gold" tier for IndyCar similar to what it offered for the PGA Tour and several other sports; for a fifty-dollar annual fee, fans could gain internet-only access to comprehensive coverage of every practice session, with bonus content in lieu of commercials and full coverage of Indy Lights and other ladder series support races.

NBC stated that viewership for its IndyCar broacasts on the NBC Sports Network cable channel (VERSUS was rebranded NBCSN in 2012) was up 78 percent since '14. Taking into account the ABC portion of the schedule, INDYCAR claimed a 38 percent overall increase in that same four-year period.

"We're excited to have NBC Sports serve as the exclusive home of INDYCAR, which represents the most competitive open-wheel racing in the world," said Jon Miller, president of programming for NBC Sports and NBCSN. "We're honored to bring the Indianapolis 500, one of the most prestigious events in all of sports, to NBC, further enhancing the NBC Sports 'Championship Season.' We've seen consistent growth for INDYCAR on NBCSN in the past decade, and we hope to continue that growth throughout the series by leveraging the television, digital, production, and marketing assets that make NBC Sports a powerful media partner."

"This arrangement brings all of INDYCAR to one home, increases our exposure, and includes our first direct-to-consumer offer for our fans," added Mark Miles, CEO of Hulman & Company and INDYCAR. "We couldn't be happier to have start-to-finish coverage of INDYCAR's season with the NBC Sports Group."

The other important development for 2019 was the arrival of a new title sponsor for the IndyCar Series after Verizon's five-year run promised much in the way of promotion but delivered little. It was similar to how CART's partnership with Federal Express in the late 1990s failed to produce significant results. Given Verizon's national name-brand recognition (35 percent of the U.S. cell phone market, compared to 34 percent for AT&T, 17 percent for T-Mobile, and 12 percent for Sprint), it is disappointing that the company did so little to activate its IndyCar sponsorship. But as often happens, a change in corporate leadership fueled Verizon's change of heart, and support waned in the latter stages of the partnership.

INDYCAR anticipated running the 2019 season unbranded, but over a three-month period in late '18, Hulman Motorsports came to terms with Nippon Telephone and Telegraph (NTT), the Japanese telecommunications company, for a multiyear title sponsorship agreement. The company's NTT Data division had sponsored one of Chip Ganassi Racing's IndyCar Series entries since '13.

On the surface, the NTT/INDYCAR partnership looked like a case of strange bedfellows, but upon deeper examination, several elements made sense for both sides. NTT, like its American counterpart AT&T, was attempting to recreate its image from the stodgy old "phone company" into a provider of cutting-edge technology and network services. Key attributes of racing, including speed and reliability, play right into marketing for a technology company—attributes that Verizon and Federal Express failed to capitalize on. NTT was also trying to build its brand outside of Japan, and IndyCar—especially the well-known Indianapolis 500—provided a solid foothold in the North American market.

IndyCar got an influx of cash to fund its Entrant Support Program, and it also achieved stronger penetration into the Japanese market, leaving some sentimental fans to dream that the NTT IndyCar Series could return to Twin Ring Motegi, whether on the road course or the oval.

Skeptics pointed out that NTT is not a recognizable consumer brand in the U.S., but FedEx and Verizon certainly were, and their notoriety provided little direct benefit to the series. INDYCAR believed that beyond its financial input, NTT could help transform the series into a technology leader in terms of fan interaction.

"Having a strong technology partner is critically important to INDYCAR's continued growth, so we are thrilled to welcome NTT as our new title sponsor," stated Miles. "INDYCAR's rise in popularity is a testament to the fact that we've made the sport as accessible as possible to our fans, and we plan to continue in that mission. We know this partnership will help us attract the next generation of fans to what remains the most competitive racing program on the planet."

"Technological innovations have the potential to change the sport and fan experience drastically, and NTT is proud to be associated with INDYCAR and accelerate the future of smart racing," added Jun Sawada, president and CEO of NTT. "Based on our lengthy and successful experience, including work in mobile applications, analytics, and user experience, we will help INDYCAR create the next generation of fans globally who aspire to enjoy racing through a more digital experience."

A ghost from the Indy Racing League era made an unexpected appearance at the now-traditional St. Petersburg opener. In his traditional pre-season meet-and-greet with reporters, Roger Penske reopened the bitter 1996 argument about guaranteed starting positions for full-time teams in the Indianapolis 500; this time coming out in favor of them. It brought back memories of the second split between CART and the Indy Racing League, when the IRL controversially reserved 75 percent of the grid spots at Indianapolis and other series races for IRL championship leaders. Penske didn't exactly endear himself to the sport's loyal veteran fans by adopting a stance that looked like the polar opposite to the one he espoused in '96.

Perhaps high-profile driver James Hinchcliffe's failure to qualify for the 2018 Indianapolis 500 had rekindled memories of the Penske team's famous Indy DNQ with champion pilots Al Unser Jr. and Emerson Fittipaldi in 1995 and Bobby Rahal's similar experience two years earlier. In any case, Penske now argued that the twenty-two full-time Indy Car Series teams benefiting from the Entrant Support Program should be granted a guaranteed place on the Indianapolis grid.

"To me, it's a whole different world," he told reporters at St Petersburg. "I think a full-time team that starts day one and runs the full season and commits with the same driver, I think they have to have [a guaranteed spot in the Indy 500 field]," Penske said. "To me, it's a sign of the times."

A few weeks later at Long Beach, Penske's most successful rival Chip Ganassi threw his support behind Penske's plan. So, too, did driver-turned-owner Michael Andretti. "Roger knows what it's like not to be in that race," Ganassi said. "Thank God I don't know what that's like. But obviously I agree with him. When you're making a commitment all year for the series, a commitment is just that."

Fan reaction to what was perceived as a remarkable flip-flop by the sport's most prominent team owners was swift and severe. The 25/8 Rule was created to protect the small, poorly funded teams that made up the 1996 IRL field; now the sport's richest organizations appeared to be demanding the same kind of protection, and the optics were bad, to say the least.

Hulman Motorsport CEO Miles stayed well above the fray, stating that no decision had been made about guaranteed starting berths at Indy moving forward. "This event has traditions that mean something to fans," Miles said. "And we believe a big part of qualifying is the drama around the possibility that a car isn't going to get in—whatever car. But we try to consider all the points of view and decide what we ought to do."

Ironically, the 2019 Indianapolis 500 featured an exciting new qualifying format that left two part-time entries (Fernando Alonso of McLaren and Patricio O'Ward of Carlin) and one full-timer (Max Chilton, also from the Carlin stable) out of the top thirty-three. Under the Penske plan, Chilton would have been added to the field even though he posted the slowest overall qualifying speed, while the shoestring Juncos Racing team and driver Kyle Kaiser—who electrified fans by bumping out the high-profile McLaren entry driven by two-time Formula 1 world champion Alonso—would have been sent home.

Rahal, who memorably failed to qualify at Indianapolis in 1993 when he was the defending CART series champion, came out against any kind of "locked in" status for the 500.

"As much as it would be nice to have a guarantee where we don't have to worry about it, especially as a long-term, season-long entrant, I think that is not loyal to the history of the Indianapolis Motor Speedway and the history of the 500," Rahal said. "Clearly, spectators have made their voices pretty clear on that. To me, you've got to go out there and work for it."

The story faded in the summer, when Newgarden won four times and had a relatively untroubled run to the championship after Dixon suffered a fluke DNF at Gateway and a poor finish at Portland. For the second year in a row with the Universal Aero Kit, no driver demonstrated a marked advantage, though Team Penske's trio combined to win nine of the seventeen races. Pagenaud ended up beating Rossi into second place in the standings. Pagenaud, the 2016 IndyCar Series champion, started the '19 season under scrutiny after going winless in '18. But he secured a new contract with Penske by repeating Will Power's achievement from '18 by sweeping the month of May at Indianapolis, claiming the Indy 500 after a tense late-race battle with Rossi.

Pocono was the site of another first-lap multicar wreck in 2019, this time involving Rossi, Ganassi Racing rookie Felix Rosenqvist, and Takuma Sato. It was the third time since '15 that the track's IndyCar Series event was marred by a serious incident, and this time, there were no serious injuries. But the violent accident ignited a fierce social media debate led by Wickens about Pocono's suitability as an Indy car track, and it was dropped from the schedule for '20.

Before the dust had settled, many blamed Sato for being overaggressive, but the Japanese driver refused to accept sole responsibility for the incident. The Twitter witch hunt that targeted Sato over the next few days was disgraceful and upsetting. Rahal Letterman Lanigan Racing ultimately defended Sato by releasing in-car video that clearly showed he held his line and did not steer into or instigate his car's sudden movement to the left. But the backlash from his fellow drivers and the public was deeply hurtful to Sato. "Unfortunately, in the world right now, with social media, people have instant reactions," he told the *Indianapolis Star*. "They make decisions without information, and that's what happened." Sato responded to his critics in the best possible way by winning the IndyCar race at Gateway Raceway just six days later, making him a winner on all four of the series's track types (speedway, short oval, road course, street course).

With the consolidation of its broadcasts under the NBC Sports umbrella, INDYCAR was hoping for a much-needed boost in television ratings. Series management secretly hoped that NBC would experience similar magic with the Indianapolis 500 that it did when it took over coverage of the Kentucky Derby from ABC in 2001 and ratings jumped 59 percent.

That proved rather optimistic. NBC reported a 9 percent overall increase for 2019 compared to '18, averaging 1.105 million viewers per event across all platforms. NBC's first Indianapolis 500 broadcast claimed an 11 percent increase over '18, to 5.48 million viewers, but the 3.4 Nielsen rating was still the second lowest in the thirty-four years the race has been televised live. The seven other free-to-air network broadcasts averaged 929,000 viewers, with the series finale at Laguna Seca Raceway pulling a 0.50 rating, representing 736,000 viewers. NBC also claimed its internet coverage drew a total of 12.9 million live minutes and an Average Minute Audience (AMA) of 6,300 viewers.

For comparative purposes, NASCAR averaged 3.3 million viewers per race in 2018 after attracting 4.5 million as recently as '16. Meanwhile, ESPN reacquired the rights to Formula 1 in '18 after several years with NBCSN and claimed a 2 percent increase to 548,000 American viewers per race. In that context, INDYCAR was actually performing comparatively well in what was generally a difficult market for motorsports.

Terms were not disclosed for the NBC deal, but suffice to say INDYCAR earned a tiny fraction of the money NASCAR continued to generate from television—admittedly with twice as many races and more robust support series. Even though ratings had already started to decline as far back as 2005 and had dropped 60 percent from their historic peak, NASCAR continued to command lucrative television contracts, with Fox committing $2.4 billion to air the first half of the season from 2015-22 and NBC getting back into the game with a ten-year package worth $4.4 billion for the second half of the slate through '24. In a rapidly changing media environment, and in light of NASCAR's declining performance in the sports marketplace, those figures are likely to be substantially reduced for the group's next television contract.

The biggest takeaway from the Universal-Aero-Kit era was that everybody—including INDYCAR management—seemed happy that Indy car racing was starting to look a lot like when the sport was at peak popularity in the 1980s and early '90s in the CART era. In truth, the retro styling for the cars matched just about everything else in the modern IndyCar Series, which in the years since its formation as the Indy Racing League had essentially morphed into the old CART series. The field was comprised of many of the same historic competitors (the

Penske, Foyt, Ganassi, Andretti, Rahal, and Coyne teams represented fifteen of the twenty-two full-time cars) and race venues from that era. Eleven of seventeen races on the 2019 schedule were staged on road or street courses, and ten of the fifteen tracks on the slate started out as CART venues, with three originating as IRL and two (the Indianapolis oval and Phoenix) dating to the USAC era. The only real differences between 1995 and 2019 were that the Indianapolis Motor Speedway (under the guise of Hulman Motorsports) was the sole and undisputed leader of the sport and the economic and fan bases were a lot smaller.

With NASCAR struggling to remain relevant and Formula 1 consumed by its first major management change in more than forty years, it looked like there was a golden opportunity for Indy car racing to finally regain the popularity and international prominence it enjoyed in the first half of the 1990s prior to the CART-IRL split. The twelve years since reunification saw the IndyCar Series demonstrate slow and steady growth, but nobody seemed to know what was needed as the catalyst to spark a major revival.

And then something totally unexpected happened.

CHAPTER 24

"WE PROBABLY HAD TAKEN IT AS FAR AS WE CAN"

"Roger S. Penske has led a life worthy of example as an accomplished business-man and humanitarian. Guided by his father's favorite phrase, 'Effort equals results,' he created and built Team Penske into the most successful motorsports group in history.

Off the track, Mr. Penske built his first car dealership into the Penske companies—great American businesses that also make their vehicles available to bring crucial supplies to people in need.

Roger Penske's passion and unrelenting drive have established him as an icon of sports and business. America is proud to honor him."

—Presidential Medal of Freedom Declaration to Roger Penske

In a White House ceremony on October 24, 2019, President Donald J. Trump presented Roger Penske with the highest possible honor for an American civilian—the Presidential Medal of Freedom.

There's no question that Penske embodies the American dream. Over the course of half a century, he built a single Philadelphia Chevrolet dealership into a worldwide transportation industry empire with sixty-four thousand associates and revenues of $32 billion. He brought the Super Bowl to Detroit, and he has devoted thousands of hours and millions of dollars to renovating and restoring the city he calls home. All that is in addition to the success achieved by his racing teams, with more than five hundred wins around the world, including eighteen triumphs in the Indianapolis 500.

LAT Images

"Roger, from racing to business to philanthropy, you have moved from one great victory to another," remarked the president. "You're a very unique person and truly a great champion and truly a winner. No matter what you do, it turns to gold. You are a legend in the speedway and you're a legend in business, and your name is revered everywhere the checkered flag flies and beyond that."

Penske said that being awarded the Medal of Freedom "to me, means more than any business success or motorsports trophy." But just eleven days later, the eighty-two-year-old tycoon revealed news about what might ultimately prove to be his proudest accomplishment. On November 4, journalists woke to a Media Advisory from INDYCAR and the Indianapolis Motor Speedway:

The Board of Directors of Hulman & Company are announcing the sale of the company and certain subsidiaries, including the Indianapolis Motor Speedway, the NTT IndyCar Series and Indianapolis Motor Speedway Productions (IMS Productions) to Penske Entertainment Corp., a subsidiary of Penske Corporation.

The official announcement, befitting a longtime Indianapolis 500 tradition, would come at eleven o'clock EST.

At the appointed hour, Hulman & Co. CEO Mark Miles led Penske and Tony George, Chairman of the Hulman board, to the dais on the fourth floor of the IMS Media Center. George spoke first. He mentioned his sisters Josie, Kathi, and Nancy by name, and acknowledged the family's longtime attorney Jack Snyder and financial advisor John Ackerman. Although George didn't mention the fact, many in the room were aware that his mother, Mari Hulman George, had died almost exactly one year earlier on November 3, 2018.

"Over the course of business through the years, we've always looked at strategic opportunities, things we might be able to do to grow and expand our capabilities here," George commented. "We're a 169-, almost 170-year-old business, and we've been in a lot of different businesses during that time. We've been distillers, we've been brewers, we've been grocers, we've been in produce, canned goods, just about everything—financials, utilities."

George noted how the family had recently divested Hulman & Co.'s longtime flagship brand, Clabber Girl baking products (for $80 million earlier in 2019 to B&G Foods), and he thought back to his grandfather Tony Hulman's acquisition of the grounds on which he stood nearly seventy-four years earlier. He paused, struggling to control his emotions.

"But now this one is extra special to all of us because we've all grown up around it," George said, fighting back tears. "Nancy and I, we came home from the hospital to home just right down the street here." Their parents Elmer and Mari George built a brick ranch home at 5424 W. 25th Street. "So, we've literally grown up around it. Our kids and grand-kids have done the same.

"Bittersweet, but very exciting for us because we know that we're passing the torch to an individual who has created an organization that is not only dynamic, but it's ideally suited, I think, to take over the stewardship—a corporation that is family-involved, much like ours. But with a track record that is really without compare."

George said he approached Penske at the 2019 IndyCar Series finale at WeatherTech Raceway Laguna Seca to congratulate the team owner on another championship. "I wanted to wish him well on the grid, and just simply said I'd like to meet with him and talk about stewardship." The approach stunned Penske. After an exchange of emails and a few meetings that included Miles, the basics of a deal were quickly put in place. "Not many things are kept under wraps around here," George deadpanned. "But this was fairly well contained."

He added, "It's obviously emotionally difficult, hence the choking up. But we all love it, and we all care deeply for it. I think we all realize that as a family and as an organization, we probably had taken it as far as we can. I think that Roger, with his structure, his resources, his capabilities that he demonstrates, is only going to take this to another level. That's what we're all about. We're supporting elevating this asset and staking a new claim on its future.

"We, with emotion, are happy to be here today."

Throughout nearly seventy-five years of Hulman family ownership, rumors constantly swirled that the Indianapolis Motor Speedway was for sale. During her lifetime, Mari Hulman George always deflected such talk, saying that the Speedway was an asset that would be passed down to her grandchildren—the children of Nancy, Tony, Kathi, and Josie George. When Mrs. Hulman died in 2018, the rumors about a potential sale accelerated, with International Speedway Corp. (which was acquired by NASCAR and taken private in '19) and new Formula 1 owner Liberty Media considered the most likely buyers.

But the Hulman-George family independently concluded that Penske was the right man to lead the historic track into the future. They essentially made him an unexpected offer that he couldn't refuse. The transaction price was not disclosed, but it is believed to be around $350 million.

People had joked for years that Penske owned the Indianapolis Motor Speedway. In 2019, he finally bought it. Transfer of ownership was completed on January 6, 2020.

"Motorsports has been the common thread through our business for many years—in fact, it helped us build our brand," Penske said. "We all know what the Indianapolis 500 has meant to our company. I've got a big commitment here to take over as the steward of this great organization and what's been done here in the past for so many decades. It's my commitment to the Hulman family. The fact that you would select us for an opportunity to take on this investment, it's amazing. I just want to thank Tony and everyone else that's been involved in this."

He retold the story of attending his first Indianapolis 500 with his father in 1951 and marveled at the path that had led him to take ownership of his spiritual home. "I think that it really says that in the United States of America, if you work hard and you're committed, and you have a great group of people, you get great success," Penske reflected. "So today I hope my Dad is looking down at me and looking at this group and saying, 'Son, you did a good job.'"

Penske noted he had been back to Indianapolis for the 500 almost every year since that 1951 baptism as a fourteen-year-old. "Every single time, until one of the poorer moves we made is when we split from the Speedway and running here for a number of years," he said, referring to '96 to '99 when Penske Racing was competing elsewhere during the month of May at CART-sanctioned events. Penske also generated forehead-smash emojis by consistently referring to the IndyCar Series as "the IRL" during the press conference, an unconscious habit he has been unable to shake in the decade since unification.

He mentioned his prior ventures in track ownership, including rescuing Michigan Speedway from bankruptcy in 1973 to building California Speedway from the ground up in '97. Indianapolis, he noted, was a much different situation.

"This business is not broken," Penske said. "This is a great business, and the leadership team that's been here has done an outstanding job. We have no plans of changing the management teams that are in place today. What we want to do is be a support tool. We've been coming to this track for fifty years. Seeing the growth of the series and understanding the technology, it's also a great business opportunity for us to grow it to the next level. We look around this one-thousand-acre property and we say, 'Can this be the entertainment capital of the world, and not just the racing capital?' We're going to invest capital. We know the economic benefit today that this race brings to the region is amazing, and we want to grow that. It's important to us."

Penske's acquisition of Hulman & Co.—and by extension, the Indianapolis Motor Speedway and the IndyCar Series—stunned the world. In the modern era of cell phone cameras and social media, the fact that he kept the transaction secret was even more impressive than the way he sprung the Mercedes-Benz 500I engine on an unsuspecting public back in 1994. "I think this one was better—and more exciting," he joked to journalist Robin Miller.

Reaction to the news was almost overwhelmingly positive. Miller, whose influence in Indianapolis spread well beyond auto racing, called it Indy car's "biggest—and best—story in fifty years."

"This is great news for the industry," stated team owner Chip Ganassi. "The news will provide a shot in the arm to both the sport of auto racing and specifically to the IndyCar Series. Roger is a good friend and a class act, and all of his businesses are run well and with integrity. I couldn't be happier for all of us that are involved with the sport."

"I can't help but think that our series and IMS are in great hands," remarked driver Graham Rahal. "If you know anything about Mr. Penske, it's that he holds his work to the highest of standards. I have no doubts that we will see INDYCAR and the Indy 500 rise to new heights."

"Today marks the start of a new chapter for the city of Indianapolis, as the torch is passed from the Hulman-George family to another leader who shares a passion for the famed Indianapolis Motor Speedway and the legacy of INDYCAR," added Indianapolis Mayor Joe Hogsett. "For decades, Hulman & Company has overseen one of Indianapolis's greatest assets, acting as community partners and stewards of our state's most prized tradition. Residents across the city and around the globe all have stories of the wonder of IMS, thanks to the dedication of the Hulman-George family. I know Roger Penske and the Penske Corporation will continue this legacy, acting as ambassadors for Indianapolis and presiding over another century of progress, innovation, and sporting excellence at the world's greatest racetrack."

The dissenters were a few hardcore Hoosier old-timers whose resentment of Penske and his polished ways dated back to the USAC era, and a small group of fans fixated on what they perceived as a conflict of interest with one of the Indy car competitors owning the series. They apparently forgot similar conflicts when series owners Tony George, Gerald Forsythe, and Kevin Kalkhoven fielded entries in the IRL and Champ Car. In any case, Penske revealed that he would step away from his longtime role as race strategist and radio man for one of his drivers. "You won't see me there on race day," he said. "I think I've got a bigger job to do now, to try to see how we can build the series to the next level."

Penske acted quickly to start physical upgrades to the IMS facility. On February 14, 2020, he announced a series of improvements to enhance the fan experience at the Speedway, including the installation of thirty new video boards and a one-hundred-foot-by-twenty-foot "Media Wall" at the base of the Pagoda. IMS became the first motorsports facility with commercial 5G internet service. Georgetown Road, closed to vehicular traffic since the 16th Street roundabout was built in '14, received a much-needed repave and was reconfigured to improve pedestrian ingress and egress.

"This is the Racing Capital of the World," Penske stated. "It is on par with some of the most historic sporting institutions in this nation and across the globe, from Churchill Downs to Augusta National. Today, we're announcing a meaningful investment in our fan experience that will produce rapid results. It's part of a long-term plan to ensure the legendary status of the Speedway continues to grow and evolve for generations to come."

For the competitors, Penske pledged a $2 million increase to the Indianapolis 500 purse, bringing it to a record $15.3 million (by comparison, the 2020 Daytona 500 paid a record purse of more than $23 million). The added funds would be paid to the twenty-two full-time IndyCar Series Leader Circle entrants and put to rest talk of guaranteed starting spots for the marquee race.

Unfortunately, the COVID-19 pandemic of 2020 prevented Penske Entertainment from showing the improvements to the facility to the world during the month of May. The Indy car race on the IMS road course was postponed until the Brickyard 400 weekend in July and run without fans in attendance. More significantly, the Indianapolis 500 was delayed until August 23, and after plans were announced to run at half and then one-quarter capacity, the 500 was finally also run without spectators (and a 50-percent purse reduction, to $7.5 million). Despite lifting the local television blackout, the NBC broadcast drew a disappointing 2.3 rating, a 33-percent decrease from '19 and by far the lowest rating in the history of the race. The addition of a doubleheader INDYCAR road-racing weekend, called the Harvest Grand Prix, in early October finally allowed IMS to open its gates to show off the facility's shiny new coat of paint.

Penske Entertainment also faced its share of challenges in terms of staging a representative slate of IndyCar Series races in 2020 as the United States government and populace were unable to get the coronavirus under control. Teams had already traveled to Florida and set up for the opening race of the season when INDYCAR made the decision on March 13 to cancel or postpone all events through the end of April. Racing finally resumed at Texas Motor Speedway on June 6, with all competitors flying together to and from the one-day event in a marathon twenty-two-hour workday. Like the early years of CART, several tracks hosted two races, though in '20 they were in the form of doubleheader weekends. Road America, Iowa Speedway, Gateway Raceway, Mid-Ohio Sports Car Course, and the IMS road course all successfully executed doubleheader weekends, allowing the IndyCar Series to stage a fourteen-race championship that concluded October 25 with the rescheduled Firestone Grand Prix of St. Petersburg.

Scott Dixon cemented his position as one of the sport's all-time greats by claiming his sixth Indy car championship. Dixon won the first three races of the season, added another victory at Gateway, then endured an untimely slump before rallying to finish third at St. Pete to edge Josef Newgarden. Dixon has now earned fifty Indy car race wins, but still only one in the Indianapolis 500. In August 2020 Dixon and Chip Ganassi Racing, the pacesetter in practice and qualifying, executed a near-perfect race, only to be beaten fair and square by Takuma Sato and Rahal Letterman Lanigan Racing. With a series of strong performances since '12, including a win in '17, the once erratic Sato has emerged as a modern-day Indy 500 specialist.

Newgarden matched Dixon's four wins, and he pushed the six-time champion to the limit with a flawless drive to victory in St. Petersburg. Already a two-time Indy car champion at age twenty-nine, Newgarden can be a solid anchor for the sport for the next decade. Will Power, Simon Pagenaud, Ryan Hunter-Reay, and Ed Carpenter are established veterans still capable of winning, along with heritage stars Graham Rahal and Marco Andretti. A strong passel of young drivers, including Alexander Rossi, Colton Herta, Felix Rosenqvist, Scott McLaughlin, and Patricio O'Ward, should keep the IndyCar Series well stocked with talent for years to come. And seven-time NASCAR Cup Series champion Jimmie Johnson gave Indy car racing an unexpected boost by retiring from full-time stock car competition and announcing his intention to join the IndyCar Series for its slate of road and street course races in 2021 and beyond.

————

In truth, the Hulman-George family could not have found a better buyer for the Indianapolis Motor Speedway and the IndyCar Series than Roger Penske. He respects and appreciates the history of the Speedway, he understands the commercial value of the Indianapolis 500 and the need for a strong, year-long series of events to support it. He has the financial capital necessary to continue the upgrades and modernization of IMS that started with Project 100. The Indianapolis 500 and Indy car racing have been a major part of Penske's life, and he is sincere in his desire to maintain and grow the sport and its most iconic event, building on more than one hundred years of history.

With Mark Miles, Jay Frye, and Doug Boles, Penske inherits a management team that reveres the majesty and importance of the

Indianapolis 500, yet understands the need for a strong series of races to strengthen the 500 and provide a workable year-long business platform for the competing teams and INDYCAR's other constituents. Thanks mainly to Frye, the working relationship between series management and competitors is the most harmonious it has ever been.

Whether the battle for control of Indy car racing started in the 1950s, the '70s or the '90s, it was a long and costly civil war that caused deep and lasting damage to the sport as a whole—even to the seemingly unbreakable institution of the Indianapolis 500. NASCAR took full advantage of Indy car racing's self-destructive tendencies to take the lead as America's most popular form of auto racing.

Open-wheel racing's infighting came to an end when the Champ Car World Series and the Indy Racing League were unified in 2008. But it was not until the announcement of Penske Corp.'s acqusition of Hulman & Co. more than a decade later that the world finally started to believe that Indy car racing could again ascend to the heights it once enjoyed.

Forty years after he helped form Championship Auto Racing Teams, Roger Penske finally admitted and acknowledged that he is the right leader for Indy car racing. In reality, he always was.

PERSPECTIVE: **JIM McGEE**

Jim McGee is the most successful chief mechanic or team manager in the history of Indy car racing. McGee broke into the sport as an assistant for legendary mechanic Clint Brawner and quickly became the cantankerous Brawner's most trusted ally. After gambling on rookie driver Mario Andretti and building a Brabham-based rear-engine car, Brawner and McGee achieved tremendous success, with Andretti winning three USAC championships between 1965 and '69 and capped by victory in the '69 Indianapolis 500. McGee held key managerial roles at Vel's Parnelli Jones Racing, Team Penske, Patrick Racing, Rahal-Hogan Racing, and PKV Racing during a forty-five-year career that netted nine national championships and ninety race wins.

I was working for a newspaper and living in Massachusetts, but I went out to Indianapolis to work the month of May 1961 for Clint Brawner, with Eddie Sachs as the driver. At the end of '61, I had to decide whether to go racing or join the union and take up the apprenticeship. I started full-time with Clint in 1962. He was my mentor. He taught me the business and he taught me right. He was tough, but he had a heart of gold. He was a real down-to-earth guy. He focused on the details. He taught you there was no pie in the sky or magic bullet, it was just good common sense, hard work, and consistency.

In those days, we all lived in the basements of people's houses during May—even some of the drivers. People in the town of Speedway would make over their basements and rent them out. They charged us a dollar a day, and pretty soon, you were part of a family. They were cooking your dinner and doing your laundry. We worked many days at the Speedway from 8:00 a.m. to 6:00 p.m. Then we'd go out and get something to eat, and come back and work from 7:30 'til 10:30 or 11:00. We'd drink until midnight or one o'clock in the morning, and then be up again first thing the next day. I don't know how we did it, but we did.

Indy was really something compared to what I was used to with modifieds up in New England. It was pretty spectacular. As the month went on, I was taking it all in, thinking, "These guys are really focused." There was so much going on, and the stakes were so high. Qualifying was really important—you had to do whatever it took to qualify. Guys were really putting their lives on the line and taking chances with the cars, loosening them up, and running them on nitro.

It was funny, because after qualifying, we got into practice and fuel runs and tire runs, and everything felt kind of normal. Then there was all that buildup before the race, with the balloons and the marching bands. It was very exciting. But when they threw the green flag, all of a sudden it hit me: this is just another automobile race. There was nothing special about it. Everybody was out there racing, but there wasn't that urgency that was there at the beginning of the month. At one point, it just sort of calmed down.

I never got goosebumps when I walked into the Speedway like some people say they do. It was just another racetrack, and I was there to do a job. In fact, it used to kind of make me mad when people would make it more than it really was. That's for the fans and maybe sponsors to get all excited like that, but I think the more successful guys took it as just another race.

One of my policies at Indianapolis was: You've got to think, not react. You want to slow it down a little bit. That set the tone for my whole career, really. Reaction was a bad thing in racing, and thinking was a good thing. The wrong reaction can lead you to doing some stupid things. I always told the people working for me, "You need to slow down." Even some drivers were reactionary drivers, where others were cool and calm and just approached it as a job.

Clint hated the rear-engine cars. The "funny cars," he used to call them. There were a lot of guys who were against them, but you could see the handwriting on the wall. They were so fast through the corners. They weren't as spectacular as the roadsters were, but you knew there was going to be a change.

The racing was great through the late 1960s and into the '70s. We had good crowds and good races. When Tony Hulman was alive, the racing was good, and we worked together like a family, trying to help each other out. You could walk through every garage, and it was kind of a wide-open deal. I can remember A.J. Watson helping us with our cars, and we sometimes rebuilt his engine. As some of the sponsors started infiltrating the series, it started changing a little. It kind of separated things.

The USAC plane crash was a tragedy. We lost a lot of good guys in that deal, which might have changed some of the thinking. The racing was still good, but the sport just stalled there for a while. The teams were getting bigger, and we had to have more employees. The series is the thing that was suffering. Indianapolis was still over the top, with big crowds and the spectacle, but USAC as a whole wasn't going anywhere.

Roger Penske and Pat Patrick and those guys were putting a lot of their own money into the teams, and it wasn't making any sense. We didn't have good television, and it wasn't commercially growing. So they started CART, and in a short period of time, it just exploded. We were running international races, we had good TV, big crowds. It's interesting to speculate about what would have happened if Roger had led CART back in 1978. I think there were some egos involved, and Pat didn't want Roger to be in charge. Maybe Roger wasn't ready at that point in time, but that probably would have been the way to go.

It was really moving along until Tony George got involved. That was too bad, because you had Roger and Pat in there with their business skills, making things happen. The Speedway really didn't have good business people. They had their connections, and they knew how to make money. The Speedway made money in spite of itself, because of its tradition. But in the interim, it kept going down the wrong road. I don't think they had the right people supporting Tony. He was the commander in chief, but you still need people to guide him. After Joe Cloutier and his generation was gone, there wasn't anybody there qualified to help him steer the ship.

It's a shame that Tony decided to start the IRL. I think he was afraid, because he had guys like A.J. Foyt telling him that Roger and Pat were going to come in and take over the Speedway and buy out the Hulman family. Business-wise, Tony had good support, but I just don't think he had the right people supporting him. Certainly, I don't think he was capable himself.

CART was on the right track, for sure. They tried to make a deal with Indianapolis in 1999, and almost got it done. They had the rules package done and everything. They went downtown to sign the deal, and at the last minute, Tony walked in and said, 'I don't want to do it.' Maybe Mari Hulman George had a lot to do with that because they didn't want to see the 500 owned by anybody but them. It's probably not a coincidence that it sold less than a year after she died.

The demise of CART was when Roger decided he was going to support Tony. Indianapolis is the only thing that mattered to Roger. Winning Indy, and getting the notoriety of being a champion at Indianapolis, he didn't want to lose that. He thought Tony was the one who was going to push Indianapolis forward. I didn't feel that way at all. Most of the teams went back with Tony because of Roger's influence.

When things were going good in CART, we got free engines, free tires, free fuel. Now the poor competitor has to buy all that stuff. The economics of the series have imploded because it's not as marketable as it used to be. It's no longer a business where a guy who made a lot of money in another business is going to spend it on racing. Owning an Indy car team is not a good business model right now. Even Chip Ganassi is feeling the pinch and cutting back because he's not getting manufacturer support. But you need something the manufacturers are going to find attractive. Formula E obviously has a big attraction to manufacturers because of electric cars. It's a changing society, and to be successful, you have to be on the curve in a way that interests people.

CART had good international races in Canada, Australia, Brazil, and Japan, and those were big deals. I still think that's the way Indy car racing needs to go. With TV and that kind of worldwide interest, that's what puts people in the grandstands back here in the USA. I'm sure Penske will put more international races on the schedule. I'm sure he will also be successful in attracting more manufacturers.

I think it's great that Roger took it over. It's the best thing that could have happened. There will be no politics anymore. It will be his way or the highway. That's why he's been so successful. Once he has control, he knows what to do, and what he does is successful.

PERSPECTIVE: **MARIO ANDRETTI**

There has perhaps never been a more versatile racer than Mario Andretti. After dreaming of competing in Formula 1 when he was a boy growing up in Italy, Andretti found a very different kind of racing after his family emigrated to America in 1955. By the early '60s, Mario was an East Coast short track hotshot, and when he was given a chance in Indy cars by Clint Brawner, he made the most of it. Andretti developed into A.J. Foyt's chief rival in the late '60s, and after three USAC championships and victory in the '69 Indianapolis 500, he branched out into F1 and sports car racing. The '70s were barren for Mario in Indy cars, but he won twelve Grands Prix and in '78 became only the second American to win the F1 World Championship. Andretti returned to Indy cars full-time in the '80s, and while he never managed to win Indy again, he added a CART-sanctioned championship in '84 and remained competitive well into his fifties. Following his "retirement," Andretti has remained a hard-working ambassador for Indy car racing, helping to broker the 2008 Champ Car–IRL unification and driving the IndyCar two-seater at many races and special events.

I became aware of Indianapolis in 1951 when I was still in Italy. It started, believe it or not, with the movie *To Please a Lady*, with Clark Gable and Barbara Stanwyck. It was primarily the story of a driver coming through the ranks, dirt tracks and all that. She was a journalist. They gravitated to each other as the story went on, and here's Indianapolis. In Italy, the title of that film was not *To Please a Lady*; it was *Indianapolis*. And that actually captured my imagination. What's Indianapolis?

Then in 1954, Bill Vukovich was the first to break the 120-miles-per-hour average, which was 200 kilometers per hour. The headlines all said, "Vukovich wins Indianapolis at over 200 kph!" and that was a huge number. In Italy, only high-end cars could achieve that, and that really appealed to me.

So, the dream had already captured me and my twin brother Aldo when we arrived here. We discovered the local Nazareth track. My objective was to get as soon as possible into those single seaters—midgets, sprint cars—and try to get up the ladder to the top level. It all worked out and suddenly I was at Indy, trying to make a name for myself and hopefully someday have an opportunity to do some Formula 1. Grand Prix racing was always the goal in the back of my mind, but Indy, for any driver of single seaters here in the United States, that's the objective, to reach that level. As NASCAR has Daytona, Indy car has Indianapolis.

It was a transition. Clint Brawner didn't like the rear-engine cars because he didn't really understand the setups or anything. The Brawner Hawk was still being built, and the car didn't arrive until the second week. I had never sat in that car anywhere—not even in a garage— before it arrived at Indianapolis. I wasn't sleeping very well, obviously, up to that point.

We played it so damn conservative and it was a learning curve, but the car was reliable and we finished third. We won the championship that year too, so it was a great beginning for me. I look back and feel blessed that I had a team with the vast experience of Clint, and with Jim McGee. He was younger, more aggressive, and fast learning, and it was a great combination for me. The results are because of that.

Indy was really the launching pad, for sure. You only have one chance to become Rookie of the Year. At the end of the year, I was invited on the Johnny Carson show, and I was introduced as the Indianapolis Rookie of the Year. They never mentioned USAC National Champion, which for me had been a huge achievement. That's when I realized how important and just how big a race the Indy 500 is. When I finally won a few years later, I'll never forget that I received mail from the Tibet region. That's how far the reach is. It's such an important race for any driver, at some point in their career, to put under their belt. And to achieve that, it feels like a big weight lifted off your shoulders.

My rookie year, I finished third and won Rookie of the Year. Next year, won the national championship, started on pole, I'm on pole in '67, and then in '68 the car wasn't as good. All three races, I was out early in the race, and I wondered, "What do I have to do to even finish?" And the next time I finished, in '69, I won it. And that's the year that I shouldn't have, because of everything I had going on throughout the month. You have no idea how relieved I was when I crossed that finish line. I thought, "At least I got this one, and God willing, if I'm still around, maybe I'll get a few more."

I look at my son Michael, how good he was there, how he dominated. Lloyd Ruby, people like that who led and never won. And yet, because of that, they're not rated at the level they should be rated because they don't have that Indianapolis trophy on the mantle. It's all about the tradition, let's face it. It's an event that's known around the world, no question. From a career standpoint, there's nothing else that brings you to a different level, whether you earn it or not.

In the late '60s when you were running for a national championship, you had road course, short ovals, superspeedways and the dirt tracks. When I look back, what a time! I count my blessings, and that's one of those things that was so meaningful to me. How lucky was I to have participated in those times. To try to understand the different categories and the skill level that you needed to be able to perform in those situations. It will never happen again. I can look back with a lot of joy.

Formula 1 in the early '70s, was basically on its knees. Bernie Ecclestone saw the opportunities. He nailed down world television rights, and all of a sudden, you got billions in your coffers. Formula 1 will never again enjoy the wealth it enjoyed in the Ecclestone era. Okay, he made himself a billionaire, so be it. But it takes someone with that vision who really understands the power of the product. If you project it properly, it's contagious.

USAC never progressed. It was so parochial. You had visionaries who wanted more. Of course, there was Roger Penske. Roger had been in sports cars, he had been around. You could see that the series wasn't going anywhere, honestly. Indy was still Indy. There was no real attraction to it. That was when the team owners decided to form CART, in 1978.

I think you immediately saw how the thing exploded. Why? Because you had people who encouraged trying to do more international work, and all of a sudden TV comes on board. It was needed, I think. The way CART was formed was probably too democratic, when you have twenty-four teams, and everyone thinks they are the CEO. That was tough, but the formula was good. You could say definitely that in the history of Indy car racing, the CART days were the golden days. No question—the diversity, the international aspect, and the interest there. I think Australia was the second-highest-paid sanction outside of Indianapolis. There was wealth in the series. For us, as drivers in the '80s when there was a lot more commercial interest, there were a lot of airplanes at the FBOs. Now even the top guys have a tough time getting first class commercial! I really feel for the drivers today.

That 1996 split was not just Tony George himself. Obviously, he had his own agenda, but he was encouraged. A.J. Foyt and some other people got in his ear and told him, "You've got Indy, you don't need the other stuff, and they need Indy." As the split went on, CART had everything but Indy. The IRL had Indy and nothing else. Neither side could prosper for long. Even if you look at Indianapolis, the glory days were when CART was the strongest. You had media there from all over the world. That had never happened before, or since.

The other thing is that there was an alternative—NASCAR. And NASCAR, they were very smart. They picked up the ball there. Honestly, and unbeknownst to him, Tony George is what made NASCAR, believe it or not. I'll tell you why. He gave them Indy, and when he gave them Indianapolis, he brought them to the mainstream immediately. From there, NASCAR blossomed in ways beyond comprehension, all at Indy car's expense. It was unfortunate for us, but great for them. Probably 80 percent of our fan base migrated to NASCAR, and sponsors and everything else. All of a sudden, we were down in the cellar.

It was frustrating that it took so long to come together, but the thing is, eventually they did. Paul Newman and I said to each other, "This thing cannot keep going on. What can we do?" It had to be kept on the QT, for obvious reasons. But we finally had our first meeting right upstairs in my dining room. That's how it started. Three airplanes came in, and Tony didn't even want to come in on a plane with any of their identification on it. It was interesting, because it was the beginning of something that started to make sense. There were some questions about engines and Cosworth and things like that. But we came away believing we had something to work with, some different factors.

Then when we were getting closer, I said to Kevin, "We've got to meet and bring this to a head." We went to Aspen for three days, just Kevin and Tony and myself trying to hash it out. It came to an agreement that it was going to come together. The sticking point was: Who's going to run it? Kevin said we need to bring in an outsider. But Tony said, "I want to run it." So all of a sudden there was a little bit of a stalemate. Kevin really wanted it to happen, so I said, "Let's hear him out." And I never, ever heard Tony sell himself so much. He really wanted to do it. I said to Kevin, "You know what, the paddock trusts Tony. If we come together, he's someone we know, not an outsider." Kevin bought that, and that's how it started.

It's really hard to understand why Tony walked away when he did. I never felt I understood the man totally. I never heard anyone sell himself as much as he did to run the series, to be the man, the way Tony did to Kevin. I thought that was the right choice. Then it was up to him to carry the ball all the way. But it was also up to him to fumble it, and that's what he did, unfortunately. I don't know whether he ran out of energy, objectives, or what. It's hard to say. It's a shame, because the Hulman family has been synonymous with Indianapolis. It started with Tony Hulman himself. They were the ones behind all of this. That's the part that's hard to explain.

People say I was too critical, but I just saw that we were destroying what we love. All of us. It took a while for the Hulman-George family to make amends with me. I felt I was very close to the family, to the girls, through our family. But I only acted out of pure love for the sport in all of it. I always supported the Speedway and never wanted to see the Indy 500 diminished in stature at all. My dispute was with the IRL. I did not support the IRL because I think that's what disrupted open-wheel racing in America. We were all pulling in different directions, and that didn't make any sense.

I give Kevin so much credit as a businessman. He understood clearly that even though he had won the court case and controlled Long Beach, he didn't have Indy and he understood that. Thank God that happened, and there was some light at the end of the tunnel then. And the light keeps getting brighter and brighter. With Roger, it's in the best possible hands. It's not with some huge investor on the other side of the planet who's coming in for business reasons instead of love. It's got to be both, and we have that right now.

Right now, the roster of IndyCar drivers is probably second to none. You look at the ages, and even the champions at the upper echelon still have time in their careers. Then you have a crop of youngsters coming in that are well prepared, thanks to the Road to Indy. Teams deep in the field are capable of winning races. But somehow the message isn't getting out there.

I love to listen to Michael. He's hanging it out there. He's got his tentacles in Formula E and Supercars, and he's looking at expanding his involvement. He looks at IndyCar to be the main business for him for the rest of his career, which could be twenty to thirty years. Because we have so much skin and blood in the game, I want to see it progressing. I want to see it prosper and see all the things that should be able to happen. Times are challenging for everyone. Look at the correction that's going on in NASCAR. The days of putting one hundred thousand people in Bristol are in the past. You don't want to hear that, but it's reality.

Could the pendulum lean in our direction? Who knows, but maybe we could share it equally? How do we come out of this pandemic, in sports and in general? My heart bleeds for Roger in how the timing really worked out. But at the same time, Roger is probably the only one who could navigate through these rough waters. I don't want to talk about a new normal. We have to be more ambitious than that. We have to get back what was normal and make it better.

The split tells such a deep story about how important it is to have everything together. It's like a race car—there's not just one thing that makes it perform. A whole lot of things make the package. When the series is strong, it's got viability because of Indy, and Indy is strong because the series is strong. They need one another. At Indy, if you don't have a strong series, you're not going to have a strong field. You're not going to invest that kind of money just for Indy. I hope Roger sees that. He's very focused on Indy itself, but the strength of the series is the strength of Indianapolis's race. Indianapolis cannot live alone, that's something we know for sure.

PERSPECTIVE: **DR. STEPHEN OLVEY**

Dr. Stephen Olvey and Dr. Terry Trammell are unsung Indy car heroes. Olvey grew up in Indianapolis and was attracted to the Indianapolis 500 from an early age. After graduating from Indiana University Medical School and establishing a local practice, he began assisting Dr. Thomas Hanna with medical services at the Indianapolis Motor Speedway. Olvey worked with CART as Medical Affairs Director from 1978 to 2003 and, together with Trammell, was instrumental in developing critical safety enhancements for cars and implementing numerous driver safety initiatives. Olvey specialized in critical care and served as the director of the Neuroscience Intensive Care Unit at the University of Miami's Jackson Memorial Hospital for twenty-five years.

We lived in Indianapolis, and my parents took me to the racetrack to a practice day when I was four years old. I remember it vividly—a red car went by, and it was louder than hell. It scared the heck out of me! So, at first, I didn't really like it. My parents thought they made a mistake and we left. But something stuck with me, because I listened to Sid Collins call the race on the radio every year with my dad. I was eleven the first time I attended the race, the year Bill Vukovich got killed. He was my favorite driver at the time. I actually followed it pretty close, so that was pretty upsetting to me. But I continued to be hooked on auto racing.

Right before I graduated from medical school, there was a notice on the bulletin board where you could sign up to work at the Speedway on race day. Of course, I ended up in the infield in a tent taking care of drunks and people with sunburn. I didn't even see a race car. But the next year, I got in another tent that was pretty close to the track, and I got to see some of it.

I got to meet Dr. Thomas Hanna, the IMS medical director, when he and my dad were in the same bowling league. At that time, I was in medical practice and doing pretty well. He said he needed help at the Speedway; he was doing it with one other guy who was an optometrist. This was a time when something like one in seven drivers got killed every year across Indy car, NASCAR, and Formula 1. As far as I am concerned, Dr. Hanna invented motorsports medicine, but he was just doing what he could with the drivers.

I got to know Dr. Hanna pretty well, and at the same time, I got more and more into critical care, taking care of really sick patients. He said, "We really need somebody out there on the racetrack." At the time, the hearse from Conkle Funeral Home doubled as the ambulance, and the guy who did the embalming was the driver.

Then Wally Dallenbach and I were on the same program at a Lion's Club or Elks Club in May, talking about our involvement at the Speedway. He told me the drivers were upset that at other tracks, when something happened, there was nobody who knew what to do and they had to pretty much take care of themselves. Long before he was chief steward for CART, Wally didn't take any BS from anybody, even when he was an active driver. When something happened, he wanted to know what the causes were, what the reasons were, what could have been done better. He asked me the question: Do you know anybody that would be willing to go to all the races? I said, "Yeah, I would." So he went to Dick King, who was the president of USAC at the time, and put the thing together in two or three days. I did it for expenses only and didn't get paid anything. Starting in 1975, I traded call with people at the hospital and went to all the races I could.

I remember I was sitting in my office when Pat Patrick called and asked me if I would go with CART. I said, "No, I need to be loyal to USAC because they got me started at the Speedway." Pat said, "We're sorry, we'd sure love to have you." Then an hour later—this is a true story—I get a call from A.J. Foyt. At that time, Foyt was going to go with CART. He said something endearing like, "Olvey, you dumb sonofabitch, CART is where it's gonna be. You can't stay in USAC, they're done. You gotta come with us!" He was my hero at the time, so I called Pat back and said, "Can I still join you guys?" It wasn't a week later that

Foyt quit CART. But we remained friends. In fact, I used to go to stock car races with him because the medical care was so bad at Daytona.

I met Terry Trammell in early 1981. At that time, he was a major race fan. He went out to the track as a photographer and took pictures at the Speedway. He was still in training and wasn't actively involved with racing, but he was involved with the hospital as a new orthopedic surgeon. I thought he was doing really fabulous work, and we got to be friends, just as two doctors at Methodist Hospital in Indianapolis.

When Danny Ongais crashed in the 1981 Indianapolis 500, Terry was on call and ended up taking care of him. He did a fabulous job, and we became closer friends. Then Rick Mears had his accident at Sanair in 1984. We got Terry involved in that and kept them from amputating Rick's feet. That's when we made a push to get Terry to go to all the races, because we had so many orthopedic injuries.

Terry and I got to being scientific about it, looking for cause and effect with the injuries. We started working with the car designers and team managers trying to get changes made to the cars to prevent injuries. That's still going on today. All these years later, we're as involved in that now as we were back then. Terry and I talk to each other two or three times a week. We still have a real close relationship, actually.

What we were doing coincided with what Dr. Sid Watkins did in Formula 1. Jackie Stewart got Sid into it, playing the role of Wally Dallenbach in F1. Through the International Council of Motorsport Sciences, which is an organization I started with Terry and Hugh Scully, we started doing things in concert with Formula 1 and that collaboration continues to this day. I'm on the FIA Medical Commission, and we do all the rules and regulations for medical care in motorsports around the world. We all work in the same direction now.

In CART, we were the first ones to make the HANS Device mandatory. Formula 1 did a year later, and NASCAR didn't until after Dale Earnhardt was killed. The SAFER Barrier was a combined thing between NASCAR and Indy, and that's been fantastic. There's no way to know how many lives it's saved. Those are the two biggest safety advances we have seen, in my experience.

I'm often asked how we separate personal friendships with the drivers when we have to tend to them professionally. Terry and I answer it the same way. When you do what we do at the hospital, day in and day out, you learn to turn everything off except what you are doing. You don't think about the guy's wife you just met, or the kids in the waiting room. You have a job to do, and you do it. You don't have those feelings until it's all over. Then you get them on the way home, when you're off call and you've had a particularly bad case. That's happened to both of us on the racetrack. We just did what we had to do. We couldn't get upset until later, when our part was done. That's when it hits you.

I have opinions about why Indy car racing stayed apart for so long, but I don't want to express them. I know people on both sides. I will say it was really sad. Horrible for the sport—just a disaster. In 1995, CART was a threat to Formula 1 worldwide. Bernie Ecclestone knew it, and he was nervous. We outdrew NASCAR at every racetrack that was common to both series. We had packed houses, standing room only crowds. But after 1996, pretty soon NASCAR was filling every place and we couldn't get anybody. It was tragic. It set the whole sport of Indy car racing back a number of years, and I think they are only now getting on a real upswing. I think the racing is the best in the world, much better than Formula 1 or NASCAR. It's really on an upward trend, and I think Roger Penske buying the Speedway is good.

Last year, we had one concussion all year in the IndyCar Series. That's unbelievable when you look at the speeds and how bad the crashes are. People can't believe that other sports have far more concussions than we do. The big safety issue now is the fencing. There's still no good answer to that. There are a whole lot of people working on the best way to deal with that. It's tough. If you have to change the fencing at all the racetracks around the world, that's going to be costly. And you can have one change that helps one area but adversely affects something else. You can't risk the spectators. You've got so many variables when a car leaves the racetrack, and you don't want to throw them back into oncoming traffic, so it's a difficult situation.

PERSPECTIVE: ARIE LUYENDYK

Dutchman Arie Luyendyk was part of Indy car racing's "Second Foreign Invasion" in the 1980s. He developed into an Indianapolis specialist, winning the 500 in '90 with a record average speed that would endure for more than twenty years. Luyendyk started from pole position three times at Indianapolis, and he still holds the one- and four-lap qualifying records he established in '96. Luyendyk added a second Indy triumph in '97, making him the only driver to win the race in CART- and IRL-formula Indy cars. He currently serves as a race steward for the IndyCar Series.

I was aware of the Indianapolis 500 and Indy car racing already at a very young age. I followed Formula 1 with Graham Hill and Jim Clark and those guys by reading articles, and they obviously ventured out into Indy. I was living in South Africa when Jim Clark won the 1965 Indy 500, and right after that, we moved back to the Netherlands. There was a lot more to read than there was in South Africa, which was a bit isolated from the world in a way.

I started racing, and I won the 1977 European Super Vee Championship. Lola had offered to give me their new Super Vee for 1978, and when I was at Lola in England to pick up the car in early 1978, I saw Al Unser's Indy car sitting there. I thought, "There's no way I could ever drive anything like this!" To me, it looked so big, so massive. Everything was so impressive compared to the little bitty Super Vee. I was very intimidated just by looking at an Indy car itself, which raised my level of respect for what those guys were doing. It's funny that later in life you end up doing all that stuff in Indy.

I competed in Formula 3 against guys like Alain Prost and Michele Alboreto in 1979, and I was quick. I could run with them and beat them every now and then, but I had a horrible season. It was make or break, but the car broke down a lot and the success didn't come. Then you fade away—you just get lost in the void.

I did a Super Vee season with an old car in 1980. I finished second in the points, and they invited all the top-five guys to go do a race in the U.S. at Phoenix International Raceway at the end of '80. I was the only one of the five to accept the offer because the only thing they paid was to ship the car. Of course, it was my first-ever oval race. I did pretty good; I finished sixth. This guy comes up to me, Wilbur Bunce was his name. He says, "I like the way you drove for a guy who has never been on an oval. Do you want to drive for me next year?" That's how I got into Super Vees in the United States. I thought to myself, "Formula 1 is never going to happen. I missed that boat a long time ago. Let's set the goal to become an Indy car driver." That was also the first time I saw an Indy car race, and it was when Johnny Rutherford went upside down in Turn Four in the Pennzoil Chaparral. In fact, I had a camera and I have a bunch of pictures of that.

In my mind, Geoff Brabham was really the guy that showed you could go to the States and drive Super Vees and go to the next level, which was Indy cars and Can-Am. I almost retired from racing altogether in 1982, but for '83, I got a call from a guy called Bertil Sollenskog, who had started up a Super Vee team using an Anson chassis. We had trouble every race, and it was getting a bit frustrating. At Elkhart Lake, the car broke down again, and the team accused me of just giving up. I said, "I'm not giving up, but I am leaving the team." Provimi Veal sponsored that race at Elkhart Lake, and I had gone to the press day before the weekend with the company owners, Aat Groenevelt and his brother Erik. We were like buddies, almost. I never really wanted to ask Aat directly for sponsorship, because he had Tony Bettenhausen and Derek Daly driving for him, and I'm not the kind of guy who tries to steal somebody else's sponsors. But when I told Aat what had happened, he suggested we do a really good season of Super Vee, with the right material and the right budget. I set up the whole team. I hired a mechanic and basically, I was the team manager, the driver ,and everything else. We won the championship in 1984, and the same year I drove my first Indy car race. I went from zero to a pretty good position in a year. Aat Groenevelt was the one who saved my ass or saved my career, and the rest is kind of history.

I started doing more CART races in 1985, and it was impressive to join the Indy car ranks. All of a sudden, I was standing there on the grid and racing against guys I read about when I was a ten-year-old kid. Foyt, Johncock, Sneva, Unser, Mears—the list goes on. The core drivers were an old guard who had stuck around, and they're the ones who made Indy car famous. To be able to come in there as a rookie and race against all those names was pretty damn cool. I always respected them, but of course I tried to out run them.

With USAC, when you would go to Indy as a CART team back in the day, it was almost like an enemy had showed up. There was no harmony at all; there was like a rift between our group and USAC. They were like, "We'll show those boys how it's done." They would give out these penalties that were sometimes just ridiculous. You could see the seeds for the 1996 split were planted a long time ago.

When I drove for Ron Hemelgarn, and even more so with Dick Simon, I started to "get" the oval setup. I started to understand what I needed from the car. I knew after running with Dick for two years that if I had a good car, I could win. Straight out of the box in 1990 with Shierson Racing, the car was really good. I had a lot of confidence throughout the month of May, which eventually led to winning the race. I hadn't won an Indy car race before that, but I should have. So it wasn't uncharted territory.

I really liked IMS. It just suited me. You have to like it to run fast there. You have to have a certain feel for the car. When you ran low downforce in qualifying, you had to let the car float through the corners, and I enjoyed that. There's a story to be told for every 500, and I can remember all of them. If I was the luckiest sonofabitch ever, I probably would have won five 500s. But a lot of people can say that. Just ask Mario Andretti.

I ran my last full season in CART in 1994 with Regency Racing. It was a small team, and unfortunately, they couldn't continue in '95. I was talking to Cal Wells about his Toyota program for 1996, and that was coming along a little bit. But I thought to myself, 'Do I really want to be the test driver for a new engine coming into the series?' Jonathan Byrd talked to me about running Indy, and then Fred Treadway called. I thought if we could put together a good deal for the IRL, that would be good for me. If I could get the right crew chief and the right engineer in Tim Wardrop, that would be a good opportunity, and I could still run my favorite race—Indy.

Believe me, I knew what the split was all about. I knew how it would fragment everything. I was in the last years of my career anyway, so I went that route. Being honest, my days were over in Champ Car. That's just the way it was. I was in my forties, and I was on the way out. Then the IRL came along, and I knew I was still good at Indy. I was selfish in my choice to go to the IRL. It extended my career by another three or four years, and it worked out good for me.

I think it's commendable that Tony George wanted to give the sprint car guys a chance to go into Indy car, because that's where they originally came from. But you saw that didn't work in CART. In the IRL it didn't work either. It's honorable to think that's what Tony wanted, but basically, he was just doing the opposite of what CART was doing. I still had a lot of respect for those guys. Some of them were pretty ballsy. They weren't the most refined drivers, but they certainly weren't lacking bravery. Tony Stewart was amazing, and you could see that he was going to be a star, which he was, right away, coming out of winning the USAC Triple Crown.

The IRL cars were a lot harder to drive than a CART car, I can tell you that. They were a lot slower, but they were pretty unpredictable cars. With the weight you had in the back, the back end never felt good. A lot of times, I was pretty close to being scared of getting in the damn thing. A lot of people got hurt in those cars, and it was kind of nerve-wracking for me at my age. I thought, "Do I really need this? No." But I had this intense desire to win Indy again. So I did it. Did I do it with a big smile on my face? I did not.

A lot of the tracks the IRL ran on were pretty dangerous, and the pack racing was pretty dangerous. But boy, they had a lot of good races. You never knew who was going to win at the end, so from that perspective, it was really good. I think that might have been kind of what kept it going.

I was definitely in the middle of a lot of the controversy. I hated the fact that there was some doubt over the fact that I won the 1997 Indy 500 because Scott Goodyear was surprised by the green. But if you look at the in-car video from my car, I was in the wrong gear. I had gone up a gear just to cruise around to the yellow. I saw the green coming out, and I'm scrambling for second gear. The first thing that flashed into my mind was, "I'm going to get passed left and right by everybody," because I was surprised like hell by it. But so was everyone else. That would have been really annoying, because it would have cost me my second 500.

At one point, I held all the records for the turbocharged car and the normally aspirated car. I felt really good about that, and I was proud of that. Going from 1978, when I thought I would be too frightened to drive one of these things, to that, was pretty cool.

I never got political. I was always respectful to both sides. I actually drove the 1997 CART finale at Fontana for Chip Ganassi when Alex Zanardi had a concussion. Arnd Meier spun in front of me, and that nearly ended everything. That was a big crash.

My relationship with Tony George has always been good. Tony often seemed protective, and he never really opened up. He's an introvert-type person. The real reasons he created the Indy Racing League have never been clear to me. The rumor was he thought CART was going to boycott the Indy 500. There's always a lot of rumors circulating in the paddock that are just rumors. It's kind of a small world with a lot of talk.

I don't really have an answer as to why it took so long to come back together. It has to do probably with money and other situations I'm not aware of. I think both sides must have been pretty headstrong. At one point, CART went public, and that made a lot of people quite wealthy. But to me, it was a nail in the coffin because I think if you lower yourself to that standard—which is basically the bottom line—then anything driven by the bottom line is never going to be any good. Sports shouldn't be run by shareholders.

We put together a deal for my son, Arie Jr., to run Indy in 2006. But we had a Honda lease program where we could run only eight hundred miles, including the race. It would have been better not to do it, but we went more with our passion than our brains. From a budget and a business side it didn't make sense, but we did it because we love racing.

When it came together in 2008, it's like the world didn't realize it. They were still thinking about the split. There was a big downturn in the economy, and a lot of factors played a role in the sport not growing as fast as we thought or hoped it might. I think the Penske acquisition is one of the best things to happen to Indy car racing in many years. It's on an upward swing, but it's still a battle to win fans over because of the multiple interests people have.

I still love racing. I still get excited about going to the track in the morning, but it's in a different position. I still really enjoy being around it. I never expected working as a race steward to be so rewarding.

I hope the sport keeps growing like this. We have a bunch of new kids coming in that will be super quick. IndyCar couldn't ask for a better representative than Josef Newgarden. He's young, he's photogenic, and he's super quick. There are a lot of great personalities in the sport and a lot of exciting new talent.

PERSPECTIVE: ANDREW CRAIG

Andrew Craig served as chief executive officer of Championship Auto Racing Teams from March 1994 to June 2000. The Switzerland-based Englishman worked in senior management for International Sports and Leisure (ISL) Marketing AG, developing global initiatives for the FIFA World Cup and the International Olympic Committee before taking the reins at CART. Craig was thrust into a difficult role: his arrival coincided with Tony George's announcement of the formation of the Indy Racing League. Craig had the misfortune of leading CART in those difficult circumstances, effectively in a no-win situation. He tallied many major accomplishments for CART, but his inability to achieve a resolution to the company's conflict with the Indianapolis Motor Speedway made his position vulnerable when CART declined in the sports marketplace. CART's downfall accelerated after Craig's ouster, and the company was bankrupt barely three years later.

I've been involved in motorsport for most of my adult life. I used to race at a very modest level when I was living in the United Kingdom and Switzerland. So I was close to the sport and knew it very well. When I worked for ISL, one of our clients was Kodak, and they invited me as a corporate guest on a couple of occasions to the Indianapolis Motor Speedway. The sheer size of the venue and the speed of the cars certainly left a very strong impression. Then CART started to have a presence on European television, and I was able to follow it there.

I read in *Autosport* that Bill Stokkan was leaving CART at the same time that I was thinking about moving on from ISL. I don't know how I got the phone numbers, but I started contacting a few of the team owners. I definitely got the impression the train had left the station, but I got a list of every team owner and I wrote letters to the whole lot. Then I got a call from Carl Hogan, out of the blue, who invited me to come meet with a selection committee, which consisted of Hogan, Dale Coyne, and Carl Haas. Tony George was meant to be on it, but he never turned up. I interviewed with them in Chicago and was incredibly unimpressed. They didn't seem to have any direction, and just seemed weird. To my surprise, within a couple hours, they got hold of me and asked me to come back. I decided I'd give them a second look and it took off from there.

Stokkan did some good things to the internal structure of the company and helped professionalize the teams, for example. He unified the purses. Before he did this, the teams could cherry pick which races they wanted to take part in. He stopped all that. He did a number of things that were very important in terms of structurally improving the organization. He did some heavy lifting, quite frankly, and he doesn't get much recognition for any of that.

My due diligence was poor in one area: I had little grasp of the extent of the troubles between the Speedway and CART. I had no concept the Speedway had a desire to break away. I knew there was an issue, but given the nature of my background, I saw that issue as primarily commercial. Of course, part of it *was* commercial. But I didn't really understand the deep visceral, emotional resentment that existed on Tony's side following the rejection of the derisory offer that he made to the teams at the end of 1991. They basically told him to take a hike and that, I'm told, is what caused him to say, "That's it! I'm forming my own series." The resentment to the very existence of Championship Auto Racing Teams existed in part of the fan base as well. There were "Speedway" fans who were convinced we were sent by the devil. I may have unwittingly been the straw that broke the camel's back. When CART rejected Tony's candidate, Cary Agajanian, and brought in this foreign guy, it might have been the final catalyst.

I had my first meeting with Tony, and I think he probably thought I was some idiot from Europe who would last six months and fade away. But it was a very civil meeting, and I was able to hear his position. There were certain resentments, and he felt the sport was going in the wrong direction. He thought it should be an all-oval series, and he didn't like all these road courses coming in. He had this extraordinary notion that rich foreign drivers were stealing seats from American drivers. The reality is that highly committed and dedicated foreign drivers were putting together the money so they could race. Frankly, some of their American contemporaries were sitting at home on their hands, waiting for someone to call up, saying "Come race!" That's the harsh reality.

Another of Tony's beliefs was that the racetracks were really unhappy with CART. I think he may have been egged on a bit by Chris Pook, who was a bit of an agent provocateur. Pook wanted to be the big man among the promoter group. There were a couple—Phoenix, more than anyone else, and New Hampshire—but Tony thought all of the racetracks hated IndyCar and would rush to a new series organized by the Speedway. Of course, that wasn't the case. Quite the opposite. The tracks thought having the Speedway in charge would do them no good whatsoever, because everything would be built around the Indy 500. They would be these little satellite races and the whole idea of a championship would collapse. It became very apparent to us that instead of wanting to team up with Tony, the promoters wanted to team up with us.

At the Detroit Grand Prix in 1994, we announced long-term contracts with the majority of our racetracks. That just chopped off one of the key areas of Tony's vision. He thought he was going to sail in and take the whole thing over. Everyone would be happy. IndyCar would collapse and the teams would come running back to him. Life would be good, and the Speedway would be king. But it didn't happen that way. The teams were clearly hanging together. All the components that Tony thought were going to cause him to become the champion of the sport just weren't there. To be fair to Tony, I think he got a lot of bad advice from a lot of people with self-serving interests.

In the months that followed, he continued to talk about how he was going to launch his series. Toward the end of 1994, I called him up. He had been getting a lot of flak and criticism from fans and the media, telling him he shouldn't be doing this. And things hadn't gone entirely to plan, for him. I went and met with Tony, and he said to me, "Just find a solution here that gets everybody out of the situation looking okay, and we'll put this thing back together." I put together a proposal that I shared with a few team owners, and part of it was that I would stand down if that's what it took to get back together. That was entirely self-serving, but I put it in there to see what would happen.

I went away for the Christmas break pretty confident that we would actually get this thing fixed. In the interim, Jack Long came in and persuaded Tony: "Don't worry, I can make your series happen." Tony just changed his view, and the whole thing fell apart. That said, I floated my idea past Roger Penske, and he hated it. So I don't know whether I'd have gotten it done with the full board. That was a bit frustrating, and I guess I kind of gave up on the idea of reconciliation at that stage. It was time to just get on and keep going.

For the next few months, pretty much nothing happened. Then came the bombshell announcement in July 1995 that restricted our ability to take part in the Indy 500. It was clear that Tony did this because he knew he didn't have enough cars for the IRL. It was obviously a troubling moment. It was the moment that made it absolutely clear that Tony wasn't abandoning his series. I guess we had probably thought the IRL would never happen. Obviously, Tony reached the same conclusion, which is why he made that rule.

By that time, the teams and the sponsors were getting a bit worried. We needed to give sponsors reassurance that we weren't going away. And we needed to give our teams somewhere to race on Indy 500 weekend. In addition, the issue with the pushrod engine and USAC really crystallized Penske's thinking and he was 100 percent on board with running our own race. That's why we launched the 1996 U.S. 500. We just had to have a race on Memorial Day weekend. The sponsors wanted it, and by controlling the environment, we were able to keep the teams on board and not drift off to whatever Tony had started.

We didn't start three cars abreast at the U.S. 500 as an act of hubris, or to copy the Indy 500—that's complete rubbish. We had started cars three abreast at Michigan before, because our promoter had asked us to do it. Gene Haskett said the fans would love it and would buy a lot of tickets. Of course, we never did it again. The accident was a fiasco, and we looked like idiots after the media talked about how all the wannabes were down at Indianapolis and we were the "Stars and Cars." We went over our TV window, the ratings were poor, and the whole thing, to use an English term, was just a damp squid. It didn't resonate at all.

We invited a number of corporate guests to the U.S. 500, one of whom was Nancy Altenburg. Nancy was head of sponsorships for Federal

Express, and I knew Nancy quite well because they had been a sponsor of the Olympic Games. She was really impressed with the number of people in the stands and that led to a conversation. We were expanding internationally at the time, and there was a transportation need, so there was some value in kind for FedEx. At the same time, PPG wanted to level off their involvement and welcomed the idea of sharing the title sponsorship with another partner. So that was a PPG-friendly move. They got all the bits they wanted without their fee going up, and we got the revenue from the FedEx deal, which was of course very welcome.

The international races were worthwhile because the sanctioning fees that we could command were vastly higher than the domestic races. The average international race was paying over $4 million, when the average domestic race was paying about $1.6 million. I pushed up the sanctioning fees quite a lot, and there were major disparities between tracks depending on who you knew. I tried to eliminate that and put everybody on a more even basis. The other thing, particularly with a growing international TV package, was I thought the teams could find more money internationally. I was probably too optimistic, thinking the teams had the skill to do that. Barry Green did well with Brahma, but most owners knew what they liked and liked what they knew. They saw themselves as domestic entries and never pursued the international opportunities.

FedEx joined at the same time the Speedway claimed we couldn't use the words "IndyCar." It morphed into an antitrust lawsuit that cost both parties a lot of money. Why the Speedway agreed to not use the term "IndyCar" until the end of 2002, I do not know. It was clear that they did not know what they signed. That was actually good for us, and I think it made it difficult for them to establish a brand outside of IRL. Our teams quickly realized that the IndyCar name just wasn't working for them anymore. They didn't race at the Indy 500. But to be honest, the Champ Car branding didn't resonate. So, there was a while where we had Champ Cars, they had IRL cars, and the IndyCar brand just kind of vanished until its revival later on.

The public offering was Pat Patrick's idea. It made a lot of sense, actually. We had been talking for a long time about how guys had spent money and built up their teams, but in the end, were left with no real value. If they stopped racing, their franchise returned to us, at IndyCar, and that was that. A franchise was very attractive. When you compare the sum of money you gave to what you got, it was a very good deal. But there was no equity if they left racing. We tried to reform the franchise system so that teams would have the right to sell franchises directly, but none of it made much sense. Pat's idea to go public did make sense, though I thought the teams would never agree to it. Some were really keen, others opposed, others didn't really understand it.

It actually did really well, and from a personal point of view, I never thought I would ring the bell to open the New York Stock Exchange! I actually enjoyed doing the road show; having momentum on the road show is really what matters, and you get a sense of whether it's going well. We knew we had the momentum. Very few sports entities had ever gone public. We would say, "We are an old-line, industrial manufacturing company. We manufacture and sell motor races." That got their attention. But it was accurate. IndyCar was a manufacturer of races, and the manufacturing process was to bring the content together, with the teams and the rules and everything, and then sell it to the promoter, who was essentially the retailer. When you put it in those business terms, it made absolute sense. The stock did very well, it was a big success, and the teams made a lot of money. They were locked into holding the stock for a certain period, but it was inevitable that some of them would choose to sell.

At the end of 1998, I called Tony and we agreed to have a meeting. He picked me up at the airport, and I went into the building through the back door. It was very clear that Tony was interested in trying to find a resolution. I think Tony was under pressure from his family by this time because of the amount of money he had spent on the IRL. It was not really going anywhere—ticket sales at the Speedway were going down, the TV ratings were declining. I think the notion that someone coming in with some money to spend was attractive to Tony. We put together a working group, which was me, Jim Hardymon, and Bobby Rahal. We met with Tony, and we put forward a proposal for something like the Daimler-Chrysler "merger of equals." The discussions went pretty well, though there were some sticking points. Nothing that couldn't be solved. I remember leaving at least one of those meetings with Bobby and Jim thinking we could get this thing done.

There was a bit of a break for the holiday, and when we went back for another meeting in the new year, who should be in the room but John Cooper. He came out of nowhere, and I thought, "This is not good." I never quite understood where he fit with anything, frankly. He basically became a negative force in the room and things started to unravel from that point. We kept on discussing things, but Tony's clear and decisive attitude had shifted and now he was more ambivalent. I was also told that the IRL teams were not receptive. Tony ran away. He didn't even call me. At the Houston weekend, I read "All talks with CART are off." It just collapsed. It was done, and that was the end of it. There was nothing I felt couldn't be resolved, but that was that. It was bad news.

I know there are some people who claim we came close to a reconciliation with the Speedway. Most of that is wishful thinking. Pat Patrick made a private initiative that went absolutely nowhere, and Penske did as well. He got Herb Fishel from General Motors involved in that. Herb Fishel will tell you, "We almost got that done," but they didn't. It didn't go anywhere at all.

Having to run a series without the Indianapolis 500 was not something that I wanted—it was forced upon me. Having had it forced upon me, what I did was keep the series alive. Quite frankly, I think if I hadn't been there, they would have just scattered. One of the major contributions I made to the company I was responsible for running was just doing a remarkable job to get those teams to stay together. Tony's view was that he would put us out of business, and he did not do that. The person who stopped us from going out of business was me.

After Greg Moore was killed at the end of 1999, I said to my wife, "I really don't want to do this anymore." But I had another year on my contract. I was tired of the whole thing by then. It was the most grueling job. It was a challenging six years. In terms of my overall career in sports, which dates to 1983, it's a relatively small part. It's extraordinary to think about that. By the end, I was pretty happy to get out of there. I think I held that position longer than anyone else. I was the only CEO who made a profit. The company I took over had no money, and the company I left had plenty of money.

Coming together was absolutely the right thing to do. I wish Roger had bought the Speedway in 1994! But his acquiring the series is great.

He'll only make it better. It will be nothing but good for the series and it's the best thing that could have happened to the Speedway. I think the Hulman-George family had taken it as far as they could, and I expect Roger will do a terrific job. His enthusiasm and commitment to this project is there for all to see. I think he will do wonderful things and put zest and life back into the property and the event.

PERSPECTIVE: CHIP GANASSI

Chip Ganassi was a promising Indy car driver until a nasty accident at Michigan Speedway in 1984 essentially ended his career. He bought into Pat Patrick's CART team in '89 and shared in winning the Indianapolis 500 with driver Emerson Fittipaldi. It took the rebranded Target Chip Ganassi Racing a few years to again find Victory Lane, but drivers Jimmy Vasser, Alex Zanardi, and Juan Montoya won four consecutive CART championships from 1996-99. Ganassi supported Reynard's entry into the Indy car chassis market, and he was the first CART team owner to return to the Indianapolis 500, winning the 2000 race with Montoya. Since then, Ganassi Racing has won nine more Indy car championships with drivers Scott Dixon and Dario Franchitti, establishing Ganassi as Roger Penske's only true on-track rival.

The first time I went to the Indianapolis Motor Speedway was 1971, when the pace car crashed into the photo stand. Al Unser won. The next time was 1981, which was an interesting time for me because I had the dream of going there as a driver in 1982. I knew some guys who were there at the time, and I went in '81 to watch, just to get a feel for what was going on. Indianapolis became my harbinger of spring. They say that about baseball, but my harbinger of spring was Indianapolis. And to this day it still is. Obviously, you go to Long Beach and some of the early races, but there's still always this anticipation about the month of May and going to Indianapolis.

Racing at Indy was a natural step in my career, and it came at a time when I was going to have to start thinking about what I was going to do for a living. I thought race driver was as good as anything at that time. I was graduating from college, so I was getting ready to do something, to go out in the world.

The crash at Michigan sort of moved up the timetable for team ownership a bit. I still wanted to drive; I wanted to leave the sport on my own terms. I was lucky to be able to do that in the end. I left on my own schedule.

Those are interesting times, when you're a young kid in your late twenties and you want to start in business. People look at you a little sideways. The sport in those days was dominated by Roger Penske and Pat Patrick and Bobby Hillin and Carl Haas. They were at least one generation in front of me, and I was this young kid that came along. It raised a lot of eyebrows, I guess.

At the time, you had Carl selling Lolas and Roger would sell you a Penske car. It dawned on me the only way to beat these guys was to go outside the box. It just so happened there was a young company that built small formula cars that was a competitor of Lola. That was Reynard. I had to do things differently to become a success, and that's what we did. We changed some of the sport. That helped shift the Lola-Penske stronghold and helped me get my own little edge. Actually, it got a big edge for a lot of people. But when you start beating those guys on the track, suddenly they don't ask you to ride on their jets anymore!

Arguably, Indy car racing rivaled Formula 1, and it probably made Formula 1 better because of what IndyCar was doing. By the late '90s, you had three or four different chassis manufacturers, three engines, and two kinds of tires all mixed up, vying for the championship. You'd be hard pressed to say that time was not the sweet spot of the sport. It was a big show, people recognized it as a big show, and they paid for it as a big show. It was a great thing to be a part of.

Tony George was in a difficult position. He had family members that wanted him to exert his power, and he wanted to make his mark. He had a family business to run, and I think he probably suffered most from just getting some bad advice on what the lay of the land looked like and what it really was. I don't fault him for that. Anybody in business, you show me a guy that's an entrepreneur and I'll show you a guy that's made some mistakes in his career. So I'm not going to fault Tony for making mistakes. He's not the first guy to do that, and he won't be the last. He did the best he could do. I think in his heart of hearts, he was doing what he thought was looking out for the sport and looking out for his family.

A lot of guys in business have the right idea at the wrong time. It's easy to do.

When the split happened, people didn't understand the difference between the two series. Sponsors didn't understand the difference between IRL and IndyCar, which CART was called at the time. People just didn't get it. Out in the real world dealing with sponsors, you had to speak their language, not the language we as racers want to hear all the time. Indy cars were Indy cars to them. I was one of the few guys out there then who was getting real sponsorship from real companies. They want real results. They don't care about political infighting in sports. We got tired of not being at the Indy 500, and I said, "Dammit, I'm going!" I'm proud that were able to win that race as a team and for our sponsors, and I think the sport needed it. I was glad to do that. We were welcomed with open arms at Indianapolis, and it was all good.

Coming together was something that had to be done. Everybody knew that if we weren't careful we would be two factions who were like two bald men arguing over a comb. I don't care what sport it is, you see the kind of damage these rifts cause. It took baseball ten years before they recovered from the 1994 strike. No sport can withstand a split, a strike, a work stoppage—whatever you want to call it. Indy car racing was a Harvard Business Review case study of how to watch ice cream melt on your plate.

Roger's involvement gives us a great story to tell and credibility. There's nobody more in tune with the sport than Roger is, and I think he understands the word "stewardship." He's got his fingers on the pulse of the sport as much as anybody. I'm very optimistic and very hopeful that we see some great changes. The Hulmans deserve a lot of credit, but it was time for somebody else to come in and take the reins.

PERSPECTIVE: **DARIO FRANCHITTI**

Mentored by Jackie Stewart, Dario Franchitti dreamed of competing in Formula 1. But his formula car career detoured into the German DTM Championship before Mercedes-Benz transferred him to the USA to race in CART. Franchitti and Team Green developed into Chip Ganassi Racing's toughest competitors in the late 1990s, but the Scotsman faced a career crossroad when Andretti Green Racing moved into the IRL in 2003. In '07, Franchitti won the Indianapolis 500 and the IRL championship, only to depart for NASCAR at the end of the year with Ganassi. For a variety of reasons, Dario's time in stock cars was brief, and he returned to Indy cars in '09 with Chip Ganassi Racing to enjoy the most successful phase of his career. He won three consecutive IRL IndyCar Series championships from 2009-11 and added a pair of Indy 500 wins in '10 and '12. Since retiring from driving at the end of '13, he has worked as an engineering consultant for the Ganassi Indy car team in a role similar to Rick Mears at Penske.

From a really early age, I remember looking at pictures of the Indy 500 in *Autosport*. I probably watched it on TV for the first time in the mid-1980s, around the Danny Sullivan "Spin and Win" time. Then my brother, Marino, got an Indy 500 computer game. It didn't even have a joystick; you used the arrow keys on the keyboard for controls. You could change the setup of the car, and I always wanted to take the Buick engine because it had the most horsepower!

My journey to America started when I did a couple seasons of DTM (German Touring Car championship) with Mercedes-Benz. That had gone well. My DTM teammate Jan Magnussen had filled in for the Hogan-Penske team in CART when Emerson Fittipaldi got hurt in the summer of 1996. He came back absolutely raving about the experience. "You've got to do this if you get the chance, it is so much fun."

Roger Penske came over to Stars & Cars, the Mercedes motorsport year-end banquet. We discussed me going over to the U.S. and being Team Penske's test driver and doing some races. I just sat there listening, wide-eyed. Then I had another conversation at Stars & Cars with Paul Morgan from Ilmor. He asked what I was going to do after DTM, and I said, "Well, there's this sports car thing. But what I really want is to go to America." He said, "Whoa! I might be able to help a bit there. Leave it with me." Sure enough, he phones me in January '97 and says, "I spoke to Carl Hogan, I've done the deal. You've got to go test for him. If Carl likes you, you're in.'"

I went to Homestead, and the test went well. The CART car was quite a step up from a DTM car in terms of speed, and certainly in terms of physical effort. Whenever I took my hand off the wheel to shift, the car would veer across the road because I couldn't hold it in a straight line with one hand. It was a baptism of fire, but luckily Carl liked what he saw.

As a young driver, the CART series was a phenomenal thing to be involved with. It was a good formula. Compared to Penske and Ganassi, we were a tiny team. But we had good engines and good engineers, and we were able to be competitive. It was a cool time. With the variety of equipment, small teams could find a way to compete.

The cars were fabulous things to drive, though slightly insane at times. If you look back through the history of racing, there are certain cars that were just monsters—the pre-war "Silver Arrows," the Porsche 917-30. I think you can put those late '90s CART Indy cars in that group. They were nuts! And the people I got to race against who became friends . . . it was just a magical time to be involved. The manufacturer support was massive, there were different cars, different tires, great sponsors.

I joined Team Green and got close to winning the CART championship in 1999, which I never really thought about until I retired. Whenever I think of '99, I think about Greg Moore's accident and not the championship. Then I had a horrendous accident at Homestead in Spring Training in 2000. It took me until the end of 2002 to really get over the head injury.

I wasn't aware of the CART/IRL politics until I walked into the paddock. The DTM was a big series, with big budgets and all that. But when I came in, I was impressed by the level of the Penske and Ganassi teams, and kind of awed by the big crowds at the first few races—Long Beach, Surfers Paradise. My guys said, "Well, if you think this is cool, you should have seen it before the split." I became more aware of it when I got involved with people who were living it, and then I became one of those people as the years went on.

When I arrived in CART in '97, the downward spiral hadn't started yet. We were still living off what happened before. It was only as time went on that you could see the decline in the crowds and the sponsor dollars and the manufacturer interest and the "man on the street" interest. You could see all of that start to slip a little bit. It took a while to see what was happening, and there are a lot of people whose livelihoods were affected by it. To take that to its conclusion, look at some of the drivers who never got to drive in the Indianapolis 500. Greg and Alex Zanardi were the most obvious examples. That was a real shame.

Obviously, the thing that was missing was racing at Indianapolis, to have the last piece of pie. We didn't have that, and I didn't realize it until I went to Indianapolis in 2002 what it would have meant to the series. To have the CART series, as it was, with the Indianapolis 500 would have been phenomenal.

As for that race, it's simple: Paul Tracy won it. I'd got a flat tire, so I was a lap down. Hélio Castroneves came up behind me, and I came on the radio and said, "Do you need me to make his life difficult?" I did—not blocking him, but not making it easy to let him past. Then the team came on the radio and said, "Let him go, he's trying to save fuel." So he went, and then Paul went past. Going into Turn Three, Paul went into the lead, and the yellow light comes on. I thought, "Wow! Paul's just won the Indy 500. How cool is that?" And then they took it away from him. I don't think the initial decision was because of political reasons, but everything that happened afterwards was pure politics of the split. That sucks for PT, and it sucks for Barry Green too.

At the end of the year, I massively struggled with the decision. At Indianapolis in 2002, I didn't enjoy driving the IRL car. I didn't think the car was that exciting to drive. I knew Michael Andretti was taking over Team Green and moving the team to the IRL, and there was a contract there ready to be signed. And it was a good contract . . . financially, it was very nice. But I liked what I was doing. I could see the decline in CART, but I didn't like the idea of an all-oval series—though they assured me that road and street courses were happening.

At the same time, I was talking to Carl Haas and Paul Newman about driving for them in CART. It was a massively confusing time. I ended up going with what I knew, and that was sticking with the team that Barry built and Michael bought, trusting Honda and hoping that road and street courses were going to come through in the IRL. My manager Julian Jakobi never told me what to do. He would always give me the options and let me make my own decision. I remember when I made the decision, he said, "That's the pragmatic choice." And that's exactly what it was.

That early period was tough, but I eventually came to enjoy it. There was a bit of fan feedback, shall we say, in the early days. And some of it was pretty cruel. I just wanted to go race cars.

I had to learn some new skills. I was learning the IRL style of racing, and my engineer Allen McDonald and I were learning about the cars. The next generation of cars were better, but straight away, I broke my back in a motorcycle accident and missed most of the 2003 season. What I saw, I didn't really like. The 1.5-mile pack races were crazy. A lot of people say they didn't require any skill, and I completely disagree. There was a skill to being quick and to racing well. But it was crazy, and not something that I enjoyed.

I loved driving the car at Indianapolis and on the short ovals, and eventually on the street and road courses. Did it have the power and the mind-blowing performance of the CART cars of the late '90s? No. But especially on ovals, that meant you drove the car more on edge. You couldn't drive a CART car in yaw like that because they bit you; Greg was the only guy who could slide those things around!

I almost lost my drive at the end of 2006. I had a pretty tough season, and I had enough of being the good teammate or the wing man or whatever. So my attitude for '07 was "maximum attack." It was time to show what we could do. It was a bit of a reset. Had a couple big flips, one of which was my fault, but we got the job done—won the Indy 500 and the championship.

Then I went off to NASCAR, which was an odd decision. I'd been doing Indy car for ten years, and I finally had done what I set out to do. I was out of motivation and needed to do something else. As soon as I drove the car—never mind competed in a race—I knew I'd made a mistake. And of course, just then Champ Car and IRL finally came together, and they were going back to Toronto and Long Beach and all those great places. Timing is everything!

When the NASCAR thing didn't work, I thought I was going to go do sports cars. Then the whole thing happened at Detroit with Chip needing a driver and me needing a drive, and that was it. That turned out to be the most successful period of my career with Indy wins in 2010 and '12 and three more championships.

Al Unser Jr. famously said, "You just don't know what Indy means." And honestly, I had no idea what it meant. When I finally raced it in 2002— even with everything that happened, with the way Paul's win got taken away—that's when I started to fall in love with it. It's the only thing I've done in my life that's made me want more success. With most things, once you've done it, you throttle back a little bit. But at Indy, the more I won, the more I wanted to win. Every time I showed up, I wanted to win more. I don't know if it gets under everybody's skin like that, but it did for me.

I think almost everybody is happy the sport finally came back together. In the end, the principals on both sides had enough. It takes a straw to break the camel's back, and I think they finally both said, "What are we doing?" If you look at any type of conflict, generally there's a winner. Even if it's the person selling the weapons to people who use them to destroy themselves, somebody wins. But I cannot think of anyone who won the Indy car split—apart from NASCAR. Nobody who was involved on either side of that argument won. It was a real shame.

When people get so entrenched in their positions, it's difficult. I mean, I love Indy car racing. Here I am, six years since I retired, and I'm still involved. But to some people, it's their life and religion and everything. The split hit a lot of people hard. It hurt them, and some people still can't get over it. That's a shame, but we have to move on.

It's really nice to see IndyCar actually have some forward momentum, some positive stuff happening. As opposed to everything being doom and gloom, it's got good momentum. Good decisions are being made, and that's cool to see. You've got to have strong leaders. Jay Frye is a strong guy, and he's done a really good job.

Roger Penske is the perfect guy to own the IndyCar Series and the Speedway. I almost started my career in America racing for Roger, and most of it was spent fighting Roger and his team. He's a guy I respect massively, and he's become a friend. He is the perfect person to own IndyCar and the Speedway. He can make things happen that other people can't. He can open doors with sponsors, manufacturers . . . you name it. The sport's decline didn't happen immediately, so the uptick might take some time. It's not like turning a steamboat, it's like turning an oil tanker. It might take a little while, but with Roger at the helm, things will happen.

BIBLIOGRAPHY

"11 Bumped Cars Can Re-Qualify Today." *Indianapolis Star*, May 26, 1979.

"CART's Next Chief Hope for 'Peace.'" *AP*, March 16, 1994.

"CART's Reply: Definite 'Maybe.'" *Indianapolis Star*, February 23, 1980.

"The Clock Winds Down, the Job Search Begins." *Indianapolis Star*, July 10, 1994.

"Cooper Quits as Speedway President." *Indianapolis Star*, May 8, 1982.

"Flat Out into the Turn (Editorial)." *Indianapolis Star*, October 2, 1995.

"Hauer Named Indy Racing League Commissioner." *AP*, September 17, 1994.

"Indy Racing League Gets New Leader." *Indianapolis News*, January 5, 1995.

"IRL Destructive, Mario Claims." *AP*, June 1, 1995.

"IRL's 1996 Opener at Disney Sparks A.J." *Indianapolis News*, January 24, 1995.

"IRL Switches Engines for '97." *Indianapolis Star*, December 15, 1995.

"Key Meeting Friday on USAC's Troubles." *National Speed Sport News*, August 16, 1978.

"Make Cloutier Talk, Court Asked." *Indianapolis Star*, May 2, 1979.

"Modified Cosworth Approved by USAC." *Indianapolis Star*, August 1, 1981.

"Scoring System Will Favor Regular IRL Drivers, Teams." *AP*, August 29, 1995.

"Speedway-CART Merger Stalls." *Indianapolis News*, November 29, 1991.

"Tony George Quits as CART Director." *Indianapolis News*, January 7, 1994.

"USAC OK's Modified Cooper Peace Plan." *Indianapolis Star*, February 21, 1980.

Anderson, William E. "Foyt Cleared of Contempt, But Not by Much: Dugan." *Indianapolis Star*, May 26, 1979.

Andretti, Mario, and Bob Collins. *What's It Like Out There?: The Story of the World's Most Famous Racing Car Driver*. Illinois: NTC/Contemporary Publishing, 1970.

AP. "USAC-CART Peace Near after Talks?" *Indianapolis News*, April 3, 1980.

AutoRacing1.com.

Autosport magazine.

AutoWeek magazine.

Beer, Matt. "After the War: Exclusive Interview with Andrew Craig." Autosport, May 21, 2008. https://www.autosport.com/general/news/after-the-war-exclusive-interview-with-andrew-craig-5078949/5078949/.

Brabham, Jack. *The Jack Brabham Story*. London: Pavilion Books, 2004.

Branham, H.A. *Bill France Jr.: The Man Who Made NASCAR*. Chicago: Triumph Books, 2010.

Cadou, Jep. "Ban a Shock for CART." *National Speed Sport News*, April 25, 1979.

——. "USAC Loses Eight Officials in Air Crash." *National Speed Sport News*, April 12, 1978.

CART: Official Champ Car Yearbook. Autocourse.

Cavin, Curt. "50 Years Ago, Tony Hulman Made the Buy of a Lifetime." *Indianapolis Star*, November 13, 1995.

Cavin, Curt. "500, IRL Drop USAC as Sanctioning Body." *Indianapolis Star*, June 17, 1997.

——. "Binford Appointed Commissioner of New Racing Group." *Indianapolis Star*, May 11, 1995.

——. "Brickyard 400 Set for IMS in '94." *Indianapolis Star*, April 15, 1993.

——. "Engines Not the Only Noise at Elkhart Lake." *Indianapolis Star*, July 9, 1995.

——. "George Out as Speedway CEO." *Indianapolis Star*, July 1, 2009.

——. "IRL Provides Smashing Debut for Texas Fans." *Indianapolis Star*, June 8, 1997.

——. "Luyendyk Declared True Victor." *Indianapolis Star*, June 9, 1997.

——. "Speedway Board Asks George for Management Plan." *Indianapolis Star*, May 28, 2009.

——. "Stewart's Road Nearly Winds Into Winner's Circle." *Indianapolis Star*, January 28, 1996.

——. "Why Did He Leave IRL, Too?" *Indianapolis Star*, July 2, 2009.

Champ Car magazine.

Champ Car: Official Champ Car Yearbook. Autocourse.

Clymer, Floyd. *Indianapolis 500 Mile Race Yearbook*.

Collins, Bob. "Rising Costs Making Owners Restless." *Indianapolis Star*, May 28, 1978.

Craig, Andrew. "Another Side to the IndyCar Controversy (Letter to the Editor)." *Indianapolis Star*, October 29, 1995.

Crowe, Steve. "Biggest Names May Not Be There, But Tony George Will Not Back Down." *Knight Ridder*, January 27, 1996.

Davidson, Donald, and Rick Shaffer. *Autocourse Official History of the Indianapolis 500*. United Kingdom: Icon Publishing Ltd, 2013.

Economaki, Chris. *Let 'Em All Go!: The Story of Auto Racing by the Man Who Was There*. Indianapolis: Books by Dave Argabright, 2006.

Edsall, Larry, and Mike Teske. *Ford Racing Century*. Motorbooks, 2003.

Ferguson, Andrew. *Team Lotus: The Indianapolis Years*. Somersest: Haynes Publishing, 1996.

Formula magazine.

Fox, Jack. *The Illustrated History of the Indianapolis 500: 1911-1994*. Carl Hungness Publishing, 1995.

Freudenthal, Kurt. "Cooper Denies Firing Reports." *Indianapolis Star*, May 11, 1982.

——. "Cooper Reveals Changes in 500." *Indianapolis Star*, April 4, 1982.

——. "'New' USAC Selected to Sanction the '500.'" *Indianapolis Star*, August 30, 1980.

Fuson, Wayne. "Racing Organizations Better Get on Track." *Indianapolis News*, May 25, 1995.

Goodyear Annual Auto Racing Attendance Report.

GordonKirby.com.

Hallbery, Andy, and Jeff Olson. *Lionheart: Remembering Dan Wheldon*. Lionheart Books LLC, 2016.

Henry, Alan. *March: The Grand Prix and Indy Cars*. Oxford: Osprey, 1989.

Higgins, Tom, and Steve Waid. *Junior Johnson: Brave in Life*. Phoenix: David Bull Publishing, 1999.

Hungness, Carl. *Indianapolis 500 Yearbook*. Carl Hungness Publishing.

Indianapolis 500 and Indy Racing League IndyCar Series Official Yearbook. Autocourse.

Indianapolis 500 "Daily Trackside Report."

Indy Car Racing magazine.

IndyCar Official Yearbook. Autocourse.

IndyCar Series magazine.

Indy Review.

Ingram, Jonathan. *Crash!: From Senna to Earnhart, How the HANS Helped Save Racing*. RJP Books, 2019.

Jones, Parnelli, and Bones Bourcier. *As a Matter of Fact, I Am Parnelli Jones*. Massachusetts: Coastal 181, 2012.

Kirby, Gordon. *Bobby Rahal: The Graceful Champion.* Phoenix: David Bull Publishing, 1999.

——. *Chris Pook and The History of the Long Beach GP.* Boston: Racemaker Press, 2020.

——. *Jim McGee: Crew Chief of Champions.* Boston: Racemaker Press, 2014.

——. *Mario Andretti: A Driving Passion.* Phoenix: David Bull Publishing, 2001.

——. *Rick Mears—Thanks: The Story of Rick Mears and the Mears Gang.* United Kingdom: Icon Publishing Ltd, 2008.

——. *Wally Dallenbach: Steward of the Sport.* Boston: Racemaker Press, 2018.

Kirby, Gordon, and John Oreovicz. *A Winning Adventure: Honda's Decade in CART Racing.* Phoenix: David Bull Publishing, 2003.

Kleinfield, Sonny. *A Month at the Brickyard.* New York: Holt, Rinehart & Winston, 1977.

Koenig, Bill, and Curt Cavin. "IRL, CART Attempt Peace Negotiations." *Indianapolis Star,* May 28, 1999.

Koenig, Bill. "Anxious Businesses Brace for Repercussions of Racing Dispute." *Indianapolis Star,* November 12, 1995.

——. "CART/IRL Split Has Stalled Sport's Economic Growth." *Indianapolis Star,* September 22, 1996.

——. "Dueling Races Could Be the Pits for Firms That Profit from '500.'" *Indianapolis Star,* December 20, 1995.

——. "Fans Shouldn't Hold Breath Waiting for CART's Return to Indianapolis." *Indianapolis Star,* May 18, 1997.

——. "IRL Officials Say They've Turned the Corner." *Indianapolis Star,* May 28, 1997.

——. "It's Not Easy to Make a Super Prix." *Indianapolis Star,* September 8, 1999.

——. "Penske Interested in a Return to Indy." *Indianapolis Star,* April 27, 1997.

——. "Race's Ratings Drop." *Indianapolis Star,* May 29, 1996.

——. "Racing League Intends to Go Full Throttle." *Indianapolis Star,* November 10, 1995.

Lawrence, Mike. *The Reynard Story: From Formula Ford to Indy Champions.* Somerset: Haynes Publishing, 1997.

Lemasters, Ron. "New Indy Proposal Leaves CART Cold." *National Speed Sport News,* June 10, 1992.

Ludvigsen, Karl. *Prime Movers: Ilmor and Its Engines.* London: Transport Bookman Publications, 1995.

Miller, Robin. "'82 USAC Rules Eliminate Cosworth." *Indianapolis Star,* January 7, 1981.

——. "500 Miles of an Unfunny Folly." *Indianapolis Star,* September 7, 1978.

——. "Angry Foyt Turns in USAC Card." *Indianapolis Star,* February 5, 1980.

——. "CART Mired in Legal Lumbering." *Indianapolis Star,* May 5, 1979.

——. "CART Not Ready to Relinquish Sovereignty to George." *Indianapolis Star,* November 10, 1991.

——. "CART Says 'Let's Go'; USAC Shows 'E-Z' Board." *Indianapolis Star,* March 2, 1980.

——. "CART's CEO Wants to Be a Manager, Not Politician." *Indianapolis Star,* January 9, 1994.

——. "CART Teams to Get Indy Invites." *Indianapolis Star,* January 25, 1980.

——. "CART Wants George's Plan Revised." *Indianapolis Star,* November 7, 1991.

——. "Cooper Declares Independence." *Indianapolis Star,* June 25, 1980.

——. "Don't Believe the Hype: Speedway Is Ruining Beloved Race." *Indianapolis Star,* May 2, 1996.

——. "Dueling 500s This May 26 More Reality Than Threat." *Indianapolis Star,* October 15, 1995.

——. "Engine Formula Angers Some, Relieves Others." *Indianapolis Star,* August 14, 1994.

——. "Even Rain Can't Dampen Joy over USAC's Cosworth Ruling." *Indianapolis Star,* August 3, 1981.

Miller, Robin. "First Court Victory Goes to CART." *Indianapolis Star*, May 4, 1979.

——. "Foyt Quits CART; Rejoins USAC." *Indianapolis Star*, February 1, 1979.

——. "George Changes Plans for IRL." *Indianapolis Star*, March 11, 1995.

——. "George Has Take it or Leave it Plan For CART." *Indianapolis Star*, October 31, 1991.

——. "George's IRL Plan Will Damage Indy's Respectability." *Indianapolis Star*, July 5, 1995.

——. "George Unveils Name, Leaders for New Circuit." *Indianapolis Star*, July 9, 1994.

——. "George vs. CART Owners: Naivete vs. Greed, Stupidity." *Indianapolis Star*, December 8, 1991.

——. "George's Move Looks More Like a Retreat." *Indianapolis Star*, March 11, 1995.

——. "Goodyear Enters Indy-Car Battle." *Indianapolis Star*, January 24, 1980.

——. "Guthrie Powers Past Goliaths of IRL." *Indianapolis Star*, March 24, 1997.

——. "If Indy 500 Passed Its Test, It Sure Didn't Make Dean's List." *Indianapolis Star*, May 29, 1997.

——. "Indy-Car Bad Guys? Try the Speedway." *Indianapolis Star*, July 3, 1980.

——. "Indy-Car Racing Faced with Imminent Civil War." *Indianapolis Star*, May 27, 1995.

——. "IndyCar Threatens to Race Elsewhere on '500' Sunday" *Indianapolis Star*, September 20, 1995.

——. "IRL Entry List Boasts Roar of Harmless Lions with Laryngitis." *Indianapolis Star*, December 8, 1995.

——. "IRL Is No Joke for IndyCar Sponsors." *Indianapolis Star*, March 20, 1996.

——. "IRL Is Working to Lure Enough Cars for Season." *Indianapolis Star*, September 10, 1995.

——. "IRL Retools the Rules, Opens Door for CART." *Indianapolis Star*, May 17, 1997.

——. "IRL Says No Time Left to Strike Deal with CART." *Indianapolis Star*, October 20, 1995.

——. "IRL Searches for Engine Consistency." *Indianapolis Star*, May 4, 1997.

——. "Is John Cooper Hero or Villain?" *Indianapolis Star*, July 17, 1980.

——. "It's IndyCar, but 1996 Schedule Has No Indy." *Indianapolis Star*, June 11, 1995.

——. "Luyendyk Passes Teammate to Win 2nd 500 as Confusion Mars Last Lap." *Indianapolis Star*, May 28, 1997.

——. "May Madness Could Seriously Damage the City." *Indianapolis Star*, September 21, 1995.

——. "NASCAR Race Irks Indy Pilots." *Indianapolis Star*, June 28, 1992.

——. "NASCAR Wows IMS Crowd with 9-Lap Exhibition." *Indianapolis Star*, June 24, 1992.

——. "Oil Slick Points to Major Engine Problems." *Indianapolis Star*, March 26, 1997.

——. "Phoenix Track Eager to Give IndyCar Boot, Welcome IRL." *Indianapolis Star*, April 2, 1995.

——. "Phony Smiles Can't Soothe Family Feud." *Indianapolis Star*, May 14, 1995.

——. "Repentant Foyt Apologizes to Luyendyk." *Indianapolis Star*, June 11, 1997.

——. "Retired Greats Can't Believe It's Gone So Far." *Indianapolis Star*, December 20, 1995.

——. "Rule Change to Put New League in Driver's Seat for '96 500." *Indianapolis Star*, July 4, 1995.

——. "Speedway, Disney Join Forces to Build Track, Promote Race." *Indianapolis Star*, January 24, 1995.

——. "Speedway Could Be Busy Venue by '93." *Indianapolis Star*, December 29, 1991.

——. "Speedway Message to CART Regulars Is 'Suite Dreams.'" *Indianapolis Star*, July 14, 1996.

——. "Speedway Opens Door to Outside for 500 Sanction." *Indianapolis Star*, June 24, 1980.

——. "Speedway Power to Be Made Equal." *Indianapolis Star*, August 11, 1994.

——. "Speedway President Offers CART, USAC Peace Plan." *Indianapolis Star*, February 16, 1980.

——. "Speedway Purse: $1 Million Crumbs." *Indianapolis Star*, December 3, 1978.

Miller, Robin. "USAC-CART Talks Flag." *Indianapolis Star*, February 1, 1980.

——. "USAC Carves Governing Board." *Indianapolis Star*, August 15, 1980.

——. "USAC Nixes CRL; Reopens War?" *Indianapolis Star*, July 1, 1980.

——. "USAC's Life Threatened by CART." *Indianapolis Star*, November 19, 1978.

——. "With Brand-New Cars, IRL Tries to Get up to Speed." *Indianapolis Star*, January 25, 1997.

Mittman, Dick. "Didn't Take Long to 'Hoosier-ize' Hauer." *Indianapolis News*, September 27, 1994.

——. "Disney World First IRL Race." *Indianapolis News*, January 23, 1995.

——. "Foyt Calls Fight a 'Misfortune,' But Still Stands Behind Boat." *Indianapolis Star*, June 29, 1997.

——. "George Awaits CART Plan." *Indianapolis News*, November 7, 1991.

——. "George Ignites Indy Car Wars." *Indianapolis Star*, March 12, 1994.

——. "George Takes Bumps in Stride." *Indianapolis News*, March 25, 1995.

——. "Goodyear Still Waiting for Perfect Ending." *Indianapolis Star*, May 28, 1997.

——. "Haas To Shun New Racing League." *Indianapolis News*, June 5, 1995.

——. "IndyCar, IRL Feud Escalates." *Indianapolis News*, June 15, 1995.

——. "IndyCar Leader Says Two Series Bad for Racing." *Indianapolis News*, February 1, 1995.

——. "IRL Ends 'Lock-In' Qualifying Rule." *Indianapolis News*, May 16, 1997.

——. "New Race League Looks for Fans." *Indianapolis News*, September 16, 1994.

——. "No Power Shortage in Auto Racing." *Indianapolis News*, April 12, 1995.

——. "Owners, Sponsors to Choose between IRL, CART." *Indianapolis Star*, December 20, 1995.

——. "Porsche Threatening to Pull Out of 500." *Indianapolis News*, March 13, 1980.

——. "Rahal Sees Racing at Crossroads." *Indianapolis News*, July 8, 1995.

——. "Rutherford Accuses USAC of 'Hiding.'" *Indianapolis News*, March 29, 1980.

——. "Sharp Passes Test, Will Drive for Foyt in Colorado 200." *Indianapolis Star*, June 23, 1997.

——. "Speedway Willing to Listen." *Indianapolis News*, March 6, 1980.

——. "Time Has Come for True Truce." *Indianapolis News*, November 8, 1991.

——. "USAC, CART to Meet." *Indianapolis News*, March 18, 1980.

Moore, George. "CART Files Suit Vs. USAC, IMS." *Indianapolis Star*, April 27, 1979.

——. "Cooper's Plan for Speedway: Evolution, Not Revolution." *Indianapolis Star*, October 19, 1979.

——. "Court Is Next for CART, USAC." *Indianapolis Star*, April 26, 1979.

——. "It's USAC's Responsibility: Cloutier." *Indianapolis Star*, April 25, 1979.

Motorsports America/CART Review. Autosport International.

Olvey, Dr. Stephen. *Rapid Response: My Inside Story as a Motor Racing Life-Saver*. Somerset: Haynes Publishing, 2006.

Overpeck, Dave, and Susan Wade. "USAC, CART Form New Racing League." *Indianapolis Star*, April 4, 1980.

Overpeck, Dave. "Feud for Thought Cooper's Creation." *Indianapolis Star*, July 13, 1980.

——. "If Chief Steward Fengler Leaves, All of Top Staff Officials May, Too." *Indianapolis Star*, July 6, 1973.

——. "Lack of Speed a Leading Cause of Starting Mess, Drivers Say." *Indianapolis Star*, July 4, 1973.

——. "No Suits, War, or Porsche as Speedway Opens to 99." *Indianapolis Star*, April 27, 1980.

——. "Racing Men Unwilling to Blame Speed, Wings for Indy Carnage." *Indianapolis Star*, July 3, 1973.

——. "Ultimate Responsibility Is Hulman's, but 'Family' Decides Many Things." *Indianapolis Star*, July 12, 1973.

Overpeck, Dave. "What's Wrong at Speedway—What Can Be Done about it?" *Indianapolis Star*, July 1, 1973.

Phillips, David. *Honda's Challenging Spirit: Adversity and Success at the Indianapolis 500*. Phoenix: David Bull Publishing, 2011.

Popely, Rick. *Indianapolis 500 Chronicle*. Illinois: Publications International Ltd., 1998.

Racecar Engineering magazine.

RaceFax.

Racer magazine.

Robson, Graham. *Cosworth: The Search for Power*. United Kingdom: Veloce Publishing, 2017.

Schittone, Guido. *Dallara: It's a Beautiful Story*. Milan: Automobilia, 2011.

Shaffer, Rick. *Autocourse Official History: CART The First 20 Years, 1979-1998*. Hazelton Publishing, 1999.

Shaw, Wilbur. *Gentlemen, Start Your Engines*. New York: Coward-McCann, 1955.

Staff and Wire Reports. "CART Hires Craig, but George Resigns." *Indianapolis Star*, January 8, 1994.

——. "IndyCar Might Boycott 500." *Indianapolis Star*, September 20, 1995.

——. "Scalpers' Pre-500 Plea: You Want Tickets? We've Got Tickets." *Indianapolis Star*, May 26, 1996.

Stewart, Tony, and Bones Bourcier. *True Speed: My Racing Life*. New York: IT Books, 2003.

UPI. "CART Is Back in Indy-Car Scene." *Indianapolis Star*, July 2, 1980.

——. "CART Visits Big Apple." *Indianapolis Star*, April 19, 1979.

——. "Penske Says Solution Close In CART-USAC Wrangling." *Indianapolis Star*, March 26, 1980.

Zimmermann, John. *Dan Gurney's Eagle Racing Cars*. Phoenix: David Bull Publishing, 2007.

INDEX